Dr. Markus Hund

ASEAN and ASEAN Plus Three

I0009536

Dr. Markus Hund

ASEAN and ASEAN Plus Three

Manifestations of Collective Identities in Southeast and East Asia?

VDM Verlag Dr. Müller

ISBN: 978-3-8364-5045-4

Abstract

East Asia is a region undergoing vast structural changes. As the region moved closer together economically and politically following the breakdown of the bipolar world order and the ensuing expansion of intra-regional interdependencies, the states of the region faced the challenge of having to actively recast their mutual relations. At the same time, throughout the 1990s, the West became increasingly interested in trans- and inter-regional dialogue and cooperation with the emerging economies of East Asia. These developments gave rise to a "new regionalism", which eventually also triggered debates on Asian identities and the region's potential to integrate. Before this backdrop, this thesis analyses in how far both the Association of Southeast Asian Nations (ASEAN), which has been operative since 1967 and thus embodies the "old regionalism" of Southeast Asia, and the ASEAN Plus Three forum (APT: the ASEAN states plus China, Japan and South Korea), which has come into existence in the aftermath of the Asian economic crisis of 1997, can be said to represent intergovernmental manifestations of specific collective identities in Southeast Asia and East Asia, respectively. Based on profiles of the respective discursive, behavioral and motivational patterns as well as the integrative potential of ASEAN and APT, this study establishes in how far the member states adhere to sustainable collective patterns of interaction, expectations and objectives, and assesses in how far they can be said to form specific 'ingroups'. Four studies on collective norms, readiness to pool sovereignty, solidarity and attitudes vis-à-vis relevant third states show that ASEAN is firmly grounded in a certain measure of a grown collective identity, though its political relevance is frequently thwarted by changes in its external environment. A study on the cooperative and integrative potential of APT yields no manifest evidence of an ongoing or incipient pan-East Asian identity formation process.

Acknowledgements

Much of the research for this doctoral thesis was carried out while I was employed as a research fellow with the Department of Political Science, University of Trier (Germany), in a project investigating political processes of regionalization in East Asia-Pacific with a view to identity-formation. The funds provided by the German Research Foundation (Deutsche Forschungs-Gemeinschaft, DFG) from February 2000 to January 2002 also gave me the opportunity to collect first-hand information in Southeast Asia. In this context, I am particularly grateful for the support received by the Institute for Strategic and International Studies Malaysia (ISIS) in Kuala Lumpur and the Institute of Southeast Asian Studies (ISEAS) in Singapore, who gave me access to their facilities. Special thanks are due to Prof. Dr. Hanns W. Maull for hiring me as a research fellow and supervising my dissertation, to Prof. Dr. Sebastian Heilmann for assessing the thesis, to Dr. Steve Wood for his friendship and his comments on some chapters, and to all colleagues and friends who contributed to the various discussions. My heart goes out to my wife Sim-Yee and my parents Marion and Gerhard who have backed me tremendously throughout the writing process.

Contents (main chapters):

Contents (chapters in detail):

Chapter 3:

From "Neighborhood Watch Group" to Community? The Case of ASEAN Institutions and the Pooling of Sovereignty

Chapter 4:

Irritable Community: Unstable Solidarity in Post-crisis ASEAN

Tables and figures

14

Acronyms

ACE	ASEAN Committee on Education
ADB	Asian Development Bank
AEM	ASEAN Economic Ministers Meeting
AEM+3	ASEAN Plus Three Economic Ministers
AEMEC	ASEAN Economic Ministers on Energy Cooperation
AFM+3	ASEAN Plus Three Foreign Ministers
AFMM	ASEAN Finance Ministers Meeting
AFMM+3	ASEAN Plus Three Finance Ministers Meeting
AFTA	ASEAN Free Trade Area
AIA	ASEAN Investment Area
AIC	ASEAN Industrial Complementation scheme
AIP	ASEAN Industrial Projects program
AIPO	ASEAN Inter-Parliamentary Organisation
ALMM+3	ASEAN Plus Three Labor Ministers Meeting
AMAF	ASEAN Ministers on Agriculture and Forestry
AMAF+3	ASEAN Plus Three Agriculture and Foreign Ministers
AMEM	ASEAN Ministers on Energy Meeting
AMF	Asian Monetary Fund (never established)
AMM	ASEAN Ministerial Meeting
AMME	ASEAN Ministers Meeting on Environment
AMMH	ASEAN Ministers Meeting on Haze
AMMTC	ASEAN Ministers Meeting on Transnational Crime
AMRPDE	ASEAN Ministers on Rural Development and Poverty Eradication
APEC	Asia Pacific Economic Cooperation
APT/	ASEAN Plus Three
ASEAN+3	(ASEAN states plus China, Japan, South Korea)
ARF	ASEAN Regional Forum
ASC	ASEAN Select Committee
ASCU	ASEAN Surveillance Coordinating Unit
ASEAN	Association of Southeast Asian Nations
ASEAN+1	ASEAN Plus One (ASEAN plus individual Dialogue Partners)
ASEAN+10	ASEAN Plus Ten (ASEAN states plus all ten Dialogue Partners)
ASEAN-10	ASEAN-Ten (all ASEAN members after the enlargement)
ASEAN-5	Five founding ASEAN members (Indonesia, Malaysia, Philippines, Thailand, Singapore)
ASEAN-6	ASEAN-5 plus Brunei (sixth ASEAN member)
ASEM	Asia-Europe Meeting
ASFOM	ASEAN Senior Financial Officials Meeting
ASOD	ASEAN Senior Officials Meeting on Drugs

ASP	ASEAN Surveillance Process
ATM	ASEAN Transport Ministers
BSA	Bilateral swap arrangements
BTFG	Bilateral Trade Financing Guarantee scheme (Singapore-Indonesia)
CCI	Coordinating Committee on Investment (ASEAN)
CEP	Closer Economic Partnership (between ASEAN, Australia and New Zealand), scheme never actually implemented
CEPT	ASEAN Common Effective Preferential Tariff agreement
CER	Closer Economic Region
CLMV	Cambodia, Laos, Myanmar, Vietnam (ASEAN newcomer states)
CMI	Chiang Mai Initiative
COCI	Committee on Communication and Information (ASEAN)
COSD	Committee on Social Development (ASEAN)
COST	Committee on Science and Technology (ASEAN)
DGI	Director-Generals on Immigration (ASEAN)
EAEC	East Asian Economic Caucus (never formally established)
EAEG	East Asian Economic Group (never established)
EAFTA	East Asian Free Trade Area (never established)
EASG	East Asia Study Group (ASEAN Plus Three)
EAWG	East Asia Working Group on... (ASEAN Plus Three)
EC	European Community
EFTA	European Free Trade Area
EPA	Economic Partnership Agreement (Japan-ASEAN)
EPG	Eminent Persons Group
EU	European Union
FDI	Foreign direct investment
FEER	*Far Eastern Economic Review*
FM	Foreign Minister
FTA	Free Trade Area; Free Trade Agreement (variably)
GDP	Gross domestic product
GMS	Greater Mekong Subregion
GNP	Gross national product
HPA	Hanoi Plan of Action (ASEAN)
HRD	Human resources development
HTTF	Haze Technical Task Force (ASEAN)
IAI	Initiative for ASEAN Integration
IAMME	Informal ASEAN Ministers Meeting on Environment
IHT	*International Herald Tribune*
IL	Inclusion List of the CEPT scheme
ILO	International Labor Organization
IMF	International Monetary Fund

IMSGT	Indonesia-Malaysia-Singapore Growth Triangle
INTERFET	International Force for East Timor
IT	Information technology
JETRO	Japan External Trade Organization
LNG	Liquefied natural gas
MFN	Most Favored Nation status
MITI	Ministry of Industry and Trade
MM	Ministerial Meeting
MOU	Memorandum of understanding
NAFTA	North American Free Trade Area
NGO	Non-governmental organization
NPC	National People's Congress (People's Republic of China)
NTB	Non-tariff barrier(s)
ODA	Overseas development assistance
PM	Prime Minister
PMC	Post-Ministerial Conference(s)
PRC	People's Republic of China
PTA	Preferential Trade Agreement
RHAP	Regional Haze Action Plan (ASEAN)
ROK	Republic of Korea
RPDE	Rural Development and Poverty Eradication
SEANWFZ	Southeast Asian Nuclear Weapon Free Zone
SEOM	Senior Economic Officials Meeting
SEOM+3	ASEAN Plus Three Senior Economic Officials Meeting
SLOM+3	ASEAN Plus Three Senior Labor Officials Meeting
SLORC	State Law and Order Restoration Council (Myanmar)
SM	Senior Minister (Singapore)
SOM	Senior Officials Meeting
SOM-AMAF	SOM on ASEAN Ministers on Agriculture and Forestry
SOM-AMAF+3	SOM on ASEAN Plus Three Ministers on Agriculture and Forestry
SOME	Senior Officials Meeting on Energy
SOME+3	ASEAN Plus Three Senior Officials Meeting on Energy
SOMRPDE	Senior Officials Meeting on Rural Development and Poverty Eradication
SPDC	State Peace and Development Council (Myanmar)
STOM	Senior Transport Officials Meeting
TAC	Treaty of Amity and Cooperation (ASEAN)
TAGP	Trans-ASEAN Gas Pipeline
TAR	Trans-Asian Railway project
TEL	Temporary Exclusion List of the CEPT scheme
TELMIN	Telecommunication Ministers

TELSOM	Senior Officials Meeting on Telecommuncation
TNI	Tentara Nasional Indonesia (Indonesian military)
U.S.	United States
UN	United Nations
UNEP	United Nations Environment Programme
UNTAET	United Nations Transitional Authority in East Timor
USSFTA	U.S.-Singapore Free Trade Agreement
WTO	World Trade Organization
ZOPFAN	Zone of Peace, Freedom and Neutrality (ASEAN)

Chapter 1:

INTRODUCTION

INTRODUCTION

0. Two waves of regionalism in East Asia

Two waves of regionalism have significantly altered the political landscape and intergovernmental relations in East Asia since the late 1960s and the late 1980s, respectively. Whereas the first wave of "old" regionalism was limited to what has become known as Southeast Asia and is represented by the Association of Southeast Asian Nations (ASEAN), the second wave of "new" regionalism has generated various intergovernmental bodies and processes that either focused on trans-regional and inter-regional dialogue and cooperation between the West and what has come to be called "East Asia" (APEC, ASEM) or represented approaches by East Asian states to enhance intra-regional dialogue and cooperation among themselves (EAEC or ASEAN Plus Three).

In this context, the Asia Pacific Economic Cooperation (APEC), established in 1989, was designed to enhance economic ties between the U.S.-centric Pacific hemisphere (including Latin American countries, Canada, Australia and New Zealand) on the one hand and Japan and the newly-industrialized and developing economies of East Asia (represented by the mainly Western-leaning ASEAN states, South Korea and, as of 1993, also Taiwan and the People's Republic of China) on the other. APEC, which was to represent an only vaguely defined "Asia Pacific" region, successively also granted membership to economies such as Russia, India and Mongolia, so that its geographic extension spread over all continents except for Africa and its member economies accounted for more than 50 percent of the world's economic output. APEC's most apparent feature was that, in the face of growing economc rivalries, it excluded the European Community (EC) and the wider Eastern and Northern European area.

The APEC process indirectly contributed to regionalism in "East Asia" in so far as it raised international awareness of East Asia as a region of exceptional economic growth and thus fuelled the debate on the coming "Pacific century" and "Asian values" that started raging through the ranks of the epistemic communities in East Asia and elsewhere after the end of the Cold War at the end of the 1980s. It also heightened ASEAN's profile as a regional actor, as it caused ASEAN member states to separately consult on, and partly also coordinate, their positions regarding the APEC process. Importantly, APEC also represented an opening for dialogue and constructive engagement with China, as ASEAN members actively promoted China's accession to APEC.

The inter-regional Asia-Europe Meeting (ASEM) process, operative since 1996 as a forum for dialogue and cooperation between the member states of the EU plus the EU Commission on the one hand and the East Asian states – comprising the ASEAN member states[1] plus mainland China (PRC), Japan and South Korea (ROK) – on the other, represented a contribution to the "new" regionalism in so far as in the context of the ASEM process, the Asian countries for the first time manifested an externally distinguishable (though at best very loosely coordinated) East Asian group on the international stage which many observers and government officials alike inofficially identified as the first materialization of the East Asian Economic Caucus (EAEC), a political phantom which, as an idea, had been variously (but only reluctantly) discussed among East Asian governments since it was first proposed by Malaysia's Prime Minister Mahathir in 1990.

The ASEAN Regional Forum (ARF), an initiative launched by ASEAN in 1993 to involve the major powers in East Asia (including the U.S.) in dialogue on regional security issues, represented a further manifestation of the "new" regionalism and expressed awareness among East Asian states of heightened interdependence in the area of political stability and security.

All three intergovernmental processes (APEC, ASEM and the ARF) thus contributed to the notion of a distinctive "East Asian" region. By adopting dialogue and cooperation mechanisms that were modeled on the so-called "ASEAN way",[2] which increasingly came to be seen as the "(East)Asian way" of political interaction, they also became complicit in cementing notions of an exclusive pan-East Asian cultural homogeneity. Non-Asian dialogue partners were required to subscribe to this "Asian way" as a prerequisite of dialogue and cooperation.

The latest, and the only distinctively East Asian, manifestation of the "new" regionalism in East Asia is represented by the so-called ASEAN Plus Three (APT) process whose participants (the ASEAN grouping plus China, Japan and South Korea) for the first time publicly identified themselves as members of this separate intergovernmental forum in 1999. The forum has received much attention, as it started out with a dynamic initiative to boost regional economic and political stability, promote regional functional and political cooperation and discuss opportunities of economic integration in in its first years of existence.

---

[1] Originally, ASEAN members had joined the ASEM process collectively, but as separate states in 1996. Despite strong protests from ASEAN, Myanmar's accession to ASEM was barred by strong opposition from many EU member states due to the suppression of the democratic opposition and crude human rights violations committed by Myanmar's junta regime.

[2] The "ASEAN way" of informality, non-interference in each other's internal affairs, unanimous and non-binding decision making based on consultation and consensus represents ASEAN's trade-mark mode of conducting intergovernmental affairs.

Unlike APEC and ASEM, whose dynamic has largely faded due to differences among their members about the purposes and future course of cooperation, APT still promises to harbor as yet largely unexplored opportunities for cooperation and integration in East Asia.

Just after the turn of the century, it appears that two regional groupings of states have emerged whose members share a common heritage of various interdependencies, economic risks and political challenges imposed upon them by geographic proximity. The first of the two is ASEAN, representative of the "old" regionalism and distinguished by its 35-years' cooperative history, which has been facing the difficult task of finding a new collective role after the changes that came about with the end of the Cold War. The other one is APT, which, as the youngest and exclusively East Asian outcome of the wave of "new" regionalism looks back onto only a very short history, but has had a promising start.

1. Objective and structure of the book

This study provides an assessment of ASEAN and ASEAN Plus Three with a view to establishing in how far these two intergovernmental processes represent, or are conducive to, processes of collective identity formation between governments in Southeast Asia and East Asia, respectively. The issue of regional collective identities deserves attention in so far as, should there indeed be evidence of prevalent regional identities, any assessment of regional cooperation and integration efforts within Southeast and East Asia would have to take into account the potential impact of this special social fabric on the conduct of regional relations.

The approach chosen here to operationlize the term "collective identity between states" is to establish a set of phenotypical reference points framing and limiting the field of what in the end has to remain a "black box", as identity can never be fully and satisfactorily be explained, no matter how hard we try. Thus, this study cannot and does not claim to be authoritatively conclusive on the issue of collective identity between governments in ASEAN and APT, but rather represents a multi-faceted approximation to its subject of analysis.

The four reference points chosen here to delimit and assess the field of collective identity between governments are all functions derived from the quintessential question of any type of collective identity, namely in how far the respective members of a collective are distinguished and distinguishable as being part of the *ingroup* (as opposed to *outgroup*). These reference points are deliberately chosen to mark a not too narrow field of phenotypical features whose observation and assessment allows a qualified statement on the strength of the common bonds generating internal cohesion and delimiting the boundaries between inside and outside:

- the prevalence of collective norms,
- readiness to "pool" sovereignty, i.e. transfer national sovereignty and authority to collective mechanisms and institutions,
- solidarity and mutual trust and reliability, and
- the perception of, and positions on, third (i.e. external) parties.

The following chapter introduces the concept of collective identity from which the categories of analysis are deduced. Subsequently, both ASEAN and APT are introduced by means of an historical overview of their respective developments, a description of their institutional structures, an outline of the general purposes and objectives they are to serve and the type of cooperation they represent.

The assessment of collective identity in ASEAN will be carried out in four separate studies, each focusing on one of the four categories of analysis. The analysis of APT follows a different pattern. A single study will take stock of the respective participants' attitudes towards the APT process and their motives for participating in it, so as to successively arrive at conclusions about the potential for the evolution of a distinctly East Asian or APT identity.

The final, conlcusive chapter will then summarize the insights gained in the individual chapters of analysis and give an overall assessment of the state of collective identity in ASEAN and APT.

2. Collective Identity Between States

The first part of this section introduces the concept of collective identity that will serve as the template and reference point for the analysis of collective identity in ASEAN and ASEAN Plus Three. Drawing on this working model, the second part identifies the particular categories of analysis that form the structural backbone of the overall study.

2. 1. A Working Model of Collective Identity

Any enquiry into the essence of collective identity first of all requires an answer to the question 'What is the essence of identity?' before the qualifier 'collective' can come into focus. The objective of this approach must be to boil the term 'collective identity' down to the smallest, intersubjectively acceptable, common denominator before, in turn, it can be constructively operationalized to match the overall subject of this book.

Identity   A term traditionally at home in the area of psychology and sociology, 'identity' has come to denote the pattern 'place of the subject in relation to other subjects', which can be expressed in the formula 'self (ego) and other (alter)'. In order to act independently ('unity of action'), a subject requires 'orientation' in relation to other subjects, i.e. the ability to differentiate between self and other. Identity therefore denotes a process of 'self-recognition', of drawing and readjusting lines or borders between self and other(s). Across all disciplines, scholars consider the delineation of 'self' and 'other' as constitutive of identity, regardless whether they are referring to natural persons, groups of individuals or an abstract unit such as a nation. Thus, identity can be intersubjectively defined as the position the subject takes in the process of drawing lines between 'self' and 'other'.

Collective identity   "When speaking of 'collective identity', then [...] we do so in the sense that an individual delineates the border between itself and such collectives it does not adhere to [...] or such it is part of, respectively."[3] The term 'collective identity' can be applied to any group of subjects (be they individual human beings or abstract units such as a nation or a group of states) who positively accept that they form a distinct unit by virtue of sharing certain commonalities or positions. Collective identities are most clearly defined by processes of exclusion and inclusion. Their impact on their members' cohesion and unity of action is greatest where they create clear notions of 'us' and 'them', as such processes generate unity and difference of norms, values and modes of behavior.[4] In Lepsius' words,

> Identity formation presupposes an object that perceives of itself as one entity, separate from others and identifying itself as such. As far as collectives are concerned, their identity is based on the object of institutionalized organizational principles representing particular norms and shaping patterns of behavior.[5] [translated from German, M.H.]

Political relevance and unity of action   The strength of a collective identity can be measured by the degree of the group members' unity of action, which determines its political relevance.[6] The unity of action and political relevance of a particular collective identity will be greater if its members are not also socialized by significant other collectives, as alternative identities may interfere with each other.[7] Generally, the political relevance of collective identities grows

---

[3] Berg (1999): 225.
[4] Schmitt-Egner (1999): 130ff. Cp. also: Weller (1999): 254.
[5] Lepsius (1999): 91.
[6] Berg (1999): 223; Weller (1999): 270f.
[7] Weller (1999): 270f.

the more effectively and comprehensively they polarize, unify or monopolize their adherents' individual views and perceptions along the dividing line between 'ingroup' and 'outgroup'. Further, for a collective to emerge as a stable and cohesive entity, the group has to prove its credentials as a trustworthy, reliable entity and, most importantly, requires a sense of common purpose and interdependence (for example as a community of fate that ensures provision of certain essential goods to the group members). Thus, collective identities take time to mature, i.e. develop their own distinctive interactive and operational structures and reassure themselves of individual members' actual commitment to the collective. Collectives whose adherents share substantial common interests and which are useful to the individuals are more stable than those whose identity is merely based on a vague sense of attachment.[8] On the other hand, strong collective identity characteristically displays such a high degree of mutual loyalty that, within certain limits, the group is sustained by its relational network even over stretches of time when the collective fails to provide benefits to individual group members or even acts against their interests.[9] Significantly, "collective identity substantiates whenever members of a collective perceive of themselves primarily as members of this same collective and thus are depersonalized both in perception and action."[10] In other terms, within certain limits, the process of collective identity formation requires individual members to give up part of their individual freedom of action (or sovereignty) for the sake of making collective organizational principles work. The more readily they do so (an act with strong implications of trust and importance of the collective to the individual member), the greater the identity of this particular collective can be said to be.

Collective identity between states   The concept of collective identity introduced here is not limited to particular types of identity subjects. Its universality enables us to assess any group of single actors with regard to their collective identity. States, represented by their respective national governments, can clearly be identified as single actors in their own right, interacting with each other at the level of international relations.[11] In this sense, Wendt asserts that

---

[8] Cp. Berg (1999): 224.

[9] Ibid.: 230.

[10] Weller (1999): 269.

[11] Naturally, the state, as an amorphous entity, cannot act by itself, but rather acts through the elites running its government. Critics therefore may object that it is the elites who act, and not the states. However, wherever the elites are representing the state and take decisions in its name or on its behalf, they are both acting and being acted upon at the same time in the sense that the constitutional, institutional, political, economic, social and historical legacies of the state as a whole both restrain their freedom of action and condition their actions. Thus, the amorphous state and its respective governing elites of the moment, which form an

"states are people too", with quasi-social identities in their own right, interacting in quasi-social networks, maintaining quasi-social relations at the international level.[12] Summing up the body of literature on identity of states, single and collective, Weller states that

> [...] a socio-psychological concept of identity can also be applied to states. Just as personal identity is formed by way of the individual interacting with his/ her social environment [...] – commonly referred to as "social identity" –, states, if perceived as single actors, may be thought of as developing their own respective identities within *their* social environment, i.e. the international order. The nearly 200 actors participating therein constitute the structure of international politics, which, in turn, procreates the respective identities of the participating actors [...]. Crucially, *this* type of state identity [...] is not shaped by developments within the state, but rests exclusively on interaction between states. [...] On the premise of the approach outlined [...] [above, M.H.], *collective identity* of states is a conceivable proposition: It seems conceivable that, based on commonalities shared by [certain] states, ties between them attain a level transcending a mere coalition of interest, that membership in a collective of states strongly influences the individual terms of existence of the participating states and that the collective of states does not merely serve the purposes of its respective members, but also shared collective purposes. This presupposes clear differentiation between members and non-members and possibly generates a we-feeling [...].[13] [translated from German, M.H.]

As Weller indicates, single actors can only interact as single actors within the limits of their specific generic properties and substrata. Thus, states, represented by their governments, are the principal and only legitimate actors in the area of inter-governmental relations, because they identify themselves, and are identified by others, as such. Presupposing that only single actors belonging to the same generic type can form collective identities, states represent the only single actors that can associate, and form collective identities, with other states. Thus, a nation cannot join a grouping of states unless it is identified as a state and represented by a government (partial identification as a state will allow a

---

inseparably intertwined entity that is in constant interaction with itself, can be considered to be the actual actor in the conduct of a state's affairs.

[12] Wendt (1999): 215ff. Cp. also: Wendt (1994).
Similarly, role models of state agency in international relations presuppose that states take roles on the basis of certain identites which they adapt in interaction with significant others. Cp. for example: Aggestam (1999).
[13] Weller (2000).

nation only limited access to *de facto* intergovernmental groupings at best, such as in the case of Taiwan's membership in APEC).

Assessing collective identity   Any assessment of collective identity needs to establish in how far the object of analysis corresponds with the criteria outlined above, which, as we recall, are the following: clear ingroup/outgroup perception, distinctive collective norms, strength of distinctive organizational principles, continuity and progressive evolution of collective relations, relevance of the collective to its individual adherents (strength of common purpose and utility of the collective), extent of alternative identities, scope of collective perceptions (degree to which the collective forms its adherents' perception of the outside world and of third parties), unity of action, readiness to yield individual freedoms or cede power over themselves to the collective, and the stability of group members' relational network in times of crisis. The parameters outlined above represent the generalized template for assessing all types of collectives with a view to their identity. In order to assess particular kinds of collectives, the parameters of this template have then to be adapted to the specifics of the respective object of analysis.

Regional collective identity between states: a matter of potential, not of method   Regional collective identity between states represents an especially distinguished and promising form of collective identity between states, as it has the highest integration potential of all possible collective identities between states. Its crucial aspect is the geographical dimension, as geographical proximity implies the possibility of a coherent geographical area (comprising land and possibly also maritime territories, as long as the latter link rather than separate states) with the potential to serve as the substrate for various forms and degrees of political, economic, legal and social cohesion and integration that may range from loose cooperative designs to the formation of supranational entities or superstates (such as the EU is in the process of becoming). Without this geographical dimension, no grouping of states has the potential to achieve similar effects of integration.[14]

However, although geographical proximity represents an essential prerequisite for the formation of regional collective identities, it does not itself *engender* the same. Far from it, all too frequently, geographical proximity even accounts for forthright hostility and perceptions of mutually exclusive identites rather than a sense of shared identity between states. Hence, as a product of quasi-social processes between states (rather than a logical consequence of geographical

---

[14] In the historical perspective, the only examples of political integration that was not based on geographical proximity are conquering empires, such as the Roman or the British Empire, which imposed their administrative system on the territories they occupied or dominated by means of military power.

proximity), the formation of regional collective identities between states is essentially subject to the same conditions as any other kind of collective identity between states. To sum up, manifest collective identities within a unified geographical area can generally be expected to have a greater integrative potential than collective identities lacking this geographical dimension. However, establishing whether or not the states of a certain region adhere to a shared collective identity depends on the template used for identifying collective identity rather than on templates defining what constitutes a region. Therefore, assessing regional relations with a view to collective identity between states must conform to the same methodological paradigms as assessing such kinds of collective identity between states that are lacking the dimension of geographical proximity.

2.2. Assessing Collective Identities Between States: Formulating Categories of Analysis

Drawing on the parameters of collective identity as specified in the previous section, assessing collective identities between states requires categories of analysis that are tailored to the specific properties of states and their specific modes of interaction. This section aims at identifying categories of analysis that can be applied profitably and meaningfully to groupings of states in order to find out more about the quality of their respective collective identities.

Collective norms First of all, states, represented by their governments, interact with each other by means of diplomatic discourse on the basis of mutually recognized conventions and codified principles. The codes and principles of interaction, however, are not universal, but differ according to political and social context and environment. If a grouping of states adopt, and reassure each other of, group-specific standards of communication and interaction which set their internal ways of interaction apart from the way states outside the collective interact in the international arena, one can speak of specific collective norms. As Finnemore and Sikkink point out, such norms are expressive of identities. "There is a general agreement on the definition of a norm as a standard of appropriate behavior for actors with a given identity."[15] Similarly, Jepperson, Wendt and Katzenstein point out that

---

[15] Finnemore and Sikkink (1998): 891.

> [...] norms either define ("constitute") identities in the first place (generating expectations about the proper portfolio of identities for a given context) or prescribe or proscribe ("regulate") behaviors for already constituted identities (generating expectations about how those identities will shape behavior in varying circumstances).[16]

Thus, norms – which transcend mere rules in that they represent a shared commitment to a certain "oughtness"[17], i.e. they represent shared ideas of order –, shared collectively by a certain self-identified group of states, can be said to be the first and foremost expression of collective identity between them. As a pattern of group-specific behavior, a set of collective norms marks the very first and positively defined dividing line constituting 'ingroup' and 'outgroup'.

Pooling of sovereignty As indicated in the previous chapter, the meaning and stability of collective identities depends largely on the collective's ability to provide certain exclusive shared goods to its individual constituents.[18] In order to optimize provision – and possibly expand the range – of collectively shared goods, collectives will have to integrate ever more closely and thereby intensify their interdependencies or, if the collective is not able to do so, seek partners outside the collective with whom they can jointly provide relevant goods (such as security, for example). Whereas in the latter case, collective identity will be contested by various other alternative identities and liaisons, in the former case, the collective will gain in importance to the constituent member states and will require them to commit themselves to an ever increasing number of codified obligations that spring from the implementation of an increasingly dense web of collective norms and objectives. The number of bilateral and collective agreements, regulatory and administrative frameworks and authoritative institutions can be expected to increase. This process may require the individual states to increasingly transfer national sovereignty to the collective level, possibly with a view to engaging in more institutionalized, regime-type forms of economic and political integration.

Whereas, clearly, collective identity between states does not necessarily entail pooling of sovereignty, one can assume that wherever states engage in pooling of sovereignty and systematic integration, this suggests the existence of a considerably mature and sustainable collective identity. Thus, we can imagine

---

[16] Jepperson, Wendt and Katzenstein (1996): 54.

[17] Finnemore and Sikkink (1998): 891.

[18] This premise applies even more to relations between states than to individual human beings, as interaction between individuals tends to be more unsystematic and unreflected than interaction between states, which is usually guided by national interests and deliberated and decided upon carefully by the respective governments.

collective identity without pooling of sovereignty, but not pooling of sovereignty without a considerably strong and mature collective identity.[19]

Thus, if there was evidence suggesting that a regional grouping of states, such as ASEAN, engages in, or seriously aims at, pooling of sovereignty, we could assume that the grouping's cooperation is based on a significant and dynamic collective identity (dynamic in the sense that we can expect further deepening and coherence).

If, on the other hand, relations between the member states of a grouping remained distant and anxiously concerned with the preservation of national sovereignty (even after a long period of cooperation) rather than the pooling of sovereignty, this would suggest a low complementarity of the respective member states' national interests and/ or an essential lack in mutual trust, reliability and coherence. Thus, though the member states may actually share in a collective identity, this identity may be considered to be not very profound and dynamic – and thus less relevant to their respective conduct of international relations.

Solidarity We cannot conceive of a community of pure egoists as anything else than a paradox. On the other hand, communities rarely consist of altruists, either. It is therefore realistic to assume that an intact community is constituted by members who are more or less willing to suspend their egoistic interests as long as this serves their superordinate interest of perpetuating the group's vital functions. Thus, an intact community is intact either because there are no conflicting interests among individual members or between members and collective (which is the more unlikely the greater the impact of community life is on its respective members) or because members actually make an effort to suppress their more immediate interests for the sake of less immediate benefits they can expect to reap from a functioning community.

A community of states that actually makes a difference to its respective members because of their mutual interdependence in vital areas will therefore evoke a degree of mutual support which distant observers may mistake as

---

[19] Significant examples of successful pooling of sovereignty are the unification processes of the United States since the 18th century and the European Union in the aftermath of the terrifying experiences of World War II. In contrast, international organizations such as the United Nations or the World Trade Organization, but also regional groupings of states such as the Asia Pacific Economic Cooperation (APEC), or the South Asian Association for Regional Cooperation (SAARC), which are clearly not based on strong collective identity, find it much more difficult to establish common norms and acquire authority over its member states. Further, at the hand of the example of NATO, a security community whose institutional set-up is in question as its formerly strong collective identity is softening, one can clearly see that the willingness of states to pool sovereignty always also indicates the state and stability of collective identities.

altruistic behavior when actually it represents self-interested action in a mutually (life-) sustaining relationship, or, to put it in one word, solidarity. Solidary behavior demands from the members of a specific collective permanent readiness to support other members in times of crisis or treat them fairly when conflicts arise between members. The minimum of fairness a group member can expect in such cases is determined by the group's underlying collective norms. Group-specific solidarity among members also marks another clear demarcation line between ingroup and outgroup. A high degree of solidarity also denotes the high value group members ascribe to the goods provided by their collective. This, in turn, provides insights into, and permits conclusions about, the quality of the respective collective identity.

Positions vis-à-vis third parties   A grouping of states can also be said to be politically relevant if its very existence clearly makes a difference to its members' conduct of relations with, and attitudes towards, significant external third parties, such as, for example, great powers or other groupings of states. The clearer and the more permanent the grouping shapes its respective members' foreign policy conduct, the clearer the division between ingroup and outgroup (and thus its collective identity) can be said to be.

Groupings whose members already share certain foreign policy dispositions with regard to significant external parties will be able to draw on synergy effects of (implicitly or explicitly) coordinated foreign policy stances much faster than such groupings who still grapple with strong differences in their respective foreign policy orientations. Thus, member states' respective foreign policy dispositions are indicative of the grouping's potential for coherence in dealing with significant third parties, and hence permit conclusions about the grouping's collective identity.

In order to assess the coherence and stability of a particular grouping's foreign policy dispositions (and thus its collective identity), it is therefore essential to assess the stability and coherence of its respective members' foreign policy dispositions and see whether the potentials have been translated into clearly distinctive (implicit or explicit) collective foreign policy stances.

3. Introducing ASEAN and ASEAN Plus Three

The two objects of analysis that are to be assessed with a view to their respective collective identities in this study are the Association of Southeast Asian Nations (ASEAN) and the pan-East Asian ASEAN Plus Three (APT) grouping. The former comprises ten sovereign states altogether, namely Brunei Darussalam, Indonesia, Singapore, Thailand, Malaysia, the Philippines,

Vietnam, Cambodia, Myanmar and Laos, whereas APT is constituted by the ten ASEAN states plus three Northeast Asian states, namely the People's Republic of China (PRC), Japan and South Korea (Republic of Korea, ROK). The two groupings will be introduced by means of an overview of their respective histories of cooperation, institutional frameworks, degree and frequency of interaction at government level, and their types and modes of operation.

3.1. The Association of Southeast Asian Nations (ASEAN)

3.1.1. Brief historical overview

The history of ASEAN can be partitioned into four phases: the formative phase as a "soft" security alliance from 1967 to 1975, the consolidation of broader regionalism in the era of the Cold War between 1976 and 1989/90, the promotion of ASEAN's economic integration from 1991 to 1997/98, and the phase of economic crisis and post-crisis realignment from 1998 to today.

1967-1975   Established in 1967 by its five founding members, the so-called ASEAN-5 (Indonesia, Singapore, the Philippines, Thailand and Malaysia), ASEAN was to meet two primary objectives.

On the one hand, the founding members intended the grouping to be a platform for dialogue and mutually beneficial cooperation as a means of easing and overcoming severe bilateral strains that had built up between them in the immediate post-colonial period, as four newly-independent countries were engaged in nation-building. The ultimate purpose was to pacify relations between the five states to a degree that they could spend their resources on domestic political stability and national economic development. In this context, cooperation between the five founding members represented primarily a means of achieving "national resilience" rather than regional integration.

On the other hand, from its inception, ASEAN's political scope also went beyond "intra-ASEAN" affairs (or rather trans-ASEAN affairs, as the ASEAN-5 did not perceive of themselves as integral parts of an entity aimed at regional integration) in that the ASEAN-5 were united in their strict opposition to the destabilizing communist threat originating in the communist systems of Indochina (particularly Vietnam and Cambodia) and China.

Thus, in the first decade of its operation, ASEAN's collective goods were the stabilization and pacification of the trans-ASEAN environment and joint opposition to external communist influences.

The ASEAN-5 governments also shared a positive disposition towards the West and its main exponent in Asia, the United States (a disposition which continued unquestioned throughout the Cold War).

Remarkably, however, despite their pro-Western inclinations, the ASEAN states collectively adopted a philosophy of collective neutrality vis-à-vis the great powers in 1971 by formally declaring their intention to establish ASEAN as a Zone of Peace, Freedom and Neutrality (ZOPFAN). Whereas Singapore and the Philippines would have preferred establishing stronger formal security ties with the U.S., strong ASEAN memers such as Malaysia, Indonesia and silently also Thailand preferred Southeast Asia to remain as independent from great power interference as possible.[20] Knowing that the logic of the Cold War obliged the U.S. to provide political, military and economic support and protection to the anti-communist ASEAN states, ASEAN could well afford to collectively "free-ride" under the American security umbrella and adopt a neutral stance so as to relax tensions and to avoid unnecessary conflict between its members and its communist environment. At later stages, ASEAN's philosophy of neutrality also gave its members more political leverage to actively engage with its communist environment and eventually even integrate communist countries into ASEAN.

Overall, one can say that, effectively, "ASEAN's major thrust then [at its formative stage, M.H.] was to contain disputes within the region and insulate it from superpower conflicts."[21] However, instead of defining ASEAN mainly as the security coalition it effectively represented (with the objective of averting external threats and internally reducing conflict potentials between ASEAN members), the member states declared development cooperation between its members to be the backbone of their association.[22] Mohd Haflah Piei points out that

> It cannot be overlooked that whatever the political motivations behind the founding of ASEAN, the stated aims, principles and purposes of the Association as explicitly stated in the Bangkok Declaration seemed primarily economic in character.[23]

Externally, the proposition of ASEAN as a grouping with primarily economic objectives was less provocative to the communist camp; internally, it represented the attempt to give ASEAN states a positive focus point for long-term constructive dialogue rather than risking to obstruct community-building from the beginning by engaging in time-consuming and potentially divisive security talks. ASEAN states thus approached their objective of providing

---

[20] Cf. Dosch (1997): 170f.

[21] Mohd Haflah Piei (2000): 3.

[22] Significantly, ASEAN's foundational Bangkok Declaration largely avoided the area of primary security issues and rather put its main emphasis on economic and development cooperation.
Cf. ASEAN Declaration (Bangkok Declaration), Bangkok, 08 August 1967.

[23] Mohd Haflah Piei (2000): 3.

peace and stability to the region from an angle imaginging economic and development cooperation (which practically did not exist at the time) while at the same time they avoided to directly address the existing problems and tensions between ASEAN members.

1976-1990   The beginning of the second phase of ASEAN regionalism coincided with the withdrawal of the U.S. from Vietnam in 1975. The withdrawal of the American hegemon and the subsequent strengthening of communist regimes in Indochina catalyzed a process of heightened regionalism, as ASEAN member states closed ranks in order to adapt and proactively respond to these new challenges.[24] Thus, in 1976, ASEAN members established the ASEAN Secretariat and adopted the Treaty of Amity and Cooperation (TAC) that featured a code of conduct guiding its signatories' bilateral relations. The fact that accession to the TAC was explicitly kept "open for accession by other States in Southeast Asia",[25] i.e. non-member states, shows that, as ASEAN became internally more cohesive, it also adopted a more proactive role in regional affairs in its own right. Brunei's accession to ASEAN in 1984 is a further indicator of ASEAN's increasing importance and prestige as a meaningful regional actor.

ASEAN's cohesion in terms of a security community continued to deepen throughout the remaining years of the Cold War, which are marked most significantly by the years of 1978, when the Vietnamese invasion in Cambodia began and 1991, when the Cambodian crisis was resolved by the Paris accord. Throughout the Cambodian crisis, ASEAN member states largely managed to coordinate their policies and act in a coherent way and thus contributed towards a satisfactory resolution of the crisis.[26] In 1987, ASEAN members, envisioning a formal dispute settlement mechanism, even amended the Treaty of Amity and Cooperation to the effect that an ASEAN High Council was to be established as a "continuing [i.e. permanent, M.H.] body" that was supposed "to settle disputes through regional processes".[27]

Beyond mere regional engagement, ASEAN also began engaging in collective dialogue at ministerial level with its official Dialogue Partners outside the region, a growing number of the world's most important political actors, such as the U.S., the European Community and Japan and several other states, to discuss economic cooperation and concerns of regional stability.

Whereas ASEAN proved to be increasingly stable and successful with a view to security, the development of its economic cooperation made only moderate

---

[24] Cf. Rüland (1995a): 4.

[25] Article 18, Treaty of Amity and Cooperation, Denpasar (Bali), 24 February 1976.

[26] Cf. Busse (2000): 133-140.

[27] Article 2, Protocol Amending the Treaty of Amity and Cooperation in Southeast Asia, Manila, 15 December 1987.

progress. Rüland states that since the late 1960s ASEAN members had seen annual growth rates of about seven percent on average and that ASEAN, despite the objectives of economic cooperation laid out in the Bangkok Declaration of 1967, had no share in these national achievements.[28]

In the course of the "renewed urgency and determination to promote regional cooperation" that originated in "the common threat [perception] of military aggression" since 1975,[29] ASEAN members had actually started to consider opportunities of economic cooperation and integration more seriously. Subsequently, they adopted the Declaration of ASEAN Concord that "formally set out the guidelines for concrete regional economic relations"[30] in 1976 and began delivering a number of documents, agreements and initiatives launching several projects of economic cooperation and integration. The most notable of these were the ASEAN Preferential Trading Agreement (PTA) aimed at liberalizing trade, the ASEAN Industrial Projects Programme (AIP) based on an intra-ASEAN import substitution approach to development and the ASEAN Industrial Complementation scheme (AIC) aimed at promoting "division of labor among the five ASEAN members" as well as avoiding "duplication of small-scale production and components and parts in several ASEAN countries".[31]

However, in the end, the ASEAN governments lacked the political will to actually substantiate and implement these projects because they perceived them to run counter to their respective national interests.[32] Indeed, the low compatibility and complementarity of ASEAN economies discouraged ASEAN governments from taking ASEAN integration further throughout the 1980s.

To sum up, as ASEAN proved to be increasingly stable and successful with a view to security, the development of its economic cooperation made only moderate progress. Clearly, as long as ASEAN served the purpose it had originally been set up for, namely to enhance peace and security in the region and, secondly, as long as ASEAN members experienced satisfactory national economic growth independently of ASEAN, there was no incentive and no strong need for collective economic action.

1991-1997/98 From a security perspective, the end of the Cold War changed the regional environment dramatically. As the Soviet Union collapsed, China lost a mighty opponent that had so far checked and curbed its potential to

---

[28] Rüland (1995a): 4f.

[29] Mohd. Haflah Piei (2000): 5.

[30] Ibid.: 5.

[31] Ibid.: 9.

For an overview of all of ASEAN's initiatives, documents and agreements of economic cooperation and integration, see Dosch (1997): 268f.

[32] Dosch (1997): 268.

emerge as a regional hegemon. All of a sudden, Southeast Asian states faced a great threat potential at their borders.

At the same time, the Indochina threat at ASEAN's borders had been largely resolved with the adoption of the Paris accord of 1991 settling Vietnam's struggle with Cambodia. Vietnam was also neutralized by the loss of its strongest ally, the USSR, and now also faced an unbound China at its borders.

The new China threat accounted for a renewed wave of regionalism among the ASEAN states. Drawing on their tradition as a prestigeous security coalition and a proactive collective actor in regional affairs and owing to their shared unease about China's uncertain political ambitions, they (implicitly and explicitly) adopted a collective dual strategy.

On the one hand, ASEAN members' position on China differed from that of the West (represented by the U.S. and the European Union) in that they, from the beginning, promoted proactive, constructive engagement with China. Whereas the West was still shocked by the human rights violations of the Tiananmen incident in 1989 and had adopted a rather hostile antagonistic stance on China and demanded political reform, ASEAN collectively sought to appease China and integrate it into regional and interregional dialogue structures. Thus, ASEAN members, though fearful of China, actively promoted China's accession to APEC (which finally took place in 1991), gave China full Dialogue Partner status and established the ASEAN Regional Forum in order to discuss security questions with all great powers, including China, from 1994 on. Here there are clear links between ASEAN's distinctive and long-standing neutrality policy and China's acceptance of ASEAN's role as host of security talks. In 1995/96, ASEAN also promoted China's participation in the Asia-Europe Meeting (ASEM).

While on the one hand, ASEAN pursued constructive relations with China, the Association at the same time also sought to limit China's increasing influence on Southeast Asia and Indochina by promoting ASEAN enlargement. ASEAN's strategy was to prevent China from developing a sphere of influence right at its borders by offering the isolated and strongly underdeveloped states a perspective of economic development as members of an internationally respected and prestigeous regional organization. Likewise, ASEAN extended full membership to Vietnam, a long-standing antagonist of China, and thus showed it a way out of its economic and political isolation.

ASEAN's enlargement policy was of course not only directed at preventing China from projecting hegemonial power into Southeast Asia, but also served as a way of tying the poorest and politically most conflict-prone nations of the region into ASEAN's stabilizing institutional and normative framework. ASEAN's decision to carry out its enlargement, even though its members faced severe pressure fom the U.S. and the European Union to deny membership to Myanmar (which acceded to the Southeast Asian grouping in 1997) on the grounds of its political regime and human rights violations, shows that ASEAN had assumed great self-confidence and was ready to prove its emancipated status. Thus, ASEAN took an ever more independent role as a proactive collective regional actor.

The period between 1990 and 1998 has come to be considered the heyday of ASEAN regionalism, as ASEAN gradually expanded the scope of its integration initiatives (such as working towards an ASEAN trade and investment area). This development was largely due to the ASEAN-5 states' interest in fueling and sustaining the exceptional growth rates of their increasingly interdependent and foreign investment-based economies and to remain competitive and sustain their international credibility in an international environment in which a trend towards forming regional free trade arrangements (or regional trading blocks) prevailed.[33] What occurred during the 1990s is nothing less than a change of economic paradigms requiring ASEAN to evolve into an institutionally integrated economic community. Initially, ASEAN members seemed to be willing and able to go along with this trend and master this transition due to their expectation of continued strong economic growth.

The year 1992 marked the formal turning point in ASEAN's transition towards an economic community, when ASEAN leaders resolved to establish the ASEAN Free Trade Area (AFTA) by 2008 and to gradually liberalize intra-ASEAN trade. The Common Effective Preferential Tariff scheme (CEPT) was to form the core of AFTA. In 1995, ASEAN also resolved on an AFTA Plus package that was supposed to bring down non-tariff trade barriers. Further, ASEAN adopted a framework for investment liberalization with the objective to establish the ASEAN Investment Area (AIA).

The *ASEAN Vision 2020* (Vision 2020) and the *Hanoi Plan of Action* (HPA) adopted at the ASEAN summits in 1997 and 1998, respectively, represent the important status ASEAN members had come to attribute to the field of economic cooperation and integration since the beginning of the 1990s. Economic integration had emerged as a primary focus of ASEAN. Thus, in the Vision 2020, ASEAN members reaffirmed their commitment to regional macroeconomic and financial stability, liberalization of trade in goods and services, financial sector liberalization, intra-ASEAN development cooperation, trans-ASEAN energy production and distribution networks (ASEAN Power Grid), and establishing an integrated harmonized transportation network. The HPA, adopted under the impression of the hot phase of the Asian economic crisis, draws on the objectives outlined in the Vision 2020 and tries to formulate a more detailed and concrete integration schedule. In the face of the pressing problems of the Asian economic crisis, the plan calls for a great number of measures aimed to implement ASEAN's existing integration initiatives and calls

---

[33] Cp. Stahl (2001): 60ff; Mohd Haflah Piei (2000): 9.

for the establishment of new crisis prevention mechanisms of regional economic cooperation, such as the ASEAN Surveillance Process (ASP) to monitor economic and monetary developments in the ASEAN member states. The HPA called for swift and wide-ranging collective action with a view to macroeconomic and financial cooperation, greater economic integration, human resources development, promoting trans-ASEAN science and technology development programs and reducing the social impact of the financial and economic crisis across ASEAN. Further, it called for a more central role of the ASEAN Secretariat in overseeing and implementing the HPA. Significantly, whereas the Vision 2020 had been the climax of ASEAN's integration drive, the adoption of the HPA merely represented the last show of coherence before ASEAN entered a phase of policy incoherence and paralysis.

1998-2002 The post-crisis period, which coincided with Indonesia's demise as a regional leader and the East Timor crisis, threatened to erode ASEAN's integration initiatives and left international observers wondering whether ASEAN could resume its pre-crisis cohesion and role as a reputable, effective collective actor, especially in the area of economic integration. Representative for the main thrust of ASEAN criticism, Rolf J. Langhammer, for example, has pointed out that

> The Asian economic crisis has supported views that ASEAN as an actor in international politics owed its reputation primarily to past non-economic achievements than to present economic achievements. Its reputation would be at risk if internal political controversies are aggravated further and if each member state sees domestic and regional stabilization as trade-offs. The implementation of AFTA would be endangered, too. This could become a vicious circle since postponing the AFTA liberalization timetable would further fuel sceptical views on the "economic teeth" of ASEAN.[34]

ASEAN itself claims to be politically as relevant as ever and points at its achievements.

In the economic area, AFTA has been formally established in 2002, two years earlier than previously envisioned. Various new initiatives have been set up, such as the ASEAN Surveillance Process (ASP) and the Initiative for ASEAN Integration (IAI), which is to help bridging the economic and development gap between old and new ASEAN members.

In the area of international relations, ASEAN credits itself for its role in initiating the ASEAN Plus Three (APT) process. In 1999, the APT has apparently made rapid progress, from issuing its Joint Declaration on East Asia

---

[34] Langhammer (2001b): 285.

Cooperation in 1999 to the establishment of an APT currency swap scheme, the discussion of East Asian economic integration in general and the establishment of both an ASEAN-China Free Trade Area and a Japan-ASEAN Free Trade Area in particular. ASEAN representatives also like to point out the impact of the APT forum on regional stability and security. Further, ASEAN also insists on its central role "in the driver's seat" of the ARF and is negotiating with China on a code of conduct concerning the South China Sea issue. However, the question remains whether ASEAN disposes of the internal coherence it needs to make intra-ASEAN institutions and initiatives work and to devise a coordinated foreign policy approach with regard to its members' external relations.

3.1.2. Institutional Framework

The institutional structure of ASEAN has grown in three main stages. The first seven to eight years after the Association's inception were marked by deliberate institutional minimalism to support a minimal political and functional cooperative agenda. In the period from 1975 to 1991, ASEAN's institutional framework gradually expanded as widening political and functional cooperation was complemented by purpose-seeking in the area of economic cooperation. The third wave of institution-building in ASEAN occurred as, starting in 1992, the Association aimed at closer economic integration.

3.1.2.1. Internal Institutional structure of ASEAN

1967-1974   Between 1967 and 1974, ASEAN formed what still constitutes its institutional backbone today. Up to 1974, the ASEAN Ministers Meetings (AMMs), attended by the foreign ministers of the ASEAN member states, represented the highest-level contact and supreme decision-making body in the intergovernmental ASEAN process. The annual meetings rotated from member state to member state and were headed by the foreign minister of the respective host country. Throughout the year, the Standing Committee, in cooperation with the ASEAN Directors-Generals of the national ASEAN Secretariats, implemented ASEAN's agenda on behalf of the AMM. The Standing Committee, which represented the link between the political and the functional level and was convened three to five times a year, was presided over by the foreign minister who had hosted the previous AMM. Its other members were the ambassadors of the respective other ASEAN states. Apart from these regularly recurring instutional meetings, ASEAN foreign ministers also began convening special and informal meetings from 1971 on, when and as the political circumstances required it. At the functional level, various experts and other committees were established to explore and devise opportunities of technical and development cooperation.[35]

1975-1991   In the second phase between 1975 and 1991, the process of political decision-making was formally shifted from the AMM to the newly-established ASEAN summit of the member states' heads of government. Convened for the first time in 1976, the ASEAN summit assumed the central and final decision-making authority, but as it met infrequently and irregularly in the first 15 years after its inception (in 1976, 1977 and 1987), the AMMs *de facto* largely remained the central decision-making body in ASEAN.[36]

In terms of ASEAN's administrative structure, the ASEAN summit of 1976 established the central permanent ASEAN Secretariat in Jakarta, with the Secretary-General at its head. However, up to 1992, the newly-established Secretariat and its Secretary-General had only a few subordinate administrative competences, disposed of only a minimal budget and only little more than a handful of staff and were dominated by the Director-Generals of the respective national ASEAN Offices who met in bimonthly intervals.[37]

In terms of functional cooperation, following the summit of 1976, ASEAN established three primary committees channeling cooperation in the areas of science and technology (COST), culture and information (COCI) and social development (COSD), which, in turn, headed the work carried out in the respective sub-committees, experts committees, working groups, etc. Cooperation and decision-making in the said areas were also mirrored by the proliferation of meetings of the respective portfolio ministers. A great number of such ministerial meetings (MMs), ususally paralleled by the respective senior official meetings (SOM), were established between the mid- to late 1970s and in the 1980s. In this period, ASEAN saw the establishment of ministerial and senior officials meetings in the areas of health, labor, social welfare, youth, science and technology, information and the environment.

In the mid-1970s, ASEAN also laid the institutional foundations for economic dialogue and cooperation. The establishment of the central annual ASEAN Economic Ministers Meeting (AEM) in 1975 represented the first institutional milestone in this area. The ASEAN summit of 1976 envisioned that the AEM should take a central role in discussing and devising ASEAN cooperation, particularly in the areas of food and energy, industrial cooperation and trade liberalization within an ASEAN Preferential Trade Area (PTA). The AEM's mission also comprised discussing the harmonization of regional development.[38]

---

[35] For details, cf. Stahl (2001): 28ff.
[36] Cf. Wichmann (1996): 22.
[37] Cf. Stahl (2001): 31.
[38] Cf. Declaration of ASEAN Concord, Denpasar, 24 February 1976, section B.

Following the establishment of the AEM, the Economic Ministers set up a separate AEM on Energy Cooperation (AEMEC, renamed AMEM when transferred to the responsibility of the ASEAN Energy Ministers in 1993), plus the corresponding SOM (SOME) in 1980. In 1979, the ASEAN Ministerial Meeting on Agriculture and Forestry (AMAF), seconded by the SOM-AMAF, was established.

Other areas of intergovernmental cooperation initiated in this phase comprised dialogue on legal cooperation, civil service and drugs. Stahl also draws attention to the fact that, apart from the intergovernmental process, ASEAN came to proliferate an ever-increasing number of informal track-two institutions bringing together representatives and experts of think tanks and NGOs on the one hand and government representatives on the other.[39]

1992 to 2002

Political Between 1992 and today, ASEAN has seen a wave of institutionalization aimed at bringing about regional economic and political integration, with the main emphasis on the economic domain. Functional and other areas of cooperation have also contributed to an ever-wider and ever-deeper network of ASEAN institutions.

In the political domain, the ASEAN summit finally assumed the leading role and factually took over control from the AMM in the 1990s. Thus, the fourth ASEAN Summit in 1992 established triannual summit meetings, with informal summits being convened in the intervening years, so that the ASEAN heads of government now meet every year. Considering that the annual AMM are held regularly in June/ July and that the annual ASEAN summits take place each year in November/ December, one can see that since 1992 the highest government representatives of the ASEAN states have been meeting in semi-annual turns. The establishment of annual ASEAN summits thus represents a more centralized and more authoritative, and at the same time also a more adaptable approach to decision making in ASEAN.

Since 1999, the ASEAN Calendar has also featured informal and formal ASEAN Foreign Ministers Retreats and SOM Retreats, which serve to discuss ASEAN's future and the coordination of the ASEAN governments' positions and agendas prior to collective meetings with third parties (such as the annual APT summits, for example).

In 1999, the ASEAN summit also made provisions for the establishment of an ASEAN Troika as an *ad hoc* body for crisis prevention and resolution, which, however, has never been convened so far. The so-called ASEAN Troika is supposed to be established when and as ASEAN countries face intra-ASEAN bilateral or domestic crises that threaten to seriously disturb regional peace and

---

[39] Stahl (2001): 31.

stability. The Troika, which would comprise the respective current, past and future Presidents of the Standing Committee, can only be formed once its formation is approved by the collective of all ASEAN foreign ministers.[40]

Further, in order to increase the efficiency of the political, economic and functional mechanisms of ASEAN, the ASEAN Secretariat has been strengthened and upgraded, while the Secretariat is no longer controlled by the Director-Generals of the national ASEAN Secretariats or ASEAN Offices. The Secretary-General has been assigned ministerial rank, which puts him formally on a par with the other ASEAN ministers. Thus, he reports, and is answerable, exclusively to the ASEAN heads of government. Since 1992, the powers and authority of the ASEAN Secretary-General have been upgraded considerably. By decision of the ASEAN summit of 1992, the Secretary-General of the ASEAN Secretariat was also renamed Secretary-General of ASEAN and thus has come to officially represent the whole of ASEAN, both internally and externally. The ASEAN Secretary-General has access to ASEAN meetings at all levels and has been commissioned with the task of reviewing, coordinating and supporting economic and functional cooperation at ASEAN level. The Secretary-General submits his annual reports on the progress of ASEAN cooperation to the ASEAN summit.[41] In the context of these changes, the office of the Secretary-General has become much more political than before and allows him to even criticize negative regional developments.

Economic and financial   The most dynamic complements to ASEAN's institutional structure since 1992 have occurred in the area of economic and financial cooperation. In order to increase the effectiveness of economic cooperation, the Singapore summit of 1992 eliminated the five economic committees subordinated to the AEM and conferred their respective responsibilities to one single body, the Senior Economic Officials Meeting (SEOM).[42] Since 1995, the SEOM also oversees the implementation of the provisions of the ASEAN Agreement on Services. The AEM itself advanced to a more central position in the 1990s, as it is at the core of ASEAN's economic integration initiatives.

The 1992 Singapore summit also kicked off the ASEAN Free Trade Area (AFTA), to create "a truly integrated market".[43] Parallel to the adoption of the Common Effective Preferential Trading Scheme (CEPT), the AFTA Ministerial Council for the Implementation of the CEPT (or AFTA Council) was

---

[40] Cp. ASEAN Secretariat (undated c): "The ASEAN Troika".
[41] For an overview of the changing role and tasks of the ASEAN Secretariat, see ASEAN Secretariat (undated b): "The ASEAN Secretariat: Basic Mandate, Functions and Composition".
[42] Cf. Wichmann (1996): 23.
[43] ASEAN Secretariat (2000): "ASEAN Free Trade Area".

established to supervise, coordinate, implement and review the AFTA agreement.[44] Nominated by the AEM, the ministerial-level AFTA Council comprises one nominee from each member state and the Secretary-General of ASEAN.[45] The SEOM is in charge of supporting the work of the AFTA Council. Since its inception, the AFTA Council has met variably once or twice a year.

In 1998, the ASEAN Investment Area (AIA) was established with the objective to liberalize the investment sector within ASEAN. Its institutional structure is similar to that of AFTA. Like AFTA, the AIA process is guided by a ministerial-level council established by the AEM, the AIA Council.[46] The AIA Council, which meets regularly, comprises the ministers responsible for investment and the Secretary-General of ASEAN. Its meetings are also attended by the the heads of the national investment agencies.[47] At Senior Officials level, the Coordinating Committee on Investment (CCI) has been set up which reports to the AIA Council through the SEOM.[48]

In 1997, ASEAN expanded its institutional framework to comprise ministerial-level dialogue and cooperation in the area of finance when it convened the first annual Finance Ministerial Meeting (AFMM). The AFMM is in charge of all matters of financial cooperation and integration both between ASEAN members and between ASEAN and its external dialogue partners.

The AFMM reviews the progress of ASEAN's financial cooperation and liberalization initiatives. In particular, it reviews the progress of the ASEAN Surveillance Process (ASP), which was established in 1998 with the objective of creating early warning mechnisms to prevent the recurrence of major financial crises by monitoring macroeconomic, structural and sectoral developments in the Southeast Asian economies. The AFMM's biannual consultations on the ASP process are based on the reports of the ASEAN Select Committee (ASC), which represents the core of the ASP and is formed by the Senior Financial Officials Meeting (ASFOM) and the ASEAN Central Bank Forum.[49]

---

[44] Cf. Framework Agreement on Enhancing Economic Cooperation, Singapore, 28 January 1992, Article A.1.

[45] Agreement on the Common Economic Effective Preferential Tariff Scheme for the ASEAN Free Trade Area, Singapore, 28 January 1992.

[46] Cf. ASEAN Secretariat (undated a): "ASEAN Investment Area: An Update". See also: Framework Agreement on the ASEAN Investment Area, Manila, 07 October 1998.

[47] Framework Agreement on the ASEAN Investment Area, Manila, 07 October 1998.

[48] Ibid.

[49] Cf. Terms of Understanding on the Establishment of the ASEAN Surveillance Process, Washington, D.C., 4 October 1998.
The Select Committee, in turn, is supported in its work by the administrative ASEAN Surveillance Coordinating Unit, ASCU, based at the ASEAN Secretariat and the ASEAN Surveillance Technical Unit, ASTU, which is supposed to give technical support and training

Further, the AFMM has taken a prominent role in representing ASEAN in the financial consultations and cooperation with China, Japan and South Korea in the context of the increasing East Asian cooperation initiatives of the ASEAN Plus One and ASEAN Plus Three processes since 1998, particularly the Chiang Mai initiative of 2001 that is aimed at establishing a net of currency swap exchanges to stabilize the regional currencies in Southeast Asia.

Further, the range of portfolio ministerial and senior officals meetings in the area of economic cooperation was complemented in the fields of transport (ATM / STOM) in 1996, tourism (Tourism MM) in 1997 and telecommunications (TELMIN / TELSOM) in 2001. In addition to this, institutionalized cooperation in all areas of ASEAN economic cooperation, namely trade, services, customs (Director-Generals on Customs working group), commerce, information technology and e-commerce, agriculture, finance, subregional growth areas, industry, intellectual property, investment, minerals and energy, services, standards, tourism, transport and communications, gradually expanded and deepened at various levels comprising task forces, experts committees, working groups, etc.

Functional and other   In the 1990s, ASEAN steadily enhanced its activities in the area of functional cooperation. In institutional terms, the 1990s saw the revival of the portfolio minsterial meetings on youth in 1997 and health in 1998, which had been discontinued in the late 1980s. Cooperation on rural development and poverty eradication was raised to ministerial and senior officials level in 1997 (AMRDPE / SOM RPDE). In the area of the environment, the traditional environment ministerial (AMME) meeting was complemented by additional irregular and informal meetings (IAMME), and due to the growing concerns about the haze issue that had been especially distressing to various ASEAN countries since 1997, the environment ministers began convening additional ministerial meetings on haze (AMMH) which met four and three times a year in the crisis years of 1998 and 1999, respectively and has since been reconvened once in 2002. In the same year, the first meeting of the ASEAN Committee on Education (ACE) was convened. Thus, the significance of cooperation on education has been upgraded from its previous status as a sub-committee of the Committee on Social Development (COSD) to a separate committee in its own right.

Two other areas of cooperation that have achieved prominence in the 1990s are immigration and fighting transnational crime. The main bodies that have emerged in these areas are the Director-Generals on Immigration (DGI)

---

to "the ASEAN Secretariat, finance ministries, central banks, and other relevant departments of the ASEAN Member Countries." The ASTU is based at the ADB and is headed either by a senior official of the ASEAN Secretariat or a senior official of a member state designated by the ASEAN Select Committee.

working group and the ministerial meetings on Transnational Crime (AMMTC). Further, the Senior Officials Meeting on Drugs (ASOD) has been established.

Figure 1: Institutional Structure of ASEAN [50]

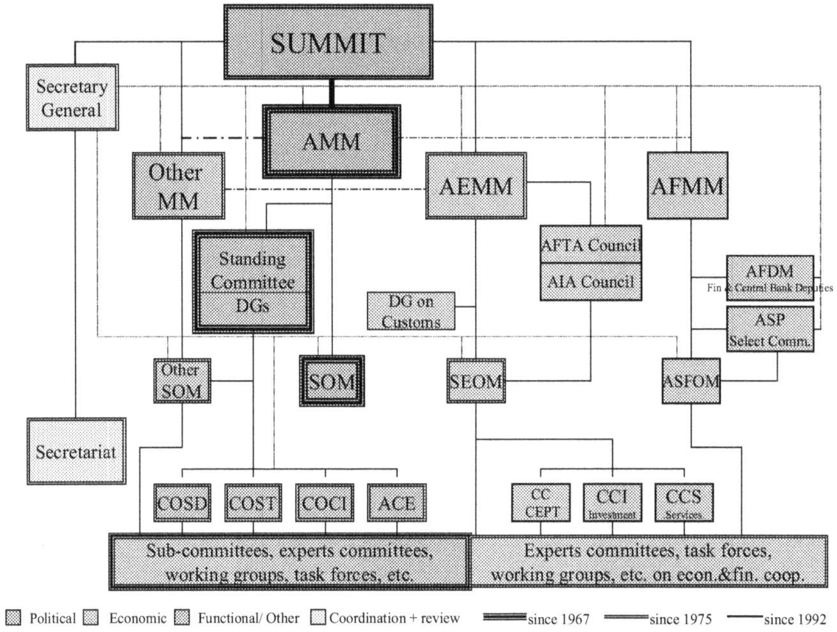

Source: author.[51]

3.1.2.2. Institutional framework for collective interaction with external partners

Following the turning point of ASEAN regionalism in 1975/76, ASEAN also started engaging in institutionalized bilateral dialogue with selected external dialogue partners at ministerial and other levels. Starting with the U.S., Japan, Australia, Canada and New Zealand in 1977, collective institutionalized

[50] ACE=ASEAN Committee on Education; AEM=ASEAN Economic Ministers Meeting; AFTA= ASEAN Free Trade Area; AFMM=ASEAN Finance Ministers Meeting; AFDM=ASEAN Finance Deputies Meeting; AIA=ASEAN Investment Area; AMM=ASEAN Ministerial Meeting; ASFOM=ASEAN Finance Officials Meeting; ASP=ASEAN Surveillance Process; CC=Coordinating Committee; CCI=Coordinating Committee on Investment; CCS=Coordinating Committee on Services; COCI=Committee on Culture and Information; COSD= Committee on Social Development; COST= Committee on Science and Technology; DG=Director-Generals; MM=Ministerial Meeting; SEOM=Senior Economic Officials Meeting; SOM=Senior Officials Meeting; Summit=ASEAN Summit of heads of the heads of government.

[51] Cp. charts on ASEAN's institutional structure in Stahl (2001): 29-33 and Wichmann (1996): 23.

dialogue was subsequently established with the European Community in 1978, India in 1980 and the Republic of Korea in 1989, followed by the People's Republic of China in 1996, Pakistan and Russia in 1997.

In 1989, ASEAN members helped found the Asia Pacific Economic Cooperation (APEC) process. Although ASEAN did not join APEC as a group and is not represented as a grouping there, ASEAN governments regularly meet to exchange views on the APEC agenda before the annual APEC meetings. Apart from the ASEAN summits and AMM, ASEAN members also discuss APEC-related matters in the ASEAN APEC SOMs which are held regularly before APEC summit meetings. However, ASEAN members at various stages of APEC's history have held quite different and uncoordinated views on the APEC process, so that it would be futile to speak of ASEAN as taking the role of a collective actor within APEC. What is more, in the course of ASEAN enlargement since the mid-1990s, not all new ASEAN members have been able to join APEC (most notably Myanmar).

Traditionally, ASEAN invites all its official Dialogue Partners to attend regular post-AMM conferences, the so-called Post-Ministerial Conferences (PMC). Since 1991, China has participated in these annual PMCs as a guest.[52] At the PMC, ASEAN engages both in separate collective bilateral talks with each Dialogue Partner (the so-called ASEAN+1 process) and in synchronous collective talks with all ten Dialogue Partners (the so-called ASEAN+10 process). In 1993, ASEAN also resolved to establish the annual post-AMM/PMC ASEAN Regional Forum (ARF) as a separate forum to promote exchange on questions of regional security with its Dialogue Partners. The first ARF was held in 1994 and has been convened regularly ever since.

In 1996, ASEAN states strongly supported Singapore's efforts to establish the Asia-Europe Meeting (ASEM) process, which was to comprise the respective member states of the European Union plus the European Commission on the European side and the ASEAN member states plus the PRC, Japan and South Korea on the Asian side. Formally, ASEAN is not represented as a collective, but *de facto* the ASEAN states have variously taken collective positions and identified themselves as a collective in the ASEM process. The ASEM is aimed at improving political, economic and cultural dialogue and cooperation between the EU and the participating Asian countries.

The most dynamic development in terms of the grouping's collective institutionalized external relations, however, is the ASEAN Plus Three (APT) process with China, Japan and South Korea. The first-ever summit of heads of government took place in 1997. Since then, summits have been reconvened annually, with the Joint Statement on East Asia Cooperation issued at the occasion of the third APT summit in 1999 marking the first joint official record

---

[52] Lee Lai To (2001): 415.

of the APT states' commitment to more permanent forms of East Asian cooperation.[53] The developments since then have shown that, in terms of institutionalization, the APT process does not stop at the annual summits, but has already proliferated further institutionalized intergovernmental meetings and mechanisms (see section on ASEAN Plus Three below).

3.1.3. Central purposes of ASEAN

Prior to 1997, observers credited ASEAN especially for its achievements in providing a politically stable regional environment conducive to the economic development of its individual member states. As Dosch pointed out in 1995, the synergies resulting from ASEAN cooperation in terms of regional security and stability came at such a low cost and represented such an invaluable collective good to the ASEAN states that, judging from a cost-benefit perspective, he deemed the ASEAN process to be irreversible.[54]

Similarly, ASEAN's economic cooperation and the benefits derived from it had come to be seen as an increasingly relevant, but largely "cost-free" logical turnout of the political cooperation process (rather than of systemic and often painful economic integration processes requiring a high degree of commitment) which, in turn, would reinforce ASEAN's political cohesion. Thus, Bilson Kurus noted in 1993 in an article on ASEAN's *raison d'être* that

> As noted earlier, the states have used ASEAN as a vehicle for dealing with extraregional trading partners, but another beneficial economic impact is tied to ASEAN's role in facilitating a more favorable investment climate within the region. It is doubtful that such an environment would have been created without ASEAN. [...]
>
> What has emerged from the discussion above is a picture of an ASEAN that has the most to show in the diplomatic and political arena. However, when the totality of the organization is taken into account, a different picture emerges – one which portrays ASEAN as both a source of, and a means to obtain benefits. *While these benefits are relatively "cost-free," they are dependent on the regional cohesion and unity of the member states.* In other words, *notwithstanding the patchy economic record in the economic sphere, the maintenance of ASEAN itself has become a logical and plausible necessity for the member states.*[55] [Emphasis added, M.H.]

---

[53] For an overview of the emergence of the APT process, cf. Hund and Okfen (2001).
[54] Cf. Dosch (1996): 106.
[55] Bilson Kurus (1993): 828, 829.

Indeed, considering the strong national economic growth rates throughout Southeast Asia prior to 1997, most ASEAN members complacently expected that explorative ventures into projects of closer economic cooperation (including AFTA) would proceed at a pace set by ASEAN's customary slow ways of decision making, which are based on paramount respect for the lowest common denominator, requiring only low-cost voluntary commitments. ASEAN governments – despite their resolve at the ASEAN Singapore summit in 1992 to intensify projects of regional political and economic cooperation – remained strongly suspicious of, and opposed to, the idea of accepting any surrender of national sovereignty to supranational ASEAN institutions or mechanisms.[56]

Since the events of the economic crisis of 1997, economic integration is no longer seen as a logical eventual outcome, but rather as an as yet unachieved necessary precondition of, regional political stability. Therefore, ASEAN's official economic objectives have been adapted accordingly. It is thus no coincidence that the ASEAN Vision 2020 of 1997 and the HPA of 1998 are the very first official ASEAN documents to feature the term "economic integration" (Vision 2020, HPA). The HPA also defines the establishment of a "highly competitive ASEAN Economic Region in which there is a free flow of goods, services and investments, a freer flow of capital, equitable economic development and reduced poverty and socio-economic disparities" as one of the main purposes of ASEAN. Although the term "integration" is nowhere clearly defined, and as supranationality is still a taboo word in ASEAN, the organization has to be measured by its ability to live up to the expectations raised by the term's implications of rules-based and legally binding trade liberalization regimes and corresponding centralized, independent authorities to oversee and implement them.

With a view to preventing future economic crises, ASEAN has also become engaged in financial and macroeconomic cooperation since 1997. The overall aims in this area are to stabilize regional currencies, establish early warning mechanisms and promote region-wide reforms in the banking sector. To this end, ASEAN has established the ASEAN Surveillance Mechanism (ASP) in cooperation with the Asian Development Bank (ADB) and has initiated consultations between member states' central banks and the ministries of finance.

The ASEAN Vision 2020 and the HPA of 1997 also reaffirmed ASEAN's willingness to expand cooperation in the area of development. Especially with a view to the CLMV countries (Cambodia, Laos, Myanmar, Vietnam), which all

---

[56] ASEAN governments – despite their resolve to intensify projects of regional political and economic cooperation at the ASEAN Singapore summit in 1992 – remained strongly suspicious of, and opposed to, the idea of accepting any surrender of national sovereignty to supranational ASEAN institutions or mechanisms (cf. Dosch 1996: 103).

acceded to ASEAN in the mid- and late 1990s, ASEAN has adopted a development assistance agenda requiring the old ASEAN members to engage in providing technical, technological and educational infrastructure development assistance to these countries. The old ASEAN members' ability to assist the newcomer states in their struggle for economic development will have a mediate and immediate impact on regional stability and security, both with a view to domestic stability in these countries, border conflicts between these and other ASEAN members (such as at the Thai-Myanmarese border), and the uncomfortable prospect of China's growing hegemonic influence in Myanmar, Laos and Cambodia.

Another major purpose of ASEAN is to enhance its members' leverage in the international arena. With respect to regional security, ASEAN is collectively promoting China's acession to a joint code of conduct for the South China Sea and is promoting the various great powers' accession to ASEAN's Treaty of Amity and Cooperation and the code of conduct for peaceful relations which is at its core. ASEAN has also involved the great powers in joint security consultations in the context of the ARF with the objective of preventing frictions and conflicts between China and the other powers. With a view to the wider East Asian environment, ASEAN, through the APT process, also seeks to contribute to the relaxation of tensions between the Northeast Asian APT participants and encourages peaceful solutions to the conflict on the Korean peninsula. With a view to collective economic relations with external parties, ASEAN has only recently started to engage in collective deliberations to negotiate bilateral free trade agreements with China, Japan and the U.S. after it has aborted AFTA-Common Economic Region (CER) talks on a joint FTA with Australia and New Zealand in 2001 due to strong differences among its members about the desirability of such an FTA. It is not clear yet, however, in how far ASEAN will be able to achieve unity and act as a single actor on external economic policy issues.

Nevertheless, ASEAN is clearly on the way to intensify its political and economic cooperation with external partners. The successive establishment of the ASEAN Plus Three process since 1997 and the preceding debate about the formation of the East Asian Economic Caucus at ASEAN level since 1994 suggests that many ASEAN states are increasingly relying on the ASEAN collective as a basis for developing external ties and cooperative relations. The establishment of so-called Retrats at AMM, AEM and senior officials level, where ASEAN members coordinate their views before meetings with external partners, is only one indicator that ASEAN's internal coordination and decision making structures are slowly adapting to the requirements of enhanced collective external relations. Still, considering the ASEAN members' strong predilection for absolute national sovereignty, a coordinated ASEAN foreign policy mechanism is nowhere near in sight.

3.1.4. Type of cooperation

In ASEAN, it is clearly the national governments calling the shots, and no-one else. The governments are the supreme decision makers and arbiters in any question. They can overturn and modify agreements and withdraw from commitments made without having to fear formal sanctions from their fellow governments. This applies to all areas of cooperation, and even to the process of economic integration, as the chapter on pooling of sovereignty in this study will show. However, whereas in the areas of political and functional cooperation ASEAN has established no formal, rules-based mechanisms of cooperation, and decision making and strictly follows the principle of unanimity, the AFTA approach to economic integration operates on a more advanced level, as it has rules-based mechanisms in place which, however, are not legally binding (or only mock-binding, respectively) and are not overseen by an independent supranational authority with the power to sanction member states for non-compliance.

Dosch, drawing on a model developed by Manfred Mols, introduces a set of criteria to evaluate the state of regional integration of a grouping of states. At the lowest level, the intergovernmental process is based on mere consultations with no decision making authority granted to the dialogue mechanism. At the second, more advanced level, decisions at the intergovernmental process are taken unanimously. At the third level, the intergovernmental process can take decisions on the basis of a qualified majority, but gives dissenters the opportunity not to accede to these decisions or accede to them later (all-minus-x principle). At the fourth level, majority decisions are binding for all participants, whereas the fifth level is distinguished by supranational bodies that are not directly controlled by the national governments and have the authority to implement and oversee mechanisms and rules agreed upon collectively by the national governments.[57] Judging by these criteria, ASEAN's political and functional cooperation is lodged at level two, whereas the intergovernmental process at AFTA level is located somewhere between levels two and three, as the "all-minus-x" rule applies to AFTA[58] and members can temporarily suspend or even reverse their accession to certain steps of liberalization (cp. the chapter on pooling of sovereignty). There are currently no signs that the status of cooperation in any of the three areas is set to shift to a higher integration level. Thus, while ASEAN is continuously striving to expand its areas of cooperation in all areas, there have been no systemic or 'constitutional' changes of the basic modes of cooperation since the mid-1990s.

---

[57] Cf. Dosch (1996): 106f.
[58] Cp. ibid.: 107.

3.1.5. Problems

The standstill of ASEAN's progress on the integration ladder, as outlined above, seems to be at odds with ASEAN's uninterrupted drive to continually expand the scope of its internal and external cooperative and integrative initiatives. Thus, ASEAN seems to be expanding horizontally without adapting the vertical structures needed to adequatly coordinate and deepen the widening scope of its increasing initiatives of cooperation and integration. As in the early 1990s, most ASEAN member states welcome synergies as long as they can be obtained at a low (political or economic) cost and as long as national commitments to the ASEAN process remain largely voluntary, unobliging and reversible. As Rüland has indicated in 1995, the low degree of transfer of sovereignty and formal, rules-based regional integration leaves ASEAN strongly vulnerable to centrifugal influences impacting on the grouping.[59] It is therefore not surprising that the economic crisis of 1997 has had a strongly centrifugal impact on the ASEAN process at large,[60] a development that has caused ASEAN think tanks to call for *Reinventing ASEAN* (thus the title of a recent collection of essays by ASEAN think tanks)[61] and let Simon Tay call for more centralized and autoritative regional mechanisms and institutions as the only solution to overcome ASEAN's incohesiveness.[62]

3.2. ASEAN Plus Three

ASEAN Plus Three (APT) represents the latest – and seemingly the most dynamic – multilateral dialogue and cooperation process ASEAN is currently engaging in. Its most apparent distinctive feature is the scope of its membership and geographic extension, which are deliberately and exclusively East Asian. It comprises the ten ASEAN states plus the People's Republic of China, Japan and the Republic of Korea. Its second remarkable feature is that, since its inception, the loosely connected grouping is making fast headway in devising and announcing new cooperation initiatives, whereas other multilateral groupings such as ASEM and notably APEC are increasingly turning out to be lame ducks in their respective efforts at striking axes of cooperation and – in the case of

---

[59] Cf. Rüland (1995a): 12

Rüland in 1995 explicitly referred to the enlargement of ASEAN's membership from ASEAN-6 to ASEAN-10 as a centrifugal force. The many crises ASEAN has been exposed to since 1997, however, can be justly considered as centrifugal forces transcending those of ASEAN enlargement by far, because they created diversion of interests that frequently divided the core member states of ASEAN.

[60] Cp. Rüland (2000a) and (2000b).

[61] Tay, Estanislao and Soesastro (eds.) (2001).

[62] Cf. Tay (2001): 19.

APEC – also free trade between East Asia and the West. This sub-chapter aims to give a brief overview of the evolution, the institutional set-up and the general purpose of the forum as well as its most apparent shortcomings.

3.2.1. Brief history of the APT process [63]

The idea of creating a forum of East Asian states was first introduced and promoted by the Malaysian Prime Minister, Mahathir Mohamad, at the occasion of a state visit of the Chinese Prime Minister Li Peng in December 1991. The East Asian Economic Grouping (EAEG) envisioned by Mahathir was to form the basis of an East Asian economic bloc which in his view was to be East Asia's answer to the uncertain outcome of the Uruguay round of the GATT and plans of economic bloc-building in North America and Western Europe (NAFTA and the European Community). At the same time, just one year after the Tianmen massacre, the proposal was a political signal to the world that Malaysia intended to act as a bridgehead in ASEAN for a constructive relationship with China.[64]

The other ASEAN members, especially Singapore and Indonesia, rejected Malaysia's unilateral EAEG proposal on the grounds that, first, Malaysia had failed to consult them before going public on the issue and, more importantly, because at that time they strictly opposed the idea of exclusive East Asian cooperation and rather preferred to cooperate with the U.S. within APEC. Nevertheless, as Mahathir insisted on his vision of East Asian cooperation and as apparently Singapore and Indonesia tried to avoid tensions with Malaysia, the AMM in 1993 agreed to work towards establishing what an East Asian Economic Caucus (EAEC) as a separate dialogue forum within APEC, which, however, never actually materialized (not at last because Japan was utterly opposed to joining a caucus that was to give a high profile to its archrival China, while the U.S. had to stay out of it).

In 1996, the idea of the EAEC experienced a renaissance as the Asian side of the first Asia-Europe Meeting was informally referred to as a manifestation of the EAEC by various observers and Asian diplomats at that time.

Another development supporting notions of closer East Asian cooeperation was that, in 1997 and 1998, informal summit meetings took place between ASEAN and China, Japan and South Korea to discuss the impact and consequences of the Asian crisis and opportunities of cooperation between ASEAN and its three Northeast Asian dialogue partners. Surprising to most observers, the very same

---

[63] This overview largely represents a reappraisal of the detailed description of the evolution of the EAEC/ ASEAN Plus Three up to 1999 by Hund and Okfen (2001).

[64] Cp. Chin (2000) on Malaysia's special relationship with China since the early 1990s, after the end of the Cold War.

thirteen states issued a Joint Statement on East Asia Cooperation at the occasion of their third joint summit in 1999 (that coincided with the third informal ASEAN summit in Manila), which is generally considered as the official beginning of the APT process. The foundational Joint Statement set the stage for a number of initiatives of (bilateral and multilateral) intergovernmental economic, monetary, financial and development cooperation and also opened a door to political and security dialogue. The heads of governemnt also "agreed to intensify coordiontion and cooperation in various international and regional fora such as the UN, WTO, APEC, ASEM, and the ARF, as well as in regional and international financial institutions."[65] In the area of culture and information, the document explicitly also addressed the shared commitment of the APT governments "to strengthen regional cooperation in projecting an Asian point of view to the rest of the world". Most remarkably, the Joint Statement called for "enhancing self-help and support mechanisms in East Asia through the ASEAN+3 Framework, including ongoing dialogue and [a] cooperation mechanism of the ASEAN+3 finance and central bank leaders and officials".[66]

In subsequent years, various contacts between the thirteen governments at ministerial and senior officials level in various portfolios increasingly complemented the annual summit meetings.

In 2000, APT drew strong attention from international observers when the APT finance ministers launched the Chiang Mai Initiative (CMI) whose main achievement so far has been the establishment of a network of bilateral currency swap and repurchase arrangement (BSA) between an increasing number of APT countries, which is designed to provide liquidity support to, and thus stabilize, regional currencies in cases of strong fluctuation. Other projects aimed to prevent the recurrence of economic and financial crises in East Asia, such as involving the Northeast Asian "Plus Three" countries in the ASEAN Surveillance Process (ASP) and initiating reforms in the financial and banking sectors, have made little headway yet.[67] However, in a first step taken in May 2001, the APT finance ministers

> agreed to update the capital flows situation in each member country and to exchange data on capital flows bilaterally among member countries on a voluntary basis [... and,] [r]ecognizing the importance of enhanced monitoring of the economic situation in our region [...,] agreed to

---

[65] Joint Statement on East Asia Cooperation, Manila, 28 November 1999.
[66] Ibid.
[67] Cp. Joint Ministerial Statement, Fifth ASEAN Finance Ministers Meeting, Kuala Lumpur, 7-8 April 2001.

establish a study group to examine ways of enhancing the effectiveness of our economic reviews and policy dialogues."[68]

The Northeast Asian "Plus Three" countries have all made commitments to training programs for ASEAN+3 Finance and Central Bank officials in one or the other form and according to their capacities. Thus, APT has not only initiated a dialogue process on financial and economic stability, but is making an effort to sustain and deepen it.

Whereas the main focus of APT has been on monetary and financial cooperation so far, functional cooperation in other areas has made steady progress. Thus, China, for example, has started to engage in Mekong development initiatives, whereas Japan has committed financial and technical assistance to various ASEAN development initiatives such as the e-ASEAN initiative and the Initiative for ASEAN Integration (IAI). Korea has also engaged in a number of functional projects and has taken over organizing the East Asia Vision Group which gave a first interims report to the APT summit in November 2001 and is to present a final report at the 2002 summit. At the 2001 summit, the heads of government also agreed to look into closer cooperation in the fight against terrorism and transnational crime.

The most spectacular and visionary, but at the same time least substantial and credible proposal of the East Asia Vision Group report is the establishment of an East Asian Free Trade Area (EAFTA), a proposal diplomatically considered as "bold yet feasible" by the Chairman of the November 2001 APT: "The report contains key proposals and concrete measures to broaden East Asia cooperation. Some are bold yet feasible such as establishing an East Asia Free Trade Area and liberalizing trade well ahead of APEC's goals."[69]

At the sidelines of the APT process, the Northeast Asian heads of government have started to engage in a separate, informal trilateral dialogue process to discuss questions of regional concern.

Parallel to, and conditioned by, the multilateral APT process, ASEAN's dialogue with the respective Northeast Asian partners, especially Japan and China, has intensified at the level of the bilateral ASEAN+1 meetings, too. In fact, China and Japan seem to be using the ASEAN+1 channels rather than the APT process to raise their individual profile and launch and carry out new cooperative initiatives with ASEAN. The most remarkable initiative in this respect is China's unilateral initiative to form a China-ASEAN Free Trade Area, a proposal that was agreed upon and endorsed in principle by the ASEAN heads of government at the ASEAN/ APT summit in Brunei in November 2001:

---

[68] Joint Ministerial Statement of the ASEAN+3 Finance Ministers Meeting, Honlulu, 09 May 2001.

[69] Chairman of the 7th ASEAN Summit and the 5th ASEAN+3 Summit: Press statement, Bandar Seri Begawan, 05 November 2001.

We endorsed the proposal for a *Framework on Economic Cooperation* and to establish an ASEAN-China Free Trade Area within 10 years with special and differential treatment and flexibility to the newer ASEAN members. The agreement should also provide for an "early harvest" in which the lists of products and services will be determined by mutual consultation. [...] We agreed to instruct our ministers and senior officials to start the negotiations with a view to conclude the agreement as soon as possible.[70]

Japan, which had been reluctant to discuss free trade agreements with ASEAN prior to the summit, clearly changed course following China's success concerning a bilateral FTA with ASEAN, but, despite a strong show of goodwill on its part with Prime Minister Koizumi commencing a tour of the capitals of Southeast Asia in early 2002, currently still seems to be very uncertain how to adapt to the new situation (see chapter on ASEAN Plus Three in this study).

To sum up, the APT, which has so far largely been a forum for dialogue and functional cooperation, has started moving into the sphere of dialogue on economic integration between ASEAN and its respective APT partners. On the other hand, there are indicators that competing strategic interests of China and Japan in Southeast Asia will leave its marks on the East Asian Cooperation (APT) process as a whole and that the ASEAN+1 processes might achieve more prominence over time. With a view to identity formation in East Asia, the analysis of the APT process carried out in this study seeks to elaborate on the cohesive and divisive forces that are impacting on the APT.

3.2.2. Institutional Framework

The number of APT meetings has increased visibly between 2001 and 2002 (see table below). Whereas the APT calendar featured 19 APT meetings in 2001, the APT process in 2002 comprised 25 such (mostly high-ranking) events. This compares to a total of 478 events (including the above-mentioned APT events

---

[70] Chairman of the 7th ASEAN Summit and the three ASEAN+1 Summits: Press Statement, Bandar Seri Begawan, 06 November 2001.

of that year) featured by the ASEAN calendar in 2002.[71] Unlike dialogue in other multilateral fora of regional and transregional dialogue and cooperation, such as APEC, ASEM and the EU-ASEAN dialogue, ASEAN has started to pair many ASEAN events with the respective APT events, so that the APT calendar increasingly resembles a replica of the ASEAN process. Thus, the annual ASEAN summits are followed by APT summits, the AMM is followed by APT Foreign Ministers Meetings, and a number of other ASEAN portfolio ministers and corresponding senior officials meetings have their equivalent in the APT calendar.

---

[71] Cf. ASEAN Calendar 2001 and ASEAN Calendar 2002, as provided by the ASEAN Secretariat, http://www.aseansec.org/general /calendar/jan02.htm , http://www.aseansec.org/general /calendar/feb02.htm, http://www.aseansec.org/general /calendar/mar02.htm, http://www.aseansec.org/general /calendar/apr02.htm, http://www.aseansec.org/general /calendar/may02.htm, http://www.aseansec.org/general /calendar/jun02.htm, http://www.aseansec.org/general /calendar/jul02.htm, http://www.aseansec.org/general /calendar/agus02.htm, http://www.aseansec.org/general /calendar/sept02.htm, http://www.aseansec.org/general /calendar/oct02.htm, http://www.aseansec.org/general /calendar/nov02.htm, http://www.aseansec.org/general /calendar/dec02.htm, http://www.aseansec.org/general /calendar/jan01.htm, http://www.aseansec.org/general /calendar/feb01.htm, http://www.aseansec.org/general /calendar/mar01.htm, http://www.aseansec.org/general /calendar/apr01.htm, http://www.aseansec.org/general /calendar/may01.htm, http://www.aseansec.org/general /calendar/jun01.htm, http://www.aseansec.org/general /calendar/jul01.htm, http://www.aseansec.org/general /calendar/agus01.htm, http://www.aseansec.org/general /calendar/sept01.htm, http://www.aseansec.org/general /calendar/oct01.htm, http://www.aseansec.org/general /calendar/nov01.htm, http://www.aseansec.org/general /calendar/dec01.htm.

Table 1: ASEAN Plus Three meetings in 2001 and 2002 (complete)

Meetings	2001	2002
APT Summit	**01 (Nov)**	**01 (Nov)**
APT Foreign Min. (AFM+3)	**01 (Jul)**	**01 (Jul)**
APT Senior Officials Meeting (SOM+3)	02 (May, Nov)	01 (May)
APT Finance Min. (AFMM+3)	**01 (May)**	**02 (May, Sep)**
APT Finance and Central Bank Deputies (AFDM+3)	02 (Apr, May)	05 (Apr, May, Sep, Oct)
APT Economic Min. (AEM+3)	**02 (May, Sep)**	**01 (Sep)**
APT Senior Economic Officials Meeting (SEOM+3)	02 (Aug, Sep)	01 (Mar)
APT SOM on Energy (SOME+3), 1st meeting in 2002		01 (Jul)
APT Agriculture&Forestry Min. (AMAF+3)	**01 (Oct)**	**01 (Oct)**
APT SOM on Agriculture & Forestry Min. (SOM-AMAF+3)	02 (Apr, Oct)	01 (Oct)
APT Labor Min. (ALMM+3)		**02 (Apr, May)**
APT Senior Labor Officials (SLOM+3)		01 (Apr)
APT Tourism Min. (1st meeting in 2002)		**01 (Jan)**
ASEAN National Tourism Organizations (NTO)+3	01 (Oct)	
APT Consultative Meeting on Science&Technology	01 (May)	
East Asia Working Group on Regional Integration (EAWG) + 3, 1st meeting in 2001	01 (Apr)	01 (Apr)
East Asia Study Group (EASG)	02 (May, Jul)	03 (Jan, May, Jun)
APT Study Group to examine ways of enhancing the effectiveness of economic reviews and policy dialogues		01 (Apr)
APT Leadership Executive Program for Youth Organizations		01 (May)

Source: ASEAN Calendars 2001 and 2002, ASEAN Secretariat, as cited above.

As table 2 shows, the institutional structure of the APT dialogue and cooperation process is institutionalizing fast. The 2001 ASEAN summit even deliberated about a proposal to establish an APT Secretariat.[72] In addition to the APT meetings listed above (see table), separate ASEAN+1 meetings with China, Japan and Korea are also increasing rapidly. Another type of meetings that is not listed here are the separate meetings between the governments of Northeast Asia, particularly the prominent informal summit talks that have been taking place annually since 2000 between the "Plus Three" countries. Thus, the main APT process in which all thirteen APT governments participate, is accompanied by various additional forms of dialogue and cooperative initiatives that are currently mushrooming in various directions, each comprising only parts of the APT membership.

3.2.3. General purpose of APT

The overall direction of the APT process is not yet very clear. Its activities so far have been directed at preventing economic crises from recurring by cooperating in the area of financial and economic monitoring and reform as well as in the area of economic development, with a focus on technical and human resources development. Further, cooperation on transnational issues, such as cross-border policing against drug smuggling, terrorism, etc. has been initiated in the context of APT. Initial efforts have been made to promote trade and investment liberalization, which points in the direction of enhanced economic cooperation and integration.

Various APT statements emphasize the importance of "mechanisms" of cooperation, suggesting that regional peace and stability in East Asia is engineerable. However, when looking at APT activism, one also needs to keep in mind that regional stability emerges foremost from more relaxed relations between the participating governments. What APT is, and can be, all about also depends largely on the respective paticipants' actual attitudes and interests.

At a first glance, the record of APT cooperation suggests that, presently, all APT partners seem resolved to position themselves so as to find and take a constructive role in the APT process and not let go of any chances of closer cooperation and (some at least) economic integration.

---

[72] Cf. Press Statement by the Chairman of the 7th ASEAN Summit and the 5th ASEAN+3 Summit, Bandar Seri Begawan, 05 November 2001.

3.2.4. Type of cooperation

APT currently represents an intergovernmental consultation process with no agreed-upon regulatory mechanisms of decision making or a collective institutional framework. Unlike ASEAN, the APT process is not based on foundational and other contractual documents (such as the Bangkok Declaration on ASEAN Cooperation, the Treaty of Amity and Cooperation, the Treaty on Southeast Asia as a Nuclear Weapon Free Zone, SEANWFZ, and the AFTA Framework) obliging its participants to follow certain modes of behavior and decision making (cf. also the chapter on ASEAN norms). So far, the APT process rests merely on joint statements issued by the heads of government and the respective ministers. The net of swap arrangements between APT countries, the most remarkable material APT achievement so far, does not represent a (pan-East Asian) collective institution, but is negotiated bilaterally between the respective participating states.

Judging by Dosch and Mols' model of progressive stages of integration (as outlined in the chapter on ASEAN above), APT therefore is still at the first (lowest) stage of integration, which is marked by government consultations with no provisions made for collective decision making.[73]

However, considering that the APT governments are already beginning to think publicly about projects of closer regional economic integration, and as they are preparing to cooperate in a number of functional and other areas, it does not seem impossible that institutional structures and formal frameworks for cooperation may be established successively as the process evolves. Possibly, the East Asia Vision Group report, which is supposed to present its report to the heads of government at the APT summit in 2002, will already devise first proposals to that effect.

3.2.5. Problems and limitations

The first and most obvious problem of the APT process is both the heterogeneity of its members and the virulent rivalries between its Northeast Asian members, particularly between the regional great powers, Japan and China. The limits set by the general opposition between these two regional poles of power and interests at the same time look set to represent the limits of APT cooperation and integration process as a whole. A plausible consequence may be that the main APT process may eventually take on the function of a loose link connecting the respective forms of cooperation and sub-regional integration, comprising only parts of the APT membership. In this case, APT

---

[73] Cp. Dosch (1996): 106f.

would not take on the role of a unified or collective regional actor or decision making body, but at best remain what it is today, namely a dialogue forum complementing other efforts to enhance political and economic stability in East Asia.

Another severe limitation to the scope and effectiveness of APT cooperation and integration is represented by most East Asian states' opposition to ceding national authority and sovereignty to regional bodies and regulatory mechanisms. The history of ASEAN relations is a case in point. As mutual distrust and fears of domination by regional hegemons is a prominent feature of intra-East Asian relations, there is no reason to expect visions of serious regional integration to materialize any time soon. Implementation of such visions (as far as they really exist at all) can be expected to be a matter of many decades at best.

Chapter 2:

THE DEVELOPMENT OF ASEAN NORMS

BETWEEN 1997 AND 2000:

A PARADIGM SHIFT?

The Development of ASEAN Norms Between 1997 and 2000: A Paradigm Shift?

1. Introduction

In line with the underlying overall concept of the thesis, this first chapter deals with the first and foremost precondition of any collective identity, namely a set of shared norms to which the respective group members subscribe and which serve as a collective bond distinguishing them as a collective.

The traditional ASEAN norms are often subsumed under the catchword phrase "the ASEAN Way", which is based on the principles of informality, quiet and non-confrontational diplomacy as well as a shared aversion to regime-building and institutionalization. In the first decade of ASEAN cooperation, the "ASEAN Way" evolved as a mode of interaction designed to preserve the *status quo* among mutually distrustful neighbors. Into the fourth decade of its existence, the "ASEAN way" remained unchallenged as the only viable and generally accepted basis of ASEAN's operation. Although the ASEAN norms represented an instrument for keeping the ASEAN member states at arms' length rather than promoting closer economic or political integration between them, ASEAN was considered to be a successful model of cooperation. Whereas ASEAN did not require its member states to transfer national sovereignty to the community level and prevented ASEAN members from interfering in each others' internal affairs, the Association had a long record of providing stability and security to the region[74] and thus provided an environment in which its members' national economies had thrived. Up to 1997, there had seemingly been no need to change the comfortable principles and norms granting individual ASEAN members a maximum of national sovereignty and a minimum of responsibilities. It was the impact of the economic meltdown of 1997 that eventually forced ASEAN members to reassess not only ASEAN's purpose and role in the region, but the adequacy of the association's normative basis, too.[75] The "flexible engagement" debate

---

[74] Observers of ASEAN generally agree that by the time of the onset of the economic crisis in 1997 ASEAN had an impressive record of implementing political stability in Southeast Asia by promoting mutual trust and establishing a culture of peaceful and cooperative relations among the originally five ASEAN members, which by then had been gradually extended to the wider region (Brunei: 1984, Vietnam: 1995, Laos and Myanmar: July 1997, Cambodia: admission delayed, but in the pipeline in 1997).

[75] Many critics emphasize that the ASEAN Way represents an obstacle to economic and political reforms, since it is designed to stabilize the fragile and sensitive relations between sovereign states in a minimalist environment rather than to provide the basis for extensive

initiated by Thailand is indicative of a previously unknown tendency to reflect on the adequacy of the traditional ASEAN norms with a view to ASEAN's challenges such as ASEAN enlargement and enhancing ASEAN's economic competitiveness.

Before this backdrop, the purpose of this chapter is, first, to take stock of ASEAN's traditional normative set-up and, second, analyze the present norms system of the Association of Southeast Asian Nations (ASEAN) with a view to the Association's normative coherence since 1997. On the one hand, it depicts the government discourse on ASEAN norms between 1997 and 2000. It thus shows in how far ASEAN's norm have been debated controversially and asks whether ASEAN's norms, catalyzed by the crisis of 1997, are presently undergoing a paradigm shift or whether the generally accepted ASEAN norms remain largely intact.

In order to identify possible changes in the collective norms system of ASEAN, I will first give an overview of ASEAN's traditional constitutive principles, procedural and behavioral norms. In a second step, I will develop a picture of the various governments' views of the principles, norms and purposes they see as relevant for the future course of ASEAN. The analysis will focus on speeches, statements and interviews of major decision makers of selected ASEAN countries in order to find out about their explicit and implicit expectations and perceptions of ASEAN.[76] Policy visions and statements of the ASEAN Secretariat (represented here by the ASEAN Secretary-General) will be considered as well. In a third step, a comparison between past and present norm patterns of ASEAN will identify changes and continuities. Finally, I will identify "emerging norms", i.e. principles and expectations that haven't been established in the collective norms system yet, but may have a good chance of being incorporated and collectively accepted over time by ASEAN members. This will show in how far the collective paradigms of ASEAN norms have (or have not) changed since 1997.

---

regime-building and regime compliance. Building a more integrated political community would require at least "some degree of surrender of sovereignty" and centralization (Khoo 2000: 298), a demand that goes well beyond the norms of the ASEAN Way and leads ASEAN members into a hitherto mostly unexplored normative territory.
Cp. also: Wesley (1999); Acharya (1999); Henderson (1999); Bessho (1999); Dosch and Mols (1998); Chang and Ramkishen (1999): 30-33.

[76] Generally, the policy makers regarded in this study are politicians of the stature and position of a prime minister or foreign minister.

2. Traditional ASEAN Norms

There is a generally accepted definition of norms as "standard of appropriate behavior for actors with a given identity" or "collective expectations about proper behaviour for a given identity", respectively.[77] In essence, this means that individuals belonging to a certain group (or share a common identity, respectively) subscribe to a collectively held set of constitutive principles, rules of behavior and procedures. A norm has been established if any member of a group can be expected by, and expect from, any other group member to behave according to this collective code. Group members will be irritated by any breaches of these norms.

ASEAN, like any other collective body, is based on a specific set of norms that will guide its way of handling internal and external affairs. Adjustment to changes in the economic and political environment is based on these norms as well. This chapter gives an overview of essential ASEAN norms as they have emerged over the thirty years of ASEAN cooperation before the crisis of 1997. This pattern of traditional norms will then serve as a foil for the set of post-crisis norms that results from the analysis of ASEAN decision makers' speeches, statements. Comparing the traditional norm set and the picture of the post-crisis norms discourse in ASEAN will deliver insights as to how far the collective expectations (i.e. ASEAN norms) have actually changed or remained stable.

2.1. ASEAN's Objectives

The core objective of ASEAN cooperation before the end of the Cold War was to pacify and stabilize relations both between the originally five (later six) ASEAN members and the wider region of Southeast Asia (including Indochina) in general. In this context, the purpose of ASEAN was to create an environment that admitted neighboring nation states which had little in common with each other (except mutual suspicion due to extensive hostilities among themselves and a shared fear of communist subversion in their respective countries) to concentrate on their own economic development rather than exhaust their resources in permanent mutual struggle. Judging from today's perspective, ASEAN represents the successful attempt to take the steam out of the explosive relations between its member states by engaging in confidence-building through consultation, cooperation, mutual assistance and even through joint action, however only "where possible and desirable"[78]. ASEAN was built on a 'don't bugger your neighbor' attitude. Its main purpose was to provide a stable

---

[77] Finnemore and Sikkink (1998): 891; Jepperson, Katzenstein and Wendt (1996): 54. Cf. also: Job (1999): 4; Boekle, Rittberger and Wagner (1999); Busse (1999): 45.
[78] Declaration of ASEAN Concord (1976).

regional environment in which the national economies of Southeast Asia could thrive and prosper. Economic cooperation was initially restricted to regional consultations on national development plans and to creating economic synergies between the countries of the region. During the second decade, there was talk of forging preferential trading arrangements, but the idea caught on only in the early 1990s. Economic cooperation was seen as an extended confidence-building measure rather than an end in itself. Leonard Unger, the U.S. ambassador in Bangkok at the time when ASEAN was founded and a long-time observer of the region, explains the original objectives of ASEAN cooperation as follows:

> The explicit emphasis of the founding fathers of ASEAN was on economic, social, and cultural issues. Their commitment was to enhance mutual cooperation in Southeast Asia in those realms. [...] In their pragmatic way, the founders said nothing of security and defense questions, which they feared would be divisive. Instead, through the work of eleven permanent committees encompassing the social and economic goals of the new association, the members focused, in the words of a later Malaysian foreign minister, on 'getting to know each other's systems, their strengths and weaknesses and their procedures.'[79]

Only in the early 1990s, under the impression of the stalled GATT negotiations, when the world economy threatened to fall apart into antagonistic and exclusive trading blocs or "fortresses" (such as NAFTA and the EC single market) did ASEAN begin to seriously discuss closer regional economic integration.[80] The beginning of this development was marked by the decision of ASEAN leaders in 1992 to establish an ASEAN Free Trade Area (AFTA). Another aspect of ASEAN cooperation had always been to gather enough political clout and standing so as to become recognized internationally as a negotiation partner in economic and trade matters[81] and to keep major powers from interfering in, and dominating, the region politically. ASEAN's long-standing effort to extend peace and stability to the wider Southeast Asian region (Vietnam, Laos, Burma/ Myanmar, Cambodia) has to be seen in this light.

It is telling that only after a decade of cooperation ASEAN extended its agenda from economic, social and cultural cooperation to political cooperation as well;[82] telling in the sense that ASEAN's declared objective was to seek

---

[79] Unger (1986): 152.

[80] Indeed, economic cooperation up to 1992 had been underdeveloped and, as a matter of fact, represented *the* weak point of ASEAN, as Rüland (1995b: 59) states.

[81] From 1971 onwards, ASEAN has gradually sought and increased contacts with its major trading partners through institutionalized dialoguepartnerships with the U.S., the European Community and various other nations.

[82] Declaration of ASEAN Concord (1976).

harmony and constructive cooperation in areas of common interest, rather than to engage in potentially divisive and controversial issues like conflict resolution or developing a strong agenda for collective action.

Generally, it can be said that ASEAN's desire to protect national sensitivities has thus strongly limited the scope and degree of regional cooperation. Regional cooperation has been viable only where it was considered to be mutually beneficial and as long as it did not oblige individual countries to assume wide-ranging responsibilities or to cede national sovereignty to the association. It was never the individual nation that was to serve a greater common good, but ASEAN cooperation, in turn, was to serve the respective national development agendas of independent, sovereign and self-reliant states.

The entire ASEAN process was thus modeled around the core objective of *national resilience*.[83] In this light, it is important to point out that "regional resilience", i.e. regional strength and self-reliance, came to be seen as merely a derivative variable of (and not the precondition for) a high degree of national resilience. This means that the habitual calls for a strong ASEAN community and ASEAN integration have to be seen in the light of a strong preference among ASEAN members for the national over the regional.[84] Balancing the struggle for community and the desire for national resilience, i.e. the question of "*How to integrate without actually integrating?*"[85] has always been ASEAN's central dilemma. To sum up, the classic ASEAN objectives can be identified as:

---

[83] Ramcharan gives a definition of *national resilience*: "Ketanan Nasional or 'national resilience' is an Indonesian concept for nation-building which is defined as 'the tenacity and resistance of a nation, bearing the capability to develop national strength and power, in responding to inside as well as outside challenges and threats that directly or indirectly endanger the national life and in achieving the national goal'. It requires a comprehensive approach to security which calls for endurance in all fields - ideology, politics, economy, socio-cultural and military." (Ramcharan 2000: 85, footnote 10).
The concept of national resilience means basically national stability, independence and sovereignty on the basis of economic growth in an environment unhampered by external and domestic security threats. For a brief description of the concept of national resilience, cf. Stahl (2001): 27f.

[84] Dosch (1997): 30f., states that the call for integration subsided and enthusiasm cooled considerably when ASEAN leaders realized that integration of the kind as the European Community practised it implicated the loss or pooling of national sovereignty and independence.

[85] Kamlin (1991), quoted in: Dosch (1997): 31.

❶ national resilience for its member states,

❷ ASEAN (regional) resilience on the basis of national resilience,

❸ peaceful co-existence, conflict prevention and stability in ASEAN and Southeast Asia through

a) building trust/ solidarity,

b) Interaction and communication in an institutionalized environment

c) economic and functional cooperation,

d) dispute avoidance,

e) establishing and keeping to a regional code of conduct,

❹ international recognition and standing of ASEAN as a unified regional entity representing Southeast Asia,

❺ independence from intervention by hegemonial and neocolonial powers,

❻ expanding peace, stability and the ASEAN code of conduct to the wider region of Southeast Asia (a development eventually leading to ASEAN-10, i.e. the integration of Vietnam, Laos, Myanmar, Cambodia into ASEAN).

Table 2: ASEAN Objectives (1967 to 1997)

Bangkok Declaration (1967)	■ close and beneficial regional cooperation (economic, social, cultural) ■ peace and stability ■ national economic development of member states ■ freedom from external influence ■ preventing national independence from subversion ■ preserving national identities
Declaration on the Zone of Peace, Freedom and Neutrality, ZOPFAN (1971)	■ lasting peace in Southeast Asia ■ relaxation of international tensions ■ freedom/ independence ■ preservation of national identities ■ forming a closer relationship between members
Declaration of ASEAN Concord (1976)	■ national and ASEAN resilience through efforts of each member to internally eliminate threats to its respective national stability ■ broadening the complementarity of ASEAN economies (by relying on regional resources) ■ intra-regional dispute settlement ■ peaceful cooperation ■ mutually advantageous relationships ■ improvement of the ASEAN "machinery" (establishing an ASEAN Secretariat) ■ political cooperation ■ preferential trade arrangements ■ consultation on national development plans (first step towards harmonizing regional development) ■ mutual assistance to members in distress (=> solidarity) ■ building a strong ASEAN community ■ awareness of regional identity
Treaty of Amity and Cooperation, TAC (1976)	■ freedom from external interference ■ freedom from national subversion ■ freedom from coercion ■ internal dispute settlement ■ solidarity ■ interaction between ASEAN peoples ■ developing a regional strategy for development and mutual assistance ■ regular contacts between members (institutionalization) ■ strenghtening national resilience ■ enhancing regional resilience ■ establishing a High Council for internal dispute settlement (=> regime-building) ■ creating harmony
Protocol ammending the TAC (1987)	■ contributing to regional dispute settlement outside of ASEAN ■ aiming at associating the non-ASEAN countries into the regional ASEAN code of conduct

Agreement on the Common Effective Preferential Tariff Scheme (CEPT) for the ASEAN Free Trade Area (AFTA), (1992)	■ enhancing intra-economic cooperation (the word *integration* does not appear) ■ "national and ASEAN Economic resilience" ■ national development ■ trade and investment liberalization regime ■ time frame for regime-building
Protocol amending the agreement on CEPT and AFTA (1992)	■ tightening the liberalization schedule (accelerating implementation of CEPT/ AFTA) ■ establishing a flexible regime (generous exemption rules, no enforcement, but setting the rules)
Treaty on the Southeast Asia Nuclear Weapon-Free Zone, SEANWFZ (1995)	■ establishing a regional regime against nuclear weapons
ASEAN Vision 2020 (December 1997)	■ foster a strong sense of community ■ concert of Southeast Asian nations ■ national and regional resilience ■ ARF: confidence-building, preventive diplomacy, conflict resolution ■ closer economic integration (regime-building): AFTA, AIA (ASEAN Investment Area) ■ closer economic cooperation: growth areas, linkages for mutual benefit, common position on problems of the world economy, infrastructure development ■ social and economic cohesion ■ enhancing institutions and mechanisms (institutionalization and integration) ■ strengthening the ASEAN Secretariat ■ macroeconomic and financial cooperation and policy coordination: ASP (Surveillance Process), transparency

(Table 2 continued)

2.2. Constitutive Principles

All classic ASEAN norms are derived from the seemingly sacrosanct objective of national resilience.[86] Traditionally, ASEAN members have assumed that each member state is able to decide what's best for itself and to define its own path to resilience. Therefore, ASEAN never tried to construct a collective or supranational good that was above the indidvidual nations. Bearing in mind that ASEAN partners have always been suspicious of each other, one can understand that ASEAN wanted to avoid at all cost forcing a member government to bow to collective decisions. The imperative of full national sovereignty and self-determination resulted in a definition of equality that included full veto power for any decision taken collectively. Cooperation between ASEAN members was to be *mutually beneficial* and of *mutual interest*. Thus, ASEAN has traditionally always put a clear emphasis on *cooperation* rather than coordination or regime-type integration, which would have demanded some transfer of sovereignty from the national to a supranational level. The dislike for regime-building also established a tradition of seeking the smallest common denominator[87] and implementing only a *minimum collective agenda*. The main purpose of ASEAN, namely peaceful co-existence thus entailed not only the principle of *sovereign equality* and each nation's territorial integrity, but also a mutual, quasi-constitutional respect for *national diversity*. If and when unity and diversity get into conflict with each other, the much-touted *unity in diversity* approach of ASEAN assigns clear priority to the latter.

Summing up, the constitutive principles of ASEAN cooperation are:

❶ imperative of mutual benefit;
❷ collective agenda restricted exclusively to concerns of mutual interest;
❸ emphasis on voluntary cooperation (not coordination or regime building);
❹ equality;
❺ absolute national sovereignty;
❻ protection of (national) diversity;
❼ absolute territorial integrity of any nation;
❽ implicit preeminence of the smallest common denominator and a minimalist collective ASEAN agenda).

---

[86] Cf. Busse (1999): 46; Dosch (1997): 30f; Rüland (1995b): 51.
[87] Cf. Dosch (1997): 39.

Table 3: Constitutive Principles of ASEAN

Bangkok Declaration (1967)	■ Equality ■ Mutual interest
ZOPFAN (1971)	■ national self-determination ■ mutually advantageous/ beneficial cooperation
Declaration of ASEAN Concord (1976)	■ mutual benefit/ mutual advantage ■ sovereign equality ■ respecting all nations
Treaty of Amity and Cooperation (1976)	■ respect for national sovereignty ■ respect for equality ■ respect for territorial integrity ■ cooperation on matters of common interest ■ mutual benefit ■ national self-reliance

2.3. Procedural Norms

The principle of equal sovereignty thus informs ASEAN's central procedural norms. Equality, as defined by ASEAN, entails the norms of *non-discrimination* and *consensus-based decision making* (rather than decision making by majority principle). The preeminence of the consensus principle does not go well with regime building or binding commitments. Changes in the status quo require that a new consensus be established.

The emphasis on equal sovereignty also entails a strong predilection for *decentralized decision making*, which – together with the principles of *informality* and *bilateral negotiation* – has traditionally formed a culture of *consultation*. This prevented ASEAN from developing formalized and institutionalized decision making bodies. *Consultation* and *consensual agreement* have been considered as so quintessentially ASEAN-style that political actors and ASEAN observers alike have referred to them by the traditional Malay terms of *musyawarah* and *mufakat*.[88] *Musyawarah* and *mufakat* in fact represent a consensus principle taken to the extreme in the sense that it not only implies coming to conclusions by consensus after mutual consultation, but that it also *a priori* excludes such issues from negotiation or debate that are unlikely to be resolved by consensus.[89] In line with the

> [...] principle of seeking agreement and harmony, the principle of sensitivity, politeness, non-confrontation and agreeability, the principle

---

[88] Cf. Dosch (1997): 39f.; Unger (1986): 160.
[89] Dosch (1997): 39f.

of quiet, private and elitist diplomacy versus public washing of dirty linen, and the principle of being non-Cartesian, non-legalistic [...][90],

ASEAN has developed a culture of political negotiation that has been dominated by the collectively shared predilection for *quiet diplomacy*, a norm that has instituted face-saving *silent peer pressure* rather than a culture of public deliberation.[91]

In a nutshell, the norms governing ASEAN procedures are:

❶ non-discrimination;
❷ consultation (*musyawarah*);
❸ consensus-based decision making (*musfakat*);
❹ decentralized decision making;
❺ informality;
❻ bilateral (rather than multilateral) negotiation;
❼ quiet diplomacy;
❽ silent peer pressure (rather than open debate or even public deliberation).

2.4. Behavioral Norms

The constitutive principles and procedural norms outlined above define the basis for any action taken by ASEAN as a collective. The behavioral norms described in this section represent a code of conduct for the bilateral relations between ASEAN members as well as between ASEAN members and other states. ASEAN's behavioral norms are set out most comprehensively in the Treaty of Amity and Cooperation of 1976, which gives a comprehensive catalog of those norms as they had emerged after nearly a decade of ASEAN cooperation. These norms are simple and few. The TAC calls for a *benevolent attitude*, *respect* and *tolerance* among members. Bilateral relations should be conducted in a way "avoiding negative attitudes which might endanger or hinder cooperation".[92] Members explicitly subscribe to the principle of *non-interference* in each other's internal affairs, and the "respect for non-interference in each other's affairs has been a cardinal principle and characteristic of ASEAN concord since ASEAN's creation."[93] All disputes and conflicts are to be settled *peacefully* and members promise to refrain from the

---

[90] Busse (1999): 47.
[91] Of course this has not always prevented governments from bickering and threatening each other in public, as the example of Malaysia and Singapore shows. Throughout the long-standing feud between those countries, there have been recurrent open and public clashes and threats. However, these incidents rather represented breaches of ASEAN norms.
[92] Treaty of Amity and Cooperation (1976).
[93] Ramcharan (2000): 60.

use of force or any other action destabilizing the security and sovereign independence of any nation. ASEAN members are also expected to show *solidarity*, to assist each other and show political *goodwill* in order to optimize mutually beneficial cooperation.

To summarize, ASEAN collectively expects each member to behave according to the following guidelines:

❶ non-interference in each others' domestic affairs;
❷ solidarity;
❸ respect/ tolerance among member states;
❹ goodwill/ benevolent attitude;
❺ avoiding negative attitudes obstructive to cooperation;
❻ non-confrontation/ seeking harmony;
❼ avoiding action that possibly destabilizes other member states;
❽ peacefulness/ refraining from threat or use of force.

3. Member States' Post-Crisis Views of ASEAN Norms

How has the Asian financial crisis affected ASEAN norms? This chapter gives an overview of member governments' stated perceptions and interpretations of, ASEAN norms. For this purpose, I will draw on speeches, statements and interviews by leading government representatives (mostly prime ministers and foreign ministers) of selected member countries in order to depict the positions they have taken in the norms debate that has been raging throughout ASEAN since the economic and financial crisis of 1997. The survey focuses on the respective positions of the original five ASEAN member countries as well as on the newcomers Vietnam, Laos and Myanmar.[94]

---

[94] Note that the number of analyzed texts varies from country to country, since not all ASEAN governments are as communicative and media-oriented as, for example, the Democratic Thai government under Prime Minister Chuan and Foreign Minister Surin. The communist newcomers in particular seem to be shying away from touting their positions publicly, but Indonesia, the one-time informal ASEAN leader, has also been relatively reluctant to take clear positions. Nevertheless, the author believes that there are a sufficient number of statements for each country to establish their respective positions regarding the present state and possible future course of collective ASEAN norms.

3.1. Thailand

Thailand has been at the forefront of promoting an overhaul of ASEAN norms and procedures since mid-1998, when Surin Pitsuwan, the foreign minister of the new, Democratic government publicly challenged the strict interpretation of the principle of non-interference in each others' domestic affairs. He demanded a *flexible engagement* policy that would allow ASEAN countries to address, criticize and consult on member states' internal problems if these impacted negatively on other countries or the region as a whole. Under his stewardship, the Thai government vociferously promoted reforms and a "new thinking" in ASEAN, such as regional *economic integration*, *political coordination*, *institutional and procedural reform* and *regime-building*, as well as *extending the collective agenda*. The call for reforms touched on a number of traditional ASEAN norms.

The following section draws on the analysis of eight ASEAN-related policy statements made by Prime Minister Chuan Leekpai and Foreign Minister Surin Pitsuwan in the time between 1998 and 2000. The texts analyzed are:

- Surin Pitsuwan: "Thailand's Foreign Policy During the Economic and Social Crisis", Keynote address at the Seminar in Commemoration of the 49th Anniversary of the Faculty of Political Science, Thammasat University, 12 June 1998.

- Ministry of Foreign Affairs, Thailand: "Press Briefing by the Foreign Minister on Flexible Engagement", Manila, 24 July 1998.

- Ministry of Foreign Affairs, Thailand: "Thailand's Non-Paper on the Flexible Engagement Approach", Bangkok, 27 July 1998.

- Chuan Leekpai: Opening Address, 6th ASEAN Summit, Hanoi, 15 December 1998.

- Surin Pitsuwan: "Heeding ASEAN's Legacy", *Far Eastern Economic Review*, 17 February 2000.

- Surin Pitsuwan: "Setting ASEAN's Future Agenda", *The Bangkok Post*, 16 July 2000.

- Chuan Leekpai: Opening Address, ASEAN Ministerial Meeting, Bangkok, 24 July 2000.

- Surin Pitsuwan: Opening Statement, ASEAN Ministerial Meeting, Bangkok, 24 July 2000.

Flexible engagement

During the 31st AMM in Manila in July 1998, Foreign Minister Surin urged his ASEAN colleagues to adopt what he had come to call the principle of "flexible engagement". He argued that, in the face of growing interdependence among Southeast Asian states, domestic affairs of ASEAN members increasingly tended to affect their neighbors in the region as well. Therefore, the strict interpretation of, and adherence to, the non-interference principle was no longer practicable:

> Many "domestic" affairs have obvious external or transnational dimensions, adversely affecting neighbours, the region and the region's relations with others. In such cases, the affected countries should be able to express their opinions and concerns in an open, frank and constructive manner, which is not, and should not be, considered "interference" in fellow-members' domestic affairs.[95]

By proposing "flexible engagement", Surin not only challenged the sacrosanct status of the principle of absolute national sovereignty, but implicitly also challenged the ASEAN norms of quiet diplomacy and silent peer pressure, as well as ASEAN's traditional disdain for controversial issues, which were to be avoided for the sake of harmony:

> ASEAN countries should have sufficient self-confidence and confidence in one another, both to discuss all issues once considered "taboos" [...] and to speak out on such issues [...] when necessary and appropriate.[96]

However, Surin attempted to camouflage his demand to diminish several central ASEAN norms by rhetorically expressing respect for exactly those ASEAN norms he actually attacked. Thus, he underlined Thailand's "continued commitment to non-interference as the cardinal principle for the conduct of [ASEAN] relations", only to state a little later that "this commitment can not and should not be absolute."[97]

From the time Surin had first introduced the concept in a speech at the Asia Pacific Roundtable on 1 June 1998 and repeated it a little later in a foreign policy speech at Thammasat University on 12 June 1998,[98] the government of Prime Minister Chuan Leekpai repeatedly reiterated the call for "flexible engagement" or "enhanced interaction" (the latter term being the more moderate

---

[95] Ministry of Foreign Affairs, Kingdom of Thailand (1998): "Thailand's Non-Paper on Flexible Engagement".

[96] Ibid.

[97] Ibid.

[98] Surin (1998a and 1998b): "Currency Turmoil in Asia: The Strategic Impact", 12th Asia Pacific Roundtable, Kuala Lumpur, 1 June; "Thailand's Foreign Policy During the Economic and Social Crisis", Thammasat University, 12 June.

compromise formula which ASEAN foreign ministers adopted formally during their annual meeting in July 1998, as a reluctant concession to Surin's "flexible engagement" initiative). The Chuan Leekpai government chose to see the concept of enhanced interaction as a norm "ASEAN Foreign Ministers have unanimously agreed to" and believed that "[f]rom now on, issues affecting each other may be brought up and discussed without being perceived as interference."[99] This suggests that, to Thailand, "flexible engagement" and enhanced interaction are equivalent and interchangeable terms. Only recently, in the running-up to the 33rd AMM in July 2000, Surin reaffirmed Thailand's "flexible engagement" policy:

> Our initiative on "flexible engagement", which has evolved into "enhanced interaction", is part of our effort to ensure that Asean is more effective, cohesive and relevant to the changing world situation.[100]

New thinking, flexibility and reform-mindedness

The debate about the "flexible engagement" approach was clearly part of an at least rhetorical commitment to a wider reform agenda. Thus, Surin announced that the adoption of enhanced interaction by the foreign ministers is not "the beginning of the end of ASEAN, but is in fact the start of a process of renewal of ASEAN"[101], and Chuan repeatedly echoed this statement by emphasizing that "[p]erhaps we do not need a new doctrine. But we do need new approaches and new thinking to keep up with the rapid pace of developments, both regionally and internationally"[102] and called for ASEAN's renewal, flexibility and adaptability.[103] Of course, such calls carry no substance by themselves. However, the strong rhetoric of change countered the discourse of ASEAN traditionalists (such as Malaysia) who defy the very idea of reforms and changes to the ASEAN way. The call for new thinking and flexibility, as I will show below, was clearly directed against the continuation of decentral decision making and against a concept of absolute national sovereignty.

Deeper Integration

At the ASEAN summit in 1998, Chuan demanded that

> ASEAN must be more than the sum of our parts. [...] The broadening of our membership must be accompanied by the deepening of our co-

---

[99] Surin (1998c): Press Briefing on Flexible Engagement, Manila, 24 July 1998.
[100] Surin (2000b): "Setting ASEAN's Future Agenda", *The Bangkok Post*, 16 July.
[101] Surin (1998c).
[102] Chuan (1998): Opening Address, 6th ASEAN Summit, Hanoi, 15 December 1998.
[103] Chuan's speech at the ASEAN Ministerial Meeting 2000 was again kept in the same reform-minded spirit and displayed a vigorous call for changes, cp. Chuan (2000): Opening Address, AMM, Bangkok, 24 July.

operation in all areas and at all levels and in building ASEAN into a *true community, and not just an association, of nations*.[104] [emphasis added]

The contrast between *community* and *association* is striking, but not explained. What kind of community was implied? What were Thailand's actual proposals for change? And how did the Chuan government hope to fill the empty word shells of terms like *new thinking, flexibility, adaptability* and *reform*? The official rhetoric seemed to imply that Thai ideas on reform focused on stronger integration of ASEAN in general and particularly on issues such as *economic integration* (in the sense of regime building), *political coordination, institutional and procedural changes* to the ASEAN way where necessary and desirable, a re-interpretation of *regional resilience* and a re-definition of the role of the individual ASEAN member state vis-à-vis the Association.

The core concern of Thailand's call on all ASEAN members "to deepen our co-operative endeavors", to move "towards closer regional integration", to "nurture ASEAN into a 'concert of nations'"[105] and ultimately to "create a true community of Southeast Asian nations"[106], was "the need for greater economic integration"[107]. Under the impression of the economic crisis, Chuan stated in 1998 that

> we must achieve *closer and deeper economic integration* be they under the ASEAN Free Trade Area (AFTA), the ASEAN Investment Co-operation Scheme (AICO) or the ASEAN Investment Area (AIA).[108] [emphasis added]

However, Chuan did not promote one-size-fits-all regime types, but took care to pay tribute to the ASEAN norms of national sovereignty, mutual benefit and agreeability by emphasizing the need for soft and flexible regimes, goodwill and the individual nations' responsibility rather than rules compliance and institutions:

> We all may not be able to achieve the same specific time-frame or move at the same pace. But as long as we redouble our efforts towards closer economic integration and seek to go at least one step beyond our pledged commitment we will create a synergy of strength, capable of propelling ASEAN back to normality and [...] renewed growth.[109]

---

[104] Chuan (1998).
[105] Chuan (2000).
[106] Surin (2000b).
[107] Chuan (2000).
[108] Chuan (1998).
[109] Ibid.

At the 33rd AMM, on 24 July 2000, apparently under the impression of rising tensions between Thailand and Malaysia over the latter country's unwillingness to meet its commitments under the ASEAN Central Economic Preferential Tariff Scheme (CEPT), Chuan seemed to put more weight on regime compliance than on tolerance. In a sharply worded statement, he called on ASEAN as a body (not on individual ASEAN members!) to prevent deviations from the collective liberalization agenda and demanded of individual countries to subject themselves to the collective agenda:

> Because of the financial crisis, there have been difficulties for some countries in meeting their objectives for liberalisation. ASEAN would need to ensure that our success would not be undermined through backtracking of our commitments. [...] While each member country may have its own priorities, there should be consonance and harmony in our actions. ASEAN must evolve into a concert of dynamism and coherence - relevant not only to itself, but also to the outside world.[110]

The ambiguous rhetorical twist in Chuan's call for harmony is that he actually subverts the norm of consensus-oriented harmony (which is based on avoiding controversial discussion) by using the term *harmony* in the sense of *harmonizing*, i.e. coordinating, straightening, unifying, and regulating. The message was clear: Individual ASEAN members could no longer afford to be complacent and go about "business as usual" (Surin)[111], and ASEAN as a collective had to impose a more rigid regime on its members by bringing them in line with a broadened collective agenda.

But deeper regional integration, according to the Democratic government's rhetoric, was not to be restricted to the economic sphere alone. In February 2000, Surin Pitsuwan demanded that ASEAN should be

> [...] accelerating the process of *economic and political reform* so vital to our recovery and renewal. [...] For ASEAN to retain its viability and relevance, it is essential that it *coordinates* more closely members' policies, especially on major political, economic and social issues of mutual concern. This entails a *stronger commitment to regionalism*, since we can no longer afford to compete individually among ourselves, and separately with the world. More *intensive interaction* [...] is clearly needed.[112] [emphasis added]

Essentially, the Thai government's rhetoric thus implied a more regime-oriented, rules-based, formalized and institutionalized ASEAN with a more

---

[110] Chuan (2000).
[111] Surin (2000a): "Heeding ASEAN's Legacy", *Far Eastern Economic Review*, 17 February.
[112] Ibid.

broadly defined, more authoritative collective agenda. Both Surin and Chuan seemed to favor rules-based "mechanisms" of cooperation over informal decision making. Thus, Surin claimed "it is imperative that ASEAN augments existing mechanisms of cooperation" such as the ASEAN Surveillance Process and AFTA,[113] whereas Chuan, in his speech at the AMM in July 2000 argued for the establishment of Surin's brainchild, an "ASEAN Troika, which will, I believe, provide our Association with a quick response and effective mechanism to deal with fast developing issues in the region".[114]

Regional Resilience

Another deviance from the traditional ASEAN way was the apparent re-interpretation of the concept of *regional resilience*. Whereas traditionally, regional resilience is interpreted as a dependent variable of national resilience, the Thai government challenged that notion. Chuan claimed that "there is a need for a suitable formula to balance regional with national interests"[115], suggesting that greater interdependence demands a more cohesive collective agenda that could be implemented only if the concern for absolute national sovereignty was relaxed. Surin went to great rhetorical lengths to merge *national resilience* and *regional resilience* into mere *resilience*, forgetting the supremacy of the national and placing the collective over the national:

> [...] at ASEAN's first summit in Bali [...] our leaders coined another phrase that has become part of ASEAN's vocabulary. They stressed the need for members to strengthen their national and regional "resilience" at a time when this part of the world faced one of its biggest crises, a result of regional tensions. Over the years, this resilience has been a source of strength for ASEAN as its members weathered many storms. [...]
> Members of ASEAN need to put their respective houses in order. [...] ASEAN can no longer afford "business as usual". Rather, we must build further resilience by accelerating the process of economic and political

---

[113] Ibid.

[114] Chuan (2000).
During the ASEAN Ministerial Meeting 2000, ASEAN foreign ministers agreed to follow a Thai initiative to establish an ASEAN Troika. But whereas Thailand had envisioned the Troika as a centralized rapid response body to resolve intra-ASEAN crises, supposed to comprise the former, present and future chairman of the ASEAN Standing Committee as central crisis managers, most foreign ministers opposed the idea of a centralized decision making body. The compromise was to set up a Troika with little powers and an as yet very diffuse mission, "as an ad hoc ministerial body which will be established in crisis situations to address issues affecting regional peace and security. [...] Elaborating on its role, Dr Surin said it was not possible to spell out, in exact terms, what the Troika would do." ("Asean creates new rapid response team", *The Straits Times*, Singapore, 26 July 2000).

[115] Chuan (2000).

reform [...]. For ASEAN it is essential that it coordinates more closely members' policies, [...] [implements] [M]ore intensive interaction [...] [and] augments existing mechanisms of cooperation.[116]

At another instance, Surin repeated his claim for a stronger collective agenda at the cost of national independence and sovereignty by drawing on the rhetoric of the Declaration of ASEAN Concord of 1976. The Concord of 1976 highlighted the absolute sovereignty and territorial integrity of each nation and the principle of non-interference in each other's domestic affairs. The passage from the Declaration of ASEAN Concord reads:

> The stability of each member state and of the ASEAN region is an essential contribution to international peace and security. Each member state resolves to eliminate threats posed by subversion to its stability, thus strengthening national and ASEAN resilience.[117]

Surin also argued that regional resilience depended on the internal state of its members. However, it was not national resilience and national sovereignty Surin placed at the center of his argument, but rather the obligation of each member to implement what was good for the collective:

> As Prime Minister Chuan Leekpai declared [...] in 1998: 'We must make Asean larger than the sum of our parts.' [...] we should recognise that events in one country may affect others and that our nations' fates are intertwined. What is also important is that each member nation has to be responsible not only to the grouping as a whole but, most importantly, to itself. Asean will not be able to withstand the pressures from outside if each country cannot manage its own problems. More significantly, we cannot become strong unless each and every one of us puts our house in order.[118]

Chuan's demand that "each of us [be] prepared to make the sacrifices and contributions [...] required" so that ASEAN, as a collective, could implement necessary action, underlines that solidarity is a duty, not a choice, and that the imperative of regional resilience overrides mere national interest and national sovereignty. Increased interdependence requires that the collective has some say over individual members' behavior and policies. And there could be no doubt about the objectives each ASEAN member should embrace for the sake of greater ASEAN resilience: "effective and transparent governance" and "further resilience by accelerating the process of economic and political reform"[119] via

---

[116] Surin (2000a).
[117] Declaration of ASEAN Concord (1976), paragraph 1.
[118] Surin (2000b).
[119] Surin (2000a).

transfer of sovereignty, coordination, centralization and collectivization through mechanisms such as AFTA, AIA, AICO, ASP, the ASEAN Troika and a rules-based regional dispute settlement body, the High Council. The process of "soul-searching and rethinking" Surin had in mind meant emphasizing the duties and responsibilities of ASEAN members over those ASEAN norms which highlight individual nations' interests and rights. The promotion of regional, rather than national, resilience seemed to be what he meant when he suggested "to move Asean's regionalism to a higher plane"[120] and to "greater heights of cooperation".[121] Seen in this light, Surin's frequently reiterated statement that ASEAN was now "mature" enough to talk about and overcome ASEAN "taboos" reflected his view that ASEAN had to take a more proactive role in managing its members' relations.

Summary

Thailand's rhetoric under the Chuan government was aimed at promoting an ASEAN that focused on economic and political integration. It favored collective regime building, institutionalizing and formalizing ASEAN's decision making processes and modes of interaction. Thailand's criticism focused on ASEAN norms designed to protect individual countries from interference and prevent public criticism by their neighbors. The norms most criticized were *national resilience* and a notion of absolute *national sovereignty* that was seen as obstructing the transfer of elements of sovereignty from the national to the collective level. Chuan and Surin seemed to favor a concept of regional resilience that emphasized the prevalence of the collective over individual interests while they de-emphasized norms such as the non-interference principle where the policies of one country threatened collective interests or interests of other ASEAN members. The Thai government claimed that ASEAN needéd to adapt its norms to the new challenges of economic integration and political coordination. However, the rhetoric of norm change remained mostly within the bounds of the criticized norms. Even where *flexible engagement* or *enhanced interaction* were promoted, Thai rhetoric assured the other ASEAN members that this did not represent a violation of the non-interference principle itself. Thus, one could argue that norm change was promoted on the basis of traditional norms. This suggests that to the Chuan government the generally accepted ASEAN norms were still relevant.

---

[120] Surin (2000b).
[121] Surin (2000c): Opening Statement, 33rd AMM, Bangkok, 24 July.

3.2. The Philippines

By backing Thai Foreign Minister Surin's call for a "flexible engagement" policy in ASEAN at the AMM in July 1998, Foreign Minister Domingo Siazon put the Philippine government clearly on the side of the reformers in ASEAN. Surin and Siazon had since been regarded as members of a new generation of politicians within ASEAN. Both Thailand and the Philippines had been at the fringes of ASEAN decision making processes before the crisis of 1997, and both had come to represent a democratic *avantgarde* among the predominantly authoritarian political systems of ASEAN member states.

The texts analyzed in the following section are speeches and interviews by President Estrada, his predecessor Ramos and Foreign Minister Siazon:

- Domingo Siazon: "ASEAN in the Next Millennium", Opening Statement, 32nd AMM, Singapore, 23 July 1999.

- Joseph Ejercitio Estrada, Opening Address, ASEAN Summit, Manila, 28 November 1999.

- "We Have To Change", interview with Domingo Siazon, *Asiaweek.com*, 10 December 1999.

- Fidel Ramos: "The World to Come: ASEAN's Political and Economic Prospects in the New Century", Address at the Economy Strategy Institute's Global Forum 2000: "The World to Come - Value and Price of Globalization", Ronald Reagan International Trade Center, Washington, D.C., 17 May 2000.

- Transcript of an interview with Domingo Siazon, *Channelnewsasia.com*, 3 February 2000.

- Domingo Siazon: "Building a Community of Peace", Opening statement, 33rd AMM, Bangkok, 24 July 2000.

Of the three Philippine politicians surveyed here, President Estrada expressed more distant visions (dreams) for ASEAN cooperation, but remained rather vague as to the present challenges facing ASEAN. At the same time, former president Fidel Ramos oscillated between articulating visions and spelling out their practical present implications for ASEAN. Finally, Foreign Minister Domingo Siazon concentrated more on near to mid-term directions for ASEAN. Nevertheless, all three seemed to share similar views.

Deeper economic and political integration

The word *integration* was by no means central to Siazon's and Estrada's rhetoric, whereas Ramos seemed to like the term a little better. Nevertheless, it is clear that the Philippines rhetorically promoted a concept of integration that is based on reform and change. Thus, Siazon claimed that

> The challenge now is to transform this collectivity into a community. We need to foster deeper and broader convergence of our respective national interests and really think, speak, and act as an organic whole.[122]

Economic cooperation was emphasized as the core of this community-building process. Estrada expressed the view that the focus and paradigm of ASEAN had steadily shifted from establishing "harmony among the member states" and "expanding functional cooperation" during the first two to three decades of ASEAN cooperation to "instituting economic cooperation as our collective approach to prosperity" as "the express mandate of our organization".[123] And Siazon, pointing to the necessity for ASEAN to adapt to the increased interdependence among Southeast Asian states and to react to the experiences of the Asian crisis, argued that "[e]conomic development is critical to building our community, especially if we look back at the past two years".[124]

The Philippines were apparently in line with the economic objectives of extending economic integration by accelerating AFTA, implementing AIA, AICO and the ASP, as laid down in the ASEAN Vision 2020 and the Hanoi Plan for Action (HPA). Beyond reminding his ASEAN colleagues that "We all agreed about the need for structural reform in the financial and other economic sectors, however painful these may be",[125] Siazon and his president also argued for closer political cooperation in ASEAN.[126]. Thus, Estrada stated that

> [...] the message we want to air is: cooperation, to be truly effective, must be comprehensive. Greater economic cooperation should lead to and accompany deeper and broader cooperation on matters of peace and security.[127]

Similarly, Ramos argued that "[a]djustments in the economy must be accompanied by adjustments in the political order",[128] while Siazon complained about the "asymmetry in both pace and direction between ASEAN economic collaboration, on the one hand, and regional security and political cooperation, on the other". He called on ASEAN to "correct the asymmetry in the pace and

---

[122] Siazon (1999a): "ASEAN in the Next Millennium", Opening Statement, 32nd AMM, Singapore, 23 July.

[123] Estrada (1999): Welcome Remarks at the Summit Opening Ceremonies, 3rd Informal ASEAN Summit, Manila, 28 November.

[124] Siazon (1999a).

[125] Ibid.

[126] Ibid.; Estrada (1999).

[127] Estrada (1999).

[128] Ramos (2000): "The World to Come: ASEAN's Political and Economic Prospects in the New Century", Washington, D.C., 17 May.

scope of political and security cooperation on the one hand, and economic integration on the other".[129] The Philippines promoted the establishment of collective ASEAN "mechanisms and structures",[130] i.e. regime building, in the field of political and security cooperation. In this respect, the Philippine government would have like to see an ASEAN code of conduct on the South China Sea passed, the ASEAN Troika established as an effective crisis task force and centralized decision maker, as well as rules of procedure finalized for an ASEAN dispute settlement body (the High Council), and generally collective mechanisms for preventive diplomacy established. The Philippines thus seemed to put great emphasis on the extension of a political and security cooperation that was commensurate with the pace of economic integration. Siazon's speech at the recent 33rd AMM in Singapore was dominated by this issue.[131] In the economic area, the Philippines called for "one ASEAN investment area" by 2010, and eventually the "even loftier dream"[132] of "a common currency, a customs union, and a common market"[133] for ASEAN and eventually for the whole of East Asia. Ramos employed such visionary vocabulary as well, and even a less dreamy Siazon presented a common East Asian currency as a viable vision:

> [Integration] will happen very quickly, faster in the next 10 years than in the last 30 years. And as that happened the only logical move would be to move towards one currency. And Japan will join and the Koreans will join [...] and China would have to come in. [...] And I think it's possible.[134]

It is important to emphasize again that deeper integration, which Siazon liked to describe as the result of an *evolutionary* process of ASEAN, was seen as a process of greater institutionalization and regime building in all fields:

> After three decades of existence, ASEAN continues to evolve its processes for dialogue and consultation, and broader political cooperation, and more inspiring possibilities lie ahead. Part of this evolution is the need to concretize the principles and values that keep

---

[129] Siazon (1999a).

[130] Ibid.

[131] Siazon (2000b): "Building a Community of Peace", Opening Statement, 33rd AMM, Bangkok, 24 July.

[132] Estrada (1999).

[133] Ramos (2000).

[134] Siazon (2000a): Transcript of an interview with Domingo Siazon, ChannelNewsAsia.com, 3 February.

ASEAN member countries together. We have to build and strengthen institutional processes and mechanisms [...].[135]

Flexible engagement/ enhanced interaction

The sense of a new degree of interdependence among ASEAN members since the crisis, as well as the ensuing demand for more ASEAN integration, led the Philippine government to support Thailand's call for "flexible engagement". Ramos defended the Philippines' position by stating that

> All our countries will have to make painful adjustments if they are to restore their economies [...] Certainly ASEAN itself will emerge from the crisis different in some ways from what it was. For instance, Thailand (supported by the Philippines) has already asked for a reexamination of ASEAN's principle of non-interference.[136]

With a view to economic and political instability in the region, the East Timor crisis and the South China Sea/ Spratly Islands issue, former president Ramos expressed his dissatisfaction with the non-interference principle: "In every one of these crises, ASEAN's non-intervention principle prevented it from taking purposeful action."[137] And only recently, Siazon confirmed the present government's view of the matter when he reiterated the view that a softening of the non-interference principle was indispensable: "We think that there are certain situations where a country or even its leaders should speak up on issues that have trans-boundaries impact on other countries".[138] That's why he saw, "above all, greater openness and closer consultation"[139] as paramount for ASEAN's culture of political interaction. Essentially, Siazon seemed to believe that a formal discussion of the subject could become superfluous as the day-to-day business in ASEAN had already set precedents for acting against the non-interference principle. Citing the examples of ASEAN's engagement in the domestic agendas of Cambodia and Indonesia (East Timor), he stated: "what's the use of arguing when de facto [it] is happening? It's interactions. The whole world is changing. ASEAN has to change".[140] And President Estrada believed that "the best paving material is openness" and that "we must learn the habits of openness"[141] as ASEAN had to learn the habits of cooperation over the first thirty years of its existence.

---

[135] Siazon (2000b).
[136] Ramos (2000).
[137] Ibid.
[138] Siazon (2000a).
[139] Siazon (1999a).
[140] Siazon (1999b): "We Have to Change", interview with Domingo Siazon, Asiaweek.com, 10 December.
[141] Estrada (1999).

However strong and explicit the Philippines' criticism of the non-interference principle, there nevertheless seemed to be a certain reluctance to step beyond the existing ASEAN norms. Thus, Siazon took care to present the Philippines' promotion of enhanced interaction or "flexible engagement" as an evolution rather than a revolution and to show that his ideas concerning enhanced interaction were commensurate with traditional ASEAN principles such as quiet, behind-the-scenes diplomacy and informality: "If we're in the family - then we should be able to talk to each other privately. You don't have to go to the press to make a point".[142] The Philippines apparently also took great care to respect the existing non-interference principle at least rhetorically. Thus, the Estrada administration was eager to declare President Estrada's public objections to the imprisonment of Anwar Ibrahim and his consequent open threats against Malaysia on this account (such as Estrada's threat to cancel his attendance at the APEC summit hosted by Malaysia) a merely personal matter that did not represent a violation of the norm of non-interference at government level:[143]

> President Estrada objected to or rather felt that when he saw Anwar Ibrahim with the blacked eye and that the person under custody was assaulted he felt [...] that's repulsive and so he made a declaration that this should not have happened - this fellow has rights [...] President Estrada always said this is my personal view. It is not the political or public official view of the government.[144]

The importance the Philippine government attributed to (at least formal and rhetorical) norm compliance suggests that it valued and respected the traditional ASEAN norms as an important collective good. Nevertheless, Siazon left no doubt as to the direction in which he wanted to see ASEAN evolve. Talking about "flexible engagement" and open criticism within ASEAN, he expressed the view that the changes happening in Indonesia in terms of openness would eventually impact on the whole of ASEAN:

> I think the rule in Asean is that everyone in Asean must be comfortable with the situation. But right now, you know, with the way things are in Indonesia, this could change quite quickly for the better. Because [...] what happens in Indonesia in terms of social mores or public acceptance of criticism will eventually have a tremendous impact on Asean.[145]

---

[142] Siazon (2000a).

[143] For a discussion of the impact of the concept of enhanced interaction on ASEAN members' behavior, see: Haacke (1999).

[144] Siazon (2000a).

[145] Ibid.

Ramos was equally careful not to step beyond the existing norms system, but clearly expressed his preference for the direction the ASEAN norms debate should take:

> Should ASEAN begin to involve itself in the political problems of its member-countries [...]? The level of mutual trust must determine the answer to that question every time it is raised - in the context of a concrete situation. But such involvement would be the natural consequence of growing [South] East Asian integration.[146]

Balancing collective and national interests

The Philippines believed that individual ASEAN members would increasingly have to rely on regional structures to effectively pursue their national interests. Therefore, primary national interests should not be allowed to obstruct regional integration, but should rather be coordinated and brought in line with the greater ASEAN objective of regional integration.

Thus, in May 2000, Ramos pleaded that unless ASEAN changed its fundamental structures and reassessed the role of national sovereignty, the organization would become meaningless:

> ASEAN is not - and was not - meant to be a supranational entity acting independently of its members. It makes no laws and it has neither powers of enforcement nor a judicial system. Having said that, I must also say that, over these next few years, ASEAN must change if it is to keep pace with [South]East Asia's evolving circumstances. Because [South] East Asia must become more closely integrated, *ASEAN's member-states must seek a new balance between national sovereignty and regional purpose.*[147] [emphasis added]

ASEAN nations, Ramos claimed, "must still learn to hold the collective spirit above their own" and to "yield [...] a [higher] measure of sovereignty than now seems possible".[148] Siazon saw ASEAN facing

> the challenge [...] to transform this collectivity into a community [...and the] need to foster deeper and broader convergence of our respective national interests, and really think, speak and act as an organic whole.[149]

Accordingly, regional integration had to be expanded, sometimes even at the cost of painful concessions from individual nations. Thus, he promoted the implementation and expansion of "structural reforms in the financial and

---

[146] Ramos (2000).
[147] Ibid.
[148] Ibid.
[149] Siazon (1999a).

economic sector, however painful these may be"; in the area of security, knowing about the reservations of many member states, he argued for regional solutions by calling for a "superstructure of peace and security" in ASEAN through furthering the "establishment of mechanisms for preventive security and conflict resolution".[150]

Challenging musyawarah and mufakat?

It is apparently not acceptable in ASEAN to officially question to the essentially central ASEAN norms of *musyawarah* and *mufakat*, i.e the ASEAN-specific modes of consensus and consultation. Informally, however, the debate about these norms seems to have begun already.[151] Thus, Fidel Ramos publicly questioned the viability of consensus and consultation as the guiding principles of ASEAN in the long run and suggested to drop them, not immediately, but over time, as ASEAN evolved into a more harmonized political body:

> Should ASEAN change its decision-making style? The time-honored insitutions of *mushawarah* and *mufakat* - consultation and consensus - still seem the best modes for organizing regional agreement on collective action by partners of diverse strengths, cultures, and methods of governance. But, as our countries themselves develop, as their fledgling democracies evolve, so must ASEAN change as it matures.[152]

Democratization

However, there are clear signs that Siazon would have liked to see ASEAN based on more democratic principles. In an interview, he explicitly denounced the undemocratic ways of ASEAN and ASEAN countries and posed as an ASEAN reformer with democratic aspirations: "[...] all of those old [ASEAN] leaders were more or less autocratic. That's not what we want to see for

---

[150] Ibid.

[151] To all those forces in ASEAN who would like to see a more integrated, institutionalized and regime-based type of cooperation established, the consensus principle represents a potential obstacle in the way of reforms. On the one hand, newcomers (Vietnam, Laos, Myanmar, Cambodia) might support the ant-reformist camp and invoke and utilize the consensus principle in order to block reforms and closer integration. On the other hand, a more centralized and institutionalized ASEAN with an extended operational range will need faster and more standardized decision making processes in order to be able to react quickly to various developments. The Thai proposal of establishing the ASEAN Troika, for example, represents an attempt at pushing ASEAN into a direction of more centralized decision making processes that don't require the consensus of all ASEAN members. Naturally, the transfer of power to ASEAN decision making bodies would not be commensurate with a consensus principle that could easily evolve into a full veto power concerning any decision for every member country. Neither would a more centralized and institutionalized mode of decision making agree with the traditional and informal consultation procedures of ASEAN.

[152] Ramos (2000).

92

ASEAN in 2020. So perhaps it's good that we don't have the old set of leaders".[153] Asked whether the democratization process in Indonesia could be expected to have an impact on ASEAN members in general, he suggested: "What happens to Indonesia happens to ASEAN in terms of this kind of change. And by 2020, there'll be a new generation of leaders".[154] According to this rhetoric, Siazon saw himself in the camp of the young generation of leaders (such as Surin Pitsuwan) who will steadily promote more democratic ideals and ways in their own countries and in ASEAN. In this context, he called on ASEAN countries to embrace the concepts of "people empowerment and the promotion of human rights"[155] and favored a more central role for ASEAN in helping to establish "the principle of good governance, such as transparency, accountability and predictability, in our institutions and policies".[156] This call was echoed and reiterated by Estrada.

Summary
Since the events of the economic crisis, the Philippines consistently promoted a reform agenda for ASEAN that centered on a concept of economic integration through the establishment of economic regimes (AFTA, AIA, AICO, ASP). The long-term objectives seemed to be an ASEAN customs union and a common market with ultimately a common (East Asian) currency. Economic regime building was to be accompanied by more intensive, institutionalized and rules-based political and security cooperation. In these areas, the Philippines called for more frequent and institutionalized forms of consultation, the establishment of a powerful ASEAN Troika, rules of procedure for an ASEAN dispute settlement mechanism through the High Council, a collective commitment to process-oriented and rules-based preventive diplomacy and a collective ASEAN code of conduct for the South China Sea. An agenda based on the collectivization and centralization of ASEAN cooperation in the economic, political and security area is what Philippine politicians have called *comprehensive cooperation*. Essentially, the Philippines promoted the view that any traditional ASEAN norms that stand in the way of closer ASEAN integration will have to be modified and adjusted to the new requirements of a region characterized by increasing interdependence. The central norms the Philippines objected to were the non-interference principle, the principle of absolute national sovereignty that grants full veto power to each country and prevents the transfer of sovereignty from the national to the ASEAN level, and the emphasis on national interest and national resilience rather than collective resilience. The Philippines expressed dissatisfaction with a lack of democracy,

---

[153] Siazon (1999b).
[154] Siazon (1999b).
[155] Siazon (2000b).
[156] Ibid.

good governance and transparency in many ASEAN countries, and there also hints suggesting that the Philippines were not happy with the consensus principle (*musyawarah*) and the ASEAN mode of consultation (*mufakat*). However, the Philippines presented ASEAN reform as an evolutionary rather than a revolutionary process, and they claimed to be moving and acting within the bounds of the common ASEAN norms. The Philippines' contribution to the norms debate therefore did not imply a break with existing ASEAN norms, but an effort to promote reforms on the basis of the existing ASEAN norms.

3.3. Singapore

Singapore, the economically most advanced country in ASEAN, has, especially since the early 1990s, been trying to open up ASEAN economically, to promote regional trade liberalization, to adapt ASEAN to world economic standards and to increase ASEAN's attractiveness as a destination for foreign capital investment. The city state has vigorously promoted the establishment of AFTA, the investment area (AIA), and the participation of ASEAN in APEC in order to secure ASEAN members' access to trans-Pacific markets. Singapore has also played a proactive part in getting ASEM off the ground as a stronger economic link with the EU. But while Singapore has been promoting economic change, the economic tiger has proved to be politically conservative, authoritarian in its style of government, a strong contributor to, and assertive promoter of, the Asian values debate, and a reliable backer of the ASEAN way and ASEAN principles. Throughout the greater part of the 1990s, at a time when Southeast Asian economies achieved remarkable economic growth rates and gained untofore unknown international recognition, Singapore, as other ASEAN members, took pride in its Asianness and its distinctive Asian values, which were presented as the key cause for economic growth in Southeast Asia. The question pursued in this chapter is whether Singapore's commitment to traditional ASEAN norms has waned in the face of the economic decline and political turbulences in the region or whether it continues to support a normative system that inhibits swift implementation of necessary structural reform. The following speeches and statements by Singapore's foreign minister Jayakumar and prime minister Goh Chok Tong will serve as references for the analysis:

- S. Jayakumar: Opening Statement, 30th AMM, Kuala Lumpur, July 1997.

- S. Jayakumar: "Stick to Basics", Opening Statement, 31st AMM, Manila, 24 July 1998.

- Goh Chok Tong: Opening Statement, 6th ASEAN Summit, Hanoi, 15 December 1998.

- S. Jayakumar: "Redefining ASEAN", Speech at the occasion of the ceremony of Cambodia's admission to ASEAN, Hanoi, 30 April 1999.

- Goh Chok Tong: Keynote Address, 32nd AMM, Singapore, 23 July 1999.

- S. Jayakumar: Remarks on return from the AMM Foreign Ministers' Retreat, Singapore, 23 July 1999.

- "Finally, Being His Own Man", Interview with Goh Chok Tong, Asiaweek.com, 25 November 1999.

- Goh Chok Tong: Transcript of remarks by the Prime Minister to the media, 3rd ASEAN Informal Summit, Manila, 28 November 1999.

- S. Jayakumar: Opening Statement, 33rd AMM, Bangkok, 24 July 2000.

During the 30th AMM in July 1997, just around the time when what was to become the Asian crisis sent Thailand's currency tumbling down, Singapore's foreign minister expressed his government's view that "the essential principles that have been responsible for ASEAN's success [...] are also the principles which indicate the direction in which ASEAN is evolving."[157] The essential principles in his view were ❶ the "principle of sovereign equality" and the related decision making modes of "consultation and consensus (musyawarah and mufakat)", ❷ "non-interference in each other's internal affairs" and ❸ refraining from "use of force to change an established government or an internationally recognised political order".[158] Jayakumar further invoked ❹ the "principle of open economies", a principle, he claimed, "that has become increasingly accepted in recent years", and ❺ making "ASEAN the cornerstone of our foreign policies", since "only collective action can ensure ASEAN's voice is heard and ASEAN's interest protected".[159] By skillfully 'smuggling' these two latter 'principles' (or what he chose to call principles) into the set of traditional core principles of ASEAN, Jayakumar Singapore's support for stronger economic and political integration, while indicating at the same time that such integration could only evolve over time on the basis of voluntary commitments and the principle of national independence and non-coercion. In

---

[157] Jayakumar (1997): Opening Statement, 30th AMM, Kuala Lumpur, July.
[158] Ibid.
[159] Ibid.

other words, Jayakumar's rhetoric here is the rhetoric of a moderate reformer who is firmly grounded in the normative system of his association.

In July 1998, under the impression of the Asian crisis, Jayakumar gave a speech at the AMM that was programmatically entitled "Stick to Basics". And indeed, the content of this speech was in clear contrast to Thailand's and the Philippines' criticism of the principle of non-interference. Jayakumar set out to confirm his position of 1997 when he stated:

> There is no denying that we face serious challenges. There is the economic and financial crisis. [...] ASEAN itself has been transformed when it expanded its membership to nine. This expansion carried an in-built challenge - whether ASEAN, no longer a small cosy club, can maintain the spirit of consultation and consensus. [...] When we met in Kuala Lumpur exactly a year ago, I set out the basic principles that shaped ASEAN's success. [...] Some of these fundamental principles are inherent in the very nature of the organisation. They have contributed to ASEAN's success in the past and will continue to do so in the future. Discarding them will not make ASEAN stronger. To the contrary, to do so may imperil ASEAN's future.[160]

Similar displays of a strong commitment to the ASEAN core norms appear in nearly all of the speeches analyzed. Thus, at the Hanoi summit in 1998, Goh considered the "habits of consultation, consensus building and working together" as the "ASEAN glue" that "must be strenghtened to hold together a more disparate ASEAN".[161] Both Jayakumar and Goh have emphasized that ASEAN is not, and will not be, a supranational body, but rather a cooperation of sovereign states. ASEAN's task is to help manage (rather than control) relations between them.[162] However, despite all commitments to traditional ASEAN principles, Singapore has left no doubt that there is urgent need for structural reform, closer economic integration and more political coordination. Rhetorically, Jayakumar and Goh have frequently juxtaposed off the commitment to the ASEAN way on the one hand and the urgency of necessary reforms on the other. They seemed to be saying *The ASEAN way? - Yes, But ....* Compare the following statement:

> Clearly, ASEAN's core principles of sovereign equality, consensus decision-making, non-interference [...] and open economies have served us well. Equally clearly, the global and regional environment is evolving

---

[160] Jayakumar (1998): "Stick to Basics", Opening Statement, 31st AMM, Manila, 24 July.
[161] Goh (1998): Opening Statement, 6th ASEAN Summit, Hanoi, 16 December.
[162] Cf. Jayakumar (1998) and Goh (1999a): "ASEAN – Meeting the Challenges Ahead", Keynote Address, 32nd AMM, Singapore, 23 July.

and ASEAN must evolve with it, preserving the core but not hesitating to modify what we must.[163]

Similarly, coming back from the ASEAN Foreign Ministers' Retreat in July 1999, Jayakumar expressed support for traditional ASEAN norms, but at the same time admitted that the ASEAN way was often not commensurate with ASEAN's challenges:

> We should not abandon them [i.e. consensus, consultation, non-interference], but without abandoning them, how can the organisation and its members face new challenges [...] such as good governance, democratisation, human rights, and so on. These are the challenges ASEAN must face and face it in a way that doesn't abandon established principles.[164]

A close reading of the statements subject to this analysis suggests that Singapore is seeking political and institutional reform, but is careful not to undermine ASEAN's relatively thin common normative basis. Thus, while Goh and his foreign minister have expressed support for the ASEAN way, they have at the same time promoted more economic and political institutionalization, more cooperation mechanisms and more integration. Yet Singapore seems afraid to discredit central principles such as national sovereignty and non-interference because it fears that "[t]his is going to divide ASEAN".[165] Knowing that countries such as Malaysia and Indonesia cannot be pushed into embracing different ASEAN modes of cooperation against their will, the city state is struggling to conciliate the objectives of economic and political coordination, institutionalization with traditional ASEAN principles. Thus, at the ASEAN summit in 1999, Goh promoted Thailand's "idea of a troika [a]s a very useful development because sometimes a crisis happens in ASEAN and you need a mechanism to deal with the crisis," claiming that "this troika is a good development"; on the other hand, he argued that, out of deference to traditional ASEAN norms, the influence of the troika as a crisis intervention body would have to be very limited: "The principle of non-interference is still there. So the troika would have to handle future crises in a very delicate way".[166] Singapore seems reluctant to demand a more rigorous ASEAN agenda for regime building and regime compliance. Instead, Singapore identifies all the things that urgently

---

[163] Goh (1999a).

[164] Jayakumar (1999b): Remarks on return from the AMM Foreign Ministers' Retreat, Singapore, 23 July.

[165] Goh (1999b):"Finally Being His Own Man", interview with Goh Chok Tong, *Asiaweek*, 25 November.

[166] Goh (1999c): Transcript of remarks by the Prime Minister of Singapore, Goh Chok Tong, to the media after the 3rd ASEAN Informal Summit, Manila, 28 November.

need to be done, but then fails to define the normative changes that would be essential to the implementation of the suggested reforms. Thus, Jayakumar on the one hand called for extending AFTA, ASEAN integration and for "mov[ing] more swiftly and decisively to deal with transnational problems" as well as for the "pooling of resources to deal with problems that countries cannot handle on their own separately but yet can affect others"; on the other hand, he emphasized that this "does not mean compromising sovereignty".[167]

Summary
Singapore continues to display strong support for what it calls the core ASEAN principles – sovereign equality, consultation and consensus (musyawarah and mufakat), non-interference, peacefulness and refraining from the use of force. The pressure of the economic crisis that hit ASEAN members between 1997 and 1999 led Singapore to call for closer economic and political integration and the restructuring of ASEAN, but only in ways which are commensurate with core ASEAN norms. In Prime Minister Goh's words, "ASEAN must evolve with it [i.e. the global and regional environment], preserving the core but not hesitating to modify what we must".[168] Nevertheless, the rhetoric of recent statements displays a strong tendency to balance core ASEAN norms with calls for flexibility and reforms.

3.4. Malaysia

Malaysia under Prime Minister Mahathir Mohammad has become notorious for its anti-Western positions, its promotion of Asian values and its belligerent support for distinctively Southeast and East Asian forms of cooperation.[169] On the other hand, Malaysia has since the onset of the economic crisis of 1997 developed a very distinctive independent national economic and political agenda that has often been at odds with policies and positions of other ASEAN members. Unlike countries such as the Philippines, Thailand and Singapore, who have called for an ASEAN dedicated to economic liberalization and transparency, willing to contemplate streamlined decision making processes, effective crisis prevention mechanisms as well as democratic reforms and the

---

[167] Jayakumar (2000): Opening Statement, 33rd AMM, Bangkok, 24 July.
[168] Goh (1999a).
[169] Thus, Mahathir has been ❶ a strong proponent of what he called the *Look East* policy, a concept of economic development for Malaysia that was modeled on the Japanese example and rested on close economic ties between Japan and Malaysia; ❷ a determined promoter of the East Asian Economic Caucus (EAEC) idea, another brainchild of his, suggesting that several Northeast Asian and ASEAN countries form an economic bloc in order to counter the economic influence of the US and the EU; ❸ a fierce opponent of Australia's participation in the Asia Europe Meeting (ASEM) as part of the Asian side.

promotion of human rights in order to regain foreign investors' confidence and to ensure the economic stability of ASEAN member countries, Malaysia has emphasized its national and economic independence and its opposition to the forces of globalization whose imperatives Mahathir feels have been imposed on Southeast Asia by the West. Therefore, it is not surprising that Malaysia continues to favor an ASEAN built on traditional ASEAN norms, as the following analysis shows.

The texts subject to analysis are:

- Abdullah Badawi: Opening Statement, 31st AMM, Manila, 24 July 1998.

- Abdullah Badawi: "'Stick To Tradition' – A top diplomat gives his views", *Asiaweek.com*, 25 December 1998.

- Mahathir Mohamad: Opening Statement, 6th ASEAN Summit, Hanoi, 15 December 1998.

- Seri Syed Hamid Albar: Speech at the occasion of the ceremony of Cambodia's admission to ASEAN, Hanoi, 30 April 1999.

- Seri Syed Hamid Albar: Opening Statement, 32nd AMM, Singapore, 23 July 1999.

- Seri Syed Hamid Albar: Opening Statement, 33rd AMM, Bangkok, 24 July 2000.

As we have seen, Singaporean politicians have been eager to emphasize their reform agenda does not contradict traditional ASEAN norms. But the emphasis has always been on reform. Looking at Malaysia's stated views, there is little to suggest that Malaysia is reform-minded. The few token calls for reforms and economic integration are offset by warnings of the dangers of globalization and an overwhelming number of instances of praise for the "time-tested" principles of the ASEAN way. Prime Minister Mahathir, for example, remarked in 1998:

> Our Association, and relations between its members, have come under some strain [...] Malaysia believes that the maintenance of *positive* interstate relations has to be consciously nurtured. ASEAN has the wherewithal to pull through this turbulent period. I am referring here to the ASEAN approach, its method of work, and the principles governing the conduct of relations between member states. These are contained in various ASEAN Declarations, Treaties and Statements [that have] evolved through the years. We should adhere to them.[170]

---

[170] Mahathir (1998): Opening Statement, 6th ASEAN Summit, Hanoi, 15 December.

Principle of non-interference maintained

Malaysia's opposition to "flexible engagement" or "enhanced interaction" has been clear from the beginning of the debate. Foreign Minister Abdullah Badawi told *Asiaweek* in 1998: "I believe in consultation, definitely not in intervention – flexible or otherwise."[171] Abdullah Badawi's entire speech at the 31st AMM in 1998 was nothing but an extensive defense of the principle of non-interference. He reminded his ASEAN colleagues that "avoiding confrontation, and not interfering in the internal affairs of other member states have been the hallmarks of ASEAN existence"; leaving this norm behind would represent a breach of the conditions that formed the very base of many members' participation in ASEAN.[172] "No single party", Foreign Minister Hamid warned in 1999, defending Malaysia's self-willed approach to handling the crisis, "should claim to have a monopoly on the solutions or try to impose them on others."[173] Taking up the issue of the "maturity" of ASEAN relations (an expression coined by Thailand's Foreign Minister Surin in order to support his call for "flexible engagement"), Abdullah claimed that

> this issue [i.e. flexible engagement] has less to do with the maturing of political systems but concerns more the level of political integration. The higher the level of integration among ASEAN countries, the less would interventionism be a problem between them. Unless ASEAN countries are ready to discuss greater integration between them, I see little benefit in discussing this divisive issue of interfering in each other's affairs.[174]

Malaysia has also consistently opposed all attempts at institutionalized approaches to settle disputes among ASEAN members and between ASEAN members and outsiders, instead recommending the tried and tired principles of informality, quiet diplomacy and bilateralism.

Consultation and consensus

The "time-tested culture of consultation, consensus and mutual respect [...] will continue to hold us in good stead as well as guide us in the right direction. "[175] This sentence by Foreign Minister Syed Hamid Albar is representative of his government's view on this issue. Similar views appear in nearly any statement analyzed here.

---

[171] Badawi (1998b):"'Stick To Tradition' – A top diplomat gives his views", *Asiaweek.com*, 25 December.

[172] Badawi (1998a): Opening Statement, 31st AMM, Manila, 24 July.

[173] Seri Syed Hamid Albar (1999b): Opening Statement, 32nd AMM, Singapore, 23 July.

[174] Badawi (1998a).

[175] Seri Syed Hamid Albar (1999a): Speech at the Ceremony of Cambodia's admission to ASEAN, Hanoi, 30 April.

Sovereign equality, national sovereignty and national resilience

Whereas the Philippines, Thailand and Singapore have all spoken of balancing national and regional resilience, meaning that individual nations should commit their agendas to the greater collective good, Malaysia has persistently invoked the principles of equal sovereignty, national resilience and national sovereignty as the basic principles. National interests and national resilience clearly range higher than the ASEAN collective. National resilience often demonstratively is mentioned first, only then regional cooperation follows, as in the following statement of 1999: "Malaysia maintains the way forward for ASEAN is to focus on the basics, namely to develop national resilience, promote economic growth and enhance regional cooperation".[176] Or as Hamid Albar put it in 2000:

> ASEAN has the capacity and resilience to emerge more united and stronger in the post crisis period. For this to be achieved, ASEAN member states must return to the basics, namely to strengthen its national resilience, to nurture positive and constructive bilateral relations while accelerating economic integration.[177]

National resilience, according to Hamid, should always be the main criterion for decisions taken at ASEAN levels. "We should not accept those [options] which are alien to our national psyche and hurtful to our national objectives. Let us adopt only those that bring real benefits [...]".[178]

Reform-mindedness?

As mentioned above, there are only very few instances where Malaysia supported ASEAN reform. Such rare remarks as Abdullah's claim that "[w]e must constantly review our efforts, persevere with measures that show promise, and dare to innovate where necessary"[179] are set off by warnings such as the one issued by Hamid at the 33rd AMM in 2000:

> While changes or adjustments may be necessary, it is important that we should not change for the sake of changing. Any change should serve the interest of ASEAN member states and be appropriate to our circumstances. It is important that ASEAN has confidence in its own convictions.[180]

This statement strongly suggests Malaysia is averse to anything that is not completely in line with traditional ASEAN principles. In other words, Malaysia essentially is opposed to structural changes to ASEAN.

---

[176] Badawi (1998a).
[177] Seri Syed Hamid Albar (2000): Opening Statement, 33rd AMM, Bangkok, 24 July.
[178] Seri Syed Hamid Albar (1999b).
[179] Badawi (1998a).
[180] Seri Syed Hamid Albar (2000).

Summary
There is little to suggest that Malaysia is interested in the reform of ASEAN. The government's rhetorical commitment to economic integration reflects Malaysia's formal support for the ASEAN agenda as adopted in the ASEAN Vision 2020 and the Hanoi Plan of Action. But Malaysia basically remains opposed to any structural changes within ASEAN, such as further institutionalization, centralization and regime-building in ASEAN. In order to keep the association from assuming supranational powers, the government strongly opposes the collectivization of decision making and conflict resolution as well as anything that would challenge the principles that mark the ASEAN way, namely national sovereignty, national resilience, consensus and consultation, non-interference, informality and bilateralism. Therefore, Malaysia can justly be considered a conservative voice in ASEAN.

3.5. Indonesia

Since the end of the Suharto era, Indonesia has experienced considerable turmoil, which makes it difficult to give an adequate picture of Indonesia's current views on ASEAN norms. Indonesia's internal conflicts have marginalized Indonesia politically within ASEAN and absorbed the administrations of presidents Habibie and Wahid in ways which have not left them much room for giving Indonesia a strong profile in ASEAN. Official government statements hardly ever formulated any controversial positions, nor did they take sides in controversial debates. The statements mostly echo the official objectives of the ASEAN Vision 2020 and the Hanoi Plan of Action.
The following texts have been subject to the analysis:

- "We Have Solidarity", Interview with Ali Alatas, *Asiaweek.com*, 25 December 1998.
- B. J. Habibie: Opening Statement, 6th ASEAN Summit, Hanoi, 15 December 1998.
- Ali Alatas: Statement at the ocasion of the Ceremony of Cambodia's admission to ASEAN, 30 April 1999.
- Ali Alatas: Opening Statement, 32nd AMM, Singapore, 23 July 1999.
- Alwi Shihab: "The Indonesian Foreign Policy Outlook", Keynote Address, Conference in Observance of the Indonesian National Press Day, Jakarta, 17 February 2000.
- Alwi Shahib: Excerpt from the Keynote Address at the CSCAP Seminar on Indonesia's Future Challenges and Implications for the Region, 8 March 2000.
- Alwi Shihab: Opening Statement, 33rd AMM, Bangkok, 24 July 2000.

In one of his last interviews in office, Ali Alatas, the long-standing foreign minister under Suharto and foreign minister of the Habibie administration, supported once more the traditional ASEAN norms he and the Suharto government had stood for in previous decades. He expressed displeasure with the disregard among the new generation of ASEAN politicians for the customary, quiet behind-the-scenes diplomacy, for the principle of non-interference and for the respect for national sovereignty. Asked about the disharmony among ASEAN countries in the aftermath of the crisis, he lamented: "Differences in public – this is a feature of modern-day diplomacy now. Nothing can be kept completely secret. Everything proceeds in public now."[181] Very subtly and diplomatically, he expressed criticism of Surin's "flexible engagement" approach, but endorsed the adopted ASEAN formula of "enhanced interaction" as a valid ASEAN norm. He acknowledged that the time was ripe for a certain measure of "reformasi", but indicated that he preferred this process to proceed slowly and on the basis of traditional ASEAN norms.

President Habibie had nothing to say on ASEAN norms at the Hanoi summit in 1998. The only statement promoting economic integration was that he "expect[ed] ASEAN in 2003 to be transformed into one vast integrated regional economy".[182] Foreign Minister Ali Alatas went a bit further when he called for "necessary economic, social and political initiatives that will make ASEAN fully a concert of Southeast Asian nations", by which he meant that ASEAN members needed to "pool our resources and collaborate" in order to become a "vast single market and investment area".[183] Alatas did not elaborate on the subject of pooling resources, and it must be doubted that he actually implied a transfer of national sovereignty to the ASEAN level. However, as far as regime building and institutionalization of political processes in ASEAN was concerned, he advocated rules of procedure for the dispute settlement mechanism of the ASEAN High Council and strengthening the ASEAN Secretariat (in his own words: to "fine-tune the structures and workings of the ASEAN Secretariat by making it focus on its role as coordinator of the substantive work of the Association").[184]

The government of President Wahid has not given major impulses to the debate about ASEAN objectives and norms. Foreign Minister Alwi Shihab expressed his country's continuing commitment to ASEAN cooperation in order to maintain political stability and to implement democratization and economic

---

[181] Alatas (1998): "We Have Solidarity", Interview with Ali Alatas, *Asiaweek.com*, 25 December.

[182] Habibie (1998): Opening Statement, 6th ASEAN Summit, Hanoi, 15 December.

[183] Alatas (1999a): Statement at the Ceremony of Cambodia's admission to ASEAN, Hanoi, 30 April.

[184] Alatas (1999b): Opening Statement, 32nd AMM, Singapore, 23 July.

integration. Concerning ASEAN norms, the new government, which had to face the military intervention of foreign nations in East Timor, has occasionally adopted a very conservative stance. Thus, Foreign Minister Alwi Shihab repeatedly invoked the principles of national sovereignty, territorial integrity and non-interference in each nation's internal affairs:

> If all powers concerned will adhere to the principles of ZOPFAN, the ASEAN region is assured that there will be no external interventions in its internal affairs and will eventually develop a capacity and a way of solving disputes and involving its members.[185]

Indonesia's strong adherence to these principles has been heightened by the crisis over Aceh and other provinces, when the Indonesian government tried to fend off intervention from the international community. In a briefing to foreign ambassadors, the Foreign Minister repeatedly pointed at Indonesia's stance in the question of non-interference:

> [...] the Government is determined to defend Indonesia's territorial integrity. [...] I would like to take this oppotunity to sincerely express our gratitude to Governments - individually or collectively - that have expressed their support to the Indonesian position on this matter.[186]

Indonesia's objectives in ASEAN sometimes seemed obscure. On one occasion, Alwi Shihab claimed that ASEAN unity served as a means to remain "independent and free from the interference of external powers", whereas on another occasion he echoed the official ASEAN formula that ASEAN cohesiveness and resilience should serve to form an "outward-looking" concert of nations. Reading the speeches, one gets the impression that the Wahid government is rather comfortable with the traditional principles, modes and procedures of ASEAN while at the same time it demands more, and more integrated, approaches to economic integration and political and social stability. In the area of security cooperation, Alwi Shihab claimed in July 2000 "that ASEAN should remain its [the ARF's] primary driving force in order to ensure its relevance", but declined to promote the adoption of a collective and more rules-oriented concept of preventive diplomacy. Instead, he demanded that the ARF "move its deliberations and activities forward on the basis of consensus and at a pace comfortable to all participants".[187] Similarly, Indonesia has given no recognizable impulses as to the necessary reforms required for implementing economic integration.

---

[185] Shihab (2000a): "The Indonesian Foreign Policy Outlook", Keynote Address, Conference in Observance of the National Press Day, Jakarta, 17 February, hereafter: IFPO2000.
[186] Shihab (2000b): Briefing by Foreign Minister Alwi Shihab to Foreign Ambassadors in Jakarta on Aceh, Maluku and Irian Jaya, Jakarta, 7 July.
[187] Shihab (2000c): Opening Statement, 33rd AMM, Bangkok, 24 July 2000.

Summary

The present government of Indonesia under President Wahid has avoided contributing publicly to the norms debate in ASEAN. Thus, Indonesia is neither promoting structutral reforms and changes to the ASEAN way nor is the government explicitly defending traditional positions. Nevertheless, there is some evidence that the Indonesian government is leaning towards the traditional approach rather than to a progressive ASEAN agenda. The few instances where norms are directly addressed in official statements are examples of a more conservative attitude to ASEAN relations that rests on the supreme importance of national sovereignty, territorial integrity and the principle of non-interference. The strong emphasis on these principles is obviously due to Indonesia's unstable domestic situation, and Indonesia's sensitivity in this respect is heightened by the precedence of foreign military intervention in East Timor. It has to be noted, however, that, while the Habibie administration had originally opposed "flexible engagement", it eventually accepted the compromise formula of "enhanced interaction". The evidence suggests that Indonesia will continue to invoke traditional ASEAN norms as far as its internal security situation is concerned. It is difficult to say whether Indonesia sees things differently with regard to economic cooperation and integration, since the government has not commented on the issue. Albeit, the Indonesian government seems prepared to follow the path to greater economic integration.

3.6. Vietnam

Vietnam joined ASEAN in 1995 as the first communist country, after decades of hostile and tense relations with the association of its anti-communist Southeast Asian neighbors. Accession to ASEAN meant that Vietnam had to subscribe to all the principles and objectives of ASEAN as laid down in the central ASEAN documents, such as the Treaty of Amity and Cooperation. To Vietnam, as well as to Myanmar, Laos and Cambodia, ASEAN's emphasis on national resilience, consensus and non-interference in the internal affairs of member states had been very attractive arguments for joining the association. In terms of security, Vietnam counted on ASEAN members' solidarity and hoped for collective approaches to regional security and especially the South China Sea issue. As the following section shows, Vietnam's views of ASEAN norms are very much determined by two factors - the desire to keep ASEAN from developing into a more centralized supranational decision making body on the one hand and an interest in developing regimes for regional security.

The following texts served as a basis for the analysis of Vietnam's norms rhetoric:

- Phan Van Khai (PM): Keynote Address, 6th ASEAN Summit, Hanoi, 15 December 1998.

- Nguyen Manh Cam (Dep. PM, FM): Statement at the Ceremony of Cambodia's admission to ASEAN, Hanoi, 30 April 1999.

- Nguyen Manh Cam: Opening Statement, 32nd AMM, Singapore, 23 July 1999.

- Nguyen Dy Nien (FM): Opening Statement, 33rd AMM, Bangkok, 24 July 2000.

Insisting on the ASEAN way

All three official speeches analyzed here display a strong commitment to the ASEAN way. Although the speakers always took care to emphasize not only national resilience, but also regional resilience, it is apparent that national sovereignty and national resilience have absolute priority on Vietnam's scale of ASEAN norms. Thus, the normative paradigm of *unity in diversity* is frequently invoked when speakers refer to the traditional ASEAN norms. PM Phan Van Khai, for example, told his ASEAN colleagues in 1998:

> In reality, unity in diversity has been and will be giving added strength to each country, promoting cooperation and enhancing ASEAN's standing in the international community. Today, against the backdrop of the economic and financial crisis, unity and one-mindedness has become more crucial than before. It is our firm belief that [...] with "the ASEAN way", we will definitely strenghten our one-mindedness while maintaining member countries' identities.[188]

In a similar vein, the foreign minister repeatedly and unambiguously voiced Vietnam's strong support for the ASEAN way when he addressed his ASEAN colleagues in 1999:

> [...] it is important to consolidate and strengthen ASEAN's unity and co-operation on the basis of the Association's fundamental principles, especially consensus, non-interference in each other's internal affairs, and unity in diversity. [...]
> the ASEAN way should be preserved and applied in resolving outstanding issues and preventing new disputes from arising.[189]

One year later, at the 33rd AMM in Bangkok, the new foreign minister of Vietnam echoed his predecessor's views. With a view to ASEAN's expanded

---

[188] Phan Van Khai (1998): Keynote Address, 6th ASEAN Summit, Hannoi, 15 December.
[189] Nguyen Manh Cam (1999b): Speech, 32nd AMM, Singapore, 23 July.

membership, he confirmed the "pursuit of the ASEAN way" as the irrefutable basis for future ASEAN cooperation. " It can be said, " he told the assembled foreign ministers,

> that solidarity, unity in diversity, in which each member's identity is maintained and developed, are both ASEAN's traditional features and an important objective that always need[s] to be respected. The Association's time-tested principles and practices, first and foremost the principle of consensus and that of non-interference [in] each other's internal affairs, have bound us together and been a source of strength. [...]
> We have every reason to firmly believe that outstanding or newly-emerging issues need to and will be effectively resolved in the ASEAN way.[190]

At several ASEAN meetings in 1999 and 2000, Vietnam also stressed the importance of "equitable development", a formula that invokes the ASEAN norm of mutually beneficial cooperation and implies the desire for a stronger engagement by the old ASEAN members in development programs for the newcomers. At the AMM 1999, the foreign minister highlighted that

> [t]he dynamism of ASEAN depends on the achievement of sustained and equitable development along the line: "Each country develops for the development of the whole region and the whole region develops for the development of each country".[191]

On another occasion, he implied that "equitable development" was among the central purposes of ASEAN: "[...] we look forward to a close cooperation [...] for ASEAN's objectives of unity and cooperation for a Southeast Asia of peace, stability and *equitable development*" [emphasis added]. His successor in office dedicated a lengthy section of his speech to the "gap" that existed between old and new members and expressed Vietnam's dissatisfaction with ASEAN's reluctance to fill that gap (see Nguyen Manh Cam 1999b). By invoking the ASEAN way and equitable development (and thereby - implicitly - the principles of equality and mutual benefit), Vietnam implies that if ASEAN ever deviated from the ASEAN way or failed to help substantially improve the economic situation of Vietnam, this would erode the basis of Vietnam's entry into ASEAN.

---

[190] Nguyen Dy Nien (2000): Statement at the Opening Ceremony, 33rd AMM, Bangkok, 24 July.
[191] Nguyen Manh Cam (1999b).

Institutionalization and regime building?

Since the adoption of the Hanoi Plan of Action (HPA) at the ASEAN summit in 1998, Vietnam has failed to repeat its calls for more economic institutionalization within ASEAN.[192] In December 1998, the prime minister had still urged more extensive coordination and crisis prevention mechanisms:

> At the regional level, ASEAN has been able to set up a mechanism for cooperation under favourable economic conditions. We, however, have not been able to create a mechanism for coordination in time[s] of crisis. We hope that this economic turmoil would give us valuable lessons to design a system for warning, preventing and handling untoward developments. This could be a mechanism for the exchange of experience, in macroeconomic management, monitoring, coordination, and mutual assistance. At the same time, practical economic, financial and monetary measures, including those related to the establishment of the ASEAN Free Trade Area (AFTA) and the ASEAN Investment Area (AIA) incorporated in the Hanoi Plan of Action, will certainly create a synergy for us to quickly overcome the crisis and move further forward.[193]

Since 1998, however, Vietnam has frequently invoked the ASEAN way, but gradually failed to mention economic mechanisms and institutionalization. For example, at the ASEAN Ministerial Meeting in 1999, the foreign minister didn't mention coordination, regime-building and institutionalization, but merely called for establishing "'hot lines' at various levels" and "increasing work visits [...] of various agencies" in order to "promote close ties and settle problems that might arise".[194] Furthermore, he emphasized that all these measures should be in line with the ASEAN way. At the Ministerial Meeting in July 2000, the foreign minister also failed to address the issue of closer cooperation in the economic sector, while at the same time commending the ASEAN way as the basis of cooperation.

Areas where Vietnam has persistently called for institutionalization and regime building, are dispute settlement and regional security. Thus, in 1999 Hanoi "support[ed] the formulation of Rules of Procedures of the High Council as envisioned in the TAC" and reiterated this view in July 2000 when the Foreign Minister claimed that the "establishment and effective functioning of the High Council is extremely necessary".[195] Vietnam has also urged a collective ASEAN approach to a Code of Conduct for the South China Sea, since this would

---

[192] This statement only holds for the body of statements at the official ASEAN level and does not necessarily represent the definite Vietnamese position.
[193] Phan Van Khai (1998).
[194] Nguyen Manh Cam (1999b).
[195] Ibid.

strengthen its position vis-à-vis China. Thus, in the area of dispute settlement and security, Vietnam seems to embrace the idea of institutionalization and rules-based decision making, whereas this does not seem to hold in the economic area.

Summary

The first communist ASEAN member puts great emphasis on all norms associated with the ASEAN way as essential to the conduct of relations within the association. With respect to economic integration, Vietnam doesn't seem to embrace the idea of ceding greater powers to collective and centralized institutions. Rather, Vietnam invokes the principles of mutually beneficial relations and equitable development. In the area of security, Vietnam has been calling for solidarity, collective policy making and regime building in order to secure its interests in the South China Sea.

3.7. Laos, Myanmar

Both Myanmar and Laos joined ASEAN in order to avoid political and economic isolation. Myanmar has been struggling with sanctions imposed by the European Union and the United States in the aftermath of the military's fierce repression of the democratic opposition. Despite ASEAN's decision to accept Myanmar's application for membership and to adopt a constructive engagement approach to Myanmar (a policy that entailed a serious deterioration of ASEAN relations with the EU and the US), Myanmar remained hostile to the idea of other ASEAN members interfering in Myanmar's domestic affairs.[196]

In addition to its repressive handling of the democracy movement and the minorities inside the country, Myanmar has also been engaged in open conflict with Thailand over cross-border drug trafficking; internal struggle between the junta and Karen rebel groups has frequently been carried across the Myanmarese-Thai border. As far as the ASEAN norms system is concerned, Myanmar obviously has no great interest in abolishing those very norms which provide protection from external interference. The communist regime of Laos, which has an almost equally disastrous human rights record and recently also has been confronted with increased internal insurgencies and instability, has as little interest in political meddling from ASEAN as has Myanmar. The

---

[196] Most recent developments since early 2001 suggest that, under the impression of an ongoing power struggle in the State Peace and Development Council (SPDC), parts of the leadership, such as General Than Shwe and Lt.-General Khin Nyunt, are increasingly ready to talk to other ASEAN members about Myanmar's democratic deficit. Cf. Siemers (2001).

following section gives an overview of Myanmar's and Laos' respective positions on ASEAN norms and ASEAN relations.

The texts analyzed here are,

for Laos:

- Sisavath Keobounphanh (PM): Statement, 6th ASEAN Summit, 15 December 1998.
- Somsavat Lengsavad (FM): Opening Statement, 32nd AMM, 23 July 1999.
- Somsavat Lengsavad: Opening Statement: 33rd AMM, 24 July 2000.

for Myanmar:

- Than Shwe (PM): Statement, 6th Summit, Hanoi, 15 December 1998.
- "We Restored Order", Interview with Khin Nyunt, 17 December 1999, *Asiaweek*, 25 (1999), 50.
- U Win Aung (FM): Opening Statement, 32nd AMM, Singapore, 23 July 1999.
- U Win Aung: Opening Statement, 33rd AMM, Bangkok, 24 july 2000.

Neither of the two governements' statements convey very much as to the actual objectives or positions these governments take. They contain what one suspects are token statements of support to such ASEAN objectives as economic integration, etc. As far as the post-crisis debate on ASEAN norms is concerned, both governments, not surprisingly, strongly lean towards a minimalist interpretation of ASEAN norms that confers national independence and sovereignty to each nation and leaves no room for centralized decision making.

Laos

At the AMM in 1999, Foreign Minister Somsavat Lengsavad stressed "holding [on] to the value[s] and fundamental principles of ASEAN".[197] So had Prime Minister Than Shwe during the ASEAN summit in December 1998, where he urged

> strong adherence to its [ASEAN's] basic principles, namely the principles of respect for the independence and identity of all nations,

---

[197] Somsavat Lengsavad (1999): Opening Statement, 32nd AMM, Singapore, 23 July.

non-interference in each other's internal affairs as well as the principle of consultation and consensus.[198]

In the same speech, he made a point of supporting the "ASEAN spirit of national resilience and self-determination" as the basis for broadening ASEAN cooperation and cooperation with other countries. At the AMM 2000 in Bangkok, Somsavat Lengsavad made clear that Laos expected ASEAN to "adapt to globalization", albeit "in conformity with the specifity of the region", and claimed that it was "ASEAN member countries' aspiration to advance and integrate their economies", but always in line with, and "pursuant to[,] the values and basic principles of ASEAN".[199] Indeed, Laos would like to see any ASEAN activities carried out in accordance with the traditional ASEAN norms. With respect to the ASEAN way, Laos' rhetoric puts the country among the conservative hard-liners who oppose any changes to the status quo of ASEAN norms.

Myanmar

Like Laos, Myanmar pays lip service to ASEAN projects such as the establishment of a free trade and investment area and all the other official objectives of ASEAN, but essentially the speeches analyzed reflect no special concern for closer economic integration and trade liberalization. It seems that to Myanmar economic integration means above all the establishment and implementation of ASEAN development assistance programs such as the Mekong Basin Development Program. Projects like AFTA and AIA are endorsed officially, since they are on the official ASEAN agenda, but Myanmar's commitment probably has to be classified as mere lip service. Thus, during the ASEAN Ministerial Meeting 2000, Foreign Minister U Win Aung briefly endorsed "economic integration" as a contribution to "maintain[ing] ASEAN's competitiveness as a single trade and investment area", but spent more time complaining about the insufficiency of ASEAN efforts to implement the Mekong Basin development program and pointing out the validity and importance of the ASEAN way in resolving the problems of the crisis.[200] In 1999, U Win Aung suggested that ASEAN would meet the challenges of integrating the new members best by "strengthen[ing] the foundation" of ASEAN, i.e. concentrating on the association's traditional and minimalist ways – such as getting to know each other in an atmosphere of

---

[198] Sisavath Keobounphanh (1998): Opening Statement, 6th ASEAN Summit, Hanoi 15 December 1998.

[199] Somsavat Lengsavad (2000): Opening Statement, 33rd AMM, Bangkok, 24 July.

[200] U Win Aung (2000): Opening Statement, 33rd AMM, Bangkok, 24 July.

tolerance for diversity and avoiding criticism ("greater accommodation and understanding based on equality and mutual respect").[201] The junta regards a conservative interpretation of existing ASEAN norms - especially national sovereignty and non-interference - as the basis of Myanmar's accession to ASEAN. Breaching these norms by institutionalizing more centralized decision making processes or by transferring sovereignty from the national to the collective level would be unacceptable. The strong man behind the junta government of Myanmar, Khin Nyunt, expressed his and Myanmar's position on ASEAN norms very clearly in an interview with *Asiaweek*:

> You must remember what its [ASEAN's] basic tenets are. It was established to increase cooperation among Southeast Asian nations. It can't, and shouldn't, be viewed in the same way as the European Union or the OSCE. [...]
> The principle of non-interference in the internal affairs of the member states is enshrined in the 1967 Bangkok Declaration, which established ASEAN. It's also in the Treaty of Amity and Cooperation, which is the basic agreement for all members. And it's a principle of international law. To re-evaluate this concept now would mean attacking the foundation of the association. [...] That's why Myanmar does not support attempts to tamper with this time-tested concept.[202]

This position implies that giving up traditional norms would erode the original conditions of Myanmar's accession to ASEAN and thereby the very basis of Myanmar's membership in the grouping. Maintaining a conservative interpretation of the ASEAN way is essential to Myanmar, since otherwise the junta would have to fear increasing intervention and embarrassment due to its democratic deficit, human rights violations, drug smuggling and recurrent violations of the Thai border. Interestingly, however, Myanmar seems to have, at least at the rhetorical level, accepted the formula of *enhanced interaction*, as officially endorsed by the ASEAN Foreign Ministers in 1998. When Prime Minister Than Shwe of Myanmar insisted on the "ASEAN way", on "sovereignty", "non-interference", "seeking consensus" and "quiet diplomacy" in December 1998, he added "enhanced interaction" to the list of principles that, as he claimed, strengthened ASEAN as a whole.[203] This means that Thailand's "flexible engagement" approach has moved even Myanmar to embrace the compromise formula of "enhanced interaction". Equally interesting is that Myanmar, despite its rejection of centralized decision making in, and institutionalization of ASEAN, spoke in favor of extending the competences of

---

[201] U Win Aung (1999): Statement, 32nd AMM, Singapore, 23 July.
[202] Khin Nyunt (1999): "We Restored Order", Interview with Khin Nyunt, *Asiaweek.com*, 17 December.
[203] Than Shwe (1998): Statement, 6th ASEAN Summit, Hanoi, 15 December.

the ASEAN Secretariat: "Without an efficient ASEAN Secretariat, the goals we leave set to realize our vision [i.e. the Hanoi Plan of Action] will, indeed, be difficult to implement".[204]   Overall, however, one can say that Myanmar's norms rhetoric suggests that if ASEAN's norms system were to change, Myanmar would be among the last to change with it.

Summary

Neither Laos nor Myanmar have contributed new impulses to ASEAN and the ASEAN norms system. Rather, the two countries have been staunch promoters of a conservative interpretation of the ASEAN way. While both subscribe to the general objectives of ASEAN and claim they support AFTA, AIA and a stronger Secretariat, they oppose more institutionalization, political and economic integration and centralization. Where Laos and Myanmar support economic integration, they are always quick to point out that these developments should be kept in line with the norms of the ASEAN way. Laos and Myanmar seem to be most happy when left alone politically, with no interference from outsiders, but they expect the more developed ASEAN members and ASEAN as an organization to support their economic development through increased economic interaction and specially designed development programs. In Laos' and Myanmar's publicized views, ASEAN has gained strength from the accession of the newcomer countries, and in turn the newcomers expect comfortable treatment in political terms as well as economic benefits. Thus, formal support for ASEAN projects in exchange for economic benefits seems to be Laos' and Myanmar's understanding of the ASEAN norm of "mutually beneficial relations".

3.8. Addendum: The Secretary-General of ASEAN

The primary role of the ASEAN Secretariat is to execute decisions made collectively by the heads of government, not to actively devise ASEAN policies. Formally, the Secretary-General has the rank of a minister, which indicates clearly his subordinate position in relation to the heads of government. Nevertheless, the Secretary-General has an exposed and relatively independent position within ASEAN: he has not only access to his own staff[205] to implement and devise ASEAN activities, but has also a mandate to develop

---

[204] Ibid.

[205] In August 1999, the ASEAN Secretariat, according to Secretary-General Rodolfo Severino, had "38 positions for openly recruited personnel and 104 for locally recruited staff." (Severino 1999a: "No Alternative to Regionalism", interview with the Secretary-General of ASEAN, Konrad Adenauer Foundation, August.)

ideas on the future of ASEAN, to relate his views to the member governments and, what is more, he has access to, and the attention of, the world media.[206] Thus, one can certainly say that the ASEAN Secretary-General is an opinion-maker in ASEAN, albeit one with very limited powers. The Secretary-General will have both a strong institutional interest in extending the Secretariat's influence within the structures of ASEAN and in ASEAN assuming an enhanced vis-à-vis its member countries. His position may deviate considerably from individual members' positions, especially of those who are critical of the association assuming a greater and more central role in Southeast Asian affairs. At the same time, the Secretary-General has to be an integrative figure and accommodate the very diverse views of the various national governments. In this respect, the Secretary-General will try to reconcile, rather than polarize, views and positions. This section focuses on the public views of Rodolfo Severino, ASEAN Secretary-General since January 1998, on ASEAN and its post-crisis norms system.

The analysis is based on the following texts by Rodolfo Severino:

- Remarks, 8th Southeast Asia Forum, Kuala Lumpur, 15 March 1998.

- "Weathering the Storm: ASEAN's Response to Crisis", Speech, *Fare Eastern Economic Review* Conference on "Weathering the Storm: Hongkong and the Asian Financial Crisis", Hongkong, 11 June 1998.

- "No Alternative to Regionalism", Interview with Wolfgang Möllers on behalf of the Konrad Adenauer Foundation, August 1999 [Konrad Adenauer Foundation "Speeches and Interviews [Reden und Gespräche] Series].

- "Thinking ASEAN", Interview, *Philippine Graphic Magazin*, 29 November 1999.

- "The Only Way for ASEAN" Interview by Serge Berthier, early 1999, ASEAN homepage.

- "Regionalism: the Stakes for Southeast Asia", Address, Institute of Defence Studies, Singapore, 24 May 1999.

- "The ASEAN Way in Manila", *FEER*, 23 December 1999.

- "Sovereignty, Intervention and the ASEAN Way", Address, ASEAN Scholar's Roundtable, Singapore, 3 July 2000.

---

[206] The present incumbent, Rodolfo Severino, by actively involving himself in ASEAN affairs and by making his voice heard in the world media, has added political weight to the role and position of the Secretary-General. Cf. for example Reyes (2000a): "Who's Afraid of a Little Candor? - ASEAN Day Four: The Secretary-General's Report", *Asiaweek.com*, 28July; Richardson (2000a): "Investment in Southeast Asia Plunges", *International Herald Tribune*, 27 July.

Rodolfo Severino, a Philippine diplomat, clearly has strong ideas of ASEAN's challenges in the future and how they should be met, but he is apparently also eager to reconcile the necessary changes with the traditional ASEAN norms system. Structurally, however, his ideas imply that some central ASEAN norms have become obsolete, and Severino sometimes admits that changes to behavioral and constitutive principles are essential to meeting the new challenges.

Solidarity - a norm between tradition and change?

The norm of solidarity among ASEAN members has traditionally exposed individual ASEAN countries to only modest demands from the group, since the concept is relatively flexible and open to interpretation. When Severino addressed the issue of solidarity in a speech in March 1998, he painted a rather conventional and unspectacular picture of ASEAN solidarity. To him, solidarity meant mutual support among individual ASEAN members:

> The leaders of individual ASEAN countries themselves have been visiting one another, helping one another with advice, counsel and resources, including financial support, rice and medicine, while working out ways of cooperatively dealing with the crisis.[207]

A few months later, in June, he spelled out a concept of solidarity which ASEAN members might find more problematic to live up to, since he made it clear that, in the future, solidarity would require individual nations to show more commitment to regional integration. He stated that

> today's crises and challenges call for tighter integration, closer cooperation and stronger solidarity in ASEAN. It requires a larger measure of regional consciousness than ever before, a deeper appreciation and stronger assertion of the regional interest.

This, he concluded, was "a delicate and complex enterprise, particularly in the absence of true supranational institutions and elaborate rules for regional behavior".[208] By thus linking solidarity to individual nations' commitment to regional integration, Severino redefined the concept of solidarity itself and made clear that solidarity had to be perceived as an objective of ASEAN rather than an achievement. His concept of solidarity would require each nation to commit itself to the cause of deepening regional integration. Failure to display

---

[207] Severino (1998a): Remarks, 8th Southeast Asia Forum, Kuala Lumpur, 15 March.
[208] Severino (1998b): "Weathering the Storm: ASEAN's Response to Crisis", *FEER* Conference on "Weathering the Storm: Hongkong and the Asian Financial Crisis", Honkong, 11 June.

such commitment would have to be interpreted as a lack of solidarity. At the 8th Southeast Asia Forum, Severino pointed out that

> [t]he financial crisis has [...] brought to the fore an emerging irony in ASEAN: The very integration envisioned and long regarded as a source of strength can be a point of weakness. ASEAN can address this irony in two ways. One is to hesitate and slow down or pause, if not retreat or reverse course, on the road to further economic integration, as individual economies seek to avoid being contaminated by the economic and financial troubles of the others. [...] The other way is to proceed, and, indeed, advance faster on the road of integration and cooperation, while ensuring that closer and faster integration is further developed as a source of strength [...].[209]

Severino here argued for solving a regional economic problem collectively, in concert, rather than individually, even if this means losing the immediate benefits of national protectionism. The new solidarity would thus mean subduing immediate national interests for the sake of (longer-term) collective solutions. But the re-interpretation of solidarity does not stop there. According to Severino,

> it is becoming clear that ASEAN solidarity also means ASEAN manifesting its concern over apparently internal developments in some members - whether they arise from ethnic conflict, political violence, or economic upheaval - if such developments threaten to spill over to neighboring countries. [...] In this sense, ASEAN is emerging as a true community or even family.[210]

Accordingly, solidarity would require ASEAN members to agree to the concept of "flexible engagement" (or "enhanced interaction" or "constructive intervention" respectively). Indeed, this extended interpretation of the norm of solidarity represents a call on all ASEAN members to accept an agenda for ASEAN reforms. Accordingly, Severino accused countries opposing such reforms as lacking solidarity: "Some in ASEAN seem to pay lip service to the ideal of regional solidarity and cooperation. They act as if they did not truly believe in the need for regional responses to regional problems."[211]

Balancing national sovereignty and collective regional interests
Severino seems to see a crucial incompatibility between the concept of national sovereignty on the one hand and the present need for ASEAN to organize

---

[209] Severino (1998a).
[210] Severino (1998a).
[211] Ibid.

political coordination and economic integration on the other. Echoing the Philippine Foreign Minister Siazon's call for a new balance between national sovereignty and collective regional interests, Severino argued in November 1999 that "[b]ecause the Southeast Asian community will be more closely integrated, a new equilibrium may have to be sought between national sovereignty and regional purpose".[212] In an earlier speech he had similarly contrasted the terms *national* and *regional* as polar opposites and given preference to the *regional* when he said "ASEAN's response to global changes has to be not greater national assertiveness, as countries might normally have reacted in the past, but greater regional integration and cooperation."[213] And with respect to multilateral dispute settlement in cases such as the crisis in East Timor, he conceded that national sovereignty had politically and historically been a highly valued norm "espeacially in the exceedingly diverse world of Southeast Asia" which therefore had to be respected. But he also arfued that "a balance has to be sought - and constantly adjusted [...] between international involvement and national sovereignty. Compromises will have to be made."[214]

Regional integration and the ASEAN way
To Severino, regional integration means both economic regime building under the roof of ASEAN and closer political coordination among ASEAN partners. As ASEAN members have always defined their association as non-legalistic and informal, the Secretary-General's demand that

> [i]n some areas, more explicit and binding rules, embodied in treaties, may be needed to complement the informal understandings that have served ASEAN so well in the past.[215]

must be considered a significant move away from this conventional ASEAN design. The fact that Severino has applied the terms "regime" and "mechanism" – with all their implications of institutionalisation, binding agreements and rules compliance – in order to describe ASEAN's objectives of economic integration and political coordination certainly confirms this impression. Statements like the following might have stirred some uneasiness among the more *status quo* – oriented, conservative ASEAN members:

> Growing trans-national problems [...] are susceptible only of regional solutions, which means more intensive ASEAN cooperation in a broader range of areas. *Agreed, enforceable rules and, at the very least, serious*

---

[212] Severino (1999c): "Thinking ASEAN", interview with R., *Philippine Graphic Magazine*, 29 November.
[213] Severino (1998b).
[214] Severino (2000): "Sovereignty, Intervention and the ASEAN Way", Address, ASEAN Scholar's Roundtable, Singapore, 3 July.
[215] Severino (1998b).

codes of conduct will probably be required in the future [...].[216]
[emphasis added]

Severino leaves no doubt as to his intention to bring ASEAN countries in line with each other, if necessary through collective pressure where one nation's policies impacted negatively on other ASEAN members or the whole region. Asked about the lessons ASEAN had learned from the crisis, Severino responded:

> The first lesson is that [...] Southeast Asia [is] more [...] interdependent than previously thought. What one country does with its economy and even with its politics almost invariably affects its neighbors. Therefore, a country's policies must have a regional outlook, and regional institutions in which to carry them out have to be developed. The days of beggar-thy-neighbor policies is past.
> The second lesson is that economic liberalization and integration within ASEAN cannot [be allowed to] falter.[217]

On the other hand, Severino has repeatedly emphasized the concept of evolution, rather than revolution, and has insisted that all of ASEAN's basic norms and the ASEAN way continue to be imperative to the operational mode of the Southeast Asian grouping. Thus, he asserted that

> [t]he challenge for ASEAN is to promote, support, and manage ASEAN cooperation in these increased areas [i.e. broader range of areas of cooperation] without over-stretching the resources of the Association or of its member states.

According to Severino, collective regime building does not imply transforming ASEAN into a supranational entity. Although one might wonder how regime building could possibly work without a degree of centralized decision making and without establishing some adequate enforcement mechanisms, Severino insisted that

> ASEAN is not and was not meant to be a supranational entity acting independently of its members. It has no parliament or council of ministers with law-making powers, no power of enforcement, no judicial system.[218]

---

[216] Severino (1998a).

[217] Severino (1999c).

[218] This statement must not, however, be taken completely as face value, since it is part of a standard reply applied by ASEAN politicians to fend off claims by ASEAN critics that ASEAN had failed to respond properly to the Asian crisis. The standard defense runs along the line that ASEAN has never been a supranational entity with a strong common agenda and

Asked whether ASEAN would evolve as an organization similar to the European Economic Community of the1950s and 1960s, Severino again denied this, stating "the idea of a supranational entity like the European Commission is for the European Parliament is not an option being considered."[219] Various statements also show that Severino, despite all his calls for regime building, regards the virtues of the ASEAN way, such as decision making by consensus and consultation, quiet diplomacy, agreeability and bilateral dispute settlement as essential prerequisites for successful cooperation within the association (cf. SAF98,).[220] Rejecting the notion that decision making by consensus was no longer viable for ASEAN, he argued that

> there is no alternative to decision making by consensus in ASEAN. Forcing a majority decision upon a dissenting minority just would not work, not in ASEAN and not in any other association of sovereign states other than the European Union.[221]

Enhanced interaction/ flexible engagement and the ASEAN way

Regarding "flexible engagement", the Secretary-General of ASEAN has been a consistent and active supporter of the Thai and Philippine line, rather than, for example, the conservative Malaysian position. This is evident from a number of statements. Severino has even promoted the idea of collective approaches to "flexible engagement" at the ASEAN level:

> Another step that ASEAN might take on the road to greater regionalism is to open itself to the possibility of taking regional action to help a member-country deal with internal difficulties that have regional or international dimensions; assist member countries in resolving disputes between them; and keep actions and policies of one member-country from seriously harming others.[222]

Astutely, Severino played on ASEAN's interventionist role as a mediator in the Cambodian peace and democratization process and asked: "Would ASEAN have done for Cambodia what it did in the 1980s and in 1997 and 1998 if Cambodia had already been a member of ASEAN then? It is an interesting

---

therefore its success or failure must not be measured in terms of a supranational entity as the EU (cp. also Alatas 1998).

[219] Severino (approx. early 1999): "The Only Way For ASEAN", R. Severino interviewed by Serge Berthier.

[220] Cf. Severino (1998a;); Severino (1999a); Severino (1999c).

[221] Severino (1999a).

[222] Severino (1999b): "Regionalism: The Stakes for Southeast Asia", Address, Institute of Defense Studies, Singapore, 24 May.

question"[223].[224] At the same time, he did not forget to indicate that the norm of national sovereignty and territorial integrity had to be respected and that ASEAN's actions had to be in line with them: "This [i.e. involvement in the internal affairs], of course, presupposes that ASEAN members would be willing to accept such involvement by their neighbors".[225] There is no doubt that Severino continues to promote more flexibility in the handling of ASEAN relations and tries to help ASEAN free itself from the corset of a restricive interpretation of norms such as national sovereignty and non-interference. In July 2000, three weeks prior to the 33rd AMM, he clearly expressed his preference for "flexible engagement" and consciously went beyond the officially endorsed consensus formula of *enhanced interaction* when he argued that "In the language of the current discussion, engagement may be more 'flexible', interaction 'enhanced'".[226] He also promoted the (originally Thai) proposal of establishing an ASEAN troika, a centralized rapid response task force designed to deal with "critical events in the region"[227] and to "address political developments more expeditiously".[228]

With all that, however, Severino has made it clear that the ASEAN way would remain the basis for all ASEAN cooperation. In 1998, and again in 1999, he claimed that

> ASEAN countries continue to regard as sacred the principle of non-interference in one another's affairs. The surest way of unraveling ASEAN is for its members to interfere in one another's affairs. However, ASEAN has now shown a willingness to express or demonstrate concern over internal developments in one country [...] if they are likely to spread to to others, to produce results that are intolerable to neighbors' well-being, or to legitimize violent methods of effecting internal change. At the same time, ASEAN has also shown that its preferred method of manifesting concern is that of friendly, quiet

---

[223] Ibid.

[224] Following Hun Sen's coup in 1997, the ASEAN Foreign Ministers had decided to postpone Cambodia's (already agreed-upon) accession to the grouping until the country complied with ASEAN's requirement to hold general elections and to form a legitimate and stable government (which finally happened in 1998).

[225] Severino (1999b).

[226] Severino (2000).

In 1998, following Thailand's "flexible engagement" initiative, ASEAN leaders had agreed to adopt the compromise formula of "enhanced interaction" rather than "flexible engagement", implying that basically ASEAN's non-intervention principle remained intact.

[227] Severino (1999d): "The ASEAN Way in Manila", *Far Eastern Economic Review,* 23 December.

[228] Severino (2000).

advice, searching but respectful questions, and mutual assistance, rather than that of public posturing or intrusive action.[229]

Severino seems to apply exactly the same tactics applied by the Chuan government and the Estrada administration insofar as he promotes reforms and changes to the ASEAN way, but always does so in a way that is in line with, and respects, the traditional ASEAN norms.

Summary

The present Secretary-General's objective is the closer economic integration and political coordination of ASEAN members. In his view, the conservative interpretation of several ASEAN norms presents an obstacle on ASEAN's way to integration that has to be removed. Therefore, he has promoted essential changes to ASEAN's *modus operandi* and called for the re-interpretation and re-assessment of central ASEAN norms such as solidarity, national sovereignty, non-interference and informality. National sovereignty and regional purpose had to be balanced in a new equilibrium. The principle of non-interference should not apply where a member country's action or policies impacted negatively on neighboring countries or the region as a whole. Informality and non-legalistic approaches to regional cooperation had to be abandoned where the formation of economic and security regimes as well as the imposition of enforceable rules were imperative for securing successful regional cooperation. At the same time, Severino made it clear that any of the steps towards a more integrated ASEAN required the consensus among ASEAN members. Decisions based on the majority principle were not viable in ASEAN. The principles of consensus, quiet diplomacy and agreeability therefore continued to be relevant as the ASEAN way of interaction and cooperation. In other words, the Secretary-General apparently favors several norms changes that would, if implemented, severely change the nature of ASEAN from a relatively informal grouping to a regimes-based organization, but he insists that these changes have to evolve in a process of mutual consultation, persuasion and general consensus, following the ASEAN way of quiet diplomacy and agreeability.

4. The Present Norms System of ASEAN: Existing and Emerging Norms

Three Insights

There are several conclusions to be drawn from this analysis. The foremost and probably most surprising insight is that traditional ASEAN norms remain

---

[229] Severino (1998a).

largely intact. Even vociferous challengers to certain norms took great care never to step outside the generally accepted norms consensus. Thailand and the Philippines, for example, promoted "flexible engagement" as a *modus operandi* in ASEAN, while at the same time they reaffirmed their general commitment to the ASEAN norm of non-interference in each other's internal affairs. Singapore has demanded more political coordination, more economic regime building and regime compliance within ASEAN, while at the same time emphasizing the validity of the ASEAN way and particularly the norms of sovereign equality, decision making by consultation and consensus, as well as non-interference in each other's internal affairs. The cautious anxiety of reform-minded ASEAN governments to avoid giving the impression they were disrespectful of existing ASEAN norms only proves the validity of the traditional norms, since it results from the pressure to live up to a set of collectively generated and shared expectations about appropriate ways of behavior (which is the classic definition of a norm).

The second insight is that the norms debate focused not so much on abolishing existing norms, but on how to interpret them. To give only a few examples, the norms debate is about defining the quality and scope of *solidarity*, about reassessing the relationship between *national sovereignty* and *collective responsibility*, and about defining *national resilience* as dependent on *regional resilience*. The challengers are trying to represent enhanced regime-building and the pooling of sovereignty as being in line with the imperative of *national sovereignty* and *mutually beneficial cooperation*, and they like to point out that adhering to the principle of *non-interference* under certain circumstances might infringe upon other ASEAN members' justified expectations about *regional stability and security*.

This process of re-interpreting norms included the re-evaluation of certain norms in their relation to others. No-one within ASEAN, for example, would seriously question national sovereignty as the basis of ASEAN cooperation or national resilience as a primary objective. Rather, the challengers argued that traditional ASEAN norms needed to be adjusted to a changing global and regional political and economic environment.

The third insight is that the norms debate since 1997, catalyzed by the economic and financial crisis, has prepared the ground for what I would like to call *emerging norms*. These emerging norms are centered around new ASEAN objectives such as the collectivization of ASEAN relations, the increasing weight ASEAN – as a body – might assume in relation to its members, and the degree of regime compliance within ASEAN. As I have shown, the emerging norms often conflict with traditional ASEAN norms. However, emerging and traditional norms are not necessarily mutually exclusive by nature – indeed, they frequently overlap.

Traditional and emerging ASEAN norms

In the following synthesis, I try to summarize the surveyed ASEAN partners' views of traditional ASEAN norms (as outlined in section 2) and present the ASEAN partners' respective positions on what I call "emerging" ASEAN norms. The four respective charts depict

Chart 1: traditional and emerging ASEAN objectives;

Chart 2: traditional and emerging constitutive principles of ASEAN;

Chart 3: traditional and emerging procedural ASEAN norms;

Chart 4: traditional and emerging behavioral ASEAN norms.

If we compare chart 1 to the others, we can clearly see a link between emerging ASEAN objectives and emerging changes in the ASEAN norms structure. In a number of instances, charts 2 to 4 depict a clear division between Thailand, the Philippines, Singapore and the Secretary-General on the one side and Malaysia, Indonesia, Vietnam, Myanmar and Laos on the other. This divide separates the reformers in ASEAN from those countries that appeared reluctant to implement essential reforms.[230]

---

[230] There is, however, a slight deficiency that challenges the representativity of these charts as far as Indonesia is concerned. The Wahid government has simply not been in power long enough and has been relatively inexplicit on a number of issues as for the analysis to make qualified definite statements on Indonesia's position concerning ASEAN norms.

Chart 1: Traditional and emerging ASEAN objectives

Traditional ASEAN objectives	Emerging ASEAN objectives
national resilience	
regional resilience on the basis of national resilience (regional resilience as a dependent variable of national resilience)	national resilience on the basis of regional resilience (national resilience as a dependent variable of regional resilience)
peaceful co-existence	economic and political coordination for economic progress, stability and peace
building trust/ solidarity	utilizing the maturity of ASEAN relations by practicing enhanced interaction/flexible engagement
interaction and communication in a weakly institutionalized environment	coordination and integration through more centralized institutions
economic & functional cooperation	economic integration and regime building
conflict/ dispute avoidance	conflict/ dispute prevention, settlement and resolution through enhanced interaction
establishing and keeping to a general regional code of conduct among ASEAN members	
international recognition as a unified regional entity	
independence from external intervention/ interference	
international recognition as a unified regional entity	
independence from external interference/ hegemons	
expanding peace and the regional ASEAN code of conduct to the wider Southeast Asian region	managing relations in an expanded ASEAN (ASEAN-10)

Chart 2 a: Positions on Constitutive Principles (surveyed ASEAN states + Secretary-General, 1998-2000)

Constitutive principles	Thailand	Philippines	Singapore	Malaysia	Indonesia	Vietnam	Myanmar/ Laos	Secretary General
mutual benefit	X	X	X	X	X	X	X	X
mutual interest	X	X	X	X	X	X	X	X
no definitive commitments, binding rules (voluntary coop)				X	X	X	X	
absolute national sovereignty			X	X	X	X	X	
Equality	X	X	X	X	X	X	X	X
absolute territorial integrity	X	X	X	X	X	X	X	X
smallest common denominator, minimalist collective agenda				X	(X)	X	X	
protection of (respect for) national diversity	X	X	X	X	X	X	X	X

"X" = continues to be valid as a constitutive principle

Chart 2 b: Positions on Emerging Constitutive Principles

Emerging Constitutive Principles	Thailand	Philippines	Singapore	Malaysia	Indonesia	Vietnam	Myanmar/ Laos	Secretary General
imperative of collective benefit	X	X	X					X
imperative of collective interests	X	X	X					X
more pol. & econ. unity, less deviance	X	X	X					X
Maximalist agenda	X	X	X					X
commitment to regimes and binding rules	X	X	X					X

Chart 3 a: Positions on Procedural Norms (surveyed ASEAN states + Secretary-General, 1998-2000)

Procedural norms/country	Thailand	Philippines	Singapore	Malaysia	Indonesia	Vietnam	Myanmar/Laos	Secretary-General
non-discrimination	O	O	O	O	O	+	+	O
consultation	+	+	+	+	O	O	+	+
decision making by consensus	O	+	+	+	O	+	+	+
decentral decision making	—	—	—	+	O	O	O	—
informality	—	—	—	O	O	O	O	—
de-emphasizing multilateralism within ASEAN	—	—	—	+	O	O	O	O
quiet diplomacy	—	+	+	+	O	O	O	O
silent peer pressure	—	O	O	O	O	O	O	O

"O" = no significant deviation from the norm; "—" = challenging or deemphasizing a norm; "+" = explicit support for a norm

Chart 3 b: Positions on Emerging Procedural Norms

emerging procedural norms/country	Thailand	Philippines	Singapore	Malaysia	Indonesia	Vietnam	Myanmar/Laos	Secretary-General
regime compliance	X	X	X					X
openness/ frankness	X	X						X
more institutionalized consultation	X	X	X	(X)		(X)		X
more institutionalized and centralized decision making	X	X	X					X
collectivization of ASEAN relations	X	X	X					X

Chart 4 a: Positions on Behavioral Norms (selected ASEAN states + Secretary-General, 1998-2000)

Behavioral norms/ country	Thailand	Philippines	Singapore	Malaysia	Indonesia	Vietnam	Myanmar/Laos	Secretary-General
non-interference	–	–	+	+	+	+	+	–/O
solidarity	+	+	+	O	O	+	+	+
respect/ tolerance among members	O	O	O	O	O	O	O	+
goodwill/ benevolent attitude	O	O	O	O	O	O	O	O
avoiding negative attitudes obstructive to cooperation	O	O	O	O	O	O	O	O
non-confrontation/ seeking harmony by excluding controversial topics	–	–	–	O	O	O	O	–
avoiding action destabilizing other members	+	+	+	O	O	O	O	+
peacefulness/ refraining from use of force	O	O	O	O	O	O	O	O

Chart 4 b: Positions on Emerging Behavioral Norms

emerging procedural norms/ country	Thailand	Philippines	Singapore	Malaysia	Indonesia	Vietnam	Myanmar/Laos	Secretary-General
addressing controversial issues	X	X	X					X
criticizing other members' behavior	X	X						X

Although the norms structure of ASEAN thus remains largely intact, the charts also show that there have been changes to the traditional norms system. As there was a heightened sense among more reform-oriented ASEAN members of the necessity of closer regional integration, coordination and collective action within ASEAN, collective benefit was often emphasized over the individual states' benefit, and regional resilience was emphasized more than national resilience. Norms entrepreneurs within ASEAN seem to favor the idea of economic regime building and more centralization within ASEAN. In the field of constitutive principles, the general consensus seems to have eroded with regard to three principles: first, the principle of voluntary and flexible cooperation, which implies no fixed obligations and binding rules for individual members; second, the imperative of absolute national sovereignty at any time, under any circumstances; and third, the common understanding to keep ASEAN and the collective agenda at a minimal organizational level, while emphasizing the centrality of the status quo and the smallest common denominator as the guiding principles. Thailand, the Philippines, Singapore and the Secretary-General adopted a rhetoric that emphasized the necessity for ASEAN members to recognize such principles as the imperative of the collective benefit, of collective interests, political and economic unity, less deviance of individual members from the collective agenda and a stronger commitment to collective regimes and binding rules. In the area of ASEAN's procedural norms, the same parties also de-emphasized the prominence of decentral decision making and the sacrosanct status of informality. In contrast, they favored the idea of regime compliance, called for more institutionalized consultation processes and emphasized the need to institutionalize and centralize decision making processes. In general, they promoted a stronger collectivization of ASEAN relations. In the area of behavioral norms, Thailand and the Philippines clearly de-emphasized the importance and relevance of the principle of non-interference in one another's internal affairs. They seemed to agree with Singapore and the ASEAN Secretariat that the traditional way of avoiding confrontation by excluding controversial topics was no longer appropriate. Only Singapore seemed to be reluctant to openly support "flexible engagement", i.e. criticize other members where their behavior infringes on regional or member states' expectations regarding economic and political security and stability.

Paradigm shift - yes or no?

As I have shown above, ASEAN's normative structures remained largely in place. However, there were a number of apparently reform-oriented ASEAN member states who advocated the adoption of norms that are in line with ASEAN's new agenda of stronger integration and collective problem resolution. These emerging norms (as outlined above) emphasize the responsibility of the individual ASEAN members for the collective and the region and downplay traditional ASEAN norms giving prominence to individual member states' agendas and interests. In this respect, they promote a paradigm shift in the ASEAN norms structure. However, the norms entrepreneurs in ASEAN did not aim to establish the emerging norms at the cost of the norms of the "ASEAN way", but rather to soften and adapt the old norms.

The question of whether, and to what degree, the emerging norms will find their place among the traditional ASEAN norms is not entirely subject to speculation. As Finnemore and Sikkink show in their "Norm Life Cycle" model (which deals with the question of how norms get established in the international arena), the successful establishment of a normative idea (or "emerging norm") as a generally accepted and valid norm is subject to a process involving three stages, leading from "norm emergence" via "broad norm acceptance" to "internalization".[231] An emerging norm may die if it fails to overcome critical stages, if it fails to reach what they call the "tipping point". Finnemore and Sikkink describe the "norm life cycle" in the following terms:

> The characteristic mechanism of the first stage, norm emergence, is persuasion by norm entrepreneurs. Norm entrepreneurs attempt to convinve a critical mass of states (norm leaders) to embrace new norms. The second stage is characterized more by a dynamic of imitation as the norm leaders attempt to socialize other states to become norm followers. [...] At the far end of the norm cascade, norm internalization occurs; norms acquire a taken-for-granted quality and are no longer a matter of broad public debate. [However,] Many emergent norms fail to reach a tipping point [...] Internalized or cascading norms may eventually become the standard of appropriateness against which new norms emerge and compete for support.[232]

According to Finnemore and Sikkink, the successful establishment of emerging norms as widely accepted and internalized norms depends to a great deal on the standing and position of the respective norms entrepreneur, i.e. his persuasiveness and ability to convince actors critical to the implementation of a specific norm to accept a proposed norm. "What happens at the tipping point" is that a critical mass of relevant actors "endorse the new norm to redefine appropriate behavior".[233] In order to maintain their shared collective identity, all other actors will fall in line with, and accept, the new norm as soon as the "tipping point", i.e. the critical mass of states supporting a norm, has been reached.

---

[231] Finnemore and Sikkink (1998): 895.
[232] Ibid.
[233] Ibid.: 900.

The question arises whether the emerging norms in ASEAN have a chance to be brought to the tipping point, i.e. to be established as valid ASEAN norms. The answer depends on two variables that are open to interpretation. 1.) Are the norms entrepreneurs in ASEAN strong enough, are they "persuasive" enough, to create a "critical mass" of ASEAN members relevant to catapulting the several emerging norms into the orbit of existing ASEAN norms? 2.) Are the major norms entrepreneurs in ASEAN as identified in this chapter – Thailand, the Philippines, Singapore and the ASEAN Secretariat – really sufficiently determined to implement the norms they have been promoting?

Chapter 3:

FROM "NEIGHBORHOOD WATCH GROUP"
TO COMMUNITY?
THE CASE OF ASEAN INSTITUTIONS AND THE POOLING OF SOVEREIGNTY

FROM "NEIGHBORHOOD WATCH GROUP" TO COMMUNITY?
THE CASE OF ASEAN INSTITUTIONS AND THE POOLING OF SOVEREIGNTY

1. Introduction

Following the preceding assessment of ASEAN norms, this chapter analyzes ASEAN with a view to the second of the four indicators of collective identities between states as identified in the intriduction to this thesis, namely ASEAN members' readiness to increasingly 'pool' sovereignty, i.e. transfer sovereignty and authority from the national level to joint regional institutions and make binding commitments to regime-type regional integration mechanisms. As states engaging in joint processes of pooling sovereignty and regime-type regional integration can reasonably be expected to identify with each other to a considerable degree, share a strong sense of interdependence, interrelatedness and common long-term interests, and must have considerable trust in each other's reliability, predictability and commitment to the process as a whole, it can be said that any serious project of regional integration is indicative of collective identity between those states (or the elites governing those states, respectively).

As collective identity between states is a prerequisite for regime-type integration, regime-type integration (or initial steps towards integration by means of pooling sovereignty) can in turn be said to be indicative of collective identity.[234] Thus, readiness of states to engage in integration is strongly indicative of a prevalent sense of collective identity.

Therefore, in order to be able to make a qualified judgement on ASEAN's collective identity, it is essential to assess ASEAN's potential to evolve from a group of only very loosely (and largely informally) associated states into a more regime-type integrated regional community.

A contributor to the journal *Contemporary Southeast Asia* convincingly paraphrased ASEAN as an "intergovernmental neighbourhood watch group" rather than a political community, stating that "the crises serve as a reminder

---

[234] Thus, we can imagine collective identity without regional integration, but not regional integration without collective identity. Further, one can assume that collective identity is necessarily substantial wherever we are able to observe regime-type integration or steps towards the same. Therefore, steps towards regime-type integration, such as various ways of pooling of sovereignty, can be said to be indicators for the prevalence of a sense of collective identity.

that an ASEAN community is still far off, and that self-interest still drives members' commitment to political, economic and social stability in the region."[235] The term 'neighborhood watch group' reflects best the character of a grouping whose members are only loosely associated, and whose preferences for cooperation are based on the "ASEAN way" of informality, personalized rather than institutionalized relations, and distrust of definite and legally binding commitments.[236]

ASEAN has been credited by critics and protagonists alike for its role in providing an environment of political stability to Southeast Asia ever since its inception in 1967. However, the crisis of 1997 has revealed that ASEAN's minimalist approach to cooperation accounts for the actors' difficulties in implementing more centralized economic, financial and political regimes and institutions to prevent economic and political disruption in the region. Indeed, as Rüland states,

> ASEAN has hardly gone beyond [...] 'negative integration'. Negative integration refers to inter-state agreements on deregulation and liberalization, while 'positive integration' signifies commonly agreed interventions in specific policy fields through the setting of rules and their subsequent implementation.[237]

This chapter argues that the central ASEAN regimes and institutions are moulded in the old ASEAN way and are therefore not capable of effectively promoting ASEAN's new objectives of deeper economic and political integration. As Rüland asserts, "much soul searching will lie ahead of ASEAN. It will include issues such as [the] political system, the degree and pace of economic liberalization and the corpus of shared values".[238] I want to show that ASEAN is not prepared for community-building (in the sense of pooling sovereignty and devising more centralized and rules-based mechanisms and institutions) and that institutions such as the ASEAN Free Trade Area (AFTA), the Investment Area (AIA), the Surveillance Process (ASP), the ASEAN Dispute Settlement mechanism, the envisioned High Council and the Troika can't be expected to contribute effectively to sustainable regional integration and stability in their present shape.

The analysis also assesses recent trends in the development of ASEAN decision-making structures and asks whether they will contribute to more pooling of sovereignty, i.e. the centralization and coordination of policy-making

---

[235] Khoo (2000): 279, 298.
[236] For the characteristics of the ASEAN way, cp. for example Busse (1999); Dosch (1997); Rüland (2000a).
[237] Rüland (2000a): 427.
[238] Ibid.: 445.

processes, in ASEAN. The role and position of the ASEAN Secretariat will be considered in this context.

The insights gathered in this analysis will serve as the basis for an outlook for the near- to mid-term prospects for ASEAN integration.

2. 'Pooling' of sovereignty — a *conditio sine qua non* for ASEAN integration

Many observers of ASEAN agree that post-crisis relations have suffered considerably from the lack of sufficiently institutionalized processes and mechanisms.

Amitav Acharya sees the need for ASEAN to move from "inclusive regionalism", a term denoting the traditional "principle of co-operative security", to "intrusive regionalism", i.e. the need for "co-operation against […] commonly faced dangers" that requires a move away from the ASEAN way, the review of the doctrine of non-interference and more institutionalization:

> [An] area of reform ASEAN has to come to terms with arises from the call to move away from the 'ASEAN Way' and to be more receptive to formal and institutionalized mechnisms for cooperation. […] the economic crisis has shown the need to supplement the 'ASEAN Way' by institutions.[…]
> The crisis has underscored the need for more transparent, rule-based institutions — institutions which are not just a club of governments and élites, but which engage national and regional civil societies […].[239]

He cites Tommy Koh of Singapore and Foreign Secretary Domingo Siazon of the Phillipines as voices promoting more rules-based integration.

Rüland, pointing out that the continued failure to establish formalized institutions can have 'spillback' effects on regional cooperation, i.e. reverse former positive effects, states that

> 'the ASEAN way' is more vulnerable to crisis than more institutionalized regional organizations such as the EU. […] Commitment to regional action and solidarity is much weaker than in cooperative arrangements based on international treaties and contractual obligations. […] ASEAN members opting out from previous agreements would not have to expect major sanctions or other forms of serious retaliation. […] the threshold for exit behaviour is comparatively low because retreat from common positions is not morally stigmatized. […]

---

[239] Acharya (1999): 19, 23.

> The 'ASEAN way' represents fair weather cooperation which flourishes under the conditions of economic boom.[240]

Calls for more centralised institutions can be heard from within ASEAN as well. Jusuf Wanandi, for example, argues that "ASEAN's integration should be rules-based and supported by better regional institutionalized regional coperation" and asserts that "Here, the region can learn from the European Union".[241]

A group of Thai scholars, in a paper intended to be "a potential departure point for the ASEAN Inter-Parliamentary Organization (AIPO) to better come to terms with the increasingly important process of economic integration" in ASEAN, call for a harmonized legislative and institutional framework.[242] They claim that such a framework would tie regional efforts at trade and investment liberalization as well as economic, monetary and fiscal cooperation into a web of "regional integration [that] is based on the concept of a point of no return" (p. 31). The group criticizes that

> So far, ASEAN has emphasized vague policy formulation with less emphasis on policy identification. [...] Future development of ASEAN requires existing mechanisms [...] to cooperate and play a better role in policy identification based on a regional perspective and an integrated approach. [...] there is a need to balance the diverse national perspectives with a regional view. [...] ASEAN institutional arrangements are still being strongly curtailed by the national interests of each member state. (pp. 45f.)

They suggest that with regard to the so far slow evolution of coordinated ASEAN mechanisms and cooperation schemes, AIPO should evolve as an inter-parliamentary process to recommend and coordinate ASEAN-wide legislative approaches to regional integration in all major areas of ASEAN cooperation. In this context, they also demand that ASEAN break with its long-cherished principles of informality and "the notion of national interest protection rather than regional mutual benefit." (p.34) With reference to the loopholes and insufficient regulations of the CEPT that underlies the AFTA, they demand "further legal commitments [...] if ASEAN intends to achieve economic integration" and overcoming "obstacles concerning domestic laws which are still an impediment to ASEAN economic integration." (p. 34)

Even the ASEAN Eminent Persons Group (EPG) carefully expressed the view that ASEAN relations require more institutionalization for the association to remain relevant as a grouping. In the section "Supranational vs. National Interestst" of their report on the ASEAN Vision 2020, they note that

---

[240] Rüland (2000a): 444.
[241] Wanandi (1999).
[242] Suthiphand et al. (1999): 28.

[...] comparisons have been made between ASEAN and the European Union, the latter of which has set up supra-national bodies [...] to enact policies and rules that affect the whole Union. [...] such comparisons must be treated with caution. In line with the precaution just expressed, we also note that so far, ASEAN governments have preferred processes to institutional structures. This obviously is based on a pragmatic, non-interventionist approach [...] [and we ask] whether there should not be some institutions in place, at least to ensure a more coherent approach [...] [and] whether the current practices are workable especially in terms of co-ordination, accountability and coherence in policy-making and implementation. [...] There is also the concern that progress in ASEAN programmes is hindered by lack of co-ordination, both at the international and national level.[243]

The underlying tenor of a recent collection of essays by leading think tank representatives across ASEAN countries is that unless ASEAN is to become inadequate, the association urgently needs to move away from the traditional principles of the ASEAN way, such as informality and the supremacy of national sovereignty, and – both with a view to political and economic integration – transform into a more rules-based, institutionalized and centralized organization.[244]

ASEAN is exposed to increasing expectations and pressure from within and outside for governments to increasingly 'pool' sovereignty, i.e. to cede additional power resources to regional institutions. Prior to the crisis, the strong economic growth of ASEAN countries seemed to confirm the association's policy of small steps and inter-governmental minimalism. Following the crisis, effective institutionalization has become the measure of ASEAN's political and economic cohesion. The following sections ask if ASEAN has started facing this challenge yet.

---

[243] ASEAN Eminent Persons Group (2000): § 2.6 Supranational vs. National Interests.

[244] Cf. Tay; Estanislao; Soesastro (eds.) (2000). The volume features contributions from Simon S.C. Tay and Chia Siow Yue (Singapore), Jesus Estanislao and Carolina G. Hernandez (Philippines), Jusuf Wanandi and Hadi Soesastro (Indonesia) as well as Nararongchai Akrasanee and Kusuma Snitwongse (Thailand).

3. All bark, no bite - regional institutions with no supranational teeth

3.1. Economic and financial cooperation mechanisms

3.1.1. ASEAN Free Trade Area (AFTA)

The Free Trade Area (AFTA) represents the most ambitious and most advanced project of economic integration in ASEAN. Officially initiated in 1992, it focuses on the gradual reduction of intra-ASEAN tariffs under the Common Effective Preferential Tariff Scheme (CEPT) and the reduction of non-tariff barriers (NTB).[245] Considered to be legally binding,[246] the CEPT agreement and later amendments set both the tariff lines for a defined range of products[247] and a clear time frame for their implementation.[248] A ministerial-level AFTA Council,[249] appointed by the respective ASEAN Economic Ministers (AEM) was set up to supervise, review and coordinate the implementation of the CEPT and mediate the settlement of disputes between member states. The AEM can, "if necessary", take the leading role in the dispute settlement procedures. The CEPT provides a basic dispute settlement and compliance mechanism that

---

[245] Agreement on the Common Effective Preferential Tariff Scheme for the ASEAN Free Trade Area, Singapore, 28 January 1992.

[246] Cf. ASEAN Secretariat (1995): 58.

[247] The CEPT comprises the Inclusion List, IL, for products already subject to tariff liberalization, the Temporary Exclusion List, TEL, for products to be liberalized within a scheduled period, the Sensitive List, SL, with products that are exempt from liberalization, but subject to a periodical review process for inclusion in the TEL, and the General Exceptions List with products interminably exempt from tariff liberalization.

[248] The time frame has been modified several times since 1992 so as to accelerate the implementation of the liberalization measures. The present schedule projects the full implementation of the CEPT by the year 2002 for the ASEAN-6 countries and 2006, 2008 and 2010 for Vietnam, Laos, Myanmar and Cambodia respectively. By the end of 2001, 55,680 tariff lines (making up for 84.74 percent of all ASEAN tariff lines) are expected to be between zero and five percent. (ASEAN Secretariat 2000; 14th AFTA Council 2000: Joint Press Statement, Chiang Mai, 4 October).

[249] Membership of the AFTA Council comprises 10 ministerial-level members from each country plus the ASEAN Secretary-General.

In 2000, Thailand, Cambodia, Laos and Vietnam delegated their finance ministers to the AFTA Council. Singapore, Malaysia, Indonesia, the Philippines and Brunei delegated their ministers of industry and trade, and Myanmar was represented by a Minister at the Office of the Chairman of the State Peace and Development Council. (14th AFTA Council: Joint Press Statement, Chiang Mai, 4 October.)

allows the parties to a dispute to withdraw concessions made under the agreement if an offender denies to follow a ruling of the AFTA Council.[250]

In typical ASEAN fashion, however, the CEPT provides several loopholes for countries to withdraw tariff concessions they are obliged to make under the agreement. What is more, the AEM is apparently prepared to modify the legal instruments of the CEPT in order to accommodate the political interests of member states. A precedent has been set by the AEM Meeting (AEMM) in October 2000, when the AEM formulated a 'lex Malaysia' enabling the country to exempt the national automotive industry from tariff liberalization. The AEMM concurred to Malaysia's demands by endorsing the "Protocol Regarding the Implementation of the CEPT Scheme Temporary Exclusion List" (as adopted by the 4th Informal ASEAN Summit) that states in Article 1:

> The objective of this protocol is to allow a Member State to temporarily delay the transfer of a product from its TEL [Temporary Exclusion List] into the Inclusion List (hereafter referred to as 'IL'), or to temporarily suspend its concessions on a product already transferred into the IL, if such a transfer or concession would cause or have caused real problems, by reasons which are not covered by Article 6 (Emergency Measures) of the Agreement.[251]

The new regulations of the protocol significantly undermine the CEPT regime, since they represent a tool for governments to withdraw tariff commitments already agreed upon under the liberalization scheme. *Asiaweek* commented on the decision:

> ASEAN's decision to allow Malaysia to delay including autos in the AFTA free-trade scheme is the latest diappointment. Other members are now poised to postpone the lifting of tariff protection for their pet sectors. AFTA could collapse.[252]

Whereas both the official consensus of ASEAN governments to gradually liberalize and eventually bring all intra-ASEAN tariffs down to 0-5 percent and AFTA's record of products already scheduled for liberalization (see table), look impressive at a first glance, there is no guarantee that by the time the various sensitive products are scheduled for liberalization, individual governments will

---

[250] See: Protocol on Dispute Settlement Mechanism, Manila, 20th November 1996; Protocol Regarding the Implementation of the CEPT Scheme Temporary Exclusion List", 4th Informal ASEAN Summit, Singapore, 23 November 2000.

[251] Protocol Regarding the Implementation of the CEPT Scheme Temporary Exclusion List, 4th Informal ASEAN Summit, Singapore, 23 November 2000.

[252] Reyes (2000c).

142

not actually backtrack from their commitments.[253] The CEPT doesn't keep them from doing so, and inconvenient regulations can be circumvented by respective decrees (or "protocols") as negotiated by the AEMM and adopted at the next ASEAN summit.

---

[253] Besides the deterring example of Malaysia's actual denial to liberalize car tariffs as scheduled, there are more severe tests to come for many ASEAN members' resolve to liberalize sensitive products. Rice, for example, a highly sensitive product for both Indonesia, Malaysia and the Philippines, is scheduled to be liberalized in 2005, but nevertheless, Malaysia is waging a newly-incited war against even small scale smuggling of the grain across the Thai-Malayisian border into the state of Kedah, the so-called 'rice bowl' of Malaysia where rice-farmers form a large part of the constituencies (see *The Sun on Sunday*, Malaysia (14 January 2001): "Rice glut may swamp farmers"; *The Star*, Malaysia (09 March 2001): "Smugglers still playing the risk game"; the information on the anti-smuggling campaign and its political context has been confirmed to the author in an interview by an official of MITI Malaysia in January 2001). Already, the MITI Malaysia announced on its homepage that for the time following the liberalization deadline, "Malaysia has reserved the right to impose a duty of 20% on rice if the need arises" (Ministry of Industry and Trade, Malaysia (2001)).
Indonesia and the Philippines may withdraw their commitments, too, the closer they get to the tariff liberalization deadline for rice and other products.

Table 4: Number of products covered by the CEPT in 2001
(Total of IL, TEL, GEL = Total of ASEAN products, excluding services)

COUNTRY	INCLU- SION LIST	TEMPO- RARY EXCLUSION LIST	SENSITIVE LIST	GENERAL EXCEPTION LIST	TOTAL
Brunei Darussalam	6,284	0	6	202	6,492
Indonesia	7,190	21	4	68	7,283
Malaysia	9,654	218	83	53	10,008
Philippines	5,622	6	50	16	5,694
Singapore	5,821	0	0	38	5,859
Thailand	9,104	0	7	0	9,111
ASEAN-6 Total	**43,675**	**245**	**150**	**377**	**44,447**
Percent (%)	**98.26**	**0.55**	**0.34**	**0.85**	**100**
Cambodia	3,115	3,523	50	134	6,822
Laos	1,673	1,716	88	74	3,551
Myanmar	2,984	2,419	21	48	5,472
Vietnam	4,233	757	51	196	5,237
New Members Total	**12,005**	**8,415**	**210**	**452**	**21,082**
Percent (%)	**56.94**	**39.92**	**1.00**	**2.14**	**100.00**
ASEAN TOTAL	**55,680**	**8,660**	**360**	**829**	**65,529**
PERCENT (%)	**84.97**	**13.22**	**0.55**	**1.27**	**100**

Source: ASEAN Secretariat

Specific tariff lines can now practically be kept out of the Inclusion List (IL) interminably.[254] What is more, products already on the IL can also be legally suspended from scheduled tariff liberalization at possibly no great political or economic cost. The CEPT basically leaves it up to affected parties to negotiate the terms of non-compliance, thus marking down tariff liberalization in AFTA

---

[254] The exemptions are due to a review after a period of two years, but it is clear already that Malaysia, for example, intends to delay the liberalization of its automotive tariffs for a few more times, if not indefinitely.

144

to an intergovernmental bazaar rather than providing a reliable and stable regime.[255] In other words, AFTA invites the continuous reassessment, renegotiation, modification and, eventually, dissolution, of the original consensus (see fig. 1), subjecting it to the changing developments in, and power-play politics of, intra-ASEAN relations.

As Stubbs notes, AFTA, like all other ASEAN initiatives, follows the "ASEAN minus X" formula, allowing individual member countries to opt out of general ASEAN policies and commitments so that the others can go ahead.[256] ASEAN-minus-X in combination with the opportunity to reverse the already agreed-upon tariff liberalization could leave AFTA ineffective.

Fig. 2: AFTA at its present state	Fig. 3 : Model of a stable AFTA regime
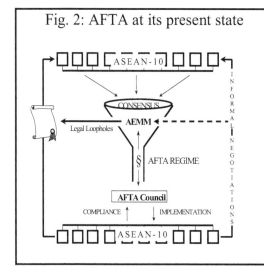	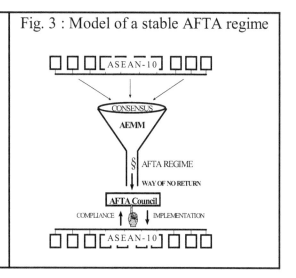

Source: author

The AFTA framework lacks the institutional structures to provide a desirable degree of stability. In order to be both effective and lasting, the influence exercised by member governments through the AEMM would have to be reduced and the AFTA Council would have to be strengthened as an independent authority with the power to oversee and enforce the commitments made by member states under the CEPT. The political unwillingness of ASEAN governments to pool sovereignty, i.e. to cede power to centralized authorities, to embrace contractual approaches and binding commitments,[257] is undermining

---

[255] The liberal exemption rules for products on the TEL of course raise doubts whether the products on the Sensitive List (SL) - mostly agricultural products - will be phased into the CEPT.

[256] Cf. Stubbs (2000): 314

[257] The fact that the acronym AFTA has been referred to as "Agree First, Talk After" by observers, reveals that the shortcoming of AFTA is that it has been styled in the typical non-leagalistic and consensus-oriented, but not always efficient, ASEAN way of agreeing on the principle first and to negotiate the details later.

AFTA's attempt at regime-type trade liberalization. This suggests that ASEAN actually does follow specific traditional norms and principles, and that they are still dominant. This also suggests that ASEAN has a specific, relatively inflexible identity that might eventually make it a political dinosaur facing extinction.[258]

3.1.2. ASEAN Investment Area (AIA)

The Investment Area (AIA) Framework was drawn up in response to the economic crisis in order to prevent the diversion of FDI from Southeast Asia to other regions, and to increase intra-ASEAN investments. It represents a wild mixture of declarations of intent, pledges, national and collective commitments. Its agenda comprises three areas, namely functional co-operation and investment facilitation programs (Schedule I), awareness-raising/promotion measures (Schedule II) and investment liberalization (Schedule III).[259] For the purposes of this analysis, only Schedule III is of interest, since it alone touches on the question of regime-building and the pooling of sovereignty.

Schedule III aims at granting national treatment in the sectors covered by the agreement to intra-ASEAN cross-border investments by 2010 and to investors from outside the region by 2020. Modeled on AFTA, the framework agreement provides an AIA Council established by the AEM that comprises "the ministers responsible for investment and the ASEAN Secretary-General" (Art. 16, 1) and is answerable to the AEM (Art. 16, 3). The agreement assigns only a subordinate role to the ASEAN Secretariat (Art. 16, 6). The AIA provides a basic schedule for the gradual liberalization of investment sectors for products on the "Temporary Exclusion List", TEL, by 2010, 2013 and 2015 respectively. Products on the "Sensitive List", SL, are merely subject to a periodical review from 2003 on. The "General Exceptions List"[260] covers products that are

---

[258] Stubbs (2000): 314, intending to defend the institutional shortcomings of AFTA, affirms that "ASEAN, and by extension AFTA, are based much more on networks of personal contacts and social obligations than on formal institutions or legal commitments." He portrays "ASEAN's flexible, informal approach" and the reluctance of member states "to give much power to a central secretariat" as the "regional cultural context [...] crucial to understanding the way in which the AFTA agreement was signed and implemented."
Stubbs makes ASEAN's dilemma of disunity a virtue by calling it "cultural context", but fails to show in how far this "cultural context" has an added value or a constructive potential for economic cooperation in Southeast Asia. As Rüland (2000a) has pointed out, obstructive cultural context can also result in a spillback effect on region-building if it hampers institution-building.

[259] Framework Agreement on the ASEAN Investment Area, Makati (Philippines), 07 October 1998.

[260] The "General Exceptions List" comprises sectors defined in Art. 13 (General Exceptions) of the agreement. It "consists of industries and investment measures that cannot be opened up

interminably exempted from th AIA.[261] Unlike AFTA, the AIA has no "Inclusion List", since all sectors not explicitly identified by the three exclusion lists are automatically subject to the liberalization scheme. The scheme obliges each ASEAN member to "open immediately all its industries for investments by ASEAN investors" and to grant investors from within ASEAN MFN status and national treatment (Articles 7,1; 8).

Regardless of the perfomance of the AIA so far, its weak spots are the institutional arrangement, the liberal exemption rules and the failure to effectively prevent non-compliance and exit behavior. The AIA is bound to fail to provide stability in the long run on three accounts:

First, the AEM-controlled AIA Council is no independent body to oversee the unconditional implementation of the AIA, but merely represents the extended arm of the national governments. The ASEAN Secretariat as an independent institution holds only one-eleventh of the votes in the Council and has no influence on decisions taken by the AEM. The AIA is thus open to massive manipulation and intervention by ASEAN governments at any given time. In times of crisis, the system is therefore at high risk to fail, since governments can easily implement the withdrawal of commitments.

Second, even an independent AIA Council would find it difficult to effectively implement compliance with AIA regulations, since ASEAN provides no supranational judiciary.

Third, the compliance mechanism of the AIA is insufficient, since non-compliance or system exit does not automatically result in punitive measures. Article 9 merely provides affected countries with the opportunity to deny the offender MFN status in the investment sector concerned:

> Where a Member State is temporarily not ready to make concessions under Article 7 of this Agreement, and another Member State has made concessions under the said Article, then the first mentioned Member State shall waive its rights to such concessions. *However, if a Member State which grants such concessions is willing to forego the waiver, then the first mentioned Member State can still enjoy these concessions.* [Emphasis added.]

In other words, whether liberalization is implemented depends not so much on pre-set rules, but largely on bilateral negotiations between individual countries. This undermines the effectiveness of the AIA as a regional regime.

---

for investment or granted national treatment because of reasons of naitonal security, public morals, public health or environmental protection." (ASEAN Secretariat: "ASEAN Investment Area: An Update" (undateda)).

[261] The three lists (TEL, SL, General Exception List) are the unmediated representations of corresponding lists submitted separately to the Council by each member state.

3.1.3. Dispute Settlement Mechanism

The conflict between the informal, bilateral approach of ASEAN and the need to increasingly establish rules-based forms of cooperation is also manifest in the Dispute Settlement Mechanism adopted in 1996 whose principles apply to all economic cooperation agreements of ASEAN, including AFTA and AIA.
The "Protocol on Dispute Settlement Mechanism",[262] while pointing out that "[a]ny differences shall, as far as possible, be settled amicably between the Member States" (Art. 2), doubtlessly provides a clear, balanced and fair mechanism for dispute settlement defining the rights of the parties, the timetables for the various procedural steps and the institutions to be addressed. It also defines the body in charge of making a final ruling on particular cases (either the SEOM or the AEM). However — and this reduces the mechanism to near meaninglessness — the system fails to provide sufficient regulations to implement these rulings. A member state that fails to comply with the ruling faces no punitive measures, but "shall [...] enter into negotiations with any party having invoked the dipute settlement procedures, with a view to developing mutually acceptable compensation" (Art. 9,1). The most severe consequence a member state faces in the case of non-compliance with ASEAN's ruling is the the re-establishment of the *status quo ante* in a particular area of cooperation:

> If no satisfactory compensation has been agreed [...], any party having invoked the dispute settlement procedures may request authorization from the AEM to suspend the application to the Member State concerned of concessions or obligations under the Agreement or any covered agreements" (Art. 9,1).

Overall, the so-called dispute settlement mechanism merely represents a rules-based procedure of dispute mediation with no power to implement its rulings vis-á-vis non-compliant member states.[263] It simply refers unsettled disputes back to the level of bilateral negotiations. In order to be effective, the dispute settlement mechanism would have to be complemented by an effective

---

[262] Protocol on Dispute Settlement Mechanism, Manila, 20 November 1996.

[263] It is telling that the "Protocol on Dispute Settlement Mechanism" alternately applies the terms "ruling" (Arts 7; 8; 9,1) and "recommendation" (Art. 9,2) for decisions taken in the course of the settlement process by the SEOM and the AEM. Whereas "ruling" suggests something more definite and irreversible, the term "recommendation" emphasizes the non-binding character of such decisions. This ambiguity underlines once more ASEAN's preference for informal, consensu-oriented decision making and ASEAN's habit to give its modes of informal cooperation a contractual, quasi-legalistic appearance.

compliance mechanism making non-compliance or exit behavior politically and economically more costly for individual member states.[264]

3.1.4. ASEAN Surveillance Process (ASP)

Set up in response to the crisis in 1997, the ASEAN Surveillance Process (ASP) is supposed to provide economic stability to the region by means of establishing an early warning system to monitor and assess potentially destabilizing financial and economic trouble spots in the region. In this context, the ASP is also supposed to assess member states' economic and financial policies and to suggest "unilateral or collective actions to prevent a crisis".[265]

The core element and at the same time the core problem of the ASP is obtaining sufficient relevant information and data from the participating countries. Even senior experts from within ASEAN have to concede that

> Since the ASP is voluntary and not compulsory, some observers fear that member countries will not comply and disclose the necessary information for the surveillance system to be effective.[266]

Generally, all ASEAN member states are obliged to provide "a set of baseline data as provided to the IMF", but otherwise the ASP has neither a clear catalog of data to be provided by participants nor a mechanism obliging participants to provide essential data. The Terms of Understanding explicitly mentions that in particular cases the ASEAN-minus-X principle can be applied (§ 6). In fact, the viability of the ASP has been questioned by many observers who point out that a number of ASEAN member states have severe reservations against releasing secret economic data. As Kraft notes,

> The efficacy of an economic surveillance and monitoring system is dependent on the willingness of the ASEAN states to provide extensive amounts of data and information regarding their economy. This seemingly innocuous requirement, however, has political implications. It requires the acceptance in principle of the need for a degree of transparency that some members of the organization have found

---

[264] A small (but still insufficient) step into this direction has been taken in AFTA, where the ASEAN Economic Ministers have determined that a party to a dispute may retaliate against a member state that disregards a ruling of the AFTA Council by withdrawing "substantially equivalent concessions", including other products than the one subject to the dispute. (Article 6, Protocol Regarding the Implementation of the CEPT Scheme Temporary Exclusion List, Singapore, 23 November 2000.)

[265] Terms of Understanding on the Establishment of the ASEAN Surveillance Process, Washington, D.C., 4 October 1998, Objectives, § 1,i-iv.

[266] Hew and Anthony (2000): 23.

objectionable. Malaysia and Singapore have opposed turning over the kind of macroeconomic data needed to sustain this policy [...]. Laos, Myanmar and Vietnam have likewise been reported as registering their misgivings about it. The plan bogged down before it had a chance to be tested.[267]

In a similar vein, Rüland states that the fact that the ASP has to rely on the voluntary submission of economic data is due to the member states' reluctance to reveal information:

> implementation [of the ASP] was agonizingly slow [...]. Moreover, whether 'peer surveillance' will work crucially depends on the quality of the data provided by members. Previous experiences raise doubts in this respect as some ASEAN members surround their economic data with an aura of secrecy and only agreed to submit them on a voluntary basis.[268]

Criticism has come from within ASEAN, too. The Secretary-General of ASEAN, Rodolfo Severino,

> reportedly stated in late 1998 that the ASEAN Secretariat's inability to manage and supervise the mechanism and the reluctance by some member economies to reveal 'too much' information and data, have been the primary reason for the initial slow progress [of the ASP, M.H.].[269]

Serge Berthier features similar criticisms by the Secretary-General.[270]
Chang and Rajan see a combination of obstacles contravening the implementation of an effective surveillance process. Among these are: the norm of national sovereignty and independence, the norm of non-interference, and the distrust in rules-based and legally binding mechanisms:

> Another possible constraint on the potential effectiveness of the ASP has to do with the *real-politik* of ASEAN. [...] the ASEAN policy of non-intervention in one another's affairs [...] may make it extremely difficult to operate a regional surveillance mechanism effectively. This is so, as criticisms of a country's misguided and unsustainable economic policies

---

[267] Kraft (2000): 458.
[268] Rüland (2000a): 430.
[269] Cf. Rajan (1999): 7.
[270] Berthier (1999), in an adjunct to the transcript of his interview with Rodolfo Severino, the ASEAN Secretary-General, notes that "As Mr. Severino outlined in a previous interview with Asian Affairs [...], members remained reluctant to share sensitive data on their real economy" due to severe economic competition in many areas and especially in the area of foreign investment.

may be perceived as being incompatible with the hitherto cherished 'ASEAN spirit'. [...]
Another potential impediment to a well-functioning surveillance mechanism [... is that...] the authorities in the region have tended to be less than forhtcoming about their economic and financial situations, and have used economic data as a strategic tool rather than a public good. The need to establish benchmarks for timely and accurate data is essential [...]
[A]vailable details suggest that the above-noted factors have constrained the speed at which the ASP has been implemented, while the initial ambitions/scope of the project also seem to have been down-sized.[271]

The institutional arrangement of the ASP is thus kept in typical ASEAN fashion, namely informal, non-mechanistic, and exclusively in the hands of the member states. Thus, the central guiding principle is "that the ASEAN Surveillance Process shall be informal, simple and based on peer review" (§ 2,ii). The ASEAN Select Committee is answerable to the ASEAN Finance Ministers Meeting (AFMM). The ASEAN Surveillance Coordinating Unit (ASCU), based at the ASEAN Secretariat, has been commissioned to coordinate the ASP process, but takes practically a subordinate executive role.
The ASEAN members' general reluctance to cede power to and invest centralized ASEAN bodies such as the Secretariat with additional prerogatives and sovereignty is very prominently represented in the structures of the ASP. This characteristic feature of ASEAN undermines (not only) the ASP. As Rajan writes,

> there is a question of whether ASEAN has the institutional capacity to develop an effective surveillance mechanism on a regular basis, given its small and poorly financed secretariat in Jakarta and loose and highly decentralised organisational structure.[272]

The handling of the ASP highlights once more the inability of ASEAN to come to terms with institutionalization and reflects the (not necessarily new) central dilemma of ASEAN, namely "How to integrate without actually integrating?"[273]
The decentralized structure and obscure program of the ASP that results from the ASEAN way neither contributes to economic and finacial stability and transparency in Southeast Asia nor does it reflect a convincing attempt at community-building. The ASP is not even convincing in terms of a mere neighborhood watch group project.

---

[271] Chang and Rajan (1999b): 9-11.
[272] Rajan (1999): 7f.
[273] See Kamlin (1991), as quoted in Dosch (1997): 31.

3.2. Mechanisms of political cooperation

3.2.1. ASEAN High Council

The phantom of the ASEAN High Council has accompanied the process of ASEAN cooperation since 1976, when the foreign ministers of ASEAN agreed to establish a regional body for the "settlement of differences or disputes by peaceful means." [274] The High Council was supposed to allow "the High Contracting Parties to take cognizance of the existence of disputes or situations likely to disturb regional peace and harmony" (Art. 14). Brought to life on paper and apparently too ambitious in scope — despite its fairly moderate profile as "a committee of mediation, inquiry or conciliation" (Art. 15) — the High Council was never implemented. Dormant for many years, the concept has been discussed again in recent years and re-appeared on the ASEAN agenda 24 years after its inception.[275] Even though ASEAN Foreign Ministers resolved on the rules of the High Council in 2001, there is little hope that the High Council will ever represent an effective mechanism for dispute settlement.[276]

3.2.2. ASEAN Troika

The idea to establish an ASEAN Troika, as proposed by Thailand in 1998, was based on the assumption that a more interdependent Southeast Asia needed a centralized and flexible political body to intervene wherever situations of local crisis and instability impacted on wider parts of the region. The implication was that a relatively independent group of three ASEAN foreign ministers — whose

---

[274] Treaty of Amity and Cooperation in Southeast Asia (1976), Articles 2.d, 14-17.

[275] In July 2000, ASEAN foreign ministers noted "the progress being made to finalise the Draft Rides of Procedure for the High Council under the TAC, and agreed to expedite efforts in this regard." (Joint Communique, 33rd ASEAN Ministerial Meeting, Bangkok, 25 July 2000.)

[276] As Dewi Fortuna Anwar (2001: 92f.) points out, ASEAN countries still prefer to deal with contentious issues bilaterally and where this is not seen as sufficient, rather seek dispute settlement through the International Court of Justice than through the ASEAN High Council. This means that ASEAN members prefer to avoid ASEAN assuming a central role in areas that could eventually undermine member states' national sovereignty. Pointing out that ASEAN is still far from bringing about regional resilience, Dewi Fortuna Anwar states that "[...] so far the existence of ASEAN has not led to the final resolution of disputes among various member states. [...] [T]o date, the High Council has never been invoked. [...] [T]he main reason has been the preference among ASEAN states to settle their differences through bilateral channels. When bilateral disputes fail [...], there is now a tendency for ASEAN members to take their cases to the International Court of Justice in the Hague. [...] These moves may be regarded as proof of the members' lack of confidence in ASEAN's ability to reolve conflicts between themselves."

membership was to be based on a rotation principle — would be better suited than the collective of ASEAN foreign ministers or a single decision maker (such as the ASEAN chairman or the Secretary-General) to decisively and authoritatively identify, and react to, situations demanding the association's diplomatic intervention and mediation. Simon Tay, chairman of the Institute of International Affairs in Singapore, welcomed the idea of a troika as ideally suited to the needs of ASEAN on the account that a body of three would balance ASEAN members' predilection for decentralized decision making on the one hand and the need for a more coordinated approach to preventive diplomacy on the other:

> There are possibilities for the troika to practice some of the tools of preventive diplomacy. [...] Such a role is likely to be more acceptable for a troika than for a single ASEAN chairman. A troika would offer more collective wisdom, political weight, less suspicion of self-interest, and greater confidence in the continuity and consistency of decision-making.[277]

Nevertheless, the debate about the ASEAN Troika divided ASEAN governments because it touched on the central ASEAN norms of national sovereignty, non-interference in each other's internal affairs and decision making by consensus.[278] Indeed, the proposal represented a precedent in ASEAN in three respects:

First, ASEAN, as an intergovernmental process, is built on the principle of *equal participation* rather than *representation*. The idea to invest three representatives, namely the former, the present and the designated next chairman of the ASEAN Standing Committee, with the power to independently decide and act on behalf of all ASEAN governments was seen as an unacceptable deviation from the ASEAN way by many.[279]

Second, many governments doubted that ASEAN relations were mature enough to endure the extension of ASEAN's role and scope in the areas of conflict resolution, dispute settlement and interference in national affairs.

Equally, the idea that ASEAN as an institution should assume superiority and fortify its position vis-á-vis individual member states, especially in areas where national interests and integrity are concerned, was opposed by a majority of ASEAN governments as well.

---

[277] Tay (2000a): 11.

[278] For an analysis of the debate and the norms involved, see chapter on ASEAN norms in this thesis.

[279] Thailand's proposal had a great symbolic impact, too, because it was explicitly modeled on the EU troika (cf. *The Straits Times*, Singapore, 19 July 2000: "Thailand to push for 'troika' plan to act in crises").

The compromise between reformers and traditionalists to adopt a greatly modified version of the original Troika proposal leaves ASEAN with a legacy of mixed signals.

The institutional arrangement for the Troika puts the collective of ASEAN foreign ministers in control of the Troika. They can, on the basis of consensus and consultation, convene the Troika *ad hoc*, "as and when the situation warrants". As a rule, the Troika normally

> comprise[s] the Foreign Ministers of the present, past and future chairs of the ASC [Standing Committee] [...]. *However, if the situation warrants, the composition of the ASEAN Troika could be adjusted upon the consensus of the ASEAN Foreign Ministers.*[280] [Emphasis added]

The Troika is accountable to the ASEAN foreign ministers and not free to take decisions or action independently. "It's not a decision-making body" and "not inteded to represent ASEAN beyond the issues assigned by the ASEAN Foreign Ministers" (ibid.) Any decisions taken are to be based on consensus and consultation. Further, it "shall refrain from addressing issues that constitute the internal affairs of ASEAN member countries" (ibid.). What is more, the Troika (i.e. the countries representing it) would have to meet its own expenses. The implication is clear: the Troika is not supposed to take over administrative power and assume dominance or permanence of any kind.

By agreeing to actually establish the Troika, traditionalists concurred to the claim that in principle ASEAN should be in the position to become more proactive in managing intra-ASEAN crisis resolution. In turn, the reformers had to accept that the Troika, in its agreed-upon institutional form, could never become an effective means of quick, unbureaucratic and effective crisis response. The newly-established Troika has therefore been portrayed by observers in terms of mere face-saving and is generally considered to be a still-born ASEAN initiative. After all, not even Surin Pitsuwan, the initiator of the original proposal, could describe the precise role and function of the modified Troika as adopted by ASEAN: "Elaborating on its role, Dr Surin said it was not possible to spell out, in exact terms, what the Troika should do."[281].

3.2.3. ASEAN Secretariat

The ASEAN Secretariat, established as late as 1981 — more as a symbolic act and about five years after its adoption in principle at the Bali summit of 1976 — has traditionally exercised little influence on ASEAN. Only in 1993, following a

---

[280] ASEAN Secretariat (undated c.)
[281] *The Straits Times*, Singapore (26 July 2000).

decision taken at the 1992 Singapore summit (a turning point towards more integration), the Secretary-General of the ASEAN Secretariat was upgraded to ASEAN Secretary-General. The change of status included the promotion from ambassadorial to ministerial level, thereby raising the Secretary-General to the level of the decision makers of the practically most important decision making body, the ASEAN Ministerial Meeting. The upgrading also gave the Secretary-General "an enlarged mandate to initiate, advise, coordinate and implement ASEAN activities" and enabled him to recruit his officers through an open selection process rather than through appointment by the national ASEAN governments.[282] Since then, the Secretariat has continually gained competence in coordinating and overseeing ASEAN policies, though its role as an active policy making body is still rather limited.[283] In recent years, and especially since the crisis of 1997 owing to both the the division of ASEAN members, his increasing involvement in reviewing and commenting on ASEAN policies and politics and the attention he enjoys from the public and the media world-wide, the Secretary-General has also assumed a role as innovator, mediator and the personified 'conscience' of ASEAN. He has thereby assumed more political independence internally and externally.[284] The fact that Rodolfo Severino apparently perceives his role to be political rather than merely administrative has certainly contributed to the prominence and independence of the office of the ASEAN Secretary-General.

However, one must not forget that the Secretariat continues to be chronically understaffed and underfinanced and faces increasing difficulties in keeping up with the mere technical challenges posed by an ever-increasing number of

---

[282] For these data and the role of the ASEAN Secretariat, cf. ASEAN Secretariat (undated b); Dosch (1997): 81ff.

[283] The ASEAN Secretariat is increasingly involved in coordinating and reviewing the several ASEAN programs and initiatives, thereby gaining competence and assuming the role of ASEAN's institutional memory. By regularly submitting reports to the decision making bodies in ASEAN that critically assess central ASEAN initiatives, the Secretariat has assumed a role in putting the finger on developments and behavior contravening ASEAN integration and in recommending policies and directions to ASEAN leaders.

[284] The Secretary-General has not only criticized developments in ASEAN publicly in many speeches and interviews and hasn't shrunk back from, in some cases, clearly hinting at certain countries he perceived as undermining ASEAN solidarity and efforts at integration. He has also made use of his institutional role in intra-ASEAN processes to exercise criticism. For example, the Secretary-General's annual report to the ASEAN Ministerial Meeting in July 2000 was so openly critical of governments' efforts at economic integration and ASEAN's subsequent failure to attract foreign investment that it was suppressed by intervention of some foreign ministers: "The annual report to 10 foreign ministers of the group by its Secretary-General, Rodolfo Severino, is normally made public. But at the meeting this year [...] some ministers objected to its release because they feared it would intensify the view that some ASEAN members are backsliding into economic crisis, delegates said [...]" (Richardson 2000a).

ASEAN initiatives.[285] Following a restructuring process initiated by the 6th ASEAN summit in 1998, the ASEAN Secretariat, according to official figures (Table 5), now employs 99 staff, including the Secretary-General himself. Deviating somewhat from these figures, the Secretary-General himself stated in an interview in Asugust 1999 that "The Secretariat has 38 positions for openly recruited personnel and 104 for locally recruited staff."[286]

Table 5: Personnel of the ASEAN Secretariat

POSITIONS	BEFORE 1999	SINCE 1999
Secretary-General	1	1
Deputy Secretary-Generals	2	2
Directors	4	4
Assistant Directors & Programme Coordinators	16	14
Senior Officers	15	23
Programme Officers	5	27
Assistant Programme Officers	21	28
TOTAL	64	99

Source: ASEAN Secretariat

This small number of about a hundred staff undoubtedly compares unfavorably to the overall 500 million people represented by ASEAN. It shows that the Secretariat simply doesn't have the capacity and the potential to assume a greater — not to mention a supranational — role in ASEAN. What is more, despite some formal autonomy, the Secretariat's role is to support and coordinate cooperative processes rather than devising them on its own. Thus, regardless of its enhanced influence, the Secretariat continues to play a subordinate (as opposed to central or even supranational) role in ASEAN.

The considerable weakness of the Secretariat is part of ASEAN's deliberate decentralist and nation-centered political program. Simon Tay, for example,

---

[285] Indeed, the Hanoi Plan of Action (HPA) of 1998, which proliferated a large number of new ASEAN initiatives and reform proposals, heaped a heavy workload of additional responsibilities onto the ASEAN Secretariat which the institution couldn't realistically be expected to manage without additional resources. In order to put the Secretariat in the position to meet its new challenges, the last enterprise on the long list of HPA initiatives was to "[r]eview the role, functions and capacity of the ASEAN Secretariat to meet the increasing demands of ASEAN and to support the implementation of the Hanoi Plan of Action." (§ 10.3).

[286] Severino (1999a).

discussing the establishment of the Troika, stated that the Secretariat was *inter alia* not suitable for taking on a central role in intra-ASEAN preventive diplomacy on the account that "while the secretary-general formally enjoys the rank of Minister, there is a tendency in ASEAN to limit the initiative of that office and its political role".[287]

4. Visions of decentralized integration

4.1. The Eminent Persons Group (EPG) Report on the ASEAN Vision 2020

The discussion of institutional reform in ASEAN since the adoption of the ASEAN Vision 2020 in 1997 and the Hanoi Plan of Action (HPA) in 1998 has been condensed in a report by the Eminent Persons Group (EPG) on Vision 2020 submitted to the ASEAN summit in November 2000.

The central premise on which the EPG based the suggestions made in the report, was that ASEAN was struggling with a problem of relevance:

> What became very clear to the EPG members is the fact that ASEAN has been facing *criticism of irrelevance both internally and externally*, especially in its failure to repond collectively to the financial crisis of 1997-99. Doubt therefore was evident in the *collective readiness and will* of ASEAN states to meet even sterner challenges in the 21ˢᵗ century [...].[288]

Interestingly, the EPG, despite shyly raising the topic of supranationality and asserting that ASEAN needs to focus more on "institutional structures" to complement the existing informal "processes", has come up with suggestions which rather reinforce the role of the individual ASEAN governments than that they express the need for more centralized, supranational ASEAN mechanisms. Further, the EPG has put much more emphasis on pointing out the need to encourage decentralized, "grassroots" and civil society networks and institutions than asking for institutional reform at the top.

In terms of integrating ASEAN politically, the EPG has suggested accelerating coordination and integration in ASEAN by shifting the emphasis of decision making structures from ministerial-level bodies to the heads of government. The EPG stated that

> Indeed, we strongly feel that the Heads of Government should take 'full ownership' of the ASEAN programme - that is, ASEAN matters should

---

[287] Tay (2000a): 11.
[288] ASEAN Eminent Persons Group (2000): § 1 "Executive Summary".

be dealt with in general at that level. [...] The ASEAN mission as it were should not be seen to be primarily moved by the respective ministries, but rather by the Heads of Government acting in concert.[289]

The last, and largest, section of § 6 ("Developing Institutions - Acting in Concert"), is dedicated to strengthening the ASEAN Secretariat (a provision made by the Vision 2020). Essentially, however, despite some provisions for additional funding and staff to keep abreast with "the challenges of an enlarged ASEAN" and adding some minor responsibilities in circulating information to the ASEAN Secretariat, the report does not suggest to greatly enhance the role of the Secretariat.

In terms of the ASEAN mechanisms and institutions surveyed in this analysis, the report merely made recommendations for enhanced cooperation, but said little to nothing on supranationalizing ASEAN mechanisms and institutions. "Institutionalization" is understood not so much in terms of establishing rules-based regimes, but rather as building more or less informal cross-border and cross-sector ASEAN networks of civil society and cultural groups and institutions promoting human resources development.

The approach chosen by the EPG clearly reflects the traditional nation-centered approach to ASEAN cooperation. By asking the heads of government to "take full ownership" of ASEAN and suggesting the disempowerment of the ministerial meetings as main decision making bodies, they actually step back behind the achievements of ASEAN in that they de-emphasize institutionalized interaction, while confirming and re-emphasizing informal, de-centralized and nation-centered decision making, based on the smallest common denominator.

To sum up, the EPG recommended the ASEAN way, complemented by a new civil society component, to empower ASEAN, but didn't give much thought to empowering centralized ASEAN institutions and mechanisms.

4.2. Trends in intergovernmental cooperation since mid-2000

The governments of Thailand, the Philippines, and Singapore, which have been promoting more institutionalized political and economic integration, haven't been able to capture or dominate the political scene in ASEAN. The events of the 33rd AMM in July 2000 and the 4th Informal ASEAN summit in November 2000 saw not only an angry Thai government protesting in vain against Malaysia's unwillingness to follow the liberalization of car tariffs. The adoption of the CEPT protocol drawing AFTA's credibility into doubt also infuriated Singapore. Thailand had to take a defeat with respect to the watering-down of the ASEAN Troika concept, while Singapore, herself frustrated by the regress

---

[289] Ibid., § 6 "Developing Institutions - Acting in Concert".

158

of AFTA, took a beating by Malaysia, the Philippines and others for negotiating bilateral free trade agreements with New Zealand, Japan, the USA and Mexico.

Indonesia made it clear that she rejected any interference in her internal affairs from fellow member countries, while the Philippines, a strong supporter of Thailand's position on the Troika since 1998, faced increased rebel insurgencies in Mindanao and also joined the chorus of ASEAN traditionalists by relapsing into a rhetoric defending the principle of non-interference. What is more, observers feared that the CEPT protocol might also tempt the Philippines and Indonesia to exempt sensitive products from the tariff liberalization schedule.

The major initiatives and declarations of intent at both meetings were related to projects mirroring the recommedations of the EPG, namely a) the call for enhancing civil society and cultural networks to promote an "ASEAN spirit" among Southeast Asian peoples, b) enhancing human resources networks across Southeast Asia, and c) enhancing technical cooperation and development programs between old and new ASEAN members. To achieve the latter, the summit initiated the so-called *Initiative for ASEAN Integration* (IAI). An ASEAN Trade Fair project and the so-called "e-ASEAN framework", intended to upgrade the region's IT capacities, were presented as highlights of ASEAN cooperation.[290] Apparently, the term "integration", frequently invoked in the ASEAN terminology, has recently lost the connotation of institutionalisation and regime-building and seems to be increasingly applied to the multitutde of initiatives of loose cooperation ASEAN has been proliferating since the crisis.

In general, the actual overall trend since the crisis, as has been frequently observed among scholars and the media, was influenced by political disintegration rather than institutionalized community-building. John Funston, a senior fellow at Singapore's Institute of Southeast Asian Studies (ISEAS), echoing similar statements by Singaporean government, was quoted as saying: "ASEAN's image has taken a real bashing in the past few years [...] Domestic politics are having a bigger impact on the way foreign policy is conducted."[291]

After the demise of PM Chuan Leekpai's government and the rise of the crew around PM Thaksin after the 2001 elections in Thailand, ASEAN has lost the energetic and reform-minded voice of former Thai foreign minister Surin Pitsuwan. His equally energetic and reform-minded colleague Domingo Siazon of the Philippines had to step down as well after the fall of president Estrada's government. The new government of the Philippines hasn't had a chance yet to prove its commitment to ASEAN integration. It seems that of the reform-oriented voices, only Singapore remains as a solemn, outspoken and vigorous promoter of economic integration mechanisms. In November 2000, PM Goh was one of the few "to hammer home the integration message". In the running-

[290] See Press Statement by the Chairman of the 4th ASEAN Informal Summit, Singapore, 25 November 2000.
[291] John Funston, quoted in: Murphy (2001).

up to the Singapore summit, he confirmed that "Singapore's primary focus will be on ASEAN integration as a medium and long-term objective".[292] And Deputy Prime Minister Lee, with regard to the regressive performance of AFTA and AIA, pointed out shortly after the summit that

> ASEAN economic cooperation was progressively gaining momentum before the crisis. However, the crisis has caused some countries to hold back, in order to give struggling domestic industries more breathing space. [...] in their anxiety to protect individual industries, countries should not lose sight of the wider benefits of ASEAN cooperation to their economies as a whole.[293]

5. The state of pooling of sovereignty and outlook for ASEAN integration

With a view to the major integration projects of ASEAN, one can conclude that ASEAN is still a far cry from deepening its relations and transferring sovereignty from the national to the ASEAN level (or even establishing supranational institutions). Most ASEAN governments are obviously too preoccupied with their immediate national agendas as to be willing or able to take the painful next step of transmutating ASEAN into a more integrated political and economic community.

The ASEAN Secretariat remains at the margins of ASEAN policy making. There are no economic, legal, financial or other regional regimes and mechanisms that command individual member states' compliance or have any authority to devise and implement common policies by their own initiative. Indeed, national governments in ASEAN are unwilling to admit any "co-pilots", guard mechanisms or supranational authorities, so that commitments made by governments under the various mechanisms can be withdrawn or modified at any time without any serious consequences. There is no pooling of sovereignty. The picture that results from this analysis is that of an organization trying to integrate without actually integrating, of nation states trying to coordinate without being coordinated. In other words, ASEAN has started to build a common house, but has failed to solidify the foundations and devise a common roof.

---

[292] Yahoo Finance News - Asian Markets, 19 November 2000.
  Singapore has repeatedly urged fellow ASEAN members to embrace political reforms and economic integration in order to keep ASEAN relevant and credible as a regional grouping. The vehemence with which Singapore has criticized fellow member governments has even intensified in 2000, as evidence of continued disunity in ASEAN mounted and left the association increasingly inoperable.
[293] Lee Hsien Loong (2000).

Recent developments in ASEAN suggest that political disunity and nation-centered navel-gazing have severely restricted ASEAN's capability to enhance and centralize its existing cooperation mechanisms and to promote community-building. The AFTA regime has been softened rather than solidified. This trend continues through 2001. In the near to mid-term, ASEAN will therefore at best remain a "neighborhood watch group".

As pointed out at the outset of this article, there is a strong sense within and outside ASEAN that the association needs to develop into a more coordinated, integrated economic and political community if it wants to remain credible and relevant as a grouping.

Indeed, ASEAN will have to prove at various fronts that it can get its act together. In economic terms, ASEAN ambitiously aims at restoring investor confidence in the Southeast Asian region, bracing up against international competitors in the area of FDI, preventing future crises through effective surveillance and early warning systems and, perhaps less importantly, increasing intra-regional trade.

However, effective surveillance and early warning systems can only work if member states are required to submit essential data. Further, ASEAN can only increase its economic clout if AFTA can stop chewing on tariff liberalization and go about deepening, i.e. pooling sovereignty, in the areas identified by what is generally referred to as AFTA-Plus.[294] As AFTA participants keep discussing the implementation of commitments made under the CEPT, they fail to make progress in the area of AFTA Plus. Thus, integrative efforts at ASEAN level could soon be rendered irrelevant by developments in the WTO.

As a political and diplomatic community, ASEAN is struggling to display cohesiveness, a sense of common purpose and the will to stabilize the region by contributing to resolve regional transnational and security issues.

Whereas in the past, national economic growth and stability ("national resilience") depended predominantly on a regional environment determined by stable inter-governmental relations, a fact that usually required ASEAN governments to look the other way or sweep problems under the carpet whenever contentious issues arose, ASEAN members' growing interdependence now increasingly requires governments to proactively *manage* intra-ASEAN transnational and security issues so as to maintain a stable regional environment

---

[294] AFTA Plus denotes closer cooperation in the banking, finance, transport and communications sectors, reduction of intra-regional non-tariff barriers (NTB), liberalization of trade in services, creating an ASEAN Investment Area, agreeing on regionwide guarantees of intellectual property rights and – increasingly – coordination of effective development cooperation programs for the poor ASEAN newcomers.

On the objectives of AFTA-Plus and ASEAN's failure so far to come to grips with the issue of deepening, cf. Menon (2000): 58ff.

conducive to economic stability.[295] The establishment of central ASEAN mechanisms and bodies for dispute resolution, mediation and flexible crisis response would be essential to demonstrate ASEAN's determination to integrate for the purpose of greater regional stability.

By launching numerous initiatives of institutionalization and regional integration, ASEAN has set the measure by which to judge its success or failure. Backtracking from commitments half-way (such as in AFTA or the ASP) and laboring on still-born institutions (such as the Troika and the High Council) leaves ASEAN increasingly less credible and relevant.

With a view to AFTA, Langhammer rightly points out that by entering the path of regional integration and institutionalization, ASEAN has redefined its status and basis of cooperation and thus has to deliver if it wants to remain credible:

> Having established AFTA, ASEAN is no longer a loose grouping based on consensus, mutual consultation, and co-operation. Instead, [...] [w]ith firm commitments and timetables, there are now risks of losing credibility once commitments are ignored and timetables are missed. Club members can produce negative externalities for other members if some do not fulfill their commitments. [...] ASEAN resources and efforts would have to be mobilized in the political arena. Economically, the costs of failure to meet commitments are low [... as long as] the ability of ASEAN to enforce sanctions against those violating the rules is unclear [...].[296]

Relying on individual ASEAN members' goodwill and more or less voluntary and renegotiable participation in AFTA and other programs of economic integration will not bring about substantial integration in ASEAN. What is needed are rules-based mechanisms demanding compliance. This will require centrally managed policies and also more independent and preferrably supranational institutions.

After a phase of controversial debate about ASEAN norms and the reform of ASEAN structures since 1997, many ASEAN members now paradoxically seem to hold on even more to the traditional norms of the ASEAN way. Whereas strong emphasis on national resilience and decentralized structures as well as on related principles such as non-interference, decision-making based on consensus and the smallest common denominator used to guarantee the stability of ASEAN as a diplomatic community throughout most of its history, this very normative setup now appears to be choking ASEAN: whereas in the past it was of paramount importance not to step on each other's toes so as to quell mutual

---

[295] In this sense, ASEAN needs to increasingly acknowledge "national resilience" as a dependent variable of "regional resilience" and thus to de-emphasize national sovereignty as the paramount paradigm governing intra-ASEAN relations. Cp. for example Anwar (2000).

[296] Langhammer (2001a): 124.

suspicion and create stable inter-governmental relations, today ASEAN fails to engage in – painful – coordination and integration processes exactly on account of the very norms of the ASEAN way.

ASEAN therefore seems to be struggling with its very identity, which is defined *ex negativo* – built around a notion of untouchable national sovereignty and keeping the neighbors at an arm's length – and apparently has not evolved much through cooperation over the last thirty-odd years. If this assumption is true, the prospects for integration and institutionalized community-building in ASEAN are not much better in the long term than they are for the near to mid-term.

Chapter 4:

IRRITABLE COMMUNITY: UNSTABLE SOLIDARITY IN POST-CRISIS ASEAN

IRRITABLE COMMUNITY: UNSTABLE SOLIDARITY IN POST-CRISIS ASEAN

1. Introduction

As the third out of four reference points chosen in this thesis to frame the "black box" of collective identity, this chapter focuses on the question of solidarity within ASEAN. It assesses contemporary ASEAN with a view to getting an insight into the overall density, depth and stability of the mutual bond of solidarity between ASEAN members after more than three decades of ASEAN cooperation.

Since the inception of the Asian economic crisis in 1997, observers from outside and within the region have charged the Association of Southeast Asian Nations (ASEAN) with failure to respond to the disruptive economic and political developments in a unified way. Many international political augurs have consequently predicted a more permanent marginalization of ASEAN.[297] David Camroux even went so far as to proclaim the impending death of ASEAN.[298] Such analyses and conclusions are usually based on the observation of ASEAN members' self-interested, non-solidary behavior in the face of economic and political crises. Rüland, for example, concludes that the events of the crisis may have brought about a more permanent spillback to regional integration in Southeast Asia, since the grouping has failed to develop appropriate norms and structures enabling collective regional – rather than national – responses in times of crisis:

> The 'ASEAN Way' represents fair weather cooperation which flourishes under the conditions of economic boom. [...] much soul searching will lie ahead of ASEAN. It will include issues such as the political system, the degree and pace of economic liberalization, and the corpus of shared values. The ensuing debates could push ASEAN to the brink of paralysis.[299]

The charges commonly held against ASEAN are the organizations's lack of coherence, the lack of a sense of common purpose and the selfish pursuit of divergent national interests. In a nutshell, ASEAN seems to be struggling with a life-choking lack of *solidarity*.

---

[297]See, for example Clad (2000); Rüland (2000b).
[298] Camroux (2001).
[299] Rüland (2000a): 444f.

This chapter intends to put the proposition to the test. It asks whether ASEAN members can rely on a net of genuine intra-ASEAN solidarity, and if so, under what circumstances and to what degree. The analysis aims to answer the question both from an ASEAN perspective and from a bird's eye (meta)perspective of solidarity as defined in chapter 2.

A first step therefore introduces both ASEAN's view of solidarity and a more comprehensive, universally applicable model of group solidarity (as outlined in section 2.2.).

In a second step, the study focuses on nine cases demanding conflict management among ASEAN members; six of these represent situations involving two or more ASEAN members, two examples represent situations demanding support from the group vis-à-vis a third party for at least one ASEAN member, and the last one explores in how far there is solidarity between the original ASEAN-6 on the one side and the new ASEAN members (Vietnam, Laos, Myanmar and Cambodia) on the other.

The cases are then assessed in terms of ASEAN's definition of solidarity. The aim is to establish in how far the analyzed situations were handled in a manner commensurable with the norms of the 'ASEAN Way'. This is followed by a second assessment in terms of the bird's eye perspective of solidarity. The two foils for the evaluation of ASEAN norms thus created will then serve as the basis for a final qualitative evaluation of ASEAN solidarity.

2. Solidarity

The term solidarity can be approached from more than one angle. The approach chosen here is to look at solidarity from two angles: firstly, solidarity as defined by ASEAN, a subject-dependent approach; and, secondly, group solidarity as a more universally applicable concept.[300] Analysis of the former requires a representation of the essence of ASEAN solidarity as perceived by ASEAN members, whereas analysis of the latter requires an operable representation of the essence of solidarity *per se*.

2.1. Solidarity as defined by ASEAN

To ASEAN members, the term solidarity – widely used within ASEAN, though never clearly defined – basically denotes norm compliance in the widest sense, i.e. compliance with a specific set of written and unwritten ASEAN norms.

---

[300] This generalized concept of solidarity is referred to as the "bird's eye view of solidarity" throughout this study.

Traditionally, the most prominent principle is not to interfere in a member countries' internal affairs by any means or destabilize other member governments in any way.

> Operationally, the noninterference norm has meant (1) that no member criticizes the actions of another toward its own population regardless of human rights violations; (2) domestic systems of governance are not a basis for deciding ASEAN membership; (3) rebel groups must be denied recognition or sanctuary by neighboring states; and (4) each member, if requested, should provide political support and material assistance to member states in their campaigns against subversive activities.[301]

Conflicts are to be kept at the bilateral level as far as possible, but member states are obliged to discuss and settle disputes by peaceful means. ASEAN as an institution should not serve as a multilateral platform for the resolution of bilateral conflicts. This way ASEAN can avoid having to take sides in disputes between its members. Therefore, ASEAN, at the official level, has tended to sweep existing tensions under the carpet and to engage primarily in non-contentious issues of common concern.

Whenever ASEAN members can't avoid addressing contentious issues, this should be done according to the norm of quiet diplomacy to save governments from public criticism and embarassment. Generally, ASEAN members are expected to cooperate on issues of mutual interest where possible, in a manner of good neighborliness and general goodwill.

ASEAN members are expected to support each other in times of crisis, although expectations must not be too high. Generally, a government of an ASEAN member state can be expected to help another ASEAN government in times of crisis with financial and humanitarian aid and diplomatic or political support, provided it has the resources to do so and provided the government in crisis has requested or allowed the support activities. In political and security terms, ASEAN has a record of supporting the front-line state in case a member is involved in a conflict with non-member states.[302]

Since 1998, in the face of the crisis, there have been tendencies in parts of ASEAN to depict commitment to political unity, economic regional integration and gradual multilateralization of ASEAN as elements of ASEAN solidarity.[303]

---

[301] Simon (1998).

[302] See Nischalke (2000): 100.

[303] For example, ASEAN Secretary-General Rodolfo Severino, supporting the position of reform-oriented countries such as Singapore, Thailand and the Philippines, tried to shed a new light on ASEAN solidarity by identifying such countries as unsolidary that, in the face of the crisis, did not commit themselves to regional integration and transnational interaction, but "seem[ed] to pay mere lip service to the ideal of regional solidarity and cooperation", since they "act[ed] as if they did not truly believe in the need for regional responses to regional

However, there are no signs that ASEAN members subscribe collectively to such attempts at redefining ASEAN solidarity.

Table 6: Essentials of ASEAN solidarity

- non-interference
- avoiding the destabilization of member governments at all costs
- peacefulness
- quiet diplomacy
- preventing multilateralization of intra-ASEAN bilateral disputes (preventing
    ASEAN from taking sides)
- quiet diplomacy
- showing goodwill/ practising good neighborliness
- bilateral political, financial and humanitarian support/ aid to member governments
    in times of crisis
supporting the frontline state in conflict with external parties

2.2. The essence of group solidarity: The bird's eye view

The model of group solidarity underlying this analysis draws strongly on two seminal analyses of group solidarity by sociologists Michael Hechter and Siegwart Lindenberg.[304] The definition of group solidarity used here extrapolates (a) Hechter's and Lindenberg's shared (rational choice) assumptions on the ultimate motivation underlying the formation of group solidarity and goes on to (b) extract the phenotypical (i.e. observable) elements of group solidarity from both models. Further, both theorists provide tools for measuring "low" and "high" solidarity (Hechter) or "weak" and "strong" solidarity (Lindenberg), respectively, which are compatible with, and complement, each other.[305] The concept of the bird's eye view concept of group solidarity used in this study draws on these two models in order to (c) generate a catalog of criteria for measuring the degree of group solidarity.

---

problems." Cf. Severino (1998a): "Remarks", 8th Southeast Asia Forum, Kuala Lumpur, 15 March 1998.

[304] Hechter (1987): 15-39, Chapter II: "The Problem"; Lindenberg (1998).

[305] Hechter uses the terms "low" and "high" solidarity as substitutes for "coalition" and "community". Lindenberg shows that "weak" and "strong" solidarity are not permanent states but are influenced by the presence/absence of what he calls "non-solidaristic governance instruments" such as rules-based regimes.

2.2.1. Reasons for solidarity

Group solidarity thrives on the principle of utility rather than altruism. It can only be maintained if it is useful to individual members in the sense that the group jointly provides/shares an (exclusive) collective good on which group members depend and which would be impossible or very difficult to gain for individual members outside the group. Interdependence among group members in this context is an important resource for sustained solidarity. Solidarity is therefore clearly interest-based.

Table 7: Reasons for collective solidarity

■ sharing/providing (rare) collective goods
■ interdependence
■ utility of the group for the purposes of the individual member (solidarity is interest-
based)

2.2.2. Phenotypical characteristics of solidarity

There are several phenotypical indicators that express the quality of a group's internal relations with respect to shared solidarity. An observer can evaluate the degree of solidarity by assessing the following characteristics.

Groups will develop specific rules and norms as they cooperate. It is therefore essential to assess the respective group members' compliance with these. Further, any kind of solidarity imposes certain solidarity costs on the participants. There is no solidarity without them. However, costs of any kind imposed on a group member can only be considered *solidarity* costs if there is no direct input/output ratio or proportional compensation for the "investor". This means the group should be based on equality rather than on equity with respect to sharing the "profit" and participating in the collective good. In this context, it is important to observe the cooperative and sharing behavior among group members. Ingroup/outgroup distinction is an equally revealing characteristic for the evaluation of group solidarity. In this context, an evaluation should also focus on shared group rituals and symbols as well as patterns of relational signaling (i.e. group-specific codes and patterns of behavior/communication). The sense of ingroup/ outgroup distinction is an equally revealing characteristic for the evaluation of group solidarity. In this context, an evaluation should also focus on shared group rituals and symbols as well as patterns of relational signaling (i.e. group-specific codes and patterns of behavior and communication).

Table 8: Phenotypical characteristics of solidarity

- compliance with group norms/rules
- solidarity costs (no direct input/gains ratio for "investments")
- equality (rather than equity) of members in participation rights
- ingroup/outgroup distinction
- group rituals and symbols
- relational signaling (group-specific)

In addition to the above criteria, the analysis of ASEAN solidarity also focuses on *five situations* of solidarity as defined by Lindenberg. Lindenberg identifies solidarity as "behavioral pattern *across* [...] five situations". Solidarity only exists if an adherent to a group can be expected to act in accordance with the model behavior in each of the five situations. He describes them as (1) common good situation, (2) sharing situation, (3) need situation, (4) breach temptation, and (5) mishap situation:

> *Common good situation*   Ego and Alter both belong to a group that produces a common good. Ego will contribute to the common good even if he could free ride (the minimal amount of contribution in terms of money, effort, time etc. expected for solidary behavior varies).

> *Sharing situation*   If there are joint divisible benefits and costs and if Ego is the one who can divide them, he will not seek to maximize what he gets from the costs but take his "fair share" of both (what the fair share is varies).

> *Need situation*   Ego will help Alter in times of need (what constitues need and how much help is minimally expected for solidary behavior varies).

> *Breach temptation*   Ego will refrain from hurting Alter even at a cost to himself (the minimal amount of cost expected for solidary behavior varies).

> *Mishap situation*   Acts can be intendedly solidary but factually turn out to go against the expectation of solidary behavior. In that case, Ego will show that he meant to act differently, that he feels sorry, [...] and he will make amends if the mishap has caused damage to others. Also, if Ego knows in advance that he will not be able to keep to the agreement, he will warn the others in advance, so that they can mitigate the damage.

> The claim is that these five situations cover all aspects of solidary behavior.[306]

---

[306] Lindenberg (1998): 64.

Table 9: Five situations of solidarity

■ Common good situation
■ Sharing situation
■ Need situation
■ Breach situation
■ mishap situation

2.2.3. Weak and strong solidarity

Generally, the solidarity model used here holds that group solidarity is strong when group members' behavior is in concordance with the five situations of solidarity (table 9).

With reference to the reasons for solidary behavior (see table 7), strong solidary requires that the value of the collective good to the individual group member is high. The more exclusive and the higher the value of the collectively provided/shared good to the individual group member, the higher the potential for strong solidarity. In other words, the lower the utility of the group for the purposes of the individual, the lower the likelyhood of strong solidarity. Equally, high interdependece between group members raises the potential for strong solidarity, whereas low interdependence reduces it.

With reference to the phenotypical characteristics of solidarity (see table 8), solidarity is stronger when both the sum of obligations imposed on group members and the frequency of compliance with group norms and rules are high. Alternatively, a high degree of "myopic opportunism"[307] (Lindenberg) and "free-riding" (Hechter) by group members is a sign of weak solidarity. Norm compliance depends to a great deal on the social/political "cost" a member faces in case of non-compliance with group norms: thus, the a respective group's cohesion and solidarity will be the stronger the higher the costs of non-compliance are and the higher the degree of members' norm compliance is.

With a view to the value of the group to its adherents, the willingness of individual group members to accept high solidarity costs is an indicator for a high degree of solidarity. Likewise, strong ingroup/outgroup distinction, pronounced cooperative and sharing behavior, steady and frequent relational signaling, frequent ritualized interaction and the use of symbols within the group are all signs of firm solidary relations.

With reference to group governance, Lindenberg states that where solidarity is "flanked" by effective "non-solidaristic" governance arrangements, i.e.

---

[307] "What threatens solidary behavior most is *myopic opportunism*, i.e. the tendency to give in to short-term temptations at the expense of long-term advantages." (Lindenberg 1998: 77.)

formalized regimes, strong solidarity is redundant, since the system takes over its cohesive and stabilizing function.[308]

2.2.4. Situations of solidarity deterioration

Solidarity tends to erode over situations of strongly diminishing returns for the group or individual group members. Likewise, severe erosion of solidarity is likely to occur in times of severe collective crisis/insecurity, when individual members' respective needs are high on the one hand and when on the other hand the frequency of incurred high solidarity costs strongly increases for each member.

> When there are fairly high costs involved in executing solidary behavior and when the situations are repetitive, then we are likely to observe, *ceteris paribus*, a decay in the overall salience of the solidarity frame.[309]

This implies that permanent severe disruption of a group's environment or the collapse of a group's basis of cooperation can be expected to diminish the group's solidarity in the sense that it enhances individual interests and competition between members and at the same time reduces the relative value attributed to the collective (jointly produced) good.

However, recurrent "need situations which hit all members (but at different times)", minor crises and a shared sense of an uncertain environment tend to enhance (rather than erode) a group's coherence and solidarity.[310]

2.3. Measuring ASEAN solidarity

2.3.1. Measuring ASEAN solidarity from the ASEAN perspective

Measuring solidarity with respect to the ASEAN view of solidarity is comparatively simple in principle. It requires merely a reality check of ASEAN members' compliance with the norms of the 'ASEAN Way' (see section 2.1.). The question of norm compliance can be answered with "yes" (behavior corresponds with the norm) or "no" (behavior does not correspond with the norm).

Following Hechter's definition of solidarity, such compliance testing, combined with a qualitative assessment of the group's underlying norms (Hechter uses the

---

[308] Lindenberg notes that traditional sociology explains this phenomenon as the transition from *community* to *society*.
[309] Lindenberg (1998): 80.
[310] Ibid.: 89.

term "obligations"), would be a valid method of measuring group solidarity.[311] However, this would mean assessing each group by its own standards, i.e. the group adopts a set of norms on the basis of which the degree of norm compliance (=solidarity) can then be assessed and measured. This approach requires any assessment of (ASEAN) solidarity to adopt the standards set by the object of its analysis (in this case ASEAN). Consequently, any assessment following this approach must be restricted to a subjective view of (ASEAN's) group solidarity. Conversely, the "bird's-eye-view" model of group solidarity introduced above evaluates ASEAN solidarity exclusively on he basis of parameters set by the analys/ observer.

2.3.2. Measuring ASEAN solidarity from the bird's-eye-view perspective

Measuring the degree of ASEAN solidarity according to the bird's-eye-view model goes beyond observing mere norm compliance (or compliance with a group's obligations, respectively). Rather, it requires taking into account the observable behavior (see criteria in table 8) of ASEAN members and relating it to both the respective external conditions (= environment) of ASEAN cooperation and the expectable motivation for ASEAN members to engage in solidarity.

(A) Observed behavior represents the degree of *absolute* solidarity in a given situation, at a given time (measurable on a continuum between high solidarity and no solidarity at all). If the observed behavior corresponds with the criteria for strong solidarity (as defined in section 2.2.3. Weak and Strong Solidarity) and is in line with the model behavior of the five situations of solidarity (see table 9), then overall (absolute) solidarity is "high". Conversely, if the observed behavior displays few or no positive attributes of solidarity and is not in line with the model behavior, then absolute solidarity is considered as "low". If the observed behavior generally to the demands of solidarity, but there is a considerable deficiency rate, absolute solidarity is considered as "deficient".

(B) The degree of *relative* solidarity is represented by the relation between *observed behavior* (*b*), *external conditions* (*c*) and members' expected (ie. model-generated) *motivation to engage in solidarity* (*m*) in a given situation, at a given time. If *b* displays an either higher or a lower degree of solidarity

---

[311] Hechter says that "a group's solidarity is a function of two independent factors: first, the extensiveness of its corporate obligations, and, second, the degree to which individual members actually comply with these obligations", or, "more formally, solidarity = $f(ab)$, where a = the extensiveness of a group's obligations and b = the rate of members' compliance to them. [...] groups only can attain high levels of solidarity when the values of both a and b are relatively high. (Hechter 1987: 18.)

than *c* and *m* suggest, then the degree of solidarity is either "relatively stable" or "defunct". In this case, *b* does not follow the solidarity model and is not a function of *c* and *m* ($b \neq f(cm)$). If *b* is proportional to *c* and *m*, i.e. *b* depends on *c* and agrees with *m*, then *b* is a function of *c* and *m* in line with the model of solidarity ($b = f(cm)$); the degree of solidarity can be considered as "relatively unstable", since solidarity can be expected to erode as the external conditions (and thus the expectable motivation to engage in solidarity) are negatively affected.

The distinction between *absolute* and *relative* solidarity permits a more effective and accurate evaluation of a group's solidarity in that it considers the respective external circumstances of observed behavior.

For example: whereas solidarity may be classified as "deficient" in absolute terms, it may still be described as "relatively high" with regard to the (adverse) external conditions under which the group operated (such as a severe and disruptive crisis threatening all members) and the subsequent (lower) degree of actors' *expectable* motivation to engage in solidary behavior.

Table 10: Measuring absolute and relative solidarity

Solidarity type	Observed behavior (*b*)	Classification
Absolute solidarity	■ *b* is in line with definition of "strong" solidarity	■ "high"
	■ *b* is generally in line with definition of solidarity, but frequently deficient	■ "deficient"
	■ *b* is clearly not in line with the definition of solidarity	■ "low"
Relative solidarity	■ *b* displays more solidarity than the model suggests with respect to the external conditions (*c*) and group members' motivation to engage in solidary behavior (*m*)	■ "relatively stable"
	■ *b* follows changes to *c* and *m*	■ "relatively unstable"
	■ *b* displays less solidarity than the model suggests with respect to *c* and *m*	■ "defunct"

3. How much solidarity for ASEAN? – The cases

The analysis focusses on nine cases, all of them displaying ASEAN members' behavior and modes of interaction in dealing with contentious issues and situations of acute crisis.

The first case, the "haze" crisis, immediately precedes ASEAN members' realization of the severe implications of the financial crisis of 1997 for the region. Similarly, the study of the South China Sea issue, tracing ASEAN's shifting position vis-à-vis China from 1992 to 2001, covers about six years of pre-cisis period altogether. All the other cases date from the years follwowing the crisis, through to 2001. Most case studies follow particular issues over a range of years, thereby establishing a longer-term perspective of ASEAN members' behavior.

In line with the criteria developed in chapter 2, each case is assessed and evaluated individually here. A conclusive assessment and evaluation of all cases with a view to a qualified statement on overall ASEAN solidarity (on the basis of the material presented) will follow in the next chapter.

3.1. The "haze" over Southeast Asia: ASEAN, Indonesia and the haze crisis of 1997

ASEAN's situation in 1997/1998: At the time the haze crisis started, in September 1997, ASEAN relations were not yet unsettled by the financial and economic crisis that had struck the region in mid-1997. Indeed, before the crisis had struck, ASEAN members had experienced decades of remarkably high economic growth and development rates, which had greatly contributed to the stability of ASEAN relations.

> In retrospect, 1997 can be seen as the organisation's high point when hopes were high that ASEAN would lead Southeast Asia into a new era of stability and cooperation fuelled by Asia's economic dynamism and a commitment to the principles of comprehensive security.[312]

In short, ASEAN operated on the basis of a notion of considerable unity, stability and shared confidence in the viability of the traditional 'ASEAN way' throughout 1997. In 1998, the impact of the economic crisis was felt throughout the region. Most remarkably, Indonesia's internal stability deteriorated fast as the crisis struck.

---

[312] Dupont (2000): 167.

The problem: From late August to early October 1997, Singapore, wide parts of Malaysia and – to a lesser degree from late September on – Thailand and the Philippines, were blanketed by heavy smoke drifting across from forest fires in the Indonesian part of Borneo, causing great distress to the populations and governments in the region. After peaking in September 1997, the fires continued to affect the region through April 1998. The so-called "haze" resulted from the large-scale "slash and burn" clearance of forests practiced by palm oil companies for the purpose of creating farmland.

Similar incidences of the so-called "haze" had occurred repeatedly throughout the 1980s and 1990s,[313] but the fellow ASEAN members – following the ASEAN norm of non-interference in the internal affairs of a member country had suffered in relative silence, and various governments actively prevented the media from reporting on the issue:

> Indeed, up to the mid 1990s, the media in some of the Southeast Asian countries (Malaysia specifically) [were] discouraged from reporting on the exact sources and extent of the air pollution.[314]

ASEAN had for the first time publicly approached the issue following the haze of 1994, when ASEAN Environment Ministers had set up a haze cooperation framework – the ASEAN Plan on Transboundary Pollution – which was followed up by the establishment of the Haze Technical Task Force (HTTF) in June 1995.[315] However, the scheme had never made any substantial progress:

> While the Co-operation Plan has the merit of recognizing the region as a single eco-system and the common interest in reducing or avoiding a recurrence of the haze, its failure was in its implementation, or the lack of it. The 1997 fires pointed to the lack of follow-up.[316]

The severity of the haze of 1997 surpassed any previous experiences and turned out to be a regional disaster.[317] Besides the enormous economic and

---

[313] Incidents of the haze clouding neighboring countries had occurred in 1982-3, 1987, 1991 and 1994, cf. Cotton (1999): 331.

[314] Chang and Rajan (2000): 10.

[315] Cf. Ramcharan (2000): 69; Tay (1997).

[316] Ramcharan (2000): 71.

[317] In Kuala Lumpur and Singapore, visibility was low and people were advised to stay indoors for weeks. In parts of East Malaysia, air pollution levels were even up to eight times higher than in the capital. Overall fire and haze-related damages to the region for August to December 1997 were valued at about US$ 4.5 billion in 1999. For more detailed accounts of the damages caused by the haze, cf. Mallet (1999): 172-77; Cotton (1999); Smith (1999); Ramcharan (2000); various reports in the editions of the *Far Eastern Economic Review* of 2, 9, 16 October 1997; EEPSEA/ WWF Research Report "The Indonesian Fires and Haze of 1997: The Economic Toll", Singapore: ISEAS, August 1999, covering the period from August-December 1999. According to a more recent figure, overall economic losses inflicted

public health damages inflicted on Indonesia's neighbors, the crisis also had major political implications for ASEAN, both at the national, the regional and international level.

Nationally, especially the governments of Singapore and Malaysia faced strong pressure from the general public to urge Indonesia to cooperate responsibly with its neighbors in regional fire fighting and prevention initiatives. At the regional level, ASEAN's profile as a relevant entity to deal with regional problems effectively was challenged. Worldwide, observers viewed ASEAN's handling of the haze as the litmus test of ASEAN's cohesion and political relevance and international standing. In the face of the events of the unfolding East Asian economic crisis since mid-July, the negative light the haze crisis shed on ASEAN's reputation was especially disconcerting.

The reaction: "Indonesian officials [had taken] a nonchalant approach to the problem intially, seeing it as a domestic and not a regional matter."[318] ASEAN members, following ASEAN's political credo of non-interference, therefore only acknowledged the problem publicly when it could not be denied any longer. At the height of the crisis, outrage in the region led President Suharto to apologize twice (on 16 September and 5 October 1997), but the general perception throughout the region was that Indonesia's words were not followed up by appropriate action, i.e. that Indonesia complied at the surface with ASEAN demands for more transparency and concerted regional action, but proved to be only insufficiently determined to implement measures to contain the fires.

Indonesia's failure to handle the haze problem adequately caused the government of Singapore to adopt an ambiguous policy: on the one side, it quite obviously launched a media campaign to step up pressure on Indonesia, while officially it remained silent and engaged in behind-the-scenes diplomacy. The Malaysian government reacted in the customary fashion adopted in the years before and after: it imposed a ban on haze-related information (which it was initially unable to enforce) and engaged in (sometimes apparently not so quiet) behind-the-scenes diplomacy with Indonesia.

Singapore's reaction in 1997   Singapore had been well aware of the heavy forest fires since May 1997 and, following regional haze warning procedures, had provided the Indonesian authorities with satellite images of so-called "hot spots". However, in the customary ASEAN manner, this had been done behind the scenes. The public was systematically kept in the dark and the press was instructed not to report on the haze (or, if this was unavoidable, to blur its origin

---

on the region from 1997 to 1998 are estimated at US$ 9.3 billion (*The Straits Times*, 17 May 2001: "ASEAN ministers meet to fight haze").

[318] Ramcharan (2000): 68.

and background) from May through well beyond mid-August 1997.[319] According to *The Straits Times* correspondent Dominic Nathan,

> A Meteorological Service officer told a reporter that fires in Sumatra were partly reponsible for the haze and his remark made it into print. The Straits Times promptly received a call from a ministry official [...]. The newspaper should not have identified Indonesia as the source of the smoke, because of regional sensitivities. [...]
>
> [W]hen parts of the island were slightly hazy on several days in mid-June, The Straits Times called it a "mystery haze" because no one seemed to know where it came from. Or, at least, no one was saying. [...] Ironically, it was only as the haze became thicker that information about it got clearer.[320]

When the haze situation began to deteriorate dramatically in late August, the Singaporean government in a press conference released satellite photos (on 29 August) identifying Indonesia as the source of the fires. However, nothing was said about the actual reasons for the fire, and the officials refrained from any kind of criticism of Indonesia. Rather, the fires were attributed to unusual heat and dryness in Indonesia.

Singapore's careful information policy vis-à-vis Indonesia changed when the haze reached new peak levels in late September. Whereas the Singaporean government still refrained from public criticism, it orchestrated a media campaign clearly exposing the Indonesian government's inaction with respect to punitive, preventive and fire fighting measures:

> On Sept 30, The Straits Times ran, in full colour, a series of satellite pictures which showed clearly that Indonesia's forest fires were no accident or act of nature. The photographs had an immediate impact. [...] people were getting fed-up with Indonesian double-speak. [...] But still, neither the Haze Task Force nor any Singapore minister had said anything publicly on the subject.[321]

From the end of September on, government-affiliated representatives of Singapore became unusuailly vocal in their public and publicized criticism of Indonesia,[322] such as Simon Tay, who claimed that there had to be limits to

---

[319] On Singapore's haze information policy in the running-up to the crisis, cf. Nathan (1997): "Diary of Disaster: People kept in the haze for too long", *The Straits Times Interactive* Haze News, Singapore, 12 October. The text is a heavily tinted report trying to depict Singapore as a faithful adherent to, and victim of, ASEAN's non-interference policy, but the essential facts appear to be reliable.

[320] Ibid.

[321] Ibid.

[322] Cf. Hiebert and McBeth (1997).

ASEAN's norm of non-interference and that Indonesia had to be held responsible for the fires, not only in a moral, but also in a legal sense.[323] The protests were clearly part of a public relations offensive orchestrated by the government. Thus, Dominic Nathan, writing in *The Straits Times*, merely spelt out Singapore's new, more proactive haze information policy when he "demanded" (or announced, rather):

> The "Asean way" of holding discreet behind-the-scenes discussions, while keeping the Asean public in the dark, may work in sorting out political, trade or diplomatic kinks. But it does not work out when it comes to a disaster like the haze [...] The way this year's haze was handled, both by Indonesia and its neighbours, suggests strongly that the next time [...] officials should come out in the open and warn the entire region [...].[324]

It is evident that the relations between Singapore and Indonesia throughout the crisis were anything but harmonious or friendly. Descriptions such as Robin Ramcharan's summary of the events therefore have to be dismissed as misleading:

> The Singapore Government [...] raised the [haze] issue in the time-honoured ASEAN way, through quiet diplomacy with Jakarta. President Soeharto took the unprecedented step of apologizing for the haze and instructed his bureaucracy to co-operate with his ASEAN partners in combating the forest fires. Singapore offered to provided technical assistance [...][325]

Rather, when the going got tough and quiet diplomacy alone proved to be insufficient, the Singaporean government apparently needed a lever to make Indonesia listen. Thus, it orchestrated public criticism, whereas officially it remained silent and carried on behind-the-scenes diplomacy with Indonesia.

Malaysia's reaction in 1997 The Malaysian government certainly felt the heat of the haze most, with the capital, Kuala Lumpur, being permanently clouded and the state of Sarawak on Borneo being exposed to extremely high pollution unequalled anywhere else in the region. Thus, on the one hand, the government had a great interest in ending the haze and moving Indonesia to act accordingly. On the other hand, however, the Malaysian leadership for various reasons had an interest in quelling reports on the origin and the actual extent of the haze: firstly, a number of companies involved in slash and burn activities in Indonesia

---

[323] Cf. Tay (1997); Tay (1998); Nathan (1997).
[324] Nathan (1997).
[325] Ramcharan (2000): 70.

were Malaysian-owned, so that business interests stood in the way of the political will to urge Indonesia to identify the culprits;[326] secondly, Malaysia itself faced some problems in enforcing the fire ban within its own territory on Borneo; thirdly, Malaysia tried to divert international attention from the environmental disaster so as to prevent further damages to the tourism industry. Therefore, Malaysia, as in the previous and following years, quelled the distribution of information on the haze throughout much of the crisis.[327] James Cotton reports

> that in November 1997 the [...] Education Minister [...] banned academics from making comments on the haze on the grounds that it tarnished the nations's image abroad. In April 1998 the Information Minister [...] admonished a local television station for using the term 'haze,' rather than reporting what it should have described as 'low-cloud, dew and smoke.'[328]

Very likely, Malaysia's restrictive information policy was also guided by ASEAN's non-interference policy. However, there were incidences when the government publicly signaled or expressed impatience with the Indonesian partner.[329]

The Malaysian government, unlike the government of Singapore, did not incite or orchestrate a media campaign against Indonesia. Rather, "[t]he Malaysian government's reaction to the media coverage was characteristic: it decided to stop academics from painting a gloomy picture of the smog disaster."[330] But the media apparently disregarded the government's restrictive information policy:

---

[326]Cp. Mallet (1999): 174; Aditjondro (2000).

[327] In 1999, Malaysia adopted the same policy again: [...] Malaysia, which, instead of preparing and protecting residents from this year's [haze] episode, opted to stop publicizing air pollution readings for fear of losing precious tourism revenue. Malaysia's environment minister Law Hieng Ding defended the move, saying the government will no longer give full pollution readings to avoid causing 'unnecessary alarm' among the public. [...] Malaysian studies about the effects of the 1997 haze, along with a World Health Organization (WHO) report compiled in 1998, also have not been published, news reports say" (Gan 1999).

[328] Cotton (1999): 347f.

[329] Thus, reportedly, the Malayisan environment minister urged Indonesia publicly to become more proactive in containing the haze in late September. Also, on 18 September (two days after the first public apology by President Suharto), Malaysia's Prime Minister Mahathir theatrically donned a haze mask during a television appearance, a gesture clearly designed to accommodate the general public, which was outraged at Indonesia's inaction. But the gesture was apparently not accompanied by verbal criticism of Indonesia (cp. Nathan 1997).

[330] Mallet (1999): 176.

In a move heavily criticized by the opposition, Malaysia took the step of forbidding scientists to comment on the "haze" problem. However, newspapers remained critical of Indonesia.[331]

Thus, in the face of the population's frustration with the continued heavy haze, the government apparently passively endured rather than actively encouraged media criticism of Indonesia.[332]

ASEAN's reaction through 1997   At the ASEAN level, the relevant ASEAN governments approached the Indonesian government to seek for regional solutions (rather than to insist on an exclusively national approach) to contain the fires and prevent future haze. However, initial concessions from Indonesia turned out to be tactical manouvers rather than longer-term commitments. Thus, in early October, the *Far Eastern Economic Review* had still commended Indonesia for its cooperative behavior and conjured up a picture of harmonious and solidary ASEAN cooperation:

> Asean's management of the smog crisis reflects the grouping's gospel of regional self-reliance. Malaysia has pledged to dispatch 400 firefighters to Sumatra and Kalimantan. Singapore is contributing satellite data. Even Thailand, which is not directly affected by the smoke, is sending two fire-fighting planes. Indonesia and Malaysia will coordinate cloud-seeding operations. In taking the lead, Indonesia is moving with unusual transparency. The environment and forestry ministers are publicizing the names of suspected companies and putting out 30-second TV spots slamming corporate irresponsibility. Provincial governors and regents were warned that their efforts to enforce the ban on burning will be reported directly to the president.[333]

Only two weeks later, the same magazine reported on the outrage throughout the societies and governments of Malaysia and Singapore about Indonesia's continued inaction.[334] Indeed, Indonesia not only failed to contain the fires in

---

[331] Smith (1999): 259.

[332] Likewise, during the haze of 2000, the usually government-controlled media bowed to public sentiment
and disregarded the government's information policy directives: Whereas the Malaysian government had imposed a "ban on the domestic media to publish air pollution readings, after Kuala Lumpur had been blanketed with dense haze from forest fires across the Malacca Strait[,] [t]he Malaysian public [...] refused to play that ostrich policy, forcing the New Straits Times, which usually supports the government initiatives unreservedly, to call for the government to publish the Air Pollution Index readings" (Aditjondro 2000).

[333] Cohen; Hiebert (1997): 29.

[334] Cf. Hiebert and McBeth (1997); cp. also Smith (1999): 245.

1997, but failed to implement any action and preventive measures in the years to come.

At the ASEAN summit in December 1997, Malaysia and Indonesia signed a memorandum of understanding for collaboration concerning the haze problem, and ASEAN Environment Ministers adopted the Regional Haze Action Plan (RHAP). The plan defined ASEAN members' roles in haze prevention and fire fighting activities and obliged especially Indonesia to draw up a national plan to significantly enhance its fire prevention and fire fighting capabilities. Progress of these national plans was to be reviewed in March 1998.[335] By the time the review of the progress of the RHAP was due, it had become clear that, while sliding into severe economic and social turmoil in the course of the crisis, "[t]he Indonesian regime ha[d] been unwilling or unable to put the interest of the neighborhood ahead of those of its closest associates."[336]

Realizing that Indonesia could not be moved to comply with the objectives of the RHAP, the ASEAN Ministerial Meeting delegated the problem to the United Nations Environmental Program (UNEP) by asking it to "continue to play a leading role in coordinating international assistance to combat and control regional fire and haze *on behalf of ASEAN* [emphasis added, M.H.].[337]

Thus, ASEAN – as an organization – acted in accordance with the classic ASEAN norms, namely: a) acting only where there is a general consensus; b) avoiding to raise controversial bilateral issues at the ASEAN level; c) respecting the principle of non-interference in a country's internal affairs.

Developments since 1998   The governments of Singapore and Malaysia have officially remained relatively silent on the haze issue ever since 1998. There has been no public posturing vis-à-vis Indonesia. Following the unsuccessful ASEAN Ministerial Meeting in April 1998, especially Singapore unilaterally stepped up its haze information policy by widely publicizing detailed satellite imagery and distributing information to NGOs. Cotton interprets this as "orchestration of NGO and interest group pressure on Indonesia" and thus as "an implicit departure from the ASEAN policy of refraining from intervening in the internal affairs of member states."[338] Indeed, ASEAN even launched its own official haze watch website in 1999 (with an extremely prominent link on the official ASEAN homepage[339]). However, in the course of the Asian economic

---

[335] ASEAN Regional Haze Action Plan, December 1997.

[336] Cotton (1999): 331.

Indonesia never implemented any effective measures to stop companies from burning forests. As a correspondent of the *Christian Science Monitor* reported in 1999, "Indonesia's current environmental laws have still many loopholes, and ministerial and local government directives banning burning have not [been] held up in court. In three years Indonesia has managed to prosecute just two of the many firms suspected of starting these forest fires. Both firms are seeking presidential pardons." (Brandon 1999)

[337] Joint Press Statement, 3rd ASEAN Ministerial Meeting on Haze, 4 April 1998.

crisis and Indonesia's multifold political turmoil, the haze issue has been put on the diplomatic backburner, both in terms of public attention and ASEAN priorities. ASEAN, in cooperation with UNEP, has continued to address and institutionalize consultation on the issue. Although the region is still regularly exposed to, and troubled by, the haze (though never again to the extent experienced in 1997), ASEAN governments have avoided destabilizing the Indonesian government further. For example, during the haze in 2000, ASEAN governments reportedly adopted a hear no evil, see no evil 'ostrich' policy:

> While in late July 2000, the smog from Indonesia's forest fires had drifted along the Malay Peninsula into southern Thailand, ASEAN government leaders did not offer any concrete steps to ameliorate the catastrophic Indonesian forest fires. On the contrary, Malaysian Prime Minister Mahathir Mohamad strongly refused to take any steps. The ten-nation ASEAN foreign ministers' summit in Bangkok also failed to address the transnational haze strongly in its final communique. Mahathir Mohamad[,] in particular, even criticised the international problem press for 'exaggerating' the haze problem.[340]

In typical ASEAN fashion, ASEAN members have engaged in a slow process of consultations. Though the process did not yield any tangible results through 1999 and 2000, it has remained on ASEAN's agenda and has made steady (if slow) progress. In April 2001, *The Straits Times* reported that

> Environment ministers from Malaysia and Singapore said here on Friday that they hope a cross-border agreement on preventing haze pollution in South-east Asia could be concluded before the year's end.[341]

---

[338] Cotton (1999): 349. Cotton also claims that Malaysia likewise engaged in a publicity campaign to influence Indonesia's handling of the issue. However, whereas Cotton provides evidence of Singapore distributing information, he fails to give any examples for Malaysia. Since research conducted in the course of this study has not resulted in any further evidence, the statement on Malaysia's information policy does not seem convincing.

[339] Official ASEAN homepage: http://www.aseansec.org.

[340] Aditjondro (2001).
Aditjondro explains ASEAN members' "lukewarm response" to the haze with concrete business interests of countries such as Malaysia and Singapore in Indonesia-based logging and palm oil companies. However, this explanation fails to take into account the strong security implications of Indonesia for the stability of Southeast Asia. In the face of the reverberations of the East Timor crisis and the current crisis in Aceh, ASEAN members must be interested in stabilizing rather than destabilizing the political and economic situation of Indonesia.

[341] *The Straits Times* (07 April 2001): "Ministers close to haze pact". On ASEAN's and UNEP's continued efforts to finalize a haze "action plan to build fire fighting capability in the region [...], including an early warning mechanism" and Indonesia's growing willingness to take legal action against companies engaged in illegal burning activities, see also: UNEP (19 March 2001): "Haze Negotiations Begin Today".

Summary: The haze crisis of 1997 hit the region as ASEAN countries slid into the Asian economic crisis. Indonesia's inflexibility and inaction therefore presented a double challenge to its neighbors: The haze not only caused high social and economic costs, but also threatened to discredit ASEAN's image as a unified and effective political entity. The high fallout of the haze crisis caused strong irritations between the Indonesian government on the one hand and the governments of countries affected by the haze on the other. Nevertheless, Singapore alone broke the ASEAN code of conduct by waging a media campaign to step up public pressure on the Indonesian government so as to move it to conform to Singapore's (and other ASEAN members') expectations. All the other governments refrained largely from provocative public action vis-à-vis Indonesia. Notably the Malaysian government suppressed rather than encouraged public reports on the haze. However, behind the scenes, all ASEAN governments engaged in (more or less) quiet diplomacy so as to move Indonesia to take effective action to contain actual and future fires. This attempt largely failed, since Indonesia made only symbolical gestures and tactical concessions lacking sincerity, substance and permanence.

As the hastily arranged Regional Haze Action Plan of December 1997 – due to Indonesia's failure to adopt and implement a national haze prevention action plan – failed to show any results by April 1998, ASEAN multilateralized consultations on haze prevention by transferring overall reponsibility for the issue to UNEP. As Indonesia's internal instability has been threatening regional security, all ASEAN governments – individually and collectively – have refrained from public posturing or exerting immoderate public pressure on Indonesia in recent years with respect to the haze issue. Quiet, behind-the-scenes diplomacy is the order of the day. The ASEAN principles of consultation, consensus and non-interference apply.

Evaluation: The case of the haze crisis allows to apply the model of the *need situation* (see section 2) to assess the Singaporean and Malaysian governments' solidarity : Did Singapore and Malaysia support Indonesia adequatley in times of need? Indonesia's solidarity can be measured according to the *mishap situation* (section 2). The question to be put is: Did Indonesia make sufficient amends for its failure to impose the ASEAN fire ban of 1995?

Certainly, Singapore and Malaysia offered technical and financial help, and especially Singapore would have been ready to invest substantially in preventive and fire fighting measures. However, it was not material resources Indonesia expected from its neighbors. What Indonesia could expect (and did expect) was its fellow ASEAN members' compliance with the norms and conventions of ASEAN cooperation, i.e. political sensitivity, quiet diplomacy, refraining from public posturing and non-interference. On the other hand,

Indonesia could not have expected other ASEAN members to permanently accept disadvantages and give up essential national interests, since this did not agree with ASEAN principles, either.

Singapore   Singapore in 1997 considerably stretched the limits of the ASEAN norms of non-interference and quiet diplomacy by orchestrating a media camapaign against Indonesia. On the other hand, the Singaporean government adopted a policy of official acquiescence on the haze issue, thereby signaling that ASEAN norms were generally still applied and valued. The Singaporean government's behavior emerges from the perception of an existential threat to regional and national stability. Thus, Singapore's partial failure to cater to the political "needs" of Indonesia (namely to be exempted from public criticism and external pressure) corresponds with Singapore's fear of diminishing political returns from ASEAN and the diminishing value of ASEAN's collectively produced good (political stability and mutual benefit). It is clearly not motivated by myopic opportunism or an egotistic interest in securing short term benefits at the cost of ASEAN neighbors. Nevertheless, it represents a partial breach of solidarity. Thus, in absolute terms, Singapore's behavior in the particular context of the events of 1997 has to be classified as ranging between "deficient" and "low". Overall, the events of 1997 mark Singapore's relative solidarity as "unstable" (but clearly not "defunct").

Malaysia   Despite the high economic and political costs the haze incurred to Malaysia, the government avoided public criticism and engaged in behind-the-scenes diplomacy. Malaysia apparently criticized Indonesia vocally in internal ASEAN talks, but overall it remained silent on the issue in pulic and even attempted to quell public criticism. There were only a few instances where government representatives showed impatience about Indonesia's inaction. Admittedly, the government had a strong direct self-interest in suppressing haze publicity, which is why the government's behavior cannot be entirely attributed to solidarity. Nevertheless, the Malayisan government's absolute solidarity performance was "high" in 1997, and so was its degree of relative solidarity.

Indonesia   While Indonesia counted on other ASEAN members' solidarity, Indonesia's own solidarity with the haze-struck countries of the region was at an all-time low. Initially, not even relational signaling worked, since Indonesia for a long time denied any regional obligations and considered the issue to be an exclusively internal matter. Once relational signaling was applied, it didn't work, since the token excuse for the impact of the fires on the region was not followed up by credible and solid haze containment action. Overall, Indonesia's handling of the haze crisis showed no commitment to regional action. Regional guidelines such as the fire ban were implemeted only half-heartedly. Business interests ranged higher than neighbor countries' interests on the Indonesian government's scale of priority. Therefore, Indonesia's absolute solidarity performance in 1997 and after was "low", and relative solidarity must be labeled "defunct".

ASEAN (overall)   Although no special emphasis has been put on other ASEAN members in this study, there is no evidence of unsolidary behavior vis-à-vis Indonesia in the crisis of 1997. In Thailand and the Philippines, public outrage was high, but public criticism was attributable to more freedom of the press and freedom of opinion in these countries rather than government orchestration. The governments only raised the issue at the intra-ASEAN level, but did not embarrass Indonesia publicly. The haze was discussed at ASEAN level, and the Regional Haze Action Plan adopted. However, ASEAN refrained from publicly embarassing Indonesia, and when Indonesia failed to implement the RHAP nationally, ASEAN reacted by transferring haze response negotiations to UNEP in order to de-emphasize internal controversies. Thus, absolute solidarity was "high", as was relative solidarity.

Singapore, Malaysia, Indonesia and ASEAN since 1998   Throughout Indonesia's several internal crises since 1998, ASEAN, and along with it Singapore, de-emphasized the haze issue in order not to destabilize the country further. While most countries in the region recovered gradually from the crisis and did not themselves face existential crises, Indonesia's stability continued to deteriorate economically and politically. These circumstances were fertile ground for solidary behavior in ASEAN. To ASEAN members, refraining from criticizing Indonesia was essential in order to secure regional stability and security (the *raison d'être* of ASEAN, and thus a highly valued collective good). By multilateralizing the haze issue, ASEAN has prevented it from featuring too prominently on the ASEAN agenda.

Thus, ASEAN's (including Singapore's and Malaysia's) level of absolute solidarity since 1998 has been "high". However, if one considers that the degree of Singapore's absolute solidarity only improved as external conditions became conducive to solidarity, Singapore's relative solidarity remained "unstable". On the other hand, relative solidarity levels of Malaysia and the other ASEAN members remained "high".

Although the Indonesian government still hasn't implemented new major haze policies, there is evidence that Indonesia has shown more readiness recently to cooperate with the region and to make more substantial concessions with respect to national and regional fire pevention and fighting efforts. Apparently, an ASEAN/UNEP haze action framework is in the pipeline at present. Absolute solidarity is still "deficient" to "low". Thus, Indonesia's relative solidarity has improved from "defunct" to "unstable".

Table 11: Solidarity levels in the haze crisis of 1997/1998

	Absolute solidarity	Relative Solidarity
Singapore	deficient to low	unstable
Malaysia	high	high
ASEAN (overall)	high	high
Indonesia	low	defunct

Table 12: Solidarity levels with respect to the haze issue since 1998

	Absolute solidarity	Relative solidarity
Singapore	high	unstable
Malaysia	high	high
ASEAN (overall)	high	high
Indonesia	deficient to low	unstable

3.2. The South China Sea dispute: ASEAN's shifting position vis-à-vis China   (1992-2001)

The situation: In the early 1990s, ASEAN faced a shake-up of the East Asian regional environment, with China emerging as a potential regional hegemon and economic competitor to ASEAN. ASEAN's position vis-à-vis China was ambiguously torn between fear of China and, on the other hand, the wish not to antagonize, but to constructively engage the big neighbor.[342] There was a sense in ASEAN that the organization needed a coherent stance vis-à-vis China in order to be able to deal with it effectively.

Internally, the shared sense of being exposed to an insecure regional environment gave new impetus to ASEAN's coherence. Providing regional stability so as to flank the strong economic growth rates ASEAN members experienced in the 1990s was regarded as a high collective good that only ASEAN could provide. The external conditions for strong solidarity were thus relatively good through the mid-1990s to 1997.

---

[342] Thus, ASEAN aimed at integrating China into various forms of regional bilateral and multilateral cooperation, such as in APEC (1992), the ASEAN Post Ministerial Meetings, the ARF (1994) and ASEM (1996). Thailand had traditionally good ties to mainland China; Malaysia since 1992 engaged in the development of good economic and political relations with the PRC and promoted the idea of an East Asian Economic Caucus for the purpose of stronger intra-regional economic cooperation; Singapore did not give up its good relations with Taiwan, but embraced a policy of developing good economic and diplomatic relations with the PRC as well; even Indonesia reversed course and gave up its strict antagonism to China.

After ASEAN cooperation had peaked in 1997, the economic crisis of 1997/8 shook the region, and as external conditions deteriorated dramatically and put strains on ASEAN relations, the seedbed for solidarity eroded the longer the crisis lasted.

As the crisis had enhanced awareness of the high degree of interdependence among ASEAN nations, and as most ASEAN countries slowly emerged from the crisis in 1999 and 2000, the *external* conditions for ASEAN coherence and solidarity improved again.

Towards the end of 2000, growth rates throughout the region started to drop again sharply due to the stalling U.S. economy, especially in Singapore and Malaysia, but also in Thailand and the Philippines.

Political stability in the region was relatively high in 1999, but 2000 and 2001 saw several discontinuities: Prime Minister Mahathir's firm political grip on the country has threatened to slip ever since 2000, a development which led to the stronger repression of oppositional forces in Malaysia; Thailand saw a landmark change of government with wide-ranging implications for the country's domestic politics and external relations in early 2001. In 2000, the Philippines faced the resurgence of strong guerilla activity, whereas early 2001 also saw the coup-like overthrow of President Estrada.

Overall, after a phase of relative stability in 1999, the major countries in the region experienced more destabilizing economic and political turmoil. This caused ASEAN members to be more self-centered and preoccupied with national interests. Thus, the external circumstances of ASEAN cooperation suggest that the potential for solidary behavior improved temporarily through 1999 and dropped again between mid-to late 2000 and 2001.

The problem: In the early 1990s, China emerged as a major claimant to maritime territories in the South China Sea. Whereas Brunei, Indonesia, Malaysia, the Philippines and Vietnam each held separate and often competing claims to the waters surrounding particular shorelines, islands and reefs, "China's claims in the South China Sea encompass[ed] [...] the entire body of waters and all its islands."[343] To underline its claims, China passed official legislation in 1992 and presented a map marking wide areas in the South China Sea as Chinese territory during a South China Sea workshop organized by Indonesia in 1993.[344]

This new assertiveness disquietened all ASEAN member states (though to varying degrees), as they feared that the projection of Chinese military power into the South China Sea would imperil free access to vital shipping lanes and

---

[343] Liow (2000): 686.
[344] Umbach (2000): 176f.

disrupt the balance of power in the region. ASEAN members thus had a certain shared interest in containing the PRC's expansionism.

Apart from their geo-strategic implications and questions of national sovereignty, China's wide-ranging claims also posed a very concrete threat to the economic interests of various Southeast Asian claimant states, since the South China Sea is supposed to harbor large natural gas and oil reserves.

In terms of territorial dispute, all Southeast Asian claimants have felt the heat of China's ambitions, although the claims of the Philippines and Vietnam have been especially exposed to incidences of Chinese covetousness in the second half of the 1990s. Notably the Philippines lacks the military capacity to protect its possessions in the Spratlys effectively. Thus, it is not surprising that ever since 1995, when China started to engage the Philippines by way of an assertive "fishing boat" diplomacy, the Philippines has been soliciting collective support from fellow ASEAN members.[345] Vietnam has also sought ASEAN backing for its claims, both in the Spratlys and the Paracels.

The essential question to be asked with regard to ASEAN solidarity is whether the following motives – (a) a shared threat perception vis-à-vis China, (b) a shared interest in containing China's expansionism in the South China Sea, and (c) complying with the ASEAN norm of backing the "front-line state" (in this case the Philippines, and Vietnam, respectively, vis-à-vis China) – offered sufficient cause to draw a unified ASEAN response to the problem. The analysis focuses on the development of ASEAN's and ASEAN members' handling of the situation from 1992 through mid-2001.

The reaction:

ASEAN 1992-1996   After China had passed a new law "declaring [...] almost all territories of the South China Sea to be within its sovereign waters" on 25 February 1992, ASEAN, in an unprecedented move, took a common stance and responded in July by passing the Manila Declaration on the South China Sea, which urged "the peaceful settlement of disputed territorial claims and the need to cooperate in order to ensure the safety of maritime navigation and communication".[346] Faced with a unified ASEAN position, China apparently felt compelled to accede to the declaration for tactical reasons.[347] ASEAN at this time also began backing Vietnam in its maritime territorial disputes with China. However, despite further signs of Chinese expansionism, ASEAN's unity

---

[345] This situation continues to today. Cp. chapter on the Philippines, in: Baker, McNally and Morrison (eds.) (2001): 135.

As Thayer reports, President Arroyo of the Philippines "characterized the South China Sea dispute as the 'number one threat to security of the region'", a statement that shows how serious the issue features for the Philippines (cf. Thayer 2001a).

[346] Umbach (2000): 176f.

[347] Cf. Tasker (1995): 15.

swayed. Non-claimant states Thailand and Singapore, but also Malaysia, were careful not to provoke China unnecessarily, which is why ASEAN, as a group, was hesitant to push China to multilateralize talks on the South China Sea. Thus, the *Far Eastern Economic Review* in August 1994 featured an article stating that

> In the past two years, Vietnam has found support within Asean for its efforts to contain China's ambitions in the South China Sea by presenting a common Southeast Asian front. [...] But in the face of China's refusal to discuss the legal issues or to engage in multilateral negotiations, that common front now appears to be fraying.[348]

In 1994, Indonesia, which had organized track-two South China Sea workshops with ASEAN members and China since 1990, launched an initiative to mutlilateralize the South China Sea issue by trying to get ASEAN behind Indonesia's proposed "doughnut formula" as a common basis for negotiations with China.[349] The attempt failed due to ASEAN members' apparent reluctance to provoke China:

> [...] a senior Indonesian diplomat, Hashim Jalal, had visited Asean countries in May and June to rally support for the proposal. [Indonesia's Foreign Minister] Alatas confirmed [...] the idea [...]. Asked the kind of reception the idea had received, he said that "everybody is sort of wary" because they don't want to be dragged into the bilateral territorial disputes pitting China against Vietnam, Malaysia and the Philippines.[350]

Especially Malaysia from early on opposed Indonesian efforts at multilateralizing negotiations:

> A senior Asean official familiar with Malaysian thinking suggested that Indonesia may be trying to contain China through multilateral means because it has few other options to ensure security. [...] Malaysia, on the other hand, can strengthen cooperative relations with Beijing by offering significant amounts of trade and investment, he said. That's part of the

---

[348] Chanda (1994): 18.

[349] The "doughnut formula" was a design attributing sovereignty over all maritime territories lying within the coastal zone (320 nautical miles off the shore) of a country to that country. Due to the oval-shaped rim of the South China Sea, this implied that "[o]nly the hole in the doughnut – the middle of [the] South China Sea, including the main islands of the disputed Spratlys chain [and parts of the Paracel Islands, M.H.] – would be discussed by competing claimants as an area for potential joint economic development" (Chanda:1994). The proposed formula would have significantly reduced the potential of the Chinese claims.

[350] Chanda (1994).

reason Malaysia has rejected Indonesia's "doughnut formula", the official said.[351]

ASEAN unity only re-emerged and was strengthened considerably when the Philippines turned to ASEAN for support after China had erected sheds and hoisted the Chinese flag on Mischief Reef on 8 February 1995: "The Ramos government wanted a statement from ASEAN censuring China's behaviour and supporting the Philippine position on the issue."[352] Vietnam – whose accesssion to ASEAN was imminent – was the only Southeast Asian country to instantly support the Philippines' position,[353] whereas the non-claimant ASEAN members, Singapore and Thailand, inofficially held the view that the Ramos government had overreacted and was trying to utilize ASEAN for domestic purposes. Nevertheless, the Mischief Reef incident hit a sensitive nerve with ASEAN members:

> Although ASEAN critics felt President Ramos had overreacted to the Chinese occupation of Mischief Reef, perhaps for domestic political reasons, discussions in Manila showed genuine surprise and dismay over the incident. [...] The sense of shock was accentuated by the feeling of military impotence.[354]

Thus, on 18 March, about 6 weeks after the Mischief Reef incident, the ASEAN Foreign Ministers came out with a joint statement and started forging a common position:

> Indonesia and Vietnam were soon followed by Malaysia, and the others [i.e. the other ASEAN members, M.H.], including Singapore, closed ranks behind the Philippines so that by the time of the annual dialogue in May [1995], ASEAN had a common position to discuss with China.[355]

In a rare case of ASEAN unity, the organization confronted China collectively in a specially arranged Senior Officials Meeting during the first ASEAN-China Forum in Hangzhou in April 1995. Thus, Storey remarks that

---

[351] Ibid.

[352] Storey (1999): 107.

[353] Tasker (1995) commented: "Vietnam publicly backed Manila's protest, despite occupying islands in the same area, some of which have been reinforced recently. The Vietnamese have been China's most vocal critics over the Spratlys issue [...]".

[354] Whiting (1997): 315.

[355] Hernandez (1996): 149.

The fact that Singapore backed the Philippines' position is all the more remarkable since relations between the countries had been strained at the time over the execution of a Philippine citizen who had been handed down a sentence of capital punishment in Singapore.

[...] the occupation of Mischief Reef elicited a strong diplomatic reaction from ASEAN, an indication of the group's growing concern over China's increasingly assertive behaviour. Given the differing perceptions of the PRC among the ASEAN countries, and the fact that not all its members are claimants in the South China Sea dispute, China probably did not expect such a strong rebuke. It shows that although ASEAN did not have a cohesive policy towards China, it came together on an issue considered important to regional stability.[356]

In deference to ASEAN's unified stance, China, in a tactical move, retreated from Mischief Reef and – for the moment being – accepted a diplomatic draw with the Philippines. Thus, China "offered bilateral use and development of the reef area and agreed with the Philippines on a 'code of conduct' that rejected the use of force to settle disputes."[357]

By December 1995, fine cracks started to show in ASEAN's unified position, with the Philippines and Vietnam assertively pitted against reluctant Malaysia and Thailand:

Asean members still find it hard to agree on how to deal with China. The Philippines and Vietnam want to press Beijing over its claims in the South China Sea. But Thailand and Malaysia seem to favour a gentler, more accommodating approach. [...] Indonesia has taken the middle path, trying to galvanize Asean on the issue while assuaging Chinese fears.[358]

Nevertheless, at the second ASEAN-China Forum in Bukittingi (Indonesia) in June 1996, ASEAN – on the initiative of the Philippines and Vietnam – again approached the PRC collectively – after the PRC's National People's Congress had reiterated China's claim to the Spratlys in May, even topping former claims by defining the Paracel Islands (claimed by Vietnam) as Chinese territory.[359] Facing a unified ASEAN, China made "tactical concessions in bilateral and multilateral exchanges",[360] i.e. ASEAN's initiative caused China to significantly engage in, and step up, dialogue at various levels. Thus, deviating from its prior course, China even addressed the South China Sea issue at an ARF conference in June 1996.

ASEAN 1996-1998 Whereas ASEAN's unity peaked in 1995 and reverberated recognizably in 1996, this period also marked a turning point towards stronger

---

[356] Storey (1999): 113.
[357] Valencia (2001).
[358] Vatikiotis and Tasker (1995): 17.
[359] Cf. Whiting (1997): 317 and Storey (1999): 108f.
[360] Whiting (1997): 320f.

disintegration of ASEAN's position. Thus, Malaysia had started shifting away from, and subverting, ASEAN solidarity by late 1995. By early 1997 (still before the crisis), ASEAN's South China Sea solidarity had become visibly fragile. Thus, Vietnam had asked for ASEAN support after China had begun oil-drilling operations in waters claimed by Vietnam on 7 March 1997. As the Thai newspaper *The Nation* reported,

> Vietnam had called on all Hanoi-based [...] Asean [...] ambassadors last week to be briefed over the dispute [...]. The meeting was seen by many observers and diplomats as a tactical move by Hanoi to put Asean solidarity to the test.[361]

But ASEAN members – especially the non-claimant states – initially were slow to react:

> While diplomats in Bangkok and Singapore played down the issue, the Philippines' embassy in Hanoi issued a statement saying that China's actions 'posed a threat to the security of the region.'[362]

Interestingly, only the Philippines, which itself had to rely on ASEAN in the Spratlys question, responded with spontaneous and vocal support for Vietnam. Also significantly, Thailand, a non-claimant state with considerably low concerns about China's assertiveness and with a strong interest in sustaining its traditionally good relations with the PRC, did nothing to support Vietnam:

> Prime Minister Chavalit Yongchaiyudh yesterday refused to support Vietnam's position in its ongoing dispute with China over drilling in disputed territorial waters, saying Bangkok is not in a position to comment. "[...] Both countries are our friends and I don't think it will be difficult to make them understand this," said Chavalit [...]. So far, only one ASEAN country, the Philippines, has publicly called on China to stop drilling.[363]

ASEAN members nevertheless got their act together eventually, since, according to Umbach, they considered the case as "yet another litmus test which forced them to react." As Umbach shows, ASEAN's collective stance – once more – made an impression on China: "Finally, the repeated calls on China to withdraw the oil exploration vessel mounted in a diplomatic defeat for Beijing [...]." However, Umbach also points out that ASEAN's collective support for Vietnam was not as genuine as ASEAN diplomats claimed it was. Rather, "the

[361] Pathan (1997).
[362] Vatikiotis and Hiebert (1997): 15.
[363] Pathan (1997).

incident underlined the fragility of the 'constructive engagement' policy of the ASEAN states towards China [...]."[364]

Once the Asian economic crisis had struck, ASEAN's unity on the South China Sea issue crumbled to an all-time low. National economic needs and interests dominated the scene, and good relations with China had priority for many Southeast Asian countries. Thus, when the Philippine government discovered China had erected military structures on Mischief Reef in late 1998, it again turned to ASEAN for support, albeit without great success. Reportedly, ASEAN "officials said that ASEAN wanted to register its concern to Beijing without upsetting cooperation in other areas, including measures to help the region recover from the financial contagion."[365] Thus, China could get away with the provocative occupation of Mischief Reef, which contravened the ASEAN Declaration on the South China Sea of 1992 and the ASEAN-mediated bilateral Sino-Philippine code of conduct. This represented a major flaw of ASEAN's South China Sea policy.

> China's maritime construction project [on Mischief Reef, M.H.] shows how much the balance of power has tipped in its favour since the onset of the region's economic crisis, which has sapped the strength and unity of the Association of Southeast Asian Nations. Since 1992, a chorus of complaints has checked Chinese aggressiveness in the Spratlys. But at their December 15-16 summit in Hanoi [1998], Asean leaders largely avoided the issue. "We have bigger problems to deal with, particularly the economy," Asean Secretary-General Rodolfo Severino told the Review [i.e. the *Far Eastern Economic Review*, M.H.], explaining that the meeting's final communique would contain only a veiled reference to the South China Sea.[366]

Lee Lai To confirms that "most, if not all" ASEAN foreign ministers meeting in 1998 attributed very low priority to the Philippines' Mischief Reef calamities with China, and only marginally and "somewhat dutifully" noted the situation in the South China Sea in their communiqué.[367] Given the disastrous circumstances of the economic crisis, Singapore and Thailand, unlike in 1995, were no longer ready to unanimously support a strong unified ASEAN stance on the issue. Malaysia's interest in, and support for, multilateral approaches to the South China Sea issue had already waned by the end of 1995; considering

---

[364] Umbach (2000): 179.

[365] Richardson (1998).

[366] *Far Eastern Economic Review* (24 December 1998): "'Tis the Season".

Cossa (1998) similarly concludes that "Unlike 1995, when a strong statement was issued by ASEAN [...], this time ASEAN has chosen to bury its head in the sand", and even speaks of ASEAN betraying the Philippines. Cp. also Richardson (1998).

[367] Lee Lai To (1999a): 49f.

further that relations between Prime Minister Mahathir and President Estrada had deteriorated dramatically over the imprisonment and physical abuse of former Malayisian Deputy Prime Minister Anwar Ibrahim in 1998, it is obvious that Malaysia had little incentive to support the Philippines. Finally, Indonesia was in dire straits economically and politically in 1998 and certainly had more urgent problems at its hands than to think about ASEAN unity and engage in political controversies with China. An observer described ASEAN's reaction to the second Mischief Reef incident of 1998 in the following terms:

> The RP [Rep. of the Philippines, M.H.] made a late effort during last December's ASEAN meeting in Hanoi to try and build a consensus to again confront China, as it had in 1995, over China's unilateralism on Mischief Reef. This time the attempt failed. ASEAN was and remains preoccupied with economic crises and the disintegration of Indonesia. [...] ASEAN, as a body, was [therefore] unwilling to multilateralize the RP's outrage toward China. [...] Since that time there has been a sense that ASEAN muffed an opportunity to confront China. [...] In any event, if it [i.e. the 1998 summit, M.H.] was a test [of ASEAN's solidarity, M.H.], it failed![368]

ASEAN 1999 The events of 1999 suggest that despite ASEAN's failure to take a collective stance in 1998, ASEAN had not given up on the idea of a collective approach. Nevertheless, throughout much of 1999, ASEAN's South China Sea consultations were dominated by internal polarization and political struggle. Three contending parties – the Philippines, Malaysia and Vietnam – held conflicting views:

Following a renewed Chinese-Philippine diplomatic spat over Scarborough Shoal in June 1999, the Philippines wanted ASEAN to collectively press China to accept multilateral talks on an ASEAN Code of Conduct for the South China Sea. The code of conduct was basically aimed both at condemning unilateral occupation and fortification of areas in the South China Sea and at multilateralizing the South China Sea dialogue. Apparently, the idea met with general approval from the ASEAN members, with the exception of Malaysia. In contrast to Malaysia, Vietnam backed the idea of a code of conduct, but insisted on the inclusion of the Paracel Islands (a group of islands way north of the Spratlys, occupied by China and claimed solely by Vietnam).[369]

---

[368] McDevitt (1999).

[369] The Paracels have a special significance to both China and Vietnam, since these islands were seized by China from Western-allied South Vietnam in the last phase of the Vietnam war, but were never returned after the communists had reunified the country. Michael Leifer states that, with a view to its maritime claims, "Vietnam [...] harbours a strong sense of

When the Philippines presented a draft code of conduct at the ASEAN Ministerial Meeting (AMM) in July 1999, Malaysia opposed the plans so strongly that ASEAN diplomats even suspected Malaysia had a secret arrangement with China:

> Plans [...] to draw China into talks over the disputed Spratly Islands have been scuppered by protests from Malaysia. A source told Reuters that senior officials of [...] ASEAN [...] had met on Tuesday to discuss a detailed regional agreement on the South China Sea, which would have drawn China into the discussions. [...] "The Philippines circulated a document [...] intended to guide the discussions but the Malaysians resisted this very strongly and it couldn't be discussed", the source said. [...] ASEAN members were surprised at Malaysia's response and speculated it had cut a deal on the side with China over the Spratly islands and would not be willing to draw the Asian giant into the discussions. "The Malaysian move was very puzzling to the senior officials [...] and the suspicion among some is there might have been a side deal," the diplomatic source said.[370]

Thus, Malaysia, as best it could, obstructed any attempt within ASEAN to forge a more cohesive position vis-à-vis China. Joseph Chin Yong Liow quotes the Philippine foreign minister, Domingo Siazon, as saying that "among ASEAN members, it is really just Malaysia now that has some second thoughts."[371]

When the Philippines again "lobbied fellow ASEAN members strongly to reach final agreement on a draft ASEAN Code of Conduct [...]" in November 1999,[372] Malaysia again sided with China. On 22 November, the Prime Ministers of Malaysia and China, Mahathir and Zhu, concluded a bilateral agreement in which they generally accepted the idea of a code of conduct, as long as it did not include any references to multilateralism and as long as its geographic scope did not include the Paracel Islands (which are claimed solely by Vietnam and China):

> [...] the two leaders [had] agreed that 'differences in this part of the world should be properly resolved through friendly (bilateral) consultations between the relevant countries...' They also agreed in general terms on a code of conduct for the Spratly Islands.[373]

---

grievance, especially over the Paracels which are totally subject to Chinese dominion [...]"
(Leifer 1999).
[370] Valerie Lee (1999).
[371] Liow (2000): 687.
[372] Thayer (1999c).
[373] Ibid.

The implication was that Malaysia (a) backed China's rejection of multilateral approaches, a position that clearly contravened ASEAN's and particularly the Philippines' interest, and (b) openly supported China's position against the claims of Vietnam:

> China wanted the code to cover only the Spratlys and Scarborough Shoal. But for ASEAN to exclude the Paracels from the code would be to undercut an ASEAN member in favor of China.[374]

Thus, Malaysia demonstratively – and this time even publicly – sided with China against fellow ASEAN members Philippines and Vietnam, even before ASEAN had consulted on the issue.

After a very controversial debate, Malaysia gave in to ASEAN's position. Vietnam's claims prevailed: the Paracels were duly included in the proposed code, whereupon China rejected it the very next day:

> During the ASEAN senior officials meeting, agreement on the Philippines' draft of conduct for the South China Sea was discussed. This proved to be so contentious that a late night meeting had to be held between Malaysia, the Philippines, and Vietnam to discuss Vietnamese insistence that the scope of the code be expanded to include the Paracel as well as Spratly Islands. After the Vietnamese proposal was accepted, a copy of the draft code was informally presented to the Chinese officials on November 25. [...] That same day it was reported that China had turned down the draft code [...]. Zhu objected to the inclusion of the Paracel Islands and warned ASEAN that China would not be rushed on the issue.[375]

Whereas Vietnam had thus won the support of ASEAN, the Philippines, because of Vietnam's insistence on the inclusion of the Paracels, had lost an opportunity to achieve fast and tangible results with China. Whereas the Philippines had nevertheless closed ranks with Vietnam (though probably grudgingly), both Malaysia and Vietnam pursued their interests to the last, knowingly driving the Philippines' initiative against the wall instead of seeking a compromise or alternative solutions.[376]

In this context, the fact that, in the running-up to the November meetings, Malaysia and Vietnam deliberately staged demonstrations of military power against the Philippines in the disputed areas is a clear indicator of the very thin

---

[374] Valencia (2001).

[375] Thayer (1999c).

[376] Considering that Vietnam's claims to the Paracels are of a completely different nature altogether than all other claims in the South China Sea, Vietnam could, for example, have agreed to exempt the Paracels from the code of conduct. This would have ensured a more successful outcome of the Philippines' initiative.

diplomatic ice ASEAN members are dancing on in their dealings vis-à-vis China. Thus, in June 1999, Malaysia provocatively occupied and fortified several reefs on Investigator Shoal in the Sratlys, which were also claimed by the Philippines and Vietnam.[377] Following a formal complaint by the Philippines, which was ignored by Malaysia "[i]n August, Philippine and Malaysian planes engaged in a standoff over Investigator Shoal [...]."[378] Similarly, Vietnam flexed its muscles and provoked the Philippines in the Spratlys in October, shortly before the negotiations of the code of conduct:

> The Spratlys also generated tension within ASEAN, with the Philippines issuing a diplomatic protest in June 1999 over Malaysia's occupation of Investigator Shoal, also claimed by Manila [...] Subsequently, in October 1999 the Philippines issued a formal protest to Vietnam over the upgrading of structures on Barque-Canada Reef and Amboyna Cay. Vietnamese troops reportedly fired on a Philippine reconnaisance aircraft overflying a Vietnamese-occupied Spratly islet.[379]

These acts clearly undermined ASEAN's credibility and unity and therefore represented a slap in the face for the Philippines' efforts at forging a common ASEAN position vis-à-vis China.

After all, it has to be noted that, despite all controversies, ASEAN – as a group – had eventually come up with a common position and represented it to China, too. What is more, the common position included a reference to the Paracel Islands and clearly condemned unilateral occupation and fortification of claimed areas.

> ASEAN's version of a code would ban the occupation of new areas or the building of new structures in the Spratlys. However, ASEAN also wants the Paracel Islands to be governed by the code. This addition was made at Vietnam's insistence and is clearly unacceptable to China, who has occuppied the islands since its forcible removal of South Vietnamese troops.[380]

---

[377] In the incident, Malaysia had installed a radar tower, a two-storey building and a helicopter platform on Erica Reef. All this had been shielded by what an ASEAN official reportedly described as "'quite a military operation' that involved six missile gunboats at one stage and coincided with the stationing of some of the country's most modern warplanes in nearby Malaysian territory" (Richardson 1999a).
  Investigator Shoal is also claimed by China; commentators assumed that China's reaction to Malaysia's occupation of the shoal was unusually mild because it played into China's hands by diminishing ASEAN unity. Cf. Liow (2000): 689.
[378] Singh (2000): 17. Due to this and other incidents, Singh speaks of "the sorry state" of ASEAN's South China Sea policy in 1999 (p. 17).
[379] Schofield (2000).
[380] Valencia and Miller Garmendia (2000).

Thus, the official ASEAN position does not preclude any member states' territorial interests. To the contrary, in the end negotiations with China risked to stall not because there was no common position, but rather because the scope of the code was too wide as to be reconcilable with the Chinese position.

ASEAN 2000-2001   The widening triangular rift between Malaysia, the Philippines and Vietnam continued to inhibit substantial progress on forging a common unified position in 2000. In March, the gap between the Philippines and Vietnam widened after China had again flexed its muscles and exposed the Philippines' military weakness and diplomatic isolation during the Scarborough Shoal incident of February 2000 and put forth its own proposal for a code of conduct.

According to the Philippines' government, the Scarborough Shoal incident had left the Philippines "'in a lose-lose' situation in dealing with Chinese fishermen because of the cost and drain of resources."[381] Thus pressed and humiliated, the Philippines were eager to see a Sino-ASEAN code of conduct passed as soon as possible. Unlike in November 1999, the Philippines was now no longer ready to see its hopes dashed by Vietnam's insistence on including the Paracels in the code of conduct. As Thayer reported in early 2000,

> It is evident that there are differences within ASEAN on the Paracels. According to [the Philippines',M.H.] Foreign Secretary Domingo Siazon at a February 2 press briefing, "if the area of coverage were limited to (the) Spratlys, I think that I would say that within three days, our diplomats would be able to find a set of words that would be acceptable to the contesting parties in the Spratlys".[382]

When China formally proposed its own draft code in March that referred exclusively to the Spratlys and Scarborough Shoal, the Philippines lobbied ASEAN members to accommodate China's demand to drop Vietnam's interests from its draft code:

> [...] at a working group session [...], the Philippines offered a new proposal that its officials said would bring together the differing stances in the two drafts. Lauro Baja [... the Philippines' Foreign Affairs Under-Secretary, M.H.] said the new proposal was likely 'to meet the concerns of China,' which wants the Paracels dropped from coverage by the code.[383]

---

[381] Reportedly, Philippine Foreign Affairs Under-Secretary Lauro Baja and Foreign Secretary Domingo Siazon had made statements to this effect (see Thayer 2000a).

[382] Thayer (2000a).

[383] Associated Press (16 March 2000): "China, Asean agree on Spratlys code".

As in November 1999, Vietnam's opposition to such plans prevented the adoption of a common Sino-ASEAN code of conduct in 2000.[384]

As the Philippines and Vietnam were thus pitted against each other, Malaysia continued its course of fundamental obstruction with regard to the South China Sea issue. Thus, at the ASEAN Foreign Ministers Meeting in July 2000, the Malaysian government successfully torpedoed yet another attempt by the Philippines to move ASEAN to jointly urge claimant countries to refrain from provocative unilateral acts in the South China Sea:

> At the Ministerial Meetings in July, the Philippines renewed its bid to have ASEAN urge all claimants to stop occupying and building structures in disputed areas in the South China Sea. Efforts to include that call in the joint communiqué issued by the foreign ministers failed when Malaysia opposed the Philippine proposal.[385]

The rift between Malaysia, the Philippines and Vietnam respectively, which had started to paralyze ASEAN's South China Sea policy more permanently since 1999, deepened in 2000 and is likely to remain irreconcilable in the future. The events of the 34th ASEAN Ministerial Meeting in July 2001 suggest that the division continues:

> Senior officials from ASEAN's member states also discussed a proposed Code of Conduct. [...] However, no agreement emerged for foreign ministers to approve next week, delegates said. [...]Vietnam said [with a view to the ARF meeting following the AMM, M.H.][...] more discussion was needed on the code of conduct, especially among ASEAN countries. However, Malaysia said the Hanoi meetings were not the appropriate forum to discuss territorial claims.[386]

Whereas the dispute between the Philippines and Vietnam carried on, Malaysia continued to play its role of fundamental obstructor.

Country profiles: The following section is to give an overview of the motivations, behavior and roles of major ASEAN member states in ASEAN's South China Sea policy. The representation of the brief profiles will contribute to the overall assessment of the quality and intensity of ASEAN's solidarity in the South China Sea question.

---

[384] Cf. Ufen (2000): 369.
[385] Labrador (2001): 228.
[386] Reuters (22 July 2001): "ASEAN finalises integration plan but stuck on Spratlys".

Malaysia It is evident that Malaysia has contributed least to a cohesive South China Sea policy and has been the only country to directly play into China's hands. As Liow (2000) convincingly shows, Malaysia has systematically abandoned and obstructed ASEAN's approach to the South China Sea problem since late 1995 and at the same time has stepped up its bilateral relations with China considerably. The reasons for this development are apparently an increasing general preference in Malaysia for bilateral over multilateral relations as well as the pursuit of good economic and political relations with China. Further, J. Chin Yong Liow assumes that Malaysia's national interests in the South China Sea are served best by siding with China and helping it to obstruct multilateralization and the formation of a coherent ASEAN position. Since "Malaysia's claims [to the areas it occupies, M.H.] seem to be weakest among ASEAN members", Malaysia has little incentive to change the status quo. Further, the areas claimed by Malaysia have only a relatively low priority in China's ranking list of territorial interests. Thus Liow concludes that

> Malaysia's interests in the South China Sea seem to be best served by preserving the status quo and having the issue remain unresolved. Malaysia's position of prolonging the status quo is similar to that of Beijing's […]. That it is in the interest of both parties that the status quo remain also paves the way for the kind of bilateral cooperation on the South China Sea issue of recent years.[387]

In his view, Malaysia's behavior – which, as he shows, contradicts various ASEAN principles – also displays an overall strongly diminished appreciation of ASEAN as a grouping:

> That Malaysia opposed ASEAN's common position on the importance of multilateral dialogue with China also warrants attention considering the position the organization holds in the hierarchy of Malaysia's diplomatic priorities.[388]

Malaysia's behavior of unilaterally occupying Investigator Shoal in 1999 has to be seen in a similar light. The incident strongly suggests that Malaysia cares little for the Association and its objectives where its national interests are at stake. ASEAN solidarity seems to have no particular value to Malaysia *per se*,

---

[387] Liow (2000): 688f.

[388] Ibid.

The interview I conducted with a minister of the Malaysian government in January 2001 confirmed the impression of Malaysia's growing general disinterest in ASEAN and an increasing appreciation of cooperative initiatives in the larger East Asian context (notably the ASEAN Plus Three process). Asked about the importance of ASEAN to Malaysia, the minister even indicated that he saw no future for ASEAN cooperation, but put great emphasis on the prospects of ASEAN Plus Three.

otherwise it wouldn't undermine it as consequently and permanently as it has done. Van Dyke and Valencia show how far-reaching the implications of the Investigator Shoal incident are:

> This surprise unilateral action by a founding member of the Association of Southeast Asian Nations [...] has several implications. First, it clearly splits ASEAN solidarity on this issue *vis-à-vis* China. Some diplomats even suspect that Malaysia cut a deal with China at the expense of ASEAN. Second, it violates and perhaps fatally undermines the ASEAN Declaration on the South China Sea [of 1992, M.H.] and the Bandung Statement [of 1995, M.H.]. And third, it may open the floodgates to a new wave of occupations by other claimants, particularly the Philippines. Clearly anticipating a negative reaction by fellow ASEAN members, Malaysia refused to discuss the issue at the ASEAN Foreign Ministers' Meeting and joined China in arguing that the South China Sea should not be on the ARF agenda. Malaysia opposed the draft code of conduct on the ground that it was more like a "treaty" and that each article needed to be carefully studied.[389]

This implies that – not only with regard to the South China Sea issue – the value Malaysia attributes to ASEAN's collective goods has diminished, and consequently Malaysia is less willing to bear the solidarity costs ASEAN cooperation requires. Rather, Malaysia seems to seek an advantage by neglecting ASEAN unity for the sake of stepping up its bilateral relations with China. Malaysia's independent South China Sea policy has lasted for too long as to be classified as "myopic opportunism". Rather, its behavior can be classified as "strategic opportunism".

Thailand As a non-claimant state, Thailand has no vested territorial interests in the South China Sea. Of all ASEAN members, Thailand is also the one country that traditionally enjoys good relations with China and was least concerned about apprehensions of longer-term Chinese hegemonial assertiveness in the South China Sea. Indeed, at the time of the Mischief Reef incident in 1995, Thailand and Singapore were at opposite ends, when apprehension of a China threat in ASEAN "ranged from very low in Thailand to very high in Singapore."[390] Although Thailand, due to its lower threat perception, objected to Philippine and Vietnamese demands to increase ASEAN pressure on China over the South China Sea issue, it took care not to take the role of an obstructor. As Whiting shows, Thailand's supportive behavior vis-à-vis ASEAN in the South China question derives partly from the experience of

---

[389] Van Dyke and Valencia (2000): 48.
[390] Whiting (1997). 299.

ASEAN solidarity vis-à-vis Thailand during the Cambodia conflict in the 1970s and partly from a desire to reassure potentially suspicious neighbors of Thailand's solidarity:

> The absence of Thai interests in Taiwan obviates any dilemma over PRC pressures there [...]. The same absence of Thai involvement holds for the Spratlys where Ramos [i.e. Fidel Ramos, then President of the Philippines, M.H.] was seen as exploiting the issue for domestic politics. But having expressed these views privately, Thai officials nevertheless acknowledged the necessity to stand by the ASEAN consensus on China achieved in 1995. In part this stems from appreciation for the invaluable support ASEAN rendered Thailand as a front-line state during the Vientamese occupation of Cambodia. [...]

> [Historically,] Bangkok has repeatedly had to "bend with the wind" from one quarter or another [...]. Pride in this record of survival is tempered by awareness of its implications for suspicious neighbors. Thus, although China is not seen as a near term problem, Bangkok shows no inclination to weaken ASEAN solidarity as a result.[391]

Thailand thus has never been a strong promoter of a unified ASEAN stance on the issue, but has generally backed ASEAN's positions.

Nevertheless, Thailand has violated ASEAN cohesion once in 1997: When Vietnam asked ASEAN members to back its protests over Chinese drillings in waters claimed by Vietnam, Thailand openly rejected to support the Vietnamese claims and remained neutral on the issue, citing its good relations with both countries. However, this behavior was an exceptional deviation from Thailand's usual practice. Notably, Thailand has never sided with China to oppose another ASEAN member, as Malaysia has done.

Yet there is no guarantee that Thailand will continue to back other ASEAN members in their South China Sea disputes in the future. More recent developments in Thai foreign policy have shown that the government of Prime Minister Thaksin Shinawatra is prepared to considerably step up relations with China, even at a high cost.[392] Thayer shows that the Thaksin government's pursuit of better relations has opened up Thailand to manipulation from China.[393] He also reports that

---

[391] Ibid.: 315.

[392] China has become ever more important to Thailand economically, and the Thaksin government stands for business rather than principles. This development gives China a strong lever to influence Thailand's policy-making. As Thayer reports, bilateral trade between China and Thailand increased from US$ 4.3 bn. in 1999 to US$ 6.2 bn. in 2000 and US$ 6.6 bn. by early 2001. (cf. Thayer (2001 b); *Asia Times Online* (23 May 2001): "China, Thailand strengthen 'family' bond".

[393] Cf. Thayer (2001a).

> [a]ccording to Kavi Chongkittavorn, ASEAN is concerned it is losing its bargaining power in dealing with Beijing [...]. [...] The new Thai government is repositioning itself to edge closer to China's strategic design. [...].[394]

Within ASEAN, Prime Minister Thaksin demonstratively sided with Malaysia directly after its inauguration in early 2001, thereby indicating a change of the course adopted by the Democratic government of Chuan Leekpai.[395] Further, the temporary Philippine-Thai axis for more democracy and the reform of ASEAN, which had developed between Thai Foreign Minister Surin Pitsuwan and Philippine Foreign Minister Domingo Siazon, now belongs to the past. Under these circumstances, Thailand's fidelity to ASEAN's South China Sea policy and in particular to Philippine territorial interests remains doubtful.

Singapore Singapore, like Thailand, is a non-claimant state. Like Thailand, Singapore has had a vested interest in maintaining good relations with China (albeit without at the same time sacrificing its friendly relations with Taiwan). Also like Thailand, Singapore attributed little meaning to the Mischief Reef incident. "On balance, Mischief Reef was seen as of little significance in itself."[396] Unlike Thailand, however, Singapore was indeed highly concerned about longer-term Chinese assertiveness in the South China Sea and the Taiwan Strait.

> In sum, although Singapore is not directly involved in the South China Sea disputes, its unique vulnerability to any destabilizing development in East Asia awards military security high priority [...]. In this context Chinese behavior in 1995 aroused special concern, amplified in 1996 [by the Taiwan Strait incident, M.H.], for both ASEAN unity and extra-ASEAN defense ties.[397]

To Singapore, the important collective good produced by ASEAN in the South China Sea question therefore has been to contain China's hegemonic potential for the sake of regional stability. Singapore therefore backed the Philippines over Mischief Reef and has always supported the idea of a unified ASEAN stance vis-à-vis China. Still, during 1998, at the height of the economic crisis, Singapore, in line with most other ASEAN states, suspended the issue

---

Thayer shows that the Thaksin government has already downgraded human rights and democracy for the sake of better relations with Beijing when it gave in to Chinese pressure to take a prohibitive stance on Falun Gong activities in Thailand.

[394] Ibid.

[395] See for example: Lau (2001).

[396] Whiting (1997): 309.

[397] Whiting (1997): 311.

temporarily and put the Philippines' call for assistance over the second Mischief Reef incident on the backburner for the time being at the ASEAN summit in 1998. As most other ASEAN governments, Singapore in 1998 was not ready to show solidarity with the Philippines, as this may have upset Singapore's bilateral relations with China.

Since the economic crisis, Singapore's foreign policy has increasingly been guided by concerns for economic security (as different from more traditional security concepts).[398] This suggests that security in the South China Sea features less prominently in Singapore's direct foreign policy interests, whereas good economic relations with China have gained in importance. Thus, maybe even more than in the past, Singapore can be expected to refrain from confronting China as long as it can help it. Nevertheless, Singapore remains basically committed to ASEAN's efforts to engage China on the South China Sea issue. After all, Singapore's concern about Chinese expansionism remains valid and its commitment to multilateral approaches to regional security remains intact.

Indonesia: Officially, China has no overlapping claims with Indonesia in the South China Sea. Nevertheless, Indonesia and China have been involved in a silent dispute concerning the Natuna Islands (owned by Indonesia) since 1993, when China had presented a map indicating basically the entire South China Sea as Chinese Territory.[399] As Johnson points out, "[...] China, long perceived as Indonesia's nemesis, could not have claimed a more sensitive, resource-loaded sea area."[400] Thus, Indonesia has had a strong national interest in containing China's expansionism. But even much earlier, Indonesia had tried to multilateralize talks by organizing annual track-two informal work shops on the South China Sea since 1990. These work shops had been attended by representatives from ASEAN member states and China. Indonesia's motivation had been general concerns over China's assertiveness:

> Indonesia is not a claimant to the Spratlys, but in the early 1990s identified the dispute as a source of regional instability and a potential military flashpoint. [...]

> As the 1990s progressed, Indonesia became more and more concerned with China's behaviour in the South China Sea. [...]

> China's increasingly assertive behaviour in the South China Sea [...] not only had implications for the Natuna Islands dispute, but was also

---

[398] Cf. Dent (2001): 20.
[399] Cf. Johnson (1997); Kreuzer (1999).
[400] Johnson (1997): 153.

interpreted as an indication of how an economically strong and militarily powerful China might act in the future.[401]

Although Indonesia – for strategical national interests and to maintain its role as "honest broker" in the informal South China Sea work shops – has taken great care to keep out of the general South China Sea dispute and deal with the Natuna Islands issue separately,[402] Indonesia has always promoted and actively supported ASEAN's South China Sea policy vis-à-vis China. In 1994, Indonesia's attempt to multilateralize the issue and get ASEAN behind the afore-mentioned "doughnut formula" as a common position vis-à-vis China failed, due to opposition from Malaysia.

> Whereas Indonesia used multilateralism as its tool, the Malaysian diplomat believed that his nation was in the position to strengthen relations with China by offering it significant trade and investment.[403]

The *Far Eastern Economic Review* similarly reported in February 1995 (prior to the Mischief Reef incident) that

> [...] analysts say that Malaysia, which has given up the idea of multilateral solution promoted by Indonesia and Vietnam, is unlikely to push for a strong stand against China.[404]

Indonesia's South China Sea policy has remained the same even during and after the crisis. Throughout the second half of the 1990s, Indonesia continued its annual South China Sea workshops and has thereby intiated, promoted and supported ASEAN's efforts at coming to terms with China:

> Notwithstanding Indonesia's shaky financial and political situation, in early December 1998 a ninth workshop was convened in Jalarta to set the agenda for 1999. The premise of the meeting was that economic recovery of the ASEAN region depended on political stability [...]
> The Indonesian workshops represent the most serious regional effort thus far for promoting peace and cooperation in the South China Sea. They have been purposefully designed to bring together representatives from concerned states in the region to discuss non-polemical issues affecting environment, navigation, pollution control, marine research, and possible means of cooperation.[405]

---

[401] Storey (2000): 157, 158, 164.

[402] For a detailed analysis of Indonesia's motives to keep the Natunas separate from the South China Sea dispute, cf. Johnson (1997), especially pp. 154-6.

[403] Ibid.: 157.

[404] Chanda, Tiglao and McBeth (1995): 15.

[405] Joyner (1999): 97f.

At the ASEAN level, Indonesia continued to support a unified ASEAN position. There are no instances of Indonesia leaving the common ASEAN ground in the South China Sea question. Indonesia therefore can be considered to be one of the pillars of ASEAN's South China Sea policy.

The Philippines   Clearly, the Philippines takes a special role in ASEAN's South China Sea policy. As the weakest claimant, it is not able to protect its claims sufficiently and is thus exposed to Chinese – and, as shown above, sometimes even Malaysian and Vientamese – covetousness. The Philippines has had to rely on – and been at the receiving end of – ASEAN solidarity against the PRC. But the Philippines itself also has actively promoted and worked hard for a unified ASEAN position. Being itself dependent on ASEAN solidarity, the Philippines has repeatedly been the first in ASEAN to line up behind Vietnam in its disputes with China.

Since 1999, however, contrary positions over the question whether or not to include the Paracel Islands in the common code of conduct have pitted the Philippines against its former natural ally. The Philippines' interest in coming to terms with China over a code of conduct has fast eclipsed solidarity with Vietnam. Indeed, in the face of China's iron opposition to the inclusion of the Paracels, Philippine solidarity with Vietnam would threaten to permanently stall the negotiations of a common Sino-ASEAN code of conduct and thus would contravene its most pressing security interest. The Philippines are not ready to accept such high solidarity costs.

Vietnam   Vietnam, like the Philippines, has been on the receiving side of ASEAN solidarity in its South China Sea disputes with China, especially in the running-up to its ASEAN membership between 1992 and 1995 and again in 1997, when it asked for, and – after immediate support from the Philippines and initial reluctance by some ASEAN members – finally received ASEAN's support against Chinese explorative oil drilling in Vietnam-claimed waters in the Spratlys.

One of the reasons for Vietnam to join ASEAN in 1995 had been strengthening Vietnam's position vis-à-vis the Chinese neighbor. Consequently, Vietnam also supported the Philippines' calls for ASEAN assistance and welcomed the Philippines' initiatives for an ASEAN code of conduct. Vietnam's own interests and its support for the Philippines' position also pitted Vietnam and the Philippines against Malaysia in the quesion of the code of conduct. Thus, the Philippines and Vietnam, up to 1999, used to be close, quasi-natural allies in the South China Sea question.

However, just at the time when a divergence of interests began to align between Vietnam and the Philippines over the Paracels issue in late 1999, Vietnam did not refrain from shooting at a Philippine surveillance plane over one of

Vietnam's fortified possessions in the Spratlys (which is apparently also claimed by the Philippines) in October 1999.[406] Possibly, this hostile act even represented a warning to the Philippines not to neglect Vietnam's Paracels claims in the November 1999 negotiations of a code of conduct. Whatever the implications, this act contravened the spirit of both ASEAN principles and ASEAN's declared South China Sea policy.

Apparently, Vietnam's close diplomatic cooperation with the Philippines in the Spratlys question had been less informed by genuine solidarity rather than the pursuit of hard national interests (which happened to coincide with those of the Philippines). Thus, Vietnam, knowing that China will never accept the inclusion of the Paracels in a common code of conduct, seemingly irreconcilably, continues to block progress on the code by insisting on the inclusion of this group of islands, regardless of the greater implications for ASEAN and the Philippines.

Summary: ASEAN for the first time displayed unity in the South China Sea question by adopting the common Declaration on the South China Sea in 1992. The Mischief Reef incident of 1995 finally caused ASEAN members to forge a common position and represent the Philippines' interests vis-à-vis China. Although fragile internally, ASEAN's position vis-à-vis China in 1996 and 1997 prompted the PRC to make tactical (though no strategic) concessions to ASEAN, such as reluctantly entering into multilateral dialoguewith ASEAN as a grouping, rather than conducting mere bilateral dialoguewith individual claimant states. In 1997, ASEAN protests over Chinese explorative oil drilling in waters claimed by Vietnam caused China to withdraw.

In 1998, in the face of the economic crisis, when several ASEAN members had a strong interest in maintaining good economic and political relations with China, ASEAN's relatively unified common stance vis-à-vis China crumbled. Thus, ASEAN largely failed to back the Philippines' urgent call for support over the second Mischief Reef incident.

Following this setback, ASEAN resumed a stronger and more unified position again in 1999, when it represented a draft code of conduct for the South China Sea to the PRC. The draft code was remarkable in that it represented maximal ASEAN positions and even included Vietnamese claims in the Paracel Islands.

The draft code was passed against obstructive opposition from Malaysia, whose government since 1995 had more and more leaned towards Chinese positions and openly opposed ASEAN's attempts to forge a common position aimed at multilateralizing and intensifying negotiations with China. Malaysia even went so far as to show open disregard for principles of both ASEAN

---

[406] The Philippine plane was not hit, so that the shots can be assumed to have been warning shots.

cooperation and ASEAN's South China Sea policy when it occupied Investigator Shoal in 1999.

At the same time, China's insistence that the Paracels be dropped from a common code of conduct, began pitting Philippine and Vietnamese interests against each other by late 1999. Since then, the 'natural' diplomatic alliance between these two ASEAN members has eroded.

Thailand, a country that has no direct claims in the South China Sea, traditionally has had good relations with China and has the lowest concerns among ASEAN members about Chinese expansionism or a China threat, has generally supported ASEAN's position. Against its own convictions, the Thai government even supported the Philippines over the Mischief Reef incident in 1995. Thailand's motivation to back ASEAN's South China Sea policy arguably derives from both its own experience of profiting from ASEAN solidarity as a frontline state in the Cambodia conflict in the 1970s and the wish to reassure other ASEAN member about its reliability. In 1997, Thailand nevertheless failed to support Vietnam against China in an oil rigging incident in Vietnamese waters out of loyalty (or deference) to China. In 1998, Thailand – as all other ASEAN members – failed to back the Philippines' call for ASEAN support in the second Mischief Reef incident.

Nevertheless, Thailand's overall record of supporting ASEAN's South China Sea positions, sometimes even against its own interests, has been good through 2000. However, the recent change of government has seen a policy shift towards accommodating China and improving relations with Malaysia, a development that could possibly soften Thailand's resolve to support a unified ASEAN position vis-à-vis China.

Singapore's motivation to seek a common ASEAN stance derived from a genuine concern about China's expansionism throughout the 1990s. However, this concern has been counterbalanced by a foreign policy increasingly moved by economic interests since the onslaught of the economic crisis, a development that has increased with Singapore's economic recession in 2001. However, so far, Singapore has backed ASEAN's South China Sea policy and has expressed its continued interest in ASEAN and ARF as means of enhancing regional security and stability.

Ever since 1990, Indonesia has been a strong initiator and promoter of multilateralizing dialogueon the South China Sea and has unilaterally hosted the annual track-two South China Sea workshops. Indonesia's motivaton stems from a strong concern about Chinese expansionism. In addition, the country since 1993 also faces latent Chinese claims to the Natuna Islands. Unless the administration of President Megawati Sukarnoputri changes course dramatically (which appears to be unlikely), Indonesia will continue its multilateral apporach and back ASEAN's positon vis-à-vis China, as long as there is one.

The Philippines, which continues to depend on ASEAN's diplomatic support against Chinese covetousness, used to be a backer of Vietnam's interests in the South China Sea question. Since Vietnam also had an interest in a unified ASEAN stance, interests of the two countries often converged. However, the Philippines would not allow Vietnamese interests to stall the ASEAN-Chinese negotiation process, as became clear in early 2000, when the Philippine government displayed its displeasure at the inclusion of Vietnam's Paracels claims in the draft code of conduct.

Vietnam, due to its interests in the Spratlys and the Paracels, has always backed ASEAN's position. It apparently formed a silent alliance of interests with the Philippines, but as soon as interests diverged from the Philippines' by late 1999, Vietnam placed its own interests above solidarity with the Philippines. The Vietnamese government even assumed a threatening posture by shooting at a Philippine surveillance plane in the Spratlys. This suggests that Vietnam's behavior is not based on genuine solidarity.

Evaluation: *ASEAN in 1992* fulfilled all the criteria for strong solidarity. Facing a situation of increased external insecurity (but not exitential crisis) based on a power shift and concrete signs of Chinese assertiveness in the South China Sea, all ASEAN members bandwagoned and represented a common position vis-à-vis China. Even Thailand, a country which had no maritime claims, little to fear and much to gain from good relations with China, showed group spirit and accepted the solidarity costs implied without receiving equitable benefits in return. To sum up, ASEAN members were ready to bear solidarity costs, displayed a clear ingroup/outgroup distinction and reassured each other about their mutual appreciation of ASEAN's collective goods (such as regional stability). ASEAN members' (especially the non-claimant states") behavior during this phase comes close to the model solidary behavior of the *common good situation* (cf. fig. 4). Thus, ASEAN's and individual ASEAN members' solidarity can be said to have been strong in absolute and relative terms.

Table 13: ASEAN solidarity on the South China Sea issue in 1992

	Absolute solidarity	Relative solidarity
ASEAN (all members)	high	stable

ASEAN 1993 - early 1995 (just before the first Mischief Reef incident)
Following the strong display of ASEAN solidarity vis-à-vis China in 1992, individual ASEAN members sent out mixed signals in the period from 1993 to just before the first Mischief Reef incident of February 1995. Whereas ASEAN backed Vietnam's claims and thereby collectively sided against Chinese

expansionism, the non-claimant states Singapore and Thailand were careful not to strain their relations with China by pressing multilateralization of South China Sea talks too vigorously. Malaysia believed to be able to resolve its disputes bilaterally and opposed Indonesia's attempts at multilateralizing the issue. Although China kept sending clear signals of its continued assertiveness and despite continued concern about the issue among ASEAN members, ASEAN cohesion swayed. Thus, Singapore and Thailand showed slight signs of myopic opportunism, whereas Malaysia clearly discounted ASEAN unity vis-à-vis China and increasingly pursued its own – separate – China policy. Clearly, Malaysia did not resist the *breach temptation* (cf. fig. 4), as solidarity would have demanded. Overall, solidarity deteriorated slightly in the observed period and thus has to be labelled "deficient". Relative overall ASEAN solidarity (excluding Malaysia) was "unstable".

Table 14: ASEAN solidarity on the South China Sea issue 1993-early 1995

	Absolute solidarity	Relative solidarity
ASEAN	deficient	unstable
Indonesia	high	stable
Philippines	high	stable
Singapore	deficient	unstable
Thailand	deficient	unstable
Malaysia	low	defunct

ASEAN February 1995-1997   In 1995, the Philippines' call for ASEAN support against China's assertiveness after the first Mischief Reef incident met with vocal support and solidarity from all ASEAN members, including Vietnam. Even the Malaysian government joined the ASEAN chorus, though by the end of the year it slowly started dissociating itself from the mainstream position again. Thailand and Singapore supported the Philippines. After the Mischief Reef incident, ingroup cohesion was stronger than ever in ASEAN and ASEAN followed its principle of supporting the "frontline" state. Clearly, ASEAN's reaction to the Philippines' *need situation* (cf. fig. 4) was in line with the model behavior of solidarity.

ASEAN by 1996 had forged a clearly distinctive position and repeatedly represented it to China so that China had felt the need to make tactical concessions to ASEAN and increasingly engage in multilateral talks. Thus, through 1996, overall absolute ASEAN solidarity was strong. In 1997, China intruded the Paracels area, which is claimed by both Vietnam and China. In this situation, which required ASEAN solidarity, the Philippines (not without self-interest) was the only country to spontaneously and unanimously support Vietnam from the start. The other ASEAN members gave diplomatic backing to its new member only after some initial reluctance. Overall, Vietnam saw the incident as a test of ASEAN's solidarity, and ASEAN finally made an effort to live up to this test. Malaysia's increasing defection from solidarity had no strong impact on ASEAN's overall position yet. Absolute solidarity therefor can be said to have been "high"; relative solidarity was (still) "stable".

Table 15: ASEAN solidarity on the South China Sea issue in 1995

	Absolute solidarity	Relative solidarity
ASEAN (overall)	high	stable
Indonesia Philippines	high	stable
Philippines	high	stable
Vietnam	high	stable
Singapore	high	stable
Thailand	high	stable
Malaysia	high	unstable

Table 16: ASEAN solidarity on the South China Sea issue in 1996-1997

	Absolute solidarity	Relative solidarity
ASEAN (overall)	high	stable
Indonesia Philippines	high	stable
Philippines	high	stable
Vietnam	high	stable
Singapore	high	stable
Thailand	high	stable
Malaysia	low	defunct

ASEAN in 1998   In 1998, ASEAN solidarity was strongly blurred by the economic crisis. The need for good relations with China and pressing economic worries in several ASEAN states prevailed in Singapore, Thailand and Malaysia. When the Philippines, as in 1995, tried to draw support from ASEAN over the second Mischief Reef incident, the general crisis cancelled out ASEAN solidarity. ASEAN made only a veiled reference to the incident in its joint communique. Vietnam's position for 1998 is not available. Remarkably, however, Indonesia, which faced the most disastrous economic and political turmoil, kept up its efforts at multilateralizing South China Sea talks between China and ASEAN.

All in all, absolute overall ASEAN solidarity in 1998 was low. Due to the strong effect of the crisis affecting more or less all countries in the region, solidarity was temporarily suspended, though not entirely defunct. Therefore, relative solidarity is considered "unstable" to "defunct".

Table 17: ASEAN solidarity on the South China Sea issue in 1998

	Absolute solidarity	Relative solidarity
ASEAN (overall)	low	unstable to defunct

ASEAN 1999   In 1999, ASEAN reinforced its efforts at negotiating a common code of conduct with China. ASEAN's continued engagement on the issue, despite Malaysian obstruction, caused China to enter direct negotiations and basically agree with ASEAN on the principles of a code of conduct. Thus, although concrete results are still few, ASEAN has persistently shown an interest in taking the issue further. This suggests that most ASEAN members' solidarity on the issue was revived after 1998, once the worst of the economic crisis had been overcome. However, whereas ASEAN displayed formal unity in 1999, a conflict of interests emerged between the Philippines and Vietnam. Nevertheless, the Philippines still backed the Vietnamese position in the negotiations for a common ASEAN position. Malaysia continued to obstruct ASEAN solidarity. This development continued to weaken ASEAN's collective stance vis-à-vis China considerably. Therefore, absolute ASEAN solidarity (including Malaysia) is deficient. Relative ASEAN solidarity has to be labeled "unstable".

Table 18: ASEAN solidarity on the South China Sea issue in 1999

	Absolute solidarity	Relative solidarity
ASEAN (overall)	deficient	unstable
Indonesia	high	stable
Philippines	high	stable
Vietnam	deficient to low	unstable
Singapore	high	stable
Thailand	high	stable
Malaysia	low	defunct

ASEAN 2000-2001   In 2000, ASEAN was considerably successful, when China for the first time officially offered to enter negotiations on a code of conduct by proposing its own draft code to ASEAN. However, disputes about the Chinese proposal have disrupted ASEAN unity rather, due to China's insistence on the exclusion of the Paracels.

The rift between Vietnam and the Philippines deepened further and pitted the two states against each other as far as their preferences for the territorial scope of the code of conduct for the South China Sea are concerned. Malaysia has continued its obstructive role. It stands to be expected that other ASEAN members' commitment to ASEAN solidarity in the South China Sea question will be subdued as long as both Singapore and Bangkok give priority to economic security and good relations with China.

The fact that the ASEAN Ministerial Meeting of 2001 was split on the subject confirms the impression that ASEAN solidarity has suffered considerably. Overall, absolute solidarity for 2000-2001 this period therefore can be labeled "deficient" to "low". Given the negative external circumstances of the region (a new wave of economic destabilization in the region and China's increasing political and economic weight), the relative stability for this period has to be labeled as "unstable".

Table 19: ASEAN solidarity on the South China Sea issue 2000-2001

	Absolute sovereignty	Relative sovereignty
ASEAN (overall)	deficient to low	unstable
Indonesia	n.a.	n.a.
Philippines	deficient	unstable
Vietnam	deficient	unstable
Singapore	n.a.	n.a.
Thailand	n.a.	n.a.
Malaysia	low	defunct

As figure 4 below shows, the overall development of ASEAN solidarity (with regard to the South China Sea issue) before the Asian economic crisis suggests that solidarity was strongest whenever a concrete crisis occurred. Conversely, after the Asian economic crisis had struck, ASEAN solidarity over the second Mischief Reef incident in 1998 displayed an all-time collective low, because ASEAN members were reluctant to confront China. After 1998, solidarity recovered only modestly and through 2001 was at about the same level as in the first years of the reluctant solidarity build- up in the period between 1993 and just before the first Mischief Reef incident in February 1995.

Fig. 4: Development of ASEAN solidarity with respect to the South China Sea issue (1992-2001)

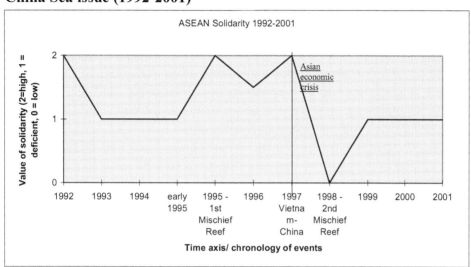

3.3. ASEAN's role in the East Timor and Aceh conflicts (1999 through 2000)

The problem: As Indonesia, which had previously been considered the anchor of ASEAN cooperation, did not recover from the Asian economic crisis after 1998, the country's economic and political instability also severely destabilized the architecture of ASEAN relations. A weakened Indonesia stood to weaken ASEAN permanently and lastingly. When Indonesia sank into political chaos in the course of the atrocities following the East Timor referendum, ASEAN governments faced the difficult question how to respond to the crisis. On the one hand, ASEAN's corporate culture suggested that other ASEAN members should keep silent on the issue and let Indonesia deal with its own affairs. After all, ASEAN was bound by the principle of non-interference, and Indonesia had initially not asked ASEAN members for mediation or support. What is more, ASEAN – in the name of ASEAN solidarity and line with the norm of refraining from destabilizing fellow ASEAN governments – had always sided with the Indonesian government against domestic and international calls for the independence of East Timor since its occupation in December 1975.[407] On the

---

[407] Cf. for example Inbaraj (1997).
ASEAN members have a long history of suppressing East Timorese activists' activities in other parts of ASEAN. For example, Ramos-Horta, the chief East Timorese activist for independence, was systematically blocked by most ASEAN states, cf. Inbaraj (2000).

other hand, there was a clear UN mandate for the intervention of international peace-keeping forces, and the international community (and also investors world wide) measured ASEAN's credibility and relevance by the organization's capability to take over regional responsibility and to contribute to the resolution of the conflict. Additionally, Australia's readiness to execute the UN mandate and to send peace-keeping forces into Indonesia put ASEAN under double strain: the engagement of this relatively small country, a direct neighbor to ASEAN and Indonesia, provided a direct measure by which ASEAN's actions and effectiveness would be judged internationally.

Measuring ASEAN solidarity in the East Timor case requires an assessment not so much of the success or failure of ASEAN's behvior in helping to resolve the crisis, but rather of the quality of relevant ASEAN members' behavior regarding (a) the cohesiveness of ASEAN's response to the crisis, (b) the agreeability of ASEAN members' behavior with Indonesian interests, (c) the solidarity costs individual members were (or were not) ready to face. Thus, the question is how ASEAN dealt with Indonesia's *need situation* (and vice versa), and whether ASEAN members resisted the *breach temptation*.

The analysis will also focus on ASEAN's attitude to the Indonesian government's handling of the secessionist developments in the Indonesian province of Aceh since 2000.

The reaction to the East Timor conflict: Following its customary "hear no evil, speak no evil" policy on East Timor, ASEAN in 1999 declined to react collectively to the deteriorating situation in East Timor. The suppression of the secessionist movement and the atrocities committed by pro-Indonesian militias and the Indonesian armed forces (TNI) in the aftermath of East Timor's vote for independence were considered to be a completely internal affair of Indonesia. Thus, ASEAN foreign ministers meeting in November 1999 made only a veiled reference to the situation in East Timor, but otherwise kept silent on the issue. Likewise, most ASEAN members individually followed the ASEAN code of conduct.

The ASEAN newcomers (Vietnam, Myanmar, Laos and Cambodia): categorically rejected any kind of interference from the start and stuck to their positions throughout the crisis. For obvious reasons, these authoritarian regimes wanted to avoid the setting of any precedences of collective intervention in member states' internal affairs, as they themselves had strong reason to fear foreign intervention in their own internal affairs.

Of the original ASEAN members, notably *Malaysia*, but also *Singapore*, took a decidedly pro-Indonesian stance and showed no regard nor sensitivity for East Timor's situation. The leaders of both countries attempted to exculpate Indonesia by portraying the country as a victim of the international community and human rights groups who had undermined Indonesia's authority in East Timor by supporting the independence movement. For examle, Singapore's Senior Minister Lee expressed the view that

> [...] East Timor is not a Southeast Asian problem. It would not have been a problem if it was left to Southeast Asia [...]. It was a problem created by Protugal, the European Union and human rights groups in America and Australia... The problem started not because of Asean, but because these other countries said: 'Look, the East Timorese are unhappy.' But there are many unhappy minorities living very uncomfortable lives in Asean. You know that, I know that. We look the other way. To go in and intervene would have the whole Asean solidarity breaking up.[408]

Prime Ministers Mahathir and Goh basically echoed this view. Malaysia and Singapore, who stood to be affected most in various ways by the threatening destabilization and disintegration of Indonesia, were ready to ignore the East Timor problem for the sake of both their own respective national stability and – more generally – regional stability.

The Philippines had considerably more scruples to consider the East Timor problem as an entirely internal affair. Public opinion and the government's pursuit of a democratic agenda both domestically and within ASEAN made it difficult for the government to justify Philippine acquiescence on the East Timor issue. Thus, the Philippine's reaction to the crisis was somewhat ambiguous and paradox. On the one hand, the government in late September opposed, and voted against, a UN resolution condemning the human rights situation in East Timor, on the other hand President Estrada felt the need to distance himself from the implications of his government's decision:

> The Philippines voted with Asian nations, including its ASEAN partners, against a resolution of the Human Rights Commission which approved by a 32-12 vote an inquiry into the massacres perpetrated by Indonesian troops and militias [...]. In this vote, lines were drawn between the Asians [...] and those who proposed the resolution introduced by the European Union. [...] In voting against the resolution, the Philippines' real reason is that, first, it does not want to alienate Indonesia, and, second, it tries to maintain the Asean fiction that in the interest of unity and solidarity, Asean members refrain from interfering in one another's internal affairs. The Philippine vote against the inquiry contradicts its own position on the call for human rights for Malaysia's Anwar Ibrahim and on the UN-sponsored inquiries into human rights

---

[408] *The Straits Times* (20 October 1999): "Lee Kuan Yew on East Timor: 'Look the other way'".

violations in Kosovo and Ruanda. President Estrada himself highlighted this inconsistency by saying that the Philippine vote was in line with the Asean policy of non-interference in the internal affairs of its members. Then, he washed his hands by saying it was not the policy of his administration.[409] [emphasis added, M.H.]

The Philippines' solidarity with ASEAN and Indonesia was limited. Thus, the Estrada government – despite its formal opposition to a referendum – welcomed the idea of a UN peace-keeping mandate in East Timor. When Indonesia was forced to formally give in to the peace-keeping mission of the Australian-led INTERFET (the International Force for East Timor) in September 1999, the Philippines contributed 600 technical (non-combat) troops. This strong representation was an *affront* against Indonesia, considering that Indonesia was actually opposed to INTERFET and had only at the last minute "invited" its deployment in order to avoid the public humiliation of facing the uninvited presence of foreign troops on East Timorese soil. Thus, the Philippines' particiption in INTERFET was formally in line with ASEAN's respect for national sovereignty and non-interference, but actually came very close to a breach of solidarity.

Thailand's position deviated most from the mainstream ASEAN position. Although formally in line with the ASEAN norms, the Democratic government of Chuan Leekpai opposed ASEAN's acquiescence on East Timor. This comes at no surprise, considering that Thai Foreign Minister Surin Pitsuwan had lobbied ASEAN hard in 1998 to allow "flexible engagement", i.e. admit exceptions to the norm of non-interference in another country's internal affairs under certain circumstances. As Alan Dupont remarks,

> East Timor has sharpened divisions within the organisation [ASEAN, M.H.] about strict adherence to ASEAN's non-interference norm. It is no coincidence that Thailand and the Philippines, the leading dissenters, have been most supportive of UN action in East Timor and have provided most of ASEAN's ground forces.[410]

The Thai government, like the Philippines, welcomed, actively promoted and vigorously supported the idea of INTERFET. Thailand deployed 1,580 combat and non-combat troops, which represented the by far the largest contribution of all ASEAN members.[411] Even more provocatively, Thailand first assumed the

---

[409] *Philippine Daily Inquirer*, (01October 1999): "Lame Excuse".

[410] Dupont (2000): 168.

[411] Whereas Malaysia sent only 30 military personnel (non-combat, mainly interpreters), Thailand participated with 1580 personnel (about 1000 of which combat troops) and the Philippines sent 600 engineers and medical staff. Numbers for Singapore unfortunately differ

deputy command and took over the command of the 9000-strong UN Transitional Authortity in East Timor (UNTAET) from October 1999 on.

Thus, Thailand broke ranks with other ASEAN members. Indeed, within and outside the region, the general perception prevailed that Thailand was leaning towards the United Nations and Australia more than to Indonesia and ASEAN. Actually, the continued strong presence of Thai troops on Indonesian soil beyond October 1999 and Australia's diplomatic praise for Thailand's cooperative behavior meant an offense to Indonesia. Thus, the international community, personified by the Australian Foreign Minister, did not tire to laud Thailand's contribution:

> As the United Nations prepares to adopt a resolution for a UN Transitional Authority in East Timor [UNTAET, M.H.], Thailand says it is willing to assume the role of force commander to lead what are expected to be almost nine thousand troops. After meeting in Bangkok [...] with Prime Minister Chuan Leekpai, Australian Foreign Minister Alexander Downer commented that participation of Southeast Asian Nations is key to the success of the East Timor peacekeeping mission. Mr. Downer also praised Thailand. He said it is seen as playing a leading role both within ASEAN [...] and in the broader international community, in helping resolve the problem of East Timor.[412]

Indeed, Thailand, in the pursuit of its peace-keeping efforts, had ventured so far beyond most other ASEAN members' commitments that "many Thais [...] worried that they might be the ones feeling the brunt of any diplomatic fallout" from Indonesia.[413]

Further proof of Thailand's solitary position in ASEAN as regards East Timor is the strong sympathy Thailand drew from East Timor's political leaders, Gusmao and Ramos-Horta. The East Timorese politicians, who on the one hand had been very critical of ASEAN due to the organization's passive role in the East Timor conflict of 1999, on the other hand praised Thailand for its exalted role in the peace-keeping efforts.

> After learning about the difficulties the Thai government encountered and went through following its decisions to dispatch peacekeepers to

---

from source to source, ranging between 20 and 240 (non-combat) troops. In comparison, Australia's contribution to INTERFET was 5,500 personnel (combat troops and technical units).

Source: Dupont (2000): 167. Cf. also: Ramcharan (2000): 88.

[412] Corben (1999).

[413] Suh (1999).

East Timor, they said they should have expressed stronger support for Thailand's policy.[414]

Thus, Gusmao and Ramos-Horta welcomed the Thai effort to take over the command of UNTAET (which started its operation in October 1999) whereas their intervention with the UN prevented Malaysia from assuming a leading role.

Thailand and Malaysia at opposite ends of the ASEAN spectrum In the context of INTERFET and UNTAET, it is important to note that Malaysia's efforts at taking over the command of the UN peace-keeping mission represented an attempt to gain international profile when it was clear that the force was going to be sent – and later to remain – in East Timor anyway. It is also important to note that from the early beginnings of INTERFET, the Indonesian government and the Indonesian armed forces (TNI) who had a strong interest in watering down the efficiency of the peace-keeping force, had wanted friendly ASEAN states to take over the operation. As Dupont points out, when it had become clear that the deployment of INTERFET was inevitable, Indonesian President

> Habibie and Foreign Minister Ali Alatas were determined [...] to seek substantial ASEAN participation in INTERFET for reasons of face and to minimise Australia's influence, which was increasingly seen as antithetical to Indonesia's interests in East Timor.[415]

Malaysia's Prime Minister Mahathir's pursuit of a leading role in INTERFET/UNTAET was aimed at carrying out exactly this strategy, i.e. to strongly curb the Australian influence and at the same time to reduce the overall number of troops deployed to East Timor. The following passage reveals Mahathir's pro-Indonesian attitude:

> He [Mahathir, M.H.] said Malaysia was taking the intiative for Asean to take over the East Timor peace-keeping job from Australia, but it did not mean that Asean countries should be sending a big force to carry out military operations there. [...]
> Dr Mahathir reiterated that Indonesia should not in the first place [have been] forced to hold a referendum at a time when the entire republic was facing problems and was very weak. ["]The referendum was held without giving Indonesia a chance to campaign, unlike the other side which was promised all kinds of support from foreigners [...]. Of

---

[414] Kavi (2000a).
[415] Dupont (2000): 166.

course, the people who wanted to be part of Indonesia felt they had been cheated and they reacted in the only way they know.[416]

Even as late as November 1999, Mahathir continued to justify Indonesia's sovereignty over East Timor.[417] In this light, it also becomes clear why Kuala Lumpur competed with Bangkok for the command of UNTAET and why it did not commit troops to the force once East Timor's leaders had successfully intervened with the UN against Malaysia taking over the command: Malaysia's agenda had been to protect Indonesian interests, whereas Thailand had aimed at resolving the East Timor conflict in favor of East Timor.

ASEAN's reaction to the Aceh conflict   If ASEAN had overall largely backed Indonesia in the East Timor crisis, the Acehnese demands for independence or autonomy met with even more opposition and silence from ASEAN members. Despite the terrifying experience of Indonesia's handling of the East Timor crisis, ASEAN saw no need to address the Aceh issue. At their summit in November 1999, ASEAN leaders insisted that the issue was clearly an internal affair of Indonesia.[418] ASEAN's non-interference policy was clearly informed by the fact that Aceh was an inseparable part of Indonesia and was thus protected from interference by ASEAN norms. Moreover, the view prevailed that the unity of Indonesia was a precious good to the region that needed to be maintained by all means. This view was confirmed at the ASEAN Ministerial Meeting in July 2000:

> Southeast Asian ministers stood united [...] in supporting the "sovereignty, territorial integrity and unity" of Indonesia against secessionist movements in Aceh and Papua. "The stability and prosperity of Indonesia would positively contribute to the peace, stability and prosperity of the Asian region as a whole", the foreign ministers [...] said in a joint statement [...] [T]he ASEAN ministers said they fully backed "the efforts and measures taken by the Indonesian government to restore peace and order. [...] Philippine Foreign Secretary Domingo Siazon said the statement spells out the ASEAN common position it "does not support any attempt to dismember Indonesia as a country." ASEAN Secretary General Rodolfo Severino

---

[416] *Antara* (01 October 1999): "Malaysia wants ASEAN to handle East Timor peace-keeping job".
[417] Cf. Richardson (1999b).
[418] Cf. Thomas (1999); cf. also Reuters (22 November 1999): "ASEAN defends hands-off policy on Aceh".

stressed […] "[…] any threat to the territorial integrity of Indonesia has to be taken very seriously as a whole."[419]

Considering that, at the same time as ASEAN rejected any interference Indonesia's internal affairs, Thailand (with support from the Philippines) actively promoted the proposal of an ASEAN Troika (which the Chuan government intended to enhance ASEAN's ability to comment on, and intervene in, ASEAN members' national affairs), one can assume that at least Thailand had reservations regarding ASEAN's Aceh policy. Ambiguous comments from the ASEAN Secretary General also show that there must have been some controversial discussion of ASEAN's stance on Aceh in November 1999:

> "What happens in Aceh would be of greatest interest to Indonesia's neighbours but as of now, I don't think any ASEAN country considers it the right time to intrude into what is essentially an internal matter". […] However, he added: "If something happens within a country that has a serious impact on others then statements or actions by other countries cannot be considered as interference." In a situation like Aceh, it is up to Indonesia and its partners in ASEAN to judge if the situation there poses an immediate threat to Indonesia's neighbors, he said."[420]

However, publicly no country deviated from the common ASEAN position.

Unsurprisingly, *Malaysia* expressed its strong opposition to any ASEAN interference and demonstratively took a strong stance against the independence of Aceh. However, in an attempt to defuse the tensions over Aceh, Prime Minister Mahathir also strongly signaled his readiness to mediate between the Acehnese independence movement and the Indonesian government and hinted that Aceh should be given more autonomy:

> Speaking in Jakarta after meeting Indonesia's President […] Wahid, he also stressed Malaysia was against Aceh receiving independence. "This is an internal problem of Indonesia. We will oppose Malaysia being used as the base-camp for activity by the separatist movement against Indonesia […]. Malaysia is quite willing to be of some help if we are asked to […]. We, in fact[,] have met some of the religious leaders of Aceh. I have personally met them and explained to them that our stand is that Aceh should remain a part of Indonesia." Mahathir said the

---

[419] *The Straits Times* (25 July 2000): "ASEAN expresses support for Indonesian unity", cp. *The Straits Times* (26 July 2000): "Asean backs Indonesia against provinces".
[420] Cf. Reuters (22 November 1999): "ASEAN defends hands-off policy on Aceh".

Acehnese leaders may want more autonomy and "it's up to them to negotiate."[421]

Thus, Mahathir formally maintained the official non-interference policy, while he actually engaged actively in Indonesia's internal affairs in order to defuse tensions over Aceh. Nevertheless, Malaysia's interference was in line with the conventions and norms of the ASEAN way, since Mahathir tried to avoid criticizing or embarassing the Indonesian government and showed strong respect for Indonesia's sovereignty.

Other ASEAN members also avoided public interference and rather approached Indonesia in the manner of ASEAN's customary behind-the-scenes diplomacy.

Summary: ASEAN – as an organization – rejected any interference on the issue of East Timor, which leaders officially considered to be Indonesia's internal affairs. The ASEAN newcomers (Vietnam, Myanmar, Laos and Cambodia), who generally harbor deep suspicion about ASEAN interfering in member states' internal affairs, rejected any ASEAN interference outright. Likewise, Malaysia and Singapore opposed any unsolicited intervention in East Timor and thus proved their solidarity with Indonesia. Particularly Malaysia opposed the deployment of the Australian-led INTERFET. The desire to push the Australian contingent out of East Timor and to limit INTERFET's and later UNTAET's presence there was the main reason why Malaysia competed with Thailand for a leading role in the international force. Once it was denied this leading role, Malaysia decided not to contribute substantially to the international force. The Philippines largely kept to ASEAN's official position and sided with ASEAN members in their vote opposing a UN Security Council resolution against Indonesia. On the other hand, the Estrada government expressed its concerns over ASEAN's inaction and deployed a large contingent of (non-combat) troops to INTERFET once Indonesia had formally "invited" ASEAN members to do so. Thailand took the most independent stance towards Indonesia throughout the East Timor crisis. Although the Democratic government officially adhered to ASEAN's neutral stance and waited until Indonesia officially removed the barrier to the deployment of troops to East Timor, it welcomed the deployment of INTERFET, contributed the largest contingent of troops and cooperated closely with the Australian government and the UN to ensure the effectiveness of the international force. Thus, Thailand earned the open respect of the international community. Thailand eventually even took over the command of UNTAET, which represented an offense to the Indonesian government.

As regards the conflict in Aceh, ASEAN officially kept out of Indonesia's internal affairs and backed Indonesia's efforts in maintaining its unity.

---

[421] *The Times of India* (10 March 2000): "Malaysia against Aceh independence".

Evaluation: The position of ASEAN – the organization – in both the East Timor and the Aceh conflict was unified, since the offcial common policy, even in the face of the adverse circumstances of Indonesian atrocities in East Timor, backed Indonesia's sovereignty claims and objected to foreign interference in Indonesia's internal affairs.

As to solidarity costs, the organization's East Timor policy entailed a strong loss of ASEAN's reputation and international standing. Thus, one could say that, for the sake of ASEAN unity and Indonesia's internal unity, ASEAN risked the deterioration of its international image (with all its political and economic implications).

Individually, certainly Singapore paid the highest price for backing Indonesia, since Singapore has been the one country in ASEAN seeking to make ASEAN more compatible with, and linking up to, the international community and its trade centers, Japan, the U.S. and the EU.

Malaysia, whose relations with the West had deteriorated since the Asian crisis and which cared little about being popular with particularly the U.S., but also the EU, has certainly had to invest less in terms of solidarity costs.

Likewise, the ASEAN newcomers , especially Myanmar and Laos, but also Vietnam and Coambodia, in terms of their respective national interests, had little to lose and much to gain from insisting on the non-interference principle. Thus, they certainly did not find it difficult to pay the price of alienating the international community and international investors.

Finally, the Philippine government of President Estrada apparently struggled hard to satisfy both ASEAN, the international community and its democratically-oriented constituency at home. Thus, it sent out conflicting signals: it voted with ASEAN against a resolution, while President Estrada emphasized that this did not agree with his government's ideas. Further, the Philippines participated in INTERFET with a large contingent of troops, as soon as the situation permitted it. Thus, one can say that the Philippines tried to keep the solidarity costs as low as possible.

Thailand, on the other hand, was not ready to face high solidarity costs. To the contrary, the Chuan government was ready to face high costs for non-compliance with ASEAN solidarity and pursued its own national policies. By siding with Australia and the international community Thailand risked the deterioration of its relations with other ASEAN members, especially Indonesia. Although Thailand formally kept to ASEAN norms, it did not go beyond the minimal requirements for compliance with the ASEAN code of conduct.

Overall, ASEAN solidarity in the East Timor case can be considered as "deficient", due to the respective "deficient" and "low" solidarity levels of Philippines and Thailand. Malaysia's and Singapore's solidarity can be calssified as "high" in absolute terms and "stable" in relative terms. The solidarity factor (in thish particular case) for the ASEAN newcomer countries can be classified as "high" in absolute terms and "stable" in relative terms (though there are strong reservations as to whether this behavior can be described as solidarity at all).

With regard to the Aceh conflict, ASEAN collectively backed Indonesia. There is no reason to doubt ASEAN members' cohesion on the issue, although there are reasons to assume that not all countries (notably Thailand) were happy with ASEAN's strict hands-off policy. It stands to be expected that, had there been a pro-interference alternative, Thailand may have joined this camp. However, this is mere speculation. Thus, overall absolute solidarity is classified as "high" and relative solidarity needs to be considered as "stable".

Table 20: ASEAN solidarity in the East Timor crisis (1999-2000)

	Absolute sovereignty	Relative sovereignty
ASEAN (overall)	deficient	unstable
Indonesia	--	--
Thailand	low	defunct
Philippines	deficient	unstable
Singapore	high	stable
Malaysia	high	stable
ASEAN newcomers (Vietnam, Myanmar, Laos, Cambodia)	high	stable

Table 21: ASEAN solidarity on the Aceh issue (1999-2000)

	Absolute sovereignty	Relative sovereignty
ASEAN (overall)	high	stable
Indonesia	--	--
Thailand	high	stable
Philippines	high	stable
Singapore	high	stable
Malaysia	high	stable
ASEAN newcomers (Vietnam, Myanmar, Laos, Cambodia)	high	stable

3.4. Myanmar in ASEAN: A case of one-way solidarity? (1997-2001)

The situation: In 1997, Myanmar acceded to ASEAN despite grave concerns from Thailand, the Philippines and Singapore and against these countries' explicit will. Indonesia and especially Malaysia had managed to enforce an accelerated schedule for Myanmar's accession.[422] Whereas Singapore had feared Myanmar might slow down the process of economic integration, the Philippines under President Ramos had had objections due to Myanmar's negative human rights record, the governing State Law and Order Council's (SLORC) lack of democratic legitimation and the suppression of the democratic opposition. Thailand, which had earlier promoted a "constructive engagement" policy and promoted Myanmars' eventual accession to ASEAN as a means of relieving the traditionally strained bilateral relations with its difficult neighbor, did not think the time was ripe yet to admit Myanmar. In the face of Thailand's unsuccessful engagement policy vis-à-vis Myanmar, the government of Prime Minister Chavalit saw Thailand's leverage slip in case the regime was admitted to ASEAN without being required to make concessions or showing goodwill with regard to the Thai-Myanmarese border conflicts.[423] In October 1996, the *FEER* reported that the Philippines and Thailand were opposed to ASEAN's constructive engagement policy vis-à-vis Myanmar:

> [...] President Fidel Ramos [...] argues that Asean's policy of engagement with Burma should be reviewed. Thailand supports this position. Thai Prime Minister Banharn Silpa-archa told the visiting Norwegian Prime Minister [...] that Asean is not ready to accept Burma. [...].[424]

Malaysia and Indonesia, on the other hand, had given up their former opposition to Myanmar's entry (which derived from Myanmar's active suppression of a 200,000 strong Muslim minority) and since 1995/6 had started throwing their

---

[422] Cp. Guyot (1997): 193.; Vatikiotis (1996): 17; McBeth (1996); Lim Kit Siang (1996).

[423] Myanmar has a long and complex record of violating Thailand's borders and carrying its own conflicts into Thai territory. Further, the borders serve as a transit for Myanmarese drug traffickers. The junta has not only failed to address this problem, but has partly even encouraged and prepared the ground for even more drug trafficking.

Buszinsky (1998) shows that by the time ASEAN decided to admit Myanmar, Thailand had abandoned its former policy of promoting Myanmar's early accession. "By then, conditions had changed. The Thai Foreign Ministry had earlier championed this objective [of Myanmar's accession, M.H.] but had recoiled from the consequences . [...] Within the Thai Foreign Ministry there were reservations about the step which was seen to be driven by Mahathir's personal ambitions rather than by any realistic assessment of the benefits" (p. 303).

[424] Vatikiotis (1996): 17.

weight around for Myanmar's early accession.[425] Eventually, Malaysia and Indonesia's aggressive lobbying prevailed over the resistance of Singapore, the Philippines and Thailand, and ASEAN decided to admit Myanmar in July 1997. The Bangkok-based newspaper *The Nation* commented:

> [...] in spite of the "consensus" nature of their decision, the Asean foreign ministers themselves only managed to arrive at an agreement after much debate. It was reported that three of the seven members, namely the Philippines, Singapore and Thailand, expressed reservations, while two other members, Indonesia and Malaysia, were in favour of an early admission. Obviously, the latter two countries prevailed. Sadly, this contest of will-power between the "determined" and "less determined is being played out again and again at Asean meertings. As long as the "determined" are adamant enough in their demand, the "less determined" will sooner or later give in.[426]

Malaysia's and Indonesia's motives for promoting Myanmar's accession had been to to enhance ASEAN's political clout in the region and prevent China's increasing and worrying grip on the country. Myanmar was seen as an important part of ASEAN's expansion design, which also included Laos and Cambodia.
The decision to admit Myanmar was made in June 1997, immediately before the onset of the Asian economic crisis. Thus, Myanmar's actual accession in November 1997 came at a time of economic and political turmoil.

The problem: Myanmar's accession raised a number of severe problems for ASEAN's external and internal relations. The move was set to ruffle relations with the U.S. and the EU, who had vehemently opposed Myanmar's accession due to the governing junta's disastrous human rights record and suppression of the democratic opposition. Internally, Myanmar's admission to ASEAN threatened to further dilute ASEAN unity and integration efforts and presented an *affront* to the more democratically-minded and reform-oriented governments of ASEAN members such as Thailand and the Philippines. Considering that the point of time and the conditions of the junta's accession to the circle of ASEAN governments had been a rather contentious issue within ASEAN and that the ASEAN members' relations with Myanmar had frequently been far from harmonious, it is all the more interesting to observe in how far the ASEAN members received and interacted with the new member in a spirit of solidarity and, conversely, whether Myanmar showed solidarity with its new ASEAN associates.

---

[425] Indonesia had bullied the Philippines into supporting Myanmar's early accession, whereas Malaysia, as ASEAN chairman, had unilaterally preset Myanmar's accession date from 2000 to 1997.

[426] Darmp (1997).

The questions to be raised with a view to ASEAN solidarity thus relate to (a) the external unity of ASEAN in the face of criticism and sanctions from U.S. and the EU, especially in times of economic crisis, (b) the readiness of ASEAN member to integrate Myanmar economically and politically into ASEAN, (c) Myanmar's efforts to become a reliable ASEAN partner, to contribute to ASEAN's agenda and to adapt to, and accommodate, ASEAN's expectations.

The ASEAN-Myanmar relationship allows the observation of members' behavior in each of the five model situations: *common good situation*, *sharing situation*, *need situation*, *breach temptation* and *mishap situation*.

The reaction:

ASEAN   In a display of ASEAN unity, the decision to admit Myanmar was represented to the international public by the governments of Singapore and the Philippines (though not Thailand) – governments who had originally opposed Myanmar's early accession, but had given in eventually. This symbolic gesture was apparently to affirm that once the decision had been made, Myanmar had been accepted by all of ASEAN. President Ramos and Prime Minister Goh left no doubt about ASEAN's collective stance on the issue:

> Singapore and the Philippines [...] defended a decision by the Association of Southeast Asian Nations (ASEAN) to admit international pariah Burma into their club, saying it would make the group stronger. [...] 'We know that the U.S. and Europe are unhappy with Myanmar's admission but we have always taken a position that the internal situation of a country is that country's concern,' Goh said [...]. 'We don't believe that sanctions will work. We haven't heard anybody come out with a better alternative than constructive engagement,' he said. [...] Philippine President Ramos [...] also defended the group's decision [...]. 'We want to uplift everyone regardless of [their] economic or political situation. As far as the internal politics within each country, well, we did not begin ASEAN by examining that and excluding those that had a different system from ours,' he said.[427]

This rhetoric was followed up by substantial support for Myamar's interests. Against strong opposition from the EU, ASEAN members closed ranks with the new member and lobbied for Myanmar's admission to the 1998 Asia Europe Meeting (ASEM). Thailand's outgoing government in 1997 spearheaded ASEAN's effort to ensure Myanmar's admission to the annual ASEAN-EU Joint Cooperation Meeting; when the EU rejected this proposal, ASEAN cancelled the meeting[428] and suspended the ASEAN-EU dialog.[429] When

---

[427] Uday (1997).
[428] Cp., for example, Guyot (1998): 192.

ASEAN and the EU debated the resumption of their bilateral dialoguein 2000, ASEAN's position was unchanged. At the ASEAN summit, Singapore's Prime Minister Goh reiterated the view that ASEAN would cancel the planned meeting in Vientiane (Laos) unless the EU went along with Myanmar's participation:

> Myanmar is a member of Asean and we will meet the EU together as an Asean group and we would go so far as even to say that if [the] EU wants to exclude Myanmar and the dialogue is going to be called off, then let it be called off, because we can't allow an external organisation to dictate who should be in Asean when we have such a dialogue [...].[430]

Likewise, ASEAN (with the exception of Thailand) closed ranks with Myanmar when the International Labor Organization (ILO) investigated against Myanmar and attempted to impose punitive measures because of cases of systematic exploitation of unpaid and forced labor in Myanmar. Whereas ASEAN, in an act of quiet diplomacy, collectively resolved to "send a team of labor and technical experts to Burma to try to get it to comply with the ILO recommendations" in August 2000,[431] individual ASEAN members predominantly objected to the ILO's stance and voted against the ILO resolution.[432] Likewise, when the ILO debated the issue again in 2001, "[o]fficials [...] indicated that ministers would agree to a unified stand in support of Myanmar's military government against persistent claims that forced labour continued in the reclusive country."[433] Reportedly, Myanmar was so sure of ASEAN members' solidarity that it even devised plans to how to evade Western ILO-imposed sanctions with the help of ASEAN members:

> In an internal memo in December [2000] reacting to the ILO's decision to impose sanctions, the SPDC characerized trade with Western countries as "insignificant" and said the sanctions were of "no serious danger" to their terms of trade. For exports that would be hit by the ILO restrictions, such as pulses and textiles, the SPDC outlined plans to

---

[429] The ASEAN-EU dialoguewas only resumed in 2001, when both sides met in Laos after a compromise formula had been found.

[430] Goh Chok Tong, quoted in: Malaysia Directory (25 November 2000): "No Myanmar, no meeting, ASEAN tells EU", http://ww8.malaysiadirectory.com/news/10/112505.html [08/05/01]; On this debate, cf. also: *The Straits Times* (04 May 2000): "No Myanmar, no EU-ASEAN talks"; Brandmaier (2000).

[431] Kavi (2000b).

[432] Cf. Agence France Press (16 November 2001): "Thailand vetos ASEAN support for Myanmar over ILO sanctions".

[433] *The Straits Times* (09 May 2001): "Group to discuss rights in Myanmar and layoffs",

employ covert trans-shipment through regional allies Malaysia and Singapore.[434]

The overall picture that results is that ASEAN has always represented Myanmar's status as an equal ASEAN member and has never let Myanmar down when it needed support against third parties.

In terms of political and economic integration, Myanmar has been treated like the other ASEAN newcomers. It acceded to all formal ASEAN conventions and codes of conduct and subjected itself to a delayed timetable for accession to the ASEAN Free Trade Area (AFTA). As all newcomers, Myanmar had expected a good deal more infrastructure development and material assistance than the more developed ASEAN members, facing their own economic difficulties throughout and after the economic crisis, were ready to give. Nevertheless, the chorus of the poor, consisting of Myanmar, Vietnam, Laos and Cambodia has been heard by the richer ASEAN members, especially at the 33rd ASEAN Ministerial Meeting (AMM) and the summit in 2000. The old ASEAN members have taken the demands seriously and followed Singapore's plan to launch the Initiative for ASEAN Integration (IAI) at the 34th AMM in 2001. The IAI is supposed to improve human resources and infrastructure development, though no miracles must be expected. Overall, richer ASEAN members have so far been reluctant to face high economic costs for the sake of the development of the newcomers, but have made an effort to reduce the economic gap between old and new ASEAN economies. Myanmar has received no more and no less economic benefits than the other newcomers.

Thailand's ambiguous role   The only country with a mixed record of solidarity with Myanmar is Thailand. From mid-to late 1997, the outgoing Chavalit government took into account high diplomatic costs when, against its own convictions, it followed and backed ASEAN's decision to admit Myanmar. Especially the U.S., but also the EU, took offence at Thailand's solidarity with ASEAN over the grouping's supportive stance vis-à-vis the junta.

> Western governments were especially critical of Thailand's demonstration of solidarity in support of Yangon's admission into ASEAN in July 1997, in spite of Bangkok's apparent own doubts about the wisdom of such a decision and in defiance of intense outside pressure not to do so. [...] the US State Department also accused Thailand of violating human rights provisions in relation to Myanmar [...] Thailand had also been at the centre of difficulties that emerged between ASEAN and the European Union, due to Thailand's adamant

---

[434] Crispin and Lintner (2001).

insistence on Myanmar's participation in EU-ASEAN dialogue meetings.[435]

Thailand's solidarity with ASEAN and Myanmar possibly came at a high cost, if, as observers of Thai-U.S. relations have claimed, it is true that due to Thailand's decision to support Myanmar's accession, the U.S. withheld financial aid to Thailand during the economic crisis.[436] Considering that the Chavalit government had its strong doubts about Myanmar's accession to ASEAN, it is remarkable that the outgoing government was ready nevertheless to accept high solidarity costs for backing ASEAN's decision.

The incoming Democratic government of Prime Minister Chuan Leekpai promoted a policy change with regard to both ASEAN's non-interference principle and the constructive engagement approach to Myanmar. On the one hand, Foreign Minister Surin Pitsuwan lobbied fellow ASEAN governments to follow Thailand's "flexible engagement" initiative and allow ASEAN to get involved in the internal affairs of member states as far as this country's policies impacted negatively on neighboring states or the entire Southeast Asian region. The Thai government intended this policy to provide a means of collectively influencing and checking Myanmar's human rights violations, government-sanctioned production and trafficking of narcotics and the continued violations of Thailand's border. On the other hand, the Chuan government took a decidedly assertive stance on Myanmar and was openly critical of the new member. Whereas Thailand continued to pay formal tribute to ASEAN's policy of "constructive engagement" of Myanmar and emphasized the importance of quiet diplomacy, the Chuan government also took over the role of Myanmar's chief critic. At a conference on "Engaging Myanmar in East Asia" in November 1998, the Thai Deputy Prime Minister demanded that "constructive engagement" be interpreted not as an excuse for looking the other way, no matter what was going on in Myanmar, but to interpret the formula as a mission to actively address Myanmar's shortcomings:

> When the Chuan Leekpai government took office in November 1997, the policy of "Constructive Engagement" had been in place for over six years. Looking back [...], we felt that, while Thailand could point to various achievements of engagement, [...] we also had to acknowledge the policy's limitations. [...] All too often there was an asymmetry between the cordial and co-operative state of governmental relations, on the one hand, and the frequency of incidents in border areas, on the other. In the minds of critics, the term "constructive" amounted to no more than tacit consent with everything that has been going on in

---

[435] Haacke (1999): 588.
[436] Cp. Suchitra (1998): 166.

Myanmar, and the term "engagement", a justification for effortss to seek economic benefits in the resource-rich country. [...] the Chuan Leekpai Government continues to endorse "Constructive Engagement" as the policy of conduct for relations with Myanmar. Nor can we do otherwise in a unilateral manner, given the priority we attach to ASEAN. Myanmar is now an ASEAN member. The clock can not be turned back, even if anyone so wishes. [...] But believing in the continued validity of the rationale underlying "Constructive Engagement" is one thing, not being prepared to do something to improve it, to fine-tune it, is quite another.[437]

In his speech, the Deputy Prime Minister further elaborated that Thailand expected Myanmar to implement policy changes in the areas of human rights, the domestic political system, Myanmar's violations of the Thai border as well as the production and trade of narcotics. The motives for Thailand's tightrope walk between constructive engagement and open criticism of Myanmar were multifold. On the one hand, it was unrealistic to expect that anyone could impose fast policy changes onto the junta government. On the other hand, Thailand's national interest weighed too heavy as to let Myanmar – protected by the ASEAN norm of non-interference – slip into self-complacent inaction. Further, due to the economic crisis, Thailand was not in a position to antagonize American and European interests regarding Myanmar; indeed, Thailand could hope to benefit from cozying up to the position of the international community. As Shawn W. Crispin commented in the *FEER*,

Some analysts belive Thailand's 1998 championing of "flexible engagement" against Burma was a way of cementing its democratic credentials with the U.S. in hopes of securing much-needed support for its flagging economy. [... Such] conflicting strategic-power loyalties threaten to deepen the divide in Asean.[438]

The Chuan government subsequently attempted to raise bilateral disputes and with Myanmar to the ASEAN level. Frequent public criticism and spars with Myanmar continued to dominate the relations between the two countries through 2000. Thus, as the controversial bilateral issues remained unresolved, the rift between Myanmar and Thailand deepened from 1997 through 2000. Whereas during this phase ASEAN governments (especially those of Malaysia, Singapore and the ASEAN "newcomers") took great care to display solidarity and unity with Myanmar's leadership, Thailand moved to the opposite direction. An open standoff occurred in the running-up to the annual ASEAN Ministerial Meeting in May 2000, when Surin Pitsuwan expressed his government's strong

---

[437] Sukhumbhand (1998).
[438] Crispin (2000).

concerns about the junta's renewed and demonstrative crackdown on the democratic opposition around Suu Kyi. When Surin held that Myanmar wrecked ASEAN's international credibility and stopped very short of claiming that Myanmar should never have been admitted to ASEAN in 1997, these charges "[drew] flak from the Burmese junta, which deemed his comments as counterproductive to Asean solidarity."[439]

Bilateral strains culminated in November 2000, when the Democratic government declined to vote with the other ASEAN members against an ILO resolution demanding punitive action against Myanmar:

> Thailand has vetoed a push by Malaysia and Singapore to muster ASEAN support for Myanmar as it faces punitive action from the International Labour Organisation [...]. A Malaysian foreign ministry official confirmed Thailand had rejected a proposal to swing the support of the Association of Southeast Asian Nations (ASEAN) behind Myanmar. "Thailand has aid it doesn't want to be on board with ASEAN on a common support for Myanmar," he told AFP.[440]

When the Thaksin government acceded to power in early 2001, Thailand's course swung back considerably. Although tensions with Myanmar continued to affect the bilateral relations, the incoming government assumed a decidedly more conciliatory posture vis-à-vis Myanmar than the predecessor government had done. Thus, in April 2001, Thai protests at a renewed case of armed border violation by Myanmarese troops overshadowed a meeting of foreign ministers in Rangoon[441] and ASEAN worried about the lack of progress of the talks between the junta and the democratic opposition; but the new Thai government tried to soften the diplomatic torrents through extensive bilateral diplomacy and shows of goodwill. Within the first few months after the new government's inauguration, apparently almost the entire cabinet – the foreign minister, the Minister of the Prime Minister's Office and the Defense Minister – and the Prime Minister himself had visited (or prepared to visit) Myanmar. The new – conservative – government's rhetoric vis-à-vis Myanmar's was diametrically opposed to the rhetoric applied by the Democratic government of Chuan Leekpai. Thus, at an ASEAN meeting in April 2001,

> Thailand's new government had already made it clear that it intended to make economics, rather than democratic progress, the guiding principle of its "forward engagement" policy [...and] Thai Foreign Minister

---

[439] *The Nation* (09 May 2000): "Asean 'not ready' to deal with Burma".

[440] Agence France Press (16 November 2001): "Thailand vetos ASEAN support for Myanmar over ILO sanctions".

[441] BBC News (30 April 2001): "Thai-Burmese tensions at ASEAN meet",

Surakiart Sathirathai [said] "Sometimes he Asian way of doing things is different from the Western way."[442]

Likewise, the Defense Minister offered his government's firendship vows on a golden tray: "Gen Chavalit warned people [in Thailand, M.H.] not to become victims of a "third hand" that might be trying to drive a wedge between Burma and Thailand." With reference to the border incidents, he reportedly also intended to "inform Burma that Thailand has no reason to support ethnic minority rebels", thus striking a conciliatory note on a long-standing point of contention and suspicions between Myanmar and Thailand.[443] Through 2001, the Thaksin government thus joined the other ASEAN countries in their demonstratively soft approaches to Myanmar. Perhaps the most remarkable outcome of this policy for Myanmar is that Thailand in 2001 sided with ASEAN against the impending ILO resolution.

Two-way solidarity? Since the country acceded to ASEAN, the State Peace and Development Council (SPDC) – formerly SLORC – junta has always insisted on strict non-interference in Myanmar's internal affairs. Consequently, the SPDC has never failed to back ASEAN members who invoked this principle for themselves (such as Indonesia in the East Timor question, for example) and has turned against anyone trying to de-emphasize this ASEAN principle. However, such a behavior can hardly be called "solidarity", since it is motivated exclusively by equity-oriented self-interest.

Generally, whereas Myanmar has generally experienced a high degree of support from ASEAN members, Myanmar has not paid back ASEAN in kind.

If the SLORC/ SPDC had actually been interested in showing its appreciation of ASEAN and proving it had a sense of ASEAN unity and cohesion, it would have had plenty opportunity to do so. However, whereas Myanmar expected ASEAN to protect it from external criticism, to introduce it into several regional and trans-regional intergovernmental processes, to link it up to the world market and to provide infrastructure development, it has not been ready (or very reluctant at best) to give ASEAN what it wanted and expected from Myanmar.

For example, the junta could have given face to ASEAN's "constructive engagement" approach to Myanmar by proving it to be superior to the Western approach of imposing economic embargoes and political sanctions. Such a policy would have helped ASEAN resume normal relations with its Western Dialogue Parttners much earlier. But the generals remained deaf to ASEAN's – and particularly Malaysia's – efforts at negotiating political reforms in Myanmar. After Myanmar's accession, Malaysia – strictly in line with the principles of quiet and inoffensive diplomacy – led ASEAN's engagement

---

[442] BBC News (03 May 2001): "Burmese talks feared stalled".
[443] Yuwadee (2001).

efforts with Myanmar, albeit without achieving much. Thus, UN special envoy to Myanmar, Razali (a Malaysian diplomat) and Malayisia's Prime Minister Mahathir engaged in long-standing secret negotiations with Myanmar to initiate some sort of dialogueprocess between the junta and the democratic opposition around Aung San Suu Kyi. After the negotiations had been fruitless for quite some time, the negotiations seemed to yield some positive outcome in 2000.[444] Eventually, in December/January 2001, Mahathir, on returning from a trip to Myanmar, announced a breakthrough and hinted that the military government had signaled its readiness to loosen the restrictions on the opposition and to engage initiate dialoguewith the opposition.[445] However, these hopes were soon dashed, as rumors spread that incipient talks between SPDC and the opposition had stalled early on and as the SPDC junta had "deferred numerous requests by United Nations special envoy Razali Ismail – the main catalyst behind the talks – to revisit Burma."[446] Indeed, the military government even seemed to use the situation for a backlash against domestic oppositional forces. The *FEER* reported that "[i]ncreasingly, the SPDC appears to be using the confusion over the talks to try to drive a wedge between Suu Kyi and her own movement."[447]

Myanmar's lack of cooperation continued to stand in the way of an early resumption of the EU-ASEAN dialogue. Since ASEAN – against its interest in resuming the talks – insisted on Myanmar's participation, and since the EU – due to the unchanged status of Myanmar – saw no room for negotiating its admission, Myanmar's behavior deferred the resumption of the meetings.

Overall, ASEAN has treated Myanmar as an equal member and has also observed the principles of non-interference and quiet, behind-the-scenes diplomacy. Whereas Myanmar expected solidarity from ASEAN members, it has not been willing to bear any solidarity costs itself.[448]

---

[444] Cf. for example Kavi (2000).

[445] In an interview I conducted with the Malaysian Minister of Human Resources, Dr. Fung, on 10 January 2001 in Kuala Lumpur, the Minister made a point of emphasizing that the Prime Minister's recent trip to Myanmar had yielded very positive results and that Mahathir had the impression the military government's stance on the opposition had become considerably more conciliatory.

[446] Crispin and Lintner (2001).

[447] Ibid.

[448] Cp. for example Kavi (2000) who lists Myanmar's failures to show solidarity and comments: "Interestingly, in the past three years Asean countries have defended in vain their decision on Burma. In private, Asean officials have expressed disappointment a the lack of progress against political oppression in Burma. [...] [Conversely, M.H.] it has been Burma that has taken the initiative to have Asean members support its regime, as at the International Labour Organisation."

The Nation, Bangkok (24 July 2000): "Regional Perspective: Asean must confront new-old member split".

Summary: Throughout and after the economic crisis, ASEAN has shielded newcomer Myanmar from external criticism. ASEAN and its members have consistently pursued a policy of "constructive engagement" with its Myanmar and have represented this position to Western countries without any compromises. Thus, the grouping developed its own, unique way of dealing with its new member. Antagonizing the West over Myanmar came at the high diplomatic cost of alienating both the U.S. and the EU. ASEAN's support for Myanmar appears to be unbreakable, no matter how little Myanmar's commitment and contribution to ASEAN's interests.

The Democratic Thai government represented the only exception to ASEAN's otherwise consistently friendly behavior vis-à-vis Myanmar. Thus, between late 1997 and early 2001, Thailand antagonized the SPDC junta and publicly criticized what was officially considered as Myanmar's internal affairs by most ASEAN members. With a view to Myanmar, Thailand also tried to de-emphasize ASEAN's principle of non-intervention and conversely promoted "flexible engagement". The Chuan government's public stance against Myanmar's calamitous democratic and human rights record and its vote in favor of an ILO resolution against Myanmar stood in clear contrast to the other ASEAN members' approach to Myanmar and presented a rare case of unsolidary behavior vis-à-vis Myanmar within ASEAN.

Myanmar itself expected much from ASEAN in terms of political support. In turn, the SPDC government itself has cared little about how it could contribute to ASEAN's international standing and has failed to face any solidarity costs whatsoever.

Evaluation: ASEAN's solidarity with Myanmar has been consistently high, especially with regard to the representation of ASEAN unity vis-à-vis external critics of Myanmar. Within ASEAN, Myanmar has been treated as an equal member and in line with ASEAN's principles of non-interference and quiet, behind-the-scenes diplomacy. When it was confronted with external pressure, ASEAN – following the principle of backing the front-line state – lined up behind Myanmar. Myanmar has experienced this high degree of equality and support regardless of its failure to live up to ASEAN's expectations.

Since ASEAN has faced high costs in taking care to introduce Myanmar to various intergovernmental forums and to integrate it into ASEAN's trade structures, it can be said that ASEAN has assisted Myanmar in its *need situation* (cf. section 2.2.2.) and has (with the exception of Thailand) resisted any *breach temptation*. Conversely, Myanmar has not lived up to the model of the *common good situation*, but rather has tried to free-ride (i.e. it has participated in an important collective good which ASEAN provided – access to intergovernmental processes –, but at the same time took into account the defacement of ASEAN's image and international standing for the sake of its own national interests). Myanmar's behavior in a *mishap situation* could not be assessed, since it never had any intentions of acting solidarically to begin with.

The one exception to ASEAN's generally good solidarity record with Myanmar is Thailand under the Chuan government (late 1997-early 2001). When Myanmar did not comply with Thailand's demands, Thailand antagonized Myanmar's junta and eventually let it down when it voted with the West (and against ASEAN) for ILO sanctions against Myanmar. The governments preceding and following the Chuan government, however, have a better solidarity record with Myanmar.

The degree of ASEAN's political solidarity was "high" in absolute and "stable" in relative terms. In economic terms, the relatively low profile of material transfers from more developed ASEAN members to Myanmar possibly represents a shortcoming of ASEAN, but in my view does not discount the overall high degree of solidarity. Thailand's solidarity under the Chuan government was "low" in absolute and "defunct" in relative terms, whereas it seems to be "high" and "stable" under the present government.

Myanmar displayed no visible sign of solidarity with ASEAN. Overall, solidarity has been "low" in absolute terms and "defunct" in relative terms.

Table 22: ASEAN's solidarity with Myanmar (1997-2001)

	Absolute sovereignty	Relative sovereignty
ASEAN (overall)	high	stable
Indonesia	high	stable
Malaysia	high	stable
Philippines	n.a.	n.a.
Singapore	high	stable
ASEAN newcomers (Vietnam, Myanmar, Laos, Cambodia)	high	stable
Thailand (Chuan govt, late 1997 - early 2001)	low	defunct
(Thaksin govt, since early 2001)	high	stable

3.5. Economic crisis and after: Singapore's assistance to Indonesia (1997-2001)

The situation: The Asian economic crisis sent Indonesia's economy and society tumbling into chaos, while Singapore's economy was least affected of all ASEAN economies. The sudden destabilization and impoverishment of its direct neighbor and core ASEAN member, Indonesia, presented a threefold challenge to Singapore: first, a destabilized Indonesia threatened to impact negatively on Singapore and the Southeast Asian region in various ways; second, as the richest ASEAN member, Singapore could be expected to contribute to the stabilization of Indonesia, and, third, Singapore's traditionally excellent economic and political ties with the Suharto administration almost obliged Singapore to help. Thus, up to May 1998 – which marked the end of the Suharto era – conditions for Singaporean assistance to, and solidarity with, Indonesia were optimal.

From mid-1998 to 1999, tensions with the government of Suharto's successor, President Habibie, strained the bilateral relations. In 2000, Singapore welcomed the shift of power in Indonesia, but relations "remained vulnerable [...] despite Singapore's efforts to develop friendly relations with the government of President Abdurrhaman Wahid."[449] Singapore's own economic difficulties peaked both in 1998, when the city state faced a technical recession and again in 2001, when it experienced the first full-year recession since 1985.[450]

The problem: Indonesia's economic crisis can be seen as a litmus test for the substance of Singapore's solidarity with Indonesia. Whereas Singapore had profited from its especially good relations with the Suharto regime and the Indonesian armed forces (TNI) throughout the past decades when Indonesia had played the leading role in ASEAN, the question to be asked with a view to solidarity is whether Singapore was also ready to support Indonesia in times of economic and political turmoil. It is especially interesting to see whether Singapore's fading political influence in Indonesia after the change of government from Suharto to Habibie, and later to Wahid, also affected the degree of its solidarity with Indonesia.

The reaction:
October 1997 to May 1998 In direct response to Indonesia's economic turmoil, Singapore pledged an overall US$ 10 billion aid package to the Suharto government on 21 October 1997. The initial package was split into two even parts: A US$ 5 billion stand-by loan represented a supplement – as a second line

---

[449] Huxley (2001).
[450] Cf. Saywell (2001).
A technical recession is defined as two consecutive quarters of contracting GDP.

of credit – to the IMF's rescue scheme for Indonesia.[451] Another US$ 5 billion stand-by credit was pledged to a currency guarantee scheme intended to protect the rupiah from severe destabilization.[452] Thus, Singapore pledged by far more aid to Indonesia than all other ASEAN members taken together. Reportedly, "[t]he extent of the aid [...] surprised many economists; in Singapore's case, amounting to one-eighth of their foreign reserves."[453]

Table 23: Major pledges from ASEAN members to Indonesia's economic recovery (by 1998)

Country	Commitment
Singapore	US$ 10 billion loan (US$ 5 billion stand-by loan as part of the IMF rescue package plus US$ 5 billion as stand-by credit for a currency guarantee scheme)
Malaysia	US$ 1.25 billion loan
Brunei	US$ 1.2 billion loan
Thailand	5,000 tons of rice; US$ 1 million's worth of medicine

When Indonesia's currency depreciated rapidly in early 1998, Singapore took the initiative to facilitate a multilateral import guarantee scheme for Indonesia. Thus, in February 1998, Prime Minister Goh attempted to drum up US$ 20 billion from G7 countries and suggested to withdraw part of its own contribution, US$ 2 billion, from the IMF rescue package in order to reallocate it to the envisioned scheme.[454] However, Singapore's efforts to help the Suharto government garner funds for short-term import facilitation measures – for which the IMF rescue package made no provisions – failed to draw support from the G7 countries.

Subsequently – at the request of President Suharto[455] – Singapore envisioned its own Bilateral Trade Financing Guarantee Scheme (BTFG), to which it intended to reallocate the US$ 5 billion previously pledged to the IMF package.[456] Phase

---

[451] Cf. Rüland (2000a): 429.

[452] Cf. Cheng et al. (1998).

[453] Asia Pacific Management News (29 October 1997): "Stir over Singaporean and Malaysian aid to Indonesia".

[454] Cf. Rüland (2000a): 429 ; Cheng et al. (1998); Dolven and McBeth (1998).

[455] Cf. Lee Lai To (1999b): 76; Cheng et al. (1998).

[456] The reference text for this information (Cheng et al. 1998) states: "BTFG will be using the loan money (US$ 5 billion) pledged for the IMF aid package." This source seems to be the only reliable one as far as the exact name, nature and origin of the funds for the BTFG are

one of the credit guarantee scheme (worth US$ 3 billion) was to cover exclusively domestic – and later also retained – exports from Singapore to Indonesia. In a second step, the BTFG was to phase in the remaining US$ 2 billion to cover "exports through Singapore by Indonesia's trading partners who do not have their own bilateral export credit scheme." The scheme's operation was to be limited to a maximum of two years.[457]

However, disbursement of the BTFG funds was strictly tied to conditions set by the IMF. Therefore, the Suharto government – which had earlier objected to the economic reforms demanded by the IMF – was apparently reluctant to accept the terms of the scheme. By the time of Suharto's resignation, the issue was still open.

May 1998 - late 1999   The incoming government of President Habibie – whose relations with Singapore's government were strained almost from day one of Habibie's inauguration – rejected the scheme straight away. "Jakarta thought the scheme had too many safeguards."[458] The basic conflict was that

> Singapore wanted guarantees [i.e. IMF criteria, M.H.] in place to prevent the money being used "unwisely", while Indonesia regarded the conditions as far too difficult to accept.[459]

The general incompatibility of the two governments, which was accompanied by rhetorical mud-slinging on both sides[460] prevented the implementation of any aid packages. Although Singapore formally still upheld a slimmed-down US$2 billion proposal for the trade financing scheme (at IMF conditions), the pledged overall funds of US$ 10 billion remained practically undisbursed.[461] Ironically, by 1999 Singapore's actual material assistance to Indonesia had been limited to aid worth Sing$ 12 million, which had been granted in June 1998, and private donations amounting to US$ 2.5 million.[462] Obviously, Singapore no longer showed any eagerness to grant financial support to Indonesia, as Indonesia did not implement economic restructuring in line with the recommendations of the IMF.

---

concerned. Other sources are less precise as to the name, origin and exact amount of the BTFG funds. Some sources even mistake the BTFG funds as complimentary funds to Singapore's US$ 5 billion IMF supplement. Therefore, Cheng et al. (1998) is seen here as authoritative in this respect.

[457] For an overview of the scheme, cf. Cheng et al. (1998).

[458] Lee Lai To (1999b): p. 76.

[459] Smith (1999): 251.

[460] Lee Kuan Yew had publicly doubted Habibie's competence, whereupon Habibie retorted in May 1998 that Singapore was merely a "tiny red dot" on the map and in May 1999 depicted the city state as being racist and anti-Malay.

[461] Cp. Dolven and McBeth (1998); Singh and Than (eds.) (1999): 15.

[462] On these two humanitarian aid packages, cf. Sim (1998).

Singapore's reluctance to disburse aid was seen as a scandal in Indonesia, especially since Indonesians felt Singapore had profited unduly from (illegal) capital flight from Indonesia and thus had a moral obligation to help, no matter whether or not Indonesia met IMF criteria. Indonesia even demanded "Singapore to sign an extradition treaty to bring back 'economic criminals' who fled Indonesia during 1998"[463], thereby playing on Singapore's role as a safe haven for (illegally) expatriated Indonesian capital (often owned by Indonesian citizens of Chinese origin, a fact which contributed to a bilateral twist among ethnic lines between Chinese-dominated Singapore and the Malay society of Indonesia). Thus, in Indonesia there was a feeling that Singapore's failure to disburse its original financial commitments represented a crude lack of solidarity.

As a consequence, many in the Habibie government, such as senior adviser to the President, Dewi Fortuna Anwar, complained about Singapore's alleged lack of solidarity.

> "Humanitarian assistance smacks of charity [...]. We want Singapore to get us investment and help us in external debt financing. [...] Who needs fair-weather friends who are by our side only when times are good?" asked Dewi. [...] Analysts here say Dewi's views are reflective of those held by the inner core of Habibie's advisers.[464]

As the Habibie government failed to accept the IMF criteria tied to Singapore's aid scheme proposals, Singapore remained tight-fisted. In the face of bilateral strains and political incompatibilities between the two governments, and as Singapore argued it was not going to pump rescue loans into an inefficient economy, Singapore completely turned off economic and financial aid to Indonesia. As Prime Minister Goh put it in an interview,

> We are profit-oriented, we are calculative, we are logical, we are rational, but that doesn't mean we are selfish. Whatever we do, we would work it out, and make sure it is useful and constructive. That doesn't mean we are selfish. Selfish means you exploit, you don't help others because you keep everything for yourself. No, when a scheme would work, we would put money in. We would put $5 billion for investments into, say Indonesia, if the scheme will work. And if $5 billion will over time be recovered, I would say we do it. But if it is just

---

[463] Smith (1999): 251.

[464] Mohan Srilal (1999).

Cp. Lee Lai To (1999b): 76, and Smith (1999): 251, who states that "[...] there is an underlying assumption among Indonesian policy-makers that Indonesia has had to look beyond ASEAN to mobilize resources to cope with its economic crisis, and that Singapore in particular has failed to provide assistance."

a matter of giving grants and financial aid which may not work, we will not do it.[465]

Trade instead of aid   Shying away from the costs of – possibly ineffective and most likely irretrievable – economic and financial aid, Singapore's efforts at stabilizing Indonesia's economy focused increasingly on mutually beneficial, profit-oriented and sustainable development projects.

Most prominently, Singapore in 1999 initiated the first two of a series of multi-billion bilateral natural gas proliferation schemes in 1999, thereby opting for Indonesia as its future main supplier of natural gas.[466] Singapore's more than 20-years' guarantee to purchase natural gas from South Sumatra and the West Natuna gas fields at a fixed price as well as a US$ 70.5 investment outlay by Singapore's SembCorp Gas[467] enabled Indonesia to finance the required pipeline infrastructure between the respective gas fields and Singapore. The gas deals also represented an active contribution to the Trans-ASEAN Gas Pipeline (TAGP) project, an integrative energy resource development program designed to provide an intra-ASEAN trans-border infrastructure of pipelines linking remote gas fields to the industrialized centers of Southeast Asia.[468] Thus, Singapore preferred cooperation and trade over aid and thus steered a more equity-oriented course, pragmatically following ASEAN's maxim of mutually beneficial cooperation. Off-record, Indonesians frequently complained that, rather than showing solidarity, Singapore had taken Indonesia's economic weakness as an opportunity to wrench inexpensive long-term deals on the delivery of natural gas from the Indonesian government.

2000-2001   AbdurrhamanWahid's accession to the presidency in late 1999 stirred new hopes in Singapore that relations with Indonesia may improve. Underlining Singapore's interest in improving relations with Indonesia, "Singapore Prime Minister Goh Chok Tong unveiled a $1.2 billion investment

---

[465] Interview with Prime Minister Goh Chok Tong, *Straits Times*, 24 January 2001.

[466] For more information on Singapore's gas deals with Indonesia, cf. for example:
- "Singapore Power secures Indonesia gas supply", *Oil&Gas Journal*, 4 October 1999, p. 38;
- McBeth and Saywell (2001).
- Michael Richardson (2001).

[467] For this figure, cf. "Singapore, Indonesia signal improved ties at gas delivery ceremony", *Oil&Gas Journal Online*, 15 January 2001.

[468] In the longer term, the so-called "gas grid" is to make ASEAN a competitive provider of natural gas to the markets of China and Japan, cf. "Economic implications of the Indonesia-Singapore gas deal", interview by Radio Singapore International with Dr. Mike Nahan, Executive Director of the Institute of Public Affairs in Melbourne, Singapore, 13 February 2001, http://rsi.com.sg/en/programmes/newsline/2001/02/13_01.htm [02/05/01].
The TAGP is part of a larger energy cooperation scheme, cf. *ASEAN Plan of Action for Energy Cooperation 199-2004*, 1 July 1999, http://www.nepo.go.th/inter/ASEAN-PlanOf%20Action.html [11/05/01].

package for Indonesia" (more precisely, the Indonesian province Riau as part of the Indonesia-Malaysia-Singapore Growth Triangle –IMSGT– zone) in January 2000.[469] However, in the face of the continued bleak prospects for the Indonesian economy, the incentives provided under the scheme failed to attract investors.

> Singapore companies have been hesitant to take part in the S$2.6 billion [US$ 1.2 billion, M.H.] economic assistance package announced by Prime Minister Goh Chok Tong during his visit to Jakarta in January. Goh's package includes an offer to participate in investment projects in Indonesia, a loan scheme for small and medium Singapore enterprises investing in Indonesia, a joint promotion effort on the tourism front and the development of Batam, Bintan and Karimun industrial islands in Indonesia. But nearly two months since the announcement, the initiative, particularly the loan scheme, has received few takers. [...] Top government officials in Singapore said they had done all they could to encourage investment in Indonesia, but ultimately it was up to the investors.[470]

Besides this scheme, Singapore provided no further aid packages in 2000. The implication was – once again – that Singapore expected Indonesia to initiate reforms first before it could expect to profit from any loan or investment schemes. Put simply, no reforms, no trust, no rescue schemes. Among Singapore's elites, the notion prevailed that Singapore should not give out a "free lunch" to Indonesia.[471] As Prime Minister Goh explained:

> We can't just be pumping aid to the poor in our neighbourhood So, sometimes we are seen by our neighbours as not being helpful enough.

---

[469] West (2000).

There seems to be some confusion regarding the actual value of the aid scheme. The American source quoted here speaks simply of $ 1.2 billion; another source (see next footnote) speaks of 2.6 billion *Singapore* dollars (the equivalent of US$ 1.2 billion). The annual review of Singapore's foreign policy in *Asia Survey* speaks of 1.2 billion *Singapore* dollars and indicates the equivalent in dollars *US in brackets* (US$ 698 million).

[470] Bayuni (2000): "Singapore investors wait for more signals from Indonesian Government", *Jakarta Post*, 7 March 2000.

[471] Cp., for example, the comments of Friedrich Wu, vice-president of DBS bank in Singapore who is quoted as saying "From Singapore's view, we're not going to give out a free lunch [...]. We want to know that the money is going to be well spent and that it's fully accounted for. It's not just going into some corrupt businessman's or politician's pocket." (quoted in: McBeth and Saywell 2001).

In the context of Singapore's domestic discourse on aid to Indonesia, it is important to note that, since the beginning of the crisis in 1997, the Singaporean public and parliamentary opposition had been very critical to the US$ 10 billion aid package announced by Singapore's government.

[...] we should actively help where we can in a meaningful, long-term, constructive way. This is to play the role of a catalyst – [...] like the loan scheme and the investment scheme that we have for Indonesia. Those are very meaningful schemes which will work. But there must be political certainty on the other side for investors to want to invest. Once there is, Singaporeans will want to invest in Indonesia.[472]

Thus, Singapore stuck to its trade-instead-of-aid policy that had already infuriated the policy makers around Habibie. This position certainly contributed further to a heightened sensitivity in Indonesia about Singapore's alleged lack of solidarity, a view expressed in vigorous and offensive terms by President Wahid when he rode a stinging attack against Singapore during the ASEAN summit in November 2000. Besides other allegations, the President charged that

From my meeting with Lee Kuan Yew, it has also become clear that Singapore is only looking to reap profits from its relations with its neighbors. You know, Singapore is a trading nation.[473]

In 2001, Singapore's "no-free-lunch" stance on assistance to Indonesia persisted. The city state continued to invest in economically and strategically promising and mutually profitable projects. Thus, Singapore concluded a major additional gas deal with Indonesia[474] and tried to secure a deal on long-term water supply from Indonesia's Riau province. Further, Singapore implemented a small agri-business investment scheme for Riau, which, as part of the Indonesia-Malaysia-Singapore Growth Triangle, carries large investments from Singapore. As reported in February,

Singapore and Riau will establish a vegetable packaging and processing centre in Pekanbaru which is expected to be a "catalyst" to attract further private sector investment in agri-business.[475]

The rest of Indonesia received no further investment or trade promotion assistance in 2001.

Summary: In response to the impact of the economic crisis on Indonesia, Singapore initially pledged a stand-by loan package worth US$ 10 billion to the

---

[472] Interview with Prime Minister Goh Chok Tong in *The Straits Times*, 24 January 2001.

[473] *The Straits Times* (27 November 2000): "Why Gus Dur is not happy with Singapore".

[474] By February 2001, the two gorvernments agreed to build a second gas pipeline from South Sumatra to Singapore. As in the other gas deals, Singapore gave long-term guarantees to purchase the natural gas coming from the respective gas fields thus linked to the city state. Altogether, Singapore now has three such gas pipeline deals with Indonesia. On the economic scope of these projects, cf. *Jakarta Post* (15 January 2001): "Indonesia and Singapore leaders launch joint energy project"; McBeth and Saywell (2001).

[475] *Times of India* (15 February 2001): "Singapore, Indonesia expand agriculture cooperation".

Suharto government. US$ 5 billion was to complement the IMF rescue package for Indonesia as a second line of credit. The other half was earmarked for a currency stabilization scheme designed to back the rupiah against major depreciation and thereby restore confidence in the Indonesian currency.

In the face of rapid economic deterioration and currrency depreciation in Indonesia, Singapore's government – unsuccessfully – lobbied G7 countries to contribute to an overall US$ 20 billion rescue fund beyond the IMF's efforts. Subsequently, at the request of President Suharto, Singapore finally resolved to convert its original contribution to the IMF rescue package into a more flexibly accessible bilateral import promotion scheme for Indonesia, the so-called Bilateral Trade Finance Guarantee Scheme (BTFG).

In the end, however, the pledged funds remained practically undisbursed. After the fall of the Suharto regime, relations with the successor government of President Habibie deteriorated quickly. Habibie rejected to accept IMF criteria tied to the disbursement of the proposed BTFG funds, while Singapore insisted on economic restructuring measures as a precondition for disbursement of the funds.

As Singapore adopted a "no-free-lunch" policy, Singapore's focus shifted from aid to a more equity-oriented approach or, bluntly, from aid to more trade. Thus, Singapore generated additional trade by concluding three long-term natural gas proliferation agreements with Indonesia. These multi-billion dollars gas deals gave Indonesia room to tap additional gas fields and set up the required marine pipeline infrastructure to get the resources to Singapore. Further, Singapore – again not unselfishly – tried to secure a long-term contract for water supplies from Riau province.

Basically, Singapore kept to its "no-free-lunch" policy and continued to de-emphasize the aid aspect throughout President Wahid's term in office. When the only attempt to initiate a US$ 1.2 billion incentive for Singaporean companies to investment in Riau largely failed to attract investors, Singapore did not reallocate any further funds to other projects, but basically told Indonesia to provide stabilizing reforms first. Singapore's strong emphasis on economic restructuring and its insistence on economic cooperation rather than on aid drew angry protests from the governments of Presidents Habibie and Wahid.

Evaluation: As outlined in section 2, solidarity does not preclude self-interest – indeed, it is even based on it to a certain degree – and is clearly not based on altruism. On the other hand, solidarity is incompatible with (myopic) opportunism, unreliability, unpredictability and a purely equity-oriented approach to cooperation.

Singapore's behavior cannot but be considered as motivated by self-interest. Strong interdependence with Indonesia left the city state no choice but to engage in some sort of assistance to stabilize the country. Initially, Singapore chose an approach based on –by any standards – generous financial aid and even engaged in diplomatic efforts to drum up additional support from G7 countries. Thus, though clearly self-interested, Singapore's initial response was strongly solidary.

When Indonesia's leadership changed, subsequent governments declined to accept the flanking measures Singapore regarded as essential for ensuring the effectiveness and recoverability of the aid funds. Since Indonesia proved unwilling or incapable of implementing sufficient economic restructuring, Singapore's pledged bilateral funds could not be expected to effectively contribute to the stabilization of the ailing Indonesian economy. The decision to defer financial aid projects neither represented a violation of ASEAN norms nor a breach of solidarity: ASEAN norms are aimed at mutually beneficial cooperation, clearly not at financial aid. More generally, solidarity required Singapore – within the limits of its capacities – to contribute adequate political and economic resources to the stabilization of Indonesia; however, solidarity did not require Singapore to single-handedly engage in economic aid adventures of questionable outcome, especially at a time when the city state faced severe economic strains itself.

Rather than on aid, Singapore focused on sustainable, mutually beneficial and market-oriented cooperation. Between 1998 and 2001, Singapore generated massive additional revenues for Indonesia when it initiated three major long-term natural natural gas supply deals and helped fund the required natural resource development and pipeline infrastructure projects. Thus, Singapore made a valuable contribution to Indonesia's economic stability and the country's integration into the trans-ASEAN gas pipeline project. With a view to solidarity, the natural gas and water deals are an ambiguous affair, as, on the one hand, they certainly created a new source of income for Indonesia, but, on the other hand, were arguably concluded at conditions that reminded many Indonesians of economic blackmailing rather than fair dealing among equal partners.

Further, looking at Singapore's demeanor vis-à-vis Indonesia between 1998 and 2001 leaves a stale aftertaste remains if one considers that all of the originally pledged US$ 10 billion rescue package remained practically undisbursed.

Apparently, Singapore's government also failed to credibly mediate its "no-free-lunch" policy to Indonesia, and the governments of Presidents Habibie and Wahid doubted Singapore's real concern for Indonesia. They obviously would have expected Singapore to extend at least part of the rescue loans at relaxed – not the strict IMF – conditions. Indonesian governments even felt entitled to, and expected Singapore to share or repatriate, the profits gained from illegally expatriated Indonesian capital invested in Singapore. Further, Singapore's adoption of an assertive stance vis-à-vis post-Suharto Indonesia – when it rather should have made humble amends for undisbursed pledges – was also probably interpreted by many Indonesians as cool arrogance and disrespect. Thus, beyond the material side of the assistance problem, relational signaling between the two countries' governments failed. Singapore certainly failed to make sufficient amends for the *mishap situation* (cf. section 2.2.) it caused by failing to follow up on its pledges of financial and economic aid.

Thus, overall, although Singapore certainly had good reasons to behave as it did, absolute solidarity has to be classified as merely "deficient" and "relatively unstable".

Table 24: Singapore's solidarity with Indonesia (with regard to economic assistance), 1997-2001.

	Absolute solidarity	Relative solidarity
1997 to mid-1998	high	stable
mid-1998 to 2001	deficient	unstable
overall, 1997-2001	deficient	unstable

3.6. Singapore and Malaysia: 'Whose solidarity?' Contending positions on AFTA and bilateral Free Trade Agreements (FTA)

The situation: As most ASEAN economies slowly emerged and recovered from the shock of the crisis in 1999, external conditions for ASEAN solidarity and for tackling regional problems at intergovernmental rather than national level improved. With the potentially devastating impact of regional interdependence fresh on ASEAN members' mind, the moment was right to engage in constructing collective defences for the future.

Indeed, ASEAN seemed to seize the moment: In order to restore confidence in the economies of Southeast Asia, ASEAN in 1999 resolved to significantly accelerate the pace of tariff liberalization under the Common Effective Preferential Tariff Scheme (CEPT), which, as the heart piece of the ASEAN Free Trade Area (AFTA), was key to further liberalization in other areas. In the same year, ASEAN also seriously started exploring possibilities of forging a Closer Economic Cooperation area by linking AFTA and CER – Australia's and New Zealand's joint Common Economic Region free trade arrangement – and moved closer to the economies of East Asia through extended ASEAN Plus Three (APT) cooperation.

By late 2000, the slowing American economy started to plunge Southeast Asian economies into renewed recession, which hit especially export-dependent Singapore very hard, as "the economy contracted 10.6% in annualized terms in the first half of the year."[476] Thus, the strained economic environment suggested more difficult times ahead for ASEAN solidarity.

The problem: Especially Singapore, seconded by Thailand, saw swift and comprehensive AFTA integration and liberalization as the key for access to other FTAs and world markets, since this represented the only way for the region to compete for foreign investment, increase intra-regional trade and sustain its exports to the world's economic centers.

However, although other major ASEAN members – Malaysia, Indonesia, and partly the Philippines – generally agreed that, in the face of the economic crisis, closer ASEAN integration was desirable, their enthusiasm for intra-ASEAN liberalization was frequently muffled by prospects of seeing their respective protected and uncompetitive national industries pushed out of the market.

Conversely, Singapore's and Thailand's enthusiasm for AFTA liberalization was all the greater: Singapore had practically no import tariffs on manufactured and agricultural goods (and thus only stood to profit from ASEAN neighbors' liberalization efforts). Thailand, due to its strategic centrality to Japanese and American car makers could hope to become the hub of the automotive industry in, and increase its exports to, Southeast Asia. Through AFTA, Thailand could also hope to increase its exports to Malaysia's (so far highly protected) rice market with its own surplus of cheaper and qualitatively better rice.

Thus, although ASEAN had collectively agreed to speed up the CEPT time frame, interests differed strongly about the actual direction AFTA was headed for. At one end of the spectrum, Singapore saw the CEPT merely as a first step towards deeper and wider AFTA integration, from Malaysia's perspective its scope was already too wide.

Another point of contention was the proposed AFTA-CER free trade agreement. Whereas Singapore initiated and Thailand welcomed the proposed link,[477] Malaysia – Australia's staunchest political opponent since the early 1990s – headed the group of objectors most vocally and decisively.

ASEAN members' interests thus differed widely on the issue of AFTA integration and the AFTA-CER link, a situation inviting the pursuit of individual interests at the cost of group solidarity. In this context, analyzing group solidarity means establishing whether

(a) ASEAN members convincingly engaged in finding common ground on the future of AFTA – in this respect, the analysis will show in how far AFTA integration actually represented a distinguished and valuable collective good to individual members; (b) the parties involved kept to their commitments under the CEPT and refrained from opportunistic behavior; (c) the consultation

---

[476] Saywell (2001).
[477] Cf. James (2000).

process went along the lines of mutually reassuring relational signaling, fairness and community-orientation.

The analysis focuses mainly on two exponents representing opposite ends of the ASEAN spectrum with regard to economic integration in AFTA, the governments of Singapore and Malaysia.

The reaction: In 2000 and 2001, Singapore was severely frustrated by decisions taken at ASEAN level. Instead of evolution towards more integration, AFTA faced devolution to the point of meninglessness when Malaysia denied to keep to its liberalization commitments and indicated its will to indefinitely delay slashing its import tariffs on cars (presently ranging from 140 to 300 percent, depending on car size and class). Malaysia's single-handed and unprecedented denial left ASEAN members with the choice to either make special allowances for countries wanting to backtrack from their commitments or to rebuke Malaysia's behavior. In order to save AFTA's image (albeit, not its substance), ASEAN leaders opted for the former, thereby undermining AFTA considerably.[478] Apparently, the Malaysian example has set a precedent and kicked off some domino effect among ASEAN members. Thus,

> Indonesia, citing its weak economic condition, has said it would not meet its commitment until others had done so. It also wants to exclude sugar to protect its farmers. The Philippines plans to ask for a delay in cutting tariffs on petrochemical products [...].[479]

Vietnam reportedly also asked for special conditions, and Thailand has threatened to retaliate against Malaysia by raising its own import tariffs for Malaysian goods. What is more, there have been indicators of rising non-tariff barriers within ASEAN.[480]

Singapore suffered a further setback when the proposed AFTA-CER link, a project which had been assessed favorably in 2000 by a specially set-up ASEAN task force,[481] was dropped (or indefinitely deferred) due to resistance

---

[478] Cp. Article 1, paragraph 1 of the "Protocol Regarding the Implementation of the CEPT Scheme Temporary Exclusion List", Fourth ASEAN Informal Summit, Singapore, 23 November 2000.
Cf. also Reyes (2000b); Salil Tripathi (2000).

[479] Wheatley (2001).
Cp. also an editorial in the *Bangkok Post*, which observed that "In the footsteps of Malaysia, the Philippines and Indonesia are planning to ask for similar delays [i.e. deferral of tariff liberalization, M.H.] to protect their petrochemicals and sugar industries." (*Bangkok Post*, 5 May 2001: "Asean must move towards integration").

[480] Cp. for example BizAsiaNews (16 May 2000): "Non-tariff Barriers rising in Asean Free Trade Area".

[481] Cf. Austria and Avila (2001): 10.

from Malaysia, Indonesia and also the Philippines.[482] In Malaysia and Indonesia, opposition to the AFTA-CER link was not only motivated by economic concerns, but also by strong cultural and political reservations vis-à-vis Australia and New Zealand.[483] Thus, "Malaysia said it does not want Australia or New Zealand to use their ties with Singapore as a way of joining the ASEAN Free Trade Area"[484] on the grounds that "[t]hey are not part of East Asia", as Malaysia's Minister of Trade, Rafidah Aziz, put it bluntly.[485]

As AFTA was actually disintegrating, Singapore started securing access to foreign markets single-handedly and engaged in negotiating bilateral free trade agreements (FTA) with the US, EFTA, Mexico, Japan, Australia and New Zealand. When Malaysia, Indonesia and the Philippines reprimanded Singapore at the 2000 summit for its FTA efforts and claimed that the city state lacked solidarity with ASEAN members, Singapore's Prime Minister Goh retorted: "Those who can run faster should run faster. They shouldn't be restrained by those who don't want to run at all."[486]

One charge frequently aired and reproduced in the Malaysian media was that Singapore attempted to liberalize AFTA through the "back door" by channeling extra-ASEAN imports through its already liberalized national market into the AFTA market. The main thrust of this charge was that Singapore's envisioned FTAs would leave the AFTA rules of origin ineffective. The following passage may serve as an example of the discourse on the subject in Malaysia:

> The Malaysian paper [*Berita Harian Malaysia*, M.H.], in a blistering editorial last week, likened Singapore's action to 'stabbing from the back' and 'hidden scissors that cut from inside'. 'If (Singapore) has drawn up a strategy to weaken other Asean countries then its move is effective,' the paper claimed. 'Singapore will become the main gateway for goods from outside the region to be sold in the Asean market and […] enjoy Afta concessions.[487]

Another charge was that Singapore took advantage of the considerable inflexibility and weakness of other ASEAN members to channel foreign investments into its own pockets.

---

[482] Cp. James (2000); *Business Recorder* (06 October 2000): "Southeast Asia struggles to defuse trade dispute".

[483] Thus, Malaysia's resentment of any kind of regional cooperation with Australia has been consistent through much of the 1990s, and this has not changed. Indonesia's relations with Australia are still shattered because of Australia's leading role in the engagement in East Timor.

[484] AFTA Watch (23 February 2001): "Malaysia blocks Australia and New Zealand".

[485] Agence France Press (21 February 2001): "Malaysia issues warning on economic links".

[486] Reyes (2000c).

[487] *The Business Times*, Singapore (3 May 2001): "Singapore won't be 'back door to Afta'".

Singapore's politicians and media did not tire to counter such charges. The line taken in Singapore's discourse (speeches, editorials, open letters to Malaysian newspapers, etc.) is that AFTA's rules of origin were not affected at all by Singapore's FTA efforts, and that, rather than diverting investments from other ASEAN members, Singapore actually attracted additional investments to the region. Singapore's government made also clear that it expected other ASEAN members to follow Singapore's example. Often, Singaporean rhetoric depicts Singapore as a catalyst "leapfrogging" the region into competitiveness, liberalization and trans-regional cooperation with external partners for the whole region's, not only Singapore's, sake.[488] Exemplary for Singapore's discourse, Prime Minister Goh stated that

> 'Singapore's Free Trade Area initiatives with key partners outside the region do not undermine Asean, but, instead, ensure those countries stay engaged with Asean [...]. [W]e hope that our fellow Asean colleagues would join when they are ready, or forge FTAs of their own with their trading partners [...]. Neither will Singapore's FTAs with other countries outside Asean provide a backdoor for entry into the Asean market. This is precisely why we have rules of origin in Afta [...].' Asean, Goh added, could not afford to be a spectator as this trend of FTAs unfolded and replicated itself elsewhere. 'We risk being shut out of these FTAs.'[489]

Malaysia's charge that bilateral FTAs might serve to bypass AFTA's trade barriers does not hold because ASEAN's rules of origin would continue to filter imports into ASEAN coming through Singapore. Therefore, bilateral FTAs would not "buy" Singapore any advantages at the price of undermining other ASEAN members' import tariffs. Rather than trade in goods, Singapore's potential FTA partners are aiming at trade in services. As Australian Foreign Minister Downer put it: "Already we have pretty much free access to the goods market in Singapore, but what we want is better access to the services sector".[490] The real issue with Singapore's bilateral FTAs is not that Singapore has been trying to undermine any AFTA agreements, but that it has flexed its economic muscles and shown protectionists their limits. By more or less dropping AFTA from its policy focus and engaging in bilateralism, Singapore used the advantages as a lean and flexible economy whose total trade flows are nevertheless roughly equivalent to the combined GDP of Malaysia and Indonesia and whose "small size and lack of an agricultural sector allow its

---

[488] Cf. "Extracts from Prime Minister Goh Chok Tong's interview with the Straits Times, as published on 24 Jan 2001", *Straits Times*, Singapore, 24 January 2001.
[489] Goh Chok Tong, quoted in: Mehta (2001a).
[490] Reuters (23 July 2001): "Australia takes bilateral tack on Asian free trade".

government to negotiate free trade deals quickly"[491] to exert pressure on countries like Malaysia. The ratio was that, the more other countries joined in the bilateral race for investment and export markets, protectionists would soon be exposed to diversion of investments and trade to more competitive neighbors. In this sense, Singpore's politicians are right when they claim they see their FTA efforts as a contribution to regional trade liberalization.

> Singapore's drive to build up a network of bilateral free-trade agreements (FTAs) has changed the dynamics for the better, and this could lead to greater competition, said Minister for Trade and Industry George Yeo in Parliament on March 8. [...] Regional FTA initiatives, he said, are creating competitive dynamics for the launch of a new round of multilateral free-trade talks.[492]

Singapore's policy is already bearing first fruits. In July 2001, Thailand confirmed it was going to look into a bilateral FTA with Australia.[493] The Philippines' position still seems to be undecided. But whereas the country had sided with Malaysia and other critics against Singapore's FTA plans at the ASEAN summit in December 2000, Domingo Siazon, the former foreign minister – now in his capacity as the designate Philippine ambassador to Japan – in July 2001 defended Singapore's decision and advised the new government to follow in Singapore's footsteps:

> Former Philippine foreign secretary Domingo Siazon Jr has urged the government to follow Singapore and seek free-trade agreements (FTAs) with countries outside South-East Asia. Mr Siazon [...] said economic integration within Asean was slowing and it would be unwise for the Philippines to wait for other member nations to get their act together. [...] Mr Siazon praised Singapore for having the sense to enter into bilateral agreements with Australia, New Zealand and Japan [...].
>
> Last year the Philippines [had still] joined Malaysia in castigating Singapore for signing separate FTAs. [...]
>
> Mr Siazon said other countries in Asean were so beset with domestic problems that it would be dificult for an economically developed nation such as Singapore to wait for free trade.[494]

There have been reports that even Malaysia is rushing now to establish its own FTA with Japan in the face of economic competition.[495] In the face of this development, AFTA has practically lost its relevance.

---

[491] *Far Eastern Economic Review* (November 28, 2000): "Singapore's trade initiatives undermine ASEAN economic policy".

[492] Singapore News (3-9 March 2001): "Bilateral FTAs spark freer trade in the region".

[493] Reuters (23 July 2001): "Australia takes bilateral tack on Asian free trade".

[494] *The Straits Times* (21 July 2001): "Manila urged to follow S'pore on FTA".

Summary: Two reasons led Singapore to leave the common AFTA ground and pursue its own bilateral FTAs with trading partners all over the world.

First, several ASEAN members displayed a strong reluctance to follow AFTA's agenda for regional integration and trade liberalization. Malaysia openly denied to implement its agreed-upon commitments under the CEPT, whereas Indonesia and the Philippines publicly aired second thoughts about theirs. Thus, the AFTA process not only stalled at a relatively low level of liberalization, but also threatened to regress behind its prior achievements. On top of all this, other ASEAN members, such as Singapore and Thailand, had to stand by and watch as ASEAN *a posteriori* legitimized Malayisia's broken CEPT pledges.

Second, the proposed link between AFTA and CER, which had been initiated by Singapore, welcomed by Thailand and been positively assessed in economic terms by an ASEAN task force, met with especially strong opposition from Malaysia, but also from Indonesia and the Philippines.
Growing protectionism, increasing incompatibility of AFTA members' economic interests and the resulting disintegration and irrelevance of AFTA led Singapore to pursue its own straight-forward, if not to say aggressive, structural bilateralism, thereby flexing its mucles to all protectionsists in ASEAN and setting a signal for a change.
Singapore's bilateralism has caused others in the region to imitate the city state's example. Whereas this development is seen as a relief from the AFTA deadlock by Thailand and, partly, as a chance in the Philippines, Malaysia apparently feels forced to become more competitive, too, if it does not want to lose out on trade and investment in the future. All this indicates that AFTA is no longer the relevant driving force for trade liberalization in Southeast Asia.

Evaluation: Clearly, solidarity has its limits in ASEAN where national economic interests and policies are concerned. The examples of both Singapore and Malaysia clearly illustrate this. Malaysia's break with its AFTA commitments cannot but be evaluated as a crude lack of solidarity. It is a strong indicator that in Malaysia's esteem ASEAN's economic integration and institutionalization is not a highly valued common good. Even Malaysia's dire economic straits would have allowed for a more solidary policy. Malaysia's solidarity with ASEAN therefore is "low" in absolute terms and "defunct" in relative terms.
Singapore, on the other hand, deserves considerable credit for initiating and promoting the process of AFTA's institutionalized approach to economic integration since the early 1990s. Further, Singapore reacted to open confrontation and uncooperative behavior rather than breaking ASEAN

---

[495] Singapore News (3-9 March 2001), "Bilateral FTAs spark freer trade in the region".

solidarity unilaterally. Its response to AFTA's stagnation, however, can hardly be called an example of solidarity. A sober assessment of the facts shows that, as a commentator put it,

> Singapore largely has written off free trade within ASEAN as a viable short-term goal, preferring instead to focus its efforts on more developed partners outside Southeast Asia. Without Singapore's leadership, an ASEAN free trade agreement and regional economic integration are doubtful.[496]

Singapore's radical turn to bilateralism also leaves little space to classify its performance as a temporary stray from solidarity. However, a lack of viable alternatives under conditions of strong recession has to be conceded. Still, Singapore followed exclusively its own interests and recommended ASEAN members to follow its competitive model, while rhetorically dressing its demands in a solidary garb. Therefore, Singapore's solidarity in this instance has to be considered as "deficient". However, there is some chance that Singapore shows some more community-orientation again once the sour economic circumstances change for the better. Therefore, relative solidarity is seen here not as "defunct", but as "unstable".

Table 24/2: Singapore's and Malaysia's solidarity with respect to AFTA and FTAs (2000-2001)

	Absolute solidarity	Relative solidarity
Malaysia	"low"	"defunct"
Singapore	"deficient"	"unstable"

3.7. ASEAN's solidarity with its new members: the aspect of development aid (1999-2001)

The situation: Prior to the Asian economic crisis, ASEAN had raised high hopes of economic growth and extensive infrastructure development with the new ASEAN member countries – Cambodia, Myanmar, Laos and Vietnam (CLMV).[497] Thailand had launched the *Golden Quadrangle* initiative to "turn battlefields into markets" in 1992. In 1994, the ASEAN Economic Ministers

---

[496] "Singapore's trade initiatives undermine ASEAN economic policy", Stratfor Analysis, 28 November 2000.

[497] Vietnam had joined ASEAN in 1995, followed by Myanmar and Laos in 1997, whereas Cambodia's accession was deferred until 1999 because of its ruptuous domestic situation.

Meeting and Japan's MITI had devised the *AEM-MITI* initiative for Indochina, "with an emphasis on infratructure development, investment, trade and industrial policies",[498] which was followed up by an ASEAN intiative for the development of the Mekong Basin area (which comprises CLMV, Thailand and China's Yunnan province) in 1995.

> *The ASEAN-Mekong Basin Development Co-operation (ASEAN-MBDC)* [...] framework was initiated by the ASEAN nations, particularly Malaysia and Singapore in 1995 [...] [,which from 1996 on was to engage in] seven areas of cooperation: agriculture, minerals and forestry, industry, transport, telecommunications and energy, education and training, tourism, and trade and investment. [499]

In this initial phase, ASEAN had kicked off a major infrastructure project for CLMV, the US$ 1.5 billion Trans-Asia Railway link. Proposed and supervised by Malaysia, the railway was to link the countries of the Greater Mekong Subregion (GMS) to Singapore, Malaysia and China.

The *Vision 2020* document, a self-confident ASEAN brainchild devised in expectation of continuing strong regional economic growth and adopted by ASEAN leaders in December 1997, still emphasized ASEAN's objetive of "narrowing the gap in the level of development among Member Countries" and promised to "intensify and expand [...] new sub-regional growth areas" etc.[500]

The problem: When the economic crisis struck, the ASEAN-6 – in the face of their own severe economic problems – dropped or indefinitely deferred the implementation of agreed-upon development projects. The question emerges in how far ASEAN has followed up on, and implemented its original commitments and pledges in the period since 1999, once the main impact of the economic crisis had been overcome in wide parts of Southeast Asia.

ASEAN's development aid to CLMV 1999-2001 The ASEAN Ministerial Meeting and the ASEAN Summit of 1999 passed without any visible outcomes in terms of development aid for the ASEAN newcomers. Indeed, the issue did not even appear on the agendas. By mid-2000, in the face of ASEAN's inaction on the issue, CLMV – supported by Thailand, their direct Mekong neighbor – began reminding other ASEAN members of their previous promises. At the AMM in July 2000,

> Asean's comparatively new members are clamouring for a piece of the region's economic action, and called [...] for funds to accelerate the

---

[498] Mya Than and Abonyi (2001): 133.
[499] Ibid.
[500] ASEAN Vision 2020, Kuala Lumpur, 15 December 1997,.

> Mekong Basin development. Foreign ministers from Cambodia, Myanmar, Thailand, Laos and Vietnam warned at the grouping's annual meeting [...] that Asean will not progress unless it bridges the economic gaps among its 10 members. [...]
> A senior Asean official said Vietnam, Cambodia, Laos and Myanmar [...] "feel they have been given big promises when they joined Asean, but little is being done" [...].[501]

Thailand's government became instrumental in reviving the ASEAN-MBDC committee and the plans for the Trans-Asian Railway (TAR), which had fallen dormant when the crisis had struck. Meanwhile, funding for the TAR has been secured through joint support from the ADB, the World Bank as well as loans from Japan and the EU. It remains the only major infrastructure development project so far.

Thailand has reportedly also been promoting the establishment of a "Mekong Fund".[502]

Following the poorer nations' complaints, the issue of "narrowing the economic gap" between rich and poor ASEAN members gained some centrality at the ASEAN summit in November 2000, as the Initiative for ASEAN Integration (IAI) was launched.

Under the IAI, especially Singapore offered to extend its cooperation with CLMV countries in the area of human resources development. In terms of concrete transfers, the scheme is rather modest and focuses predominantly on vocational training, education of multipliers of knowledge from CLMV countries, and assistance in the area of information technology (as part of the e-ASEAN scheme). Altogether, these programs will involve about 90 additional scholarships from Singapore. Contributions from other countries have not been specified. The respective declaration vaguely states that "[t]o catalyse the IAI, ASEAN members will contribute what they can."[503]

Further, the IAI strongly focuses on drawing support from ASEAN's "Plus-Three" partners, China, Japan and Korea, who agreed on working towards an "Asian IT Belt". Under the initiative, China offered US$ 5 million and Korea altogether US$ 7 million additional funds. Japan "pledged to give priority to ASEAN countries in the disbursement of its US$ 15 billion 'Comprehensive Cooperation Package' on IT for Asia."[504]

---

[501] *The Straits Times*, Singapore (26 July 2000): "New Asean members want development".
[502] Cf. Mya Than and Abonyi (2001): 133.
[503] Chairman, 4th ASEAN Informal Summit: "The Way Forward: Initiative For ASEAN Integration", Press Statement, Singapore, 25 November 2000.
[504] For these figures, cf. "The Way Forward: Initiative For ASEAN Integration", Press Statement by the Chairman, 4th ASEAN Informal Summit, Singapore, 25 November 2000, and Anuraj Manibhandu (2000).

Further, the 7th ASEAN Economic Ministers' Retreat in May 2001 "agreed to implement an ASEAN GSP Scheme to provide preferences [i.e. tariff preferences, M.H.] to the new members […]" and "encouraged the ASEAN-6 to respond positively to these requests." The scheme, whose general concept has not been clearly specified, was reportedly likely to be implemented in the course of 2001.[505]

The scheme is to be based on special tariffs granted unilaterally by the respective developed ASEAN members.[506]

Despite ASEAN's unexpected and laudable focus on integrating its newer members, the fact remains that the IAI unmistakably represents a low-cost approach to integration. Singapore has already announced that its emphasis will continue to remain on non-financial development aid, and other countries have been unspecific about their commitments so far. Interestingly, Singapore's Prime Minister Goh also seems to apply its aid for trade stance already adopted vis-à-vis Indonesia in previous years: During a recent visist to Cambodia, he made clear that Singapore offered to invest in Cambodia's tourism industry in exchange for concrete concessions to Singapore.[507]

Already, the apologists of ASEAN, such as Margot Cohen writing in the *FEER*, are forthcoming with slogans of the "ideas are more valuable than money" kind. Though Cohen admitted that "it might be tempting to see the latest self-help kick by the Association of Southeast Asian nations as little more than Prozac-induced rhetoric", she refers to recent studies by the World Bank and statements by ASEAN officials to defend her point that, given the poor economic condition of Southeast Asia, low-cost, but sustainable skills and human resources development plus trade preferences will contribute more to regional integration than expensive railway projects.[508] However, one should not get the proportions wrong: the 90 additional scholarships Singapore plans to award to poor neighbors annually will hardly contribute to strong economic growth in the riparian countries of the Mekong Basin.

Summary: After even the discussion of development aid to its new members had stalled through mid-2000, the CLMV countries demanded that the old ASEAN members start remembering their promises made in the good years before the crisis. Thailand joined in to the wake-up call of its poorer Mekong

---

[505] Cf. Mehta (2001).

[506] Joint Statement, Press Conference of the 7th ASEAN Economic Ministers Retreat, AEM Chair, 3 May 2001.

[507] Reportedly, Goh said that in return for investments in Cambodia's tourism industry, he expected that "Cambodia must play its part." As to the nature of the deal, it was also reported that the "[s]ources said that Silk Air is interested in obtaining the right to fly passenger directly from Siem Reap to Phnom Penh, a right now reserved for Cambodia's airlines […]." (*The Straits Times*, 09 May 2001: "S'pore and Phnom Penh to boost ties".

[508] Cohen (2001).

Basin neighbors, and together they successfully promoted the revival of the MBDC and the Trans-Asia Railway project. Following the complaints of the CLMV coutries, Singapore initiated the Initiative for ASEAN Integration and promised to upgrade its existing human resources development efforts and implement new initiatives. Other ASEAN members have been slow to follow the initiative and failed to specify their respective commitments. The IAI also focuses on the "Plus Three" partners for support and has brought about a vague commitment to establish a Generalized System of Preferences (GSP) to reduce tariffs for CLMV imports into repsective ASEAN-6 countries in May 2001.

Evaluation: Overall, ASEAN's high-level rhetoric can't hide the fact that IAI represents only a low-cost approach to integration of the newcomers that hardly will improve CLMV's economic situation much. The only excuse for ASEAN-6 is that they themselves have been facing harsh economic times. The unwillingness of ASEAN-6 to engage in comprehensive development aid seems to be rather low. The exception seems to be Thailand, which, as part of the Mekong Basin Growth Triangle and direct neighbor to CLMV, feels the heat of the of its underdeveloped neighbors' economic problems most, has apparently been more proactive in the area of develpment aid than most other ASEAN members. To sum up, in the area of development aid, absolute solidarity of ASEAN-6 with the CLMV countries is rather "deficient to low" and relative solidarity can be considered "unstable".

Table 25: ASEAN's solidarity with CLMV countries in the area of development assistance (1999-2001).

	Absolute solidarity	Relative solidarity
Singapore	deficient	unstable
Thailand	high (with limitations)	unstable
other ASEAN-6	low	unstable

3.8. The case of Anwar Ibrahim: Reactions from ASEAN (1998)

The situation: In 1998, at the height of the economic crisis and in the midst of demands for political reforms in Malaysia, Prime Minister Mahathir deposed Anwar Ibrahim, Deputy Prime Minister and Mahathir's own long-time favorite aspirant as his eventual successor in office. Mahathir had him apprehended under the Internal Security Act (a relict from the early days of the cold war, which allows apprehension of any person for reasons of internal security without a formal trial). Eventually, Anwar was tried and sentenced to several years in prison on account of various charges, most prominently featuring the charge of sodomy. The affair took place under the eyes of the world media and criticism around the world intensified when Anwar Ibrahim appeared in court with apparent signs of physical abuse while in custody (a high-ranking police officer had beaten him and blackened his eye). Apparently, Mahathir had removed Anwar from the political scene because Anwar had begun promoting a strongly reformist and populist agenda and was seen as prematurely reaching out for the party presidency and the post of Prime Minister.

The problem: The affair around Anwar did not only throw a negative light on Malaysia, but also threatened to rub off onto ASEAN's already scratched political image and ran counter to some ASEAN government's explicitly democratic credentials.[509] Basically, all other original ASEAN members were appalled by the Malaysian government's despotic defiance of the rule of law. What is more, "Anwar was a popular figure in the region, with a network of contacts unmatched by any other ASEAN leader"[510] with apparently excellent connections to presidents Estrada and Habibie.

Further, the Anwar incident came at a time of increasing strains in the bilateral relations among ASEAN members that went along with problems of coordinating ASEAN's response to the crisis. In this context, the deposition of the reform-oriented Deputy Prime Minister (who had put some emphasis on improving human rights and democratic structures in Malaysia and ASEAN) to a certain degree also signaled Malaysia's insistence on national rather than regional crisis responses in the economic area. Thus, "Anwar had been a leading figure in co-ordinating the response of finance ministers to the economic crisis; ASEAN's effectiveness in this area declined notably after his departure."[511]

ASEAN members' handling of the Anwar issue is especially revealing for the state of ASEAN solidarity insofar as it is interesting to see if, in the face of heightened bilateral tensions in the course of the crisis, ASEAN members stuck to the principles of quiet diplomacy, non-interference in one another's internal affairs and refraining from destabilizing other ASEAN governments. The Anwar case also touches on the question of intra-ASEAN relational signaling.

---

[509] These were the Thai Democratic government of Prime Minister Chuan Leekpai and Foreign Minister Surin Pitsuwan, the administration of the Philippine President Estrada and his influential Foreign Secretary Domingo Siazon, as well as Indonesia's admistration under President Habibie.

[510] Funston (1999): 210.

[511] Ibid: 210f.

The reaction: As Haacke shows, ASEAN was split into two camps with regard to member countries' reactions to the incident.[512] Singapore reacted in a manner commensurate with the spirit of the ASEAN norms. *Asian Survey*'s annual review of Singapore's foreign relations in 1998 confirms that

> To promote goodwill and demonstrate that there was room for co-operation, Singapore refrained from commenting (not to say criticizing) publicly the removal and arrest of [...] Anwar Ibrahim.[513]

Likewise, the Democratic government of Thailand initially not only refrained from public criticism, but also advised the media not to provoke Malaysia. It also reassured Malaysia to prevent "fugitive opposition figures from entering into Thailand" and, with a view to the APEC summit that was due that year in Kuala Lumpur, advised APEC members to "articulate privately all complaints they might have in relation to Kuala Lumpur's human rights record, as Thailand had done." However, "[a]s the diplomatic exchanges between the Mahathir government and others threatened to derail the APEC government and others threatened to derail thee APEC Summit and affect US relations with Southeast Asian countries, [...] the Thai Foreign Minister [Surin Pitsuwan, M.H.] suggested that the Anwar trial was endangering the economic resuscitation of the Association."[514] On the other hand, the Philippines' and Indonesia's behavior deviated clearly from Singapore's and Thailand's rather careful approaches in that they publicly and vociferously criticized Malaysia's behavior.

> In the case of the Anwar affair [...] in September 1998, a serious breach in ASEAN unity seemed to have occurred. Then Indonesian President Habibie and Philippine President Joseph Estrada expressed sympathy for Anwar, and both even contemplated boycotting the APEC summit in Kuala Lumpur scheduled for November that year. Other ASEAN leaders also commented on the issue, if less outspokenly.[515]

As Haacke reports, Philippine congressmen officially solicited an invitation to Anwar's trial and President Estrada had plans of visiting Anwar in prison while attending the APEC summit.[516] Both Habibie and Estrada also demonstratively met with Anwar's wife and daughter and left out no opportunity to point at Prime Minister Mahathir's dissatisfactory handling of the affair.

Conscious of the incompatibility of their actions with ASEAN's conventions and norms, both Estrada and Habibie undertook the rhetorical attempt to

---

[512] Haacke (1999).
[513] Lee Lai To (1999b): 78.
[514] Cf. Haacke (1999): 599.
[515] Khoo (2000): 294.
[516] Haacke (1999): 602.

separate their own postures from the official position of their respective administrations by pointing out they only acted in their private capacities.[517]

The Malaysian government, in turn, threatened to retaliate against the Philippines' and Indonesia's offensive behavior. Thus, Prime Minister Mahathir deliberated publicly whether he should meet with President Estrada for bilateral talks at all during the APEC summit. He also hit a sensitive nerve with both the Philippines and Indonesia when he hinted Malaysia may retaliate by strongly limiting the inflow of Filipinos and Indonesians seeking employment in Malaysia.[518] Further, Mahathir publicly discredited Habibie and Estrada personally as well as politically and ushered

> veiled threats [...] that Malaysia might also consider flouting the 'ASEAN way' if other means of the Association failed to desist from continuous infringements of its core principles vis-à-vis Kuala Lumpur.[519]

Summary: The respective ASEAN members' reaction to the Anwar affair was quite different. On the one hand, Singapore and Thailand complied with the typical ASEAN norms and rather reassured Malaysia of their goodwill and political support, whereas the governments of the Philippines and Indonesia broke with all ASEAN conventions and took a vehement public stance against Malaysia. Estrada and Habibie even threatened to boycott the upcoming APEC summit in Kuala Lumpur. In turn, Malaysia retaliated in an equally offensive and public manner and even threatened to impose concrete sanctions against these two countries. Remarkably, as the political and economic costs of the Anwar affair increased in that it threatened to damage ASEAN's international image, Thailand, though much more modestly than Indonesia and the Philippines, also started criticizing Malaysia's stance.

Evaluation: Indonesia's and the Philippines' behavior is telling for ASEAN relations insofar as the two governments not only failed to mediate their protests by subtle diplomatic means and thus strongly disregarded any ASEAN norms, but revealed the apparent lack of a genuine bilateral fabric of mutual trust, respect and goodwill. Malaysia's response to its ASEAN neighbors' criticism was no more in line with the ASEAN way than theirs. Notably, the Anwar issue did not represent a major threat to the vital economic and political interests of

---

[517] Thus, both the Philippines' Foreign Secretary, Domingo Siazon, and the Indonesian Foreign Minister, Ali Alatas, argued that their respective governments had not violated ASEAN norms, since their respective presidents' personal positions did not reflect the official government view.

[518] Cf. Haacke (1999): 602.

[519] Ibid.

the Philippines and Indonesia, a fact that underlines the explosive potential of bilateral relations between ASEAN members in 1998. In terms of relational signaling, the incident was thus a complete failure and did in no way reflect the long history of more than thirty years of ASEAN cooperation.

In this context, it is all the more remarkable that Singapore, despite its frequent other spars with Malaysia, de-emphasized the issue and thereby contributed to the Malaysian government's stability. Likewise, Thailand's initial reaction diaplays a high level of norm compliance and neighborly goodwill, although later criticism of Malaysia revealed that there were limits to Thailand's readiness to back Malaysia.

Overall, Singapore's solidarity can be considered as "high" in absolute terms and "stable" in relative terms. Thailand's solidarity was "high" in absolute terms, but proved to be "unstable" in relative terms. Indonesia's and the Philippines' behavior was clearly "low" and "defunct", respectively.

Table 26: ASEAN members' solidarity with a view to the Anwar Ibrahim issue (1998)

	Absolute solidarity	Relative solidarity
Singapore	high	stable
Thailand	high	unstable
The Philippines	low	defunct
Indonesia	low	defunct

3.9. Indonesia's outbursts against Singapore (1999 –2001)

The situation: In the post-Suharto era, Indonesia has struggled with economic decline, erosion of the political system, the East Timor disaster and various forms of social unrest. Indonesia's national resilience and pride suffered substantially through foreign intervention in Indonesia and pressure from the international lenders to reform its economy. This humiliating situation contributed to the explosive political sensitivity that fermented everywhere in Indonesia. After more than 30 years of steady rule, the country saw four presidents inaugurated (including Megawati Sukarnoputri), three of them appointed witin the span of four years. Especially presidents Habibie and Wahid had no backing from TNI, the all-powerful Indonesian military, and were challenged by strong domestic opponents.

The problem: In this precarious situation, Singapore's leadership around Prime Minister Goh and Senior Minister Lee adopted a very assertive stance vis-à-vis Indonesia. Singapore's government, doubting the stability of the governments of Habibie and Wahid, and seeking to maintain its political influence and connections with potential successor governments and the military as the only predictable stronghold of political power, strengthened ties with both the political opposition under Megawati Suikarnoputri and the TNI.[520] Such previously unheard-of moves would have been unthinkable in Suharto's times. Had Singapore engaged in such manoeuvres in the Suharto era, this could have caused very serious strains within ASEAN. Singapore also withheld financial and economic aid to Habibie which it had previously been willing to grant to Suharto (see case 5 above).

Singapore's leaders strongly disapproved of the personal styles and policies of presidents Habibie and Wahid. Particularly Senior Minister Lee did not hide his preference for a change of leadership in Indonesia, which further undermined relations between the two countries.

Before this backdrop, it is revealing to observe the manner and tone Habibie and Wahid adopted in dealing with Singapore's criticism and interference. It shows how very thin the ice is on which this relationship floats.

The reaction: Both President Habibie and President Wahid resorted to unusually blunt, racially biased and prejudiced rhetorical outbursts against Singapore when they faced diplomatic problems with the city state between 1999 and 2001.

Habibie became infamous in February 1999 for publicly calling Singapore a "little red dot" on the map. He also claimed Singapore and especially the Singaporean military was discriminating against its Malay population, a charge that hit a sensitive nerve in Singapore. In the same month, the Indonesian government threatened to withdraw passports from (usually ethnic Chinese) Indonesian nationals who enlisted in the national service of the Singaporean armed forces.[521] Such statements were not merely expression of one of the president's passing moods, but are representative of a wide-spread and deep-seated anti-Singapore sentiment in Indonesia, which have re-emerged violently again after Indonesia's destabilization. Habibie's remarks were clearly aimed at hitting Singapore at its most sensitive spot.

President Wahid even topped Habibie's spiteful remarks and took out an even bigger rhetorical club with the intention to harm when Indonesia faced contention with Singapore on a number of counts.[522] In a now notorious speech

---

[520] Cf. Dolven (1999).
[521] Cf. Mohan Srilal (1999).
[522] Alwi Shihab, Indonesia's foreign minister, at the time traced Wahid's outbursts against Singapore back to a number of contentious issues: firstly, remarks by Lee Kuan Yew that

at the Indonesian embassy, held at the sidelines of the ASEAN summit in November 2000 in Singapore, President Wahid raved against the city-state, bringing charges of racism against the Chinese majority of Singapore. Depicting the neighbor country as being merely interested in exploiting Indonesia, he also threatened to form a coalition with Malaysia to cut Singapore's water supplies, to let ASEAN die and form a "West Pacific" forum instead with Malaysia, the Philipines and Indonesia at the core.[523]

Many Indonesian elites and especially Indonesian diplomats were shocked by Wahid's speech and objected to this unproductive violation of the code of conduct among ASEAN members. Nevertheless, this second incident of an Indonesian head of state threatening and offending the ASEAN neighbor shows that outbursts against Singapore are not merely unconnected, accidental slips of the tongue. In the Indoenesian public and the elites, anti-Singaporean sentiments are common and naturally impact on the bilateral relations between the two countries. Irawan Abidin, Indonesia's former ambassador to Greece and the Holy See, addressed the problem of racism and anti-Singaporean stereotypes as the core obstacle to improving Indonesian-Singaporean relations:

> Of President Abdurrhaman Wahid's tirade against Singapore [...], much was said by Indonesians, most of it by way of lamentation, rebuke and outright condemnation. Yet Singaporeans, according to the Straits Times, should worry that the President might have been dressed down by his countrymen *not for the substance* of his remarks but for the undiplomatic way in which he exploded. That is a very valid distinction and therefore a real concern among Singaporeans. Unfortunately for them and for Indonesians who would like to see their country adhere to the best moral position possible under the circumstances, no assurances have been conveyed that the President has been soundly rebuked by legislators and the media for both the *substance and the manner* of his attack against Singapore. [...]

---

suggested Wahid was incompetent and not able to reform the economy; secondly, quarrels about an extradition treaty with Singapore concerning Indonesian "economic criminals" who had illegally transferred their capital to Singapore; thirdly, Singapore's unwillingness to curb speculation in the rupiah in its financial market; fourth, the perceived lack of Singapore's economic and financial assistance to Indonesia, which had already led the previous government to consider Singapore a "fair weather friend". (Cf. Guerin 2000.)

[523] Whereas Foreign Minister Alwi Shihab attempted to play down the incident as "a little row between a married couple", Jürgen Rüland, professor of political science and a senior expert on Southeast Asia, sees Wahid's angry outburst against Singapore not as a singular incident, but rather as an expression of the increasing rifts and dividing lines running through a crisis-struck ASEAN. John Mc Beth commented in the *Far Eastern Economic Review* that "With his threats on November 25 to cut off Singapore's water supply and take Indonesia out of Asean, Wahid's outbursts went beyond the mildly eccentric. They represent a dangerous road to travel [...]." (Cf. West 2000; Rüland 2000b; McBeth 2000.)

Indonesia should [...] be making a review of the history of its relations with Singapore. [...] One of the finest adjustments the Indonesian political elite can give to the country's relationship with Singapore is to stop regarding it as a Chinese state and accept it for what it is striving hard to be: a multiracial meritocracy. During the past several years, well before the ascendancy of Abdurrahman's administration, some powerful individuals succeeded in introducing a heavy dose of racism into our national politics. [...] Many Singaporeans will not sleep easy as long as they believe that they do not have the goodwill of a giant just a few strides away.[524] [emphasis added]

One crucial aspect to be considered is the apparent split between positions in the presidential office and the diplomatic service of the country. Whereas the senior diplomats have mostly started their careers under Suharto's long-time foreign minister Ali Alatas, and seem to have internalised the importance of stable relations with Singapore and ASEAN in general, nationalism and national chauvinism in the administration appears to be growing.[525] So, while on the one hand the diplomatic memory of Indonesia is governed by insight in the importance of good bilateral relations with Singapore, the administrations since 1998 have been closer to Indonesia's troubled and humiliated soul.

So far, President Megawati Sukarnoputri has been much more moderate, cooperative and relatively conciliatory vis-à-vis Singapore. Thus, in a recent spat over allegations from Singapore concerning Indonesia's lack of commitment to the war on terrorism in February 2002, Megawati's administration resolved to tone down the problem in the ASEAN way rather than pouring additional oil into the fire. After an initial flare-up of angry retorts in reply to public outrage in Indonesia,

[t]he two governments [...] reached an agreement not to settle their dispute openly, but to settle their differences quietly following a row over claims by Senior Minister Lee Kuan Yew that terrorists are at large in Indonesia, Foreign Minister Hassan Wirajuda said [...]".[526]

---

[524] Irawan Abidin (2000).

[525] During an interview with a senior Indonesian diplomat in Singapore in November 2001, I stumbled over this issue quite frequently. The diplomat frequently implied that the diplomatic service did its best to bring home the message of the importance of a conciliatory and pragmatic approach to the conduct of relations with Singapore, but that the government's view of Sigapore relations was frequently different form the diplomats' view. The diplomat also confirmed that Ali Alatas' spirit was still very much alive in the Indonesian diplomatic community.

[526] News report based on material from the *Jakarta Post*: "Minister: Indonesia, Singapore agree to settle differences quietly", Country Watch homepage.

Nevertheless, it is not altogether unlikely that her administration might lash out against Singapore in a similar way as her predecessors have done, if her administration should destabilize. The potential and undercurrent tensions with Singapore are omnipresent. A comment by Bantarto Bandoro, director of the Centre for Strategic and International Studies (CSIS) Indonesia, illustrates the deep-seated distrust most Indonesian elites still share: "Indonesia and Singapore are friends who will never be close to each other. We have different races and Singaporean leaders always harbor distrust about the ability of Indonesians to handle regional problems".[527]

Evaluation: Presidents Habibie and Wahid publicly and deliberately shook the bilateral relations in its foundation by publicly and deliberately playing the race card against Singapore and threateningly reminding the small ASEAN neighbor of its physical inferiority and vulnerability. Indonesia's desastrous economic and domestic political situation alone is no sufficient explanation of these crude breaks with not only ASEAN norms but all norms of proper diplomatic conduct. Doubtlessly, "you cannot make a threat to the water supply of a country without threatening the very life of its people, no matter how small that country, and no matter how unrealistic the threat."[528] The shows of racism and chauvinism that seems to be characteristic for wide parts of the Indonesian public and elites point to a serious structural inferiority complex. Such complexcs cannot be eradicated in a short period of time and will therefore continue to affect Indonesia's relations with other ASEAN countries, especially so at times of economic or political crisis. President Megawati's presently more conciliatory approach to the conduct of bilateral relations is therefore no guarantee against similar recurrences of Indonesian chauvinism.

Overall, the unusually sharp outbursts in 1999 and 2000 reveal that trust and solidarity were practically non-existent at that time. Conversely, the situation improved recognizably under Megawati's administration, but remains unstable.

Table 27: Solidarity: Indonesia's outbursts against Singapore (1999-2001)

	Absolute solidarity	Relative Solidarity
Indonesia (1999-2001)	low	unstable to defunct
Indonesia (from 2001)	deficient	unstable

---

[527] Bantarto Bandoro, quoted in: Fabiola Desy Unijadijaja; Tiarma Siboro (2002).
[528] Irawan Abidin (2000).

4. Final Assessment

This chapter gives an overall assessment of ASEAN solidarity, based on the analysis of ASEAN members' behavior. In a first step, it sets out to scan ASEAN members' behavior with a view to the criteria of solidary behavior (as outlined in section 2.2.1., see fig. 3 and the *five situations of solidarity*) and indicate how it compares with these. In a second step, this chapter will provide some conclusions as to the overall degree and stability of ASEAN solidarity, the circumstances under which solidarity prospers or falters, the areas in which solidarity is strongest and weakest, respectively, and, finally, the implications of these insights for assessing the significance individual member states attribute to ASEAN's collective goods.

4.1. Assessment of indicators of solidarity

4.1.1. Norm compliance

The above case studies suggest that ASEAN members' overall compliance with (the spirit of) ASEAN norms is clearly deficient. This means that ASEAN members generally acknowledge the validity of these norms, but frequently fail to behave accordingly. With a view to the individual norms, the following compliance pattern results:

Non-interference in the internal affairs of a member state Whereas this norm generally applied in the cases of *the haze* (case 1), *East Timor/Aceh* (case 3) and *Myanmar* (case 4), strong deviances occurred in the cases of:
the haze (case 1), when Singapore – after initial acquiescence – lost patience with Indonesia's inaction in the haze crisis of 1997/98 and exposed Indonesia to strong criticism; *East Timor* (case 3), when especially Thailand, but also the Philippines acted against Indonesia's explicit interests by strongly supporting the INTERFET and UNTAET efforts; *Myanmar* (case 4), when Thailand publicly exposed Myanmar to severe criticism, worked towards raising the bilateral dispute to the ASEAN level and failed to vote with ASEAN members against ILO resolutions and embargos; *Singapore's assistance to Indonesia* (case 5), when Singapore insisted on economic restructuring in Indonesia as a prerequisite for financial aid; and *the Anwar Ibrahim issue* (case 8), when in 1998/99 the Philippines and Indonesia publicly, vocally and repeatedly embarassed the Malaysian government over the deposition and illegitimate imprisoning of Anwar Ibrahim.

Avoiding to destabilize governments of ASEAN member states   Compliance with this norm was generally high as far as the case studies are concerned. In the case of *the haze* (case 1), Singapore's government largely discontinued its public campaign and complaints against Indonesia and avoided to embarass the Indonesian government as the crisis in Indonesia intensified. Overall, ASEAN largely avoided pressuring Indonesia on the issue throughout the crisis. In the case of *East Timor/Aceh* (case 3), ASEAN avoided to interfere collectively (as an organization) in East Timor and backed Indonesia's position. Especially Malaysia made it clear to the Acehnese independence movement that they could expect neither support nor refuge on Malaysian territory. Although Thailand's and the Philippines' engagement in INTERFET and UNTAET ran counter to Indonesian interests, there was in my view no intention of destabilizing the Indonesian government. With respect to Aceh, ASEAN collectively (without any exceptions) backed Indonesia's sovereignty claims and territorial integrity. In the case of *Myanmar* (case 4), ASEAN collectively backed the government of Myanmar; only Thailand's outspoken support of ILO sanctions against Myanmar can be seen as an attempt to expose and destabilize the junta government. In the case of *Singapore's assistance to Indonesia* (case 5), Singapore's failure to disburse financial aid was partly made up by the initiation of extensive gas deals with long-term guarantees; it by no means represented an attempt to destabilize Indonesia. However, in the case of *the Anwar Ibrahim issue* (cases 8), the Philippines and Indonesia actively contributed to the discreditation of the Mahathir government in that their acerbic public protests and threats gave new impetus to wide-spread opposition to Anwar's detention in the Malaysian society; clearly, the Estrada and Habibie governments discredited the Malaysian government's international standing by threatening to cancel their attendance at the APEC summit in November 1998. Likewise, the case of *Indonesia's outbursts against Singapore* (case 9), when Presidents Habibie and Wahid touched on sensitive issues with strong implications for Singapore's domestic stability and security.

Imperative of peacefulness and refraining from the use of force Compliance with this norm is a very sensitive issue with far-ranging implications for intra-ASEAN relations, trust and relational signaling. Even minor cases of non-compliance have the potential of discrediting ASEAN relations. Since the behavior observed in the case studies displayed some cases of non-compliance, compliance with this norm has to be labeled deficient.

Two case studies reveal that peacefulness is not imperative to all ASEAN members by all means. As the case study on the *South China Sea* (case 2) reveals, both Malaysia and Vietnam have engaged in military operations directed against the Philippines in the Spratly islands area. Thus, in the running-up to negotiations about an ASEAN code of conduct for the South China Sea,

Malaysia's occupation of Investigator Shoal and the fortification of Erica Reef in 1999 touched on Vietnamese and Philippine sovereignty claims; the Philippines and Malaysia subsequently engaged in a minor armed clash over the incident, whereas Vietnamese troops stationed on one of the islands deliberately shot at a Philippine reconaissance plane. As mentioned in the case study on *Myanmar* (case 4), Myanmarese troops, in pursuit of trans-border operations, have continued to violate Thailand's borders and sovereignty and even engaged in clashes with the Thai military on Thai territory. Despite severe protests from Thailand, the government of Myanmar took no action to discontinue such operations.

Quiet diplomacy   This much-touted element of the "ASEAN way" has suffered considerably throughout the crisis. As the case studies indicate, ASEAN members' compliance with this norm is strongly deficient, though it is generally regarded as a valid norm throughout ASEAN.

In the case of *the haze* (case 1), Singapore's government rather avoided publicity and returned to quiet diplomacy on the haze issue after Indonesia had slid into deeper economic troubles in 1998. All other ASEAN governments, especially Malaysia, have practised quiet diplomacy on the issue throughout. In the case of *Aceh* (case 3), ASEAN also complied with the norm. Except for Thailand, ASEAN also kept to quiet diplomacy in the case of *Myanmar* (case 4).

On the other hand, ASEAN members failed to comply with the norm in the case of *the Anwar Ibrahim issue* in 1998. Disregard for quiet diplomacy can also be observed in the case of *the South China Sea issue* (case 2), when Malaysia visibly sided with China against the Philippines in 1999 and occupied areas in the Spratlys in the running-up to South China Sea negotiations, when the Philippines publicly protested Malaysia's occupation and fortification of several reefs and shoals, when Vietnam shot at a Philippine reconnaissance plane in the Spratly area, and when the Philippines publicly expressed its dissatisfaction with Vietnam's insistence on the inclusion of the Paracels into the code of conduct on the South China Sea. In the case of *Myanmar* (case 4), Thailand aired vocal and open criticism of the junta and argued in favor of an ILO embargo. As indicated in the case studies on *Singapore's assistance to Indonesia* (case 5) and *Indonesia's outbursts against Singapore* (case 9), Singaporean leaders publicly aired doubts as to President Habibie's political and economic competence, and the Habibie administration retaliated publicly in crude terms. Likewise, due to policy differences with Singapore's government, President Wahid in late 2000 ushered severe threats and offenses carrying racist undertones against Singapore. Although the tone of Wahid's remarks was generally deemed inacceptable throughout the capitals of ASEAN, the incident gave an insight into the deepening rifts between ASEAN governments since

1998. As the case of *Singapore's and Malayisa's positions on AFTA and bilateral FTA* (case 6) shows, Malaysia and other ASEAN members (such as the Philippines) deviated strongly from the imperative of quiet diplomacy when they publicly and sharply condemned Singapore's efforts at forging bilateral FTA in the running-up and during the ASEAN summit of 2000.

Preventing multilateralization of bilateral disputes (preventing ASEAN from taking sides)   One of the essentials of ASEAN is that ASEAN (as an organization) is supposed to remain neutral and take no collective stance with regard to bilateral disputes between members. Since ASEAN sees itself as a forum for mutually beneficial cooperation and not so much as a body for conflict resolution, it (as an organization) prefers to sweep controversial issues under the carpet. Compliance with this norm has been generally high.

In the case of *the haze* (case 1), ASEAN's efforts at multilateralizing the issue have been limp, and when Indonesia was unwilling or incapable of acting on the issue, ASEAN handed the problem over to UNEP for mediation, presumably in order not to enhance conflicts between ASEAN members. Likewise, ASEAN, due to differences among its members, made no attempts at adopting a decisive collective stance on *East Timor* (case 3). In the case of *Myanmar* (case 4), Malaysia for some time successfully turned down Thailand's requests to multilateralize talks on the major contentious issues between Myanmar and Thailand. However, Thailand seems to have been more successful recently in addressing issues such as drug trafficking and border issues at ASEAN level.

Showing goodwill/ good neighborliness   Although there are many examples of good neighborliness and goodwill, there are as many opposite examples. Compliance with this norm therefore can also said to be deficient.

In the case of *the haze* (case 1), the norm applied almost throughout; interestingly enough, members showed substantial goodwill even though Indonesia did not pay them back in kind and remained inactive. *The South China Sea issue* (case 2) shows that ASEAN over long stretches followed the Philippines' initiatives for a common ASEAN stance against China, even if the issue did not have high priority for some countries, especially Thailand. However, Malaysia has frequently let the Philippines down over the issue, and Vietnam showed that its goodwill an good neighborliness had narrow limits. Further, ASEAN let the Philippines completely down in 1998, at the time of the second Mischief Reef incident. Thailand's and the Philippines' ambiguous role in the *East Timor* case (case 3) also deviated from this norm. With regard to *Aceh* (case 3), ASEAN acted in accordance with the norm. With regard to *Myanmar* (case 4), the old ASEAN members had a good overall record of compliance with the norm of good neighborliness, although Thailand clearly didn't comply with it. Myanmar, on its side, continues to be involved in frequent political and military conflicts at the Thai-Myanmarese border. Singapore's "no free lunch" attitude in the case of *Singapore's assistance to Indonesia* (case 5) leaves some doubts about the city state's goodwill and neighborly spirit. With respect to *solidarity with CLMV countries* (case 7), only Thailand clearly deserves the merit of good neighborliness, whereas ASEAN was very hesitant to engage in development aid. When Singapore finally kicked off the Initiative for ASEAN Integration, most countries failed to make clear commitments, and Singapore's contributions remained insubstantial. In the case of *the Anwar Ibrahim issue* (case 8), Singapore and Thailand were in line with the norm, whereas Indonesia and the Philippines crudely disregarded it. In the case of *Indonesia's outbursts against Singapore* (case 9), Indonesia repeatedly disregarded the norm. Likewise, Singaporean leaders' disrespectful and destabilizing comments on President Habibie were out of tune.

Bilateral political, financial and humanitarian aid in times of crisis The kind of aid ASEAN members have given to each other in times of a crisis was frequently not unambiguous. In a number of cases, the kind of support offered was not the kind of aid expected. Overall, ASEAN members' compliance therefore has to be labeled as deficient.

In *the haze* crisis of 1997/98 and after, Malaysia and Singapore formally offered to dispatch fire fighters and contribute surveillance technology when Indonesia was not at all interested in material assistance. Malaysia also complied with Indonesia's wish for political acquiescence, whereas Singapore, at least in the initial phase (1997/98), did not. In the case of *East Timor* (case 3), Thailand's and the Philippines' massive deployment of troops to INTERFET and later UNTAET represented a contribution Indonesia essentially disapproved of. In the case of *Aceh* (case 3), especially Malaysia offered its assistance in mediating between the independence movement and the Indonesian government and made it clear to the rebels that they could not expect any support from Malaysia for their pursuit of independence. In the case of *Singapore's assistance to Indonesia* (case 5), Singapore effectively failed to disburse the financial aid initially promised. Rather, Singapore adopted a "no free lunch" policy and tried to stabilize Indonesia's economy by generating resource deals. Singapore did dispatch humanitarian aid, but in the face of the undisbursed overall US$ 10 billion in aid and currency funds, political elites in Indonesia felt humanitarian aid of a few million dollars represented an insult rather than actual assistance. Likewise, Singapore's "no free lunch" policy and ASEAN's hesitant and rather modest contributions to the IAI in the case of *solidarity with the CLMV countries* (case 7) reveal that there is little willingness to face real costs to fight poverty in the CLMV countries.

Supporting the "frontline" state   ASEAN members complied only partly with this norm. Therefore, overall compliance has to be considered as deficient and frequently unstable.

In the case of the *South China Sea issue* (case 2), ASEAN generally supported the "frontline" states, the Philippines and Vietnam, in their struggle against China. However, support was given only reluctantly in some periods and failed completely during and after the second Mischief Reef incident in 1998. In 1999, Vietnam even engaged in a minor armed clash with the Philippines in the Spratlys, and Malaysia used its navy to occupy and fortify maritime territories that were also claimed by Vietnam and the Philippines. thus destabilizing ASEAN unity. Malaysia's South China Sea policy also undermined the Philippines' position vis-à-vis China in that it actively obstructed ASEAN's efforts at taking a collective stance on the South China Sea issue. In the case of *East Timor* (case 3), especially Thailand cooperated with the international community (and particularly Australia) rather than fronting up for the Indonesian government. In this case, Malaysia, but also Singapore, took a much more supportive and proactive stance for Indonesia's interests in its conflict with the international community. The case of *Myanmar* (case 4) is ASEAN's most impressive example of backing and defending the "frontline" state's interests against political heavy weights such as the U.S. and the EU. In this context, Thailand occasionally declined from joining the ASEAN chorus. Finally, the Philippines and Indonesia failed to support Malayisa's international standing in the case of *the Anwar Ibrahim issue* of 1998 (case 8); they also discredited Malaysia's role as host of APEC.

4.1.2. The five situations of solidarity

Common good situation   The case of *Myanmar* (case 4) touches upon the *common good situation* or the problem of free-riding, respectively. Thus, Myanmar profited from ASEAN's support and unified solidarity vis-à-vis the EU, the U.S. and the ILO, but in turn failed to accommodate ASEAN's engagement policy and failed to acknowledge its responsibilities. Thus, after its accession to ASEAN, Myanmar escalated rather than de-escalated human rights situation, stepped up the repression of the opposition and continued to engage in drug-trafficking and to violate Thailand's borders.

In the case of *the South China Sea issue* (case 2), Malaysia, for the sake of improved bilateral relations with China and to better secure its interests in the South China Sea, opportunistically undermined ASEAN's efforts at forging a common ASEAN position vis-à-vis China by demonstratively siding with the potential regional hegemon. Thus, when Malaysia could have contributed to ASEAN's role in providing regional stability (a good generally cherished by all

ASEAN members), the Mahathir government increasingly failed to contribute to this collective good. Given that Malaysia is interested in ASEAN's general effectiveness in enhancing regional security, its behavior with respect to the South China Sea issue has to be considered as a case of free-riding. Besides these two cases, free-riding did not seem to be a major problem in ASEAN.

Sharing situation The model behavior of the *sharing situation* requires that, "if there are joint divisible benefits and costs and Ego […] can divide them, he will not seek to maximize what he gets from the costs but take his 'fair share'. This situation touches upon group members' readiness to bear solidarity costs in return for equitable (not equity-oriented) participation in collective goods.

In pecuniary and economic terms, ASEAN members' readiness to bear solidarity costs was relatively limited.
Especially Singapore's "no free lunch" behavior displayed a tendency to maximize the returns of the financial input given to its neighbors, even in times of crisis. Thus, in the case of *Singapore's assistance to Indonesia* (case 5), Singapore withheld its announced bilateral financial aid and relied on the benefits of bilateral trade instead. In the case of *solidarity with CLMV* (case 7), Singapore chose an extremely low-cost approach to human resources development in CLMV countries and seems to apply its "no free lunch" policy as well. Other ASEAN members' contribution to the Initiative for ASEAN Integration, whose declared objective it is to reduce the development gap between ASEAN members, remained even more modest than Singapore's.
With respect to economic integration through AFTA, most ASEAN members' readiness to bear the cost imposed on their national industries or to their national markets is extremely limited. The case of *Singapore's and Malaysia's position on AFTA/FTA* (case 6) is representative of this tendency.
In terms of political stability, there is genrally a stronger tendency to accept solidarity costs. The examples of *the haze* (case 1), *the South China Sea* (case 2), *Aceh* (case 3) and *Myanmar* (case 4) confirm this. Nevertheless, there clearly are limits to accept solidarity costs, such as Thailand and the Philippines in the case of *East Timor* (case 3), Thailand in the case of *Myanmar* (case 4), and both the Philippines and Indonesia in the case of *the Anwar Ibrahim issue* (case 8).

Need situation Generally, ASEAN members acknowledged a certain responsibility for each other. Support in situations of emergency or concrete need was forthcoming, as the cases of *the haze* (case 1), *the South China Sea issue* (case 2), *East Timor/Aceh* (case 3), *Myanmar* (case 4), *Singapore's assistance to Indonesia* (case 5) and *solidarity with CLMV* (case 6) show. However, the willingness to help in times of need seemed to be strongly limited as far as high solidarity costs were involved. Thus, Thailand and the Philippines found it difficult to face the political costs of acquiescing on Indonesia's East

Timor policy and, unlike the rest of ASEAN, supported INTERFET and UNTAET (case 3); Singapore saw the need to expose Indonesia to recriminatory public criticism when the haze smog choked the country in 1997/98 (whereas Malaysia continued to acquiesce on the issue) (case 1); despite the rhetoric on reducing the economic gap in ASEAN, ASEAN's aid in response to CLMV countries' call for assistance remained insubstantial (case 6); Singapore's aid to Indonesia remained undisbursed (case 5); and ASEAN collectively disregarded the Philippines' need for support after the second Mischief Reef incident so as not to risk provoking China (case 2).

Breach temptation   Various ASEAN members have occasionally breached ASEAN solidarity for the sake of securing national benefits. Thus, ASEAN in 1998 failed collectively to support the Philippines after the second Mischief Reef incident of 1998, because ASEAN members had a strong interest in improving political and economic ties with China in times of regional economic crisis (case 2). Malaysia opportunistically failed to support the Philippines and undermined ASEAN's efforts to form a common position on a code of conduct for the South China Sea in order to maintain its good bilateral relations with China and pursue its own territorial interests in the South China Sea. Thailand contributed strongly to Australia's and the international community's INTEFET and UNTAET efforts partly to prove its democratic credentials and partly to reassure the U.S. and the West of Thailand's political reliability. By doing so, it was clearly out of tune with both Indonesia's and most ASEAN members' interests. In the case of *Myanmar* (case 4), Thailand breached ASEAN's solidarity with Myanmar because of severe bilateral tensions.
Malaysia crudely breached ASEAN solidarity in 2000 when it unilaterally denied to keep to its commitments under the the tariff liberalization scheme of AFTA and thus undermined the overall credibility of the AFTA project of economic integration (case 6).

Mishap situation   The case studies featured two situations that can be assessed in terms of a mishap situation, i.e. a situation where an intendedly solidary act turns out to go against solidarity (so that solidary behavior would require that appropriate amends be made for the solidarity failure). Thus, Indonesia (*the haze*, case 1) failed to make amends for not complying with ASEAN's fire ban of 1995 and for covering parts of the region in heavy smog for weeks and months in 1997/98. Suharto apologized to the region for the effects of the haze smog on Indonesia's neighbors, but effectively Indonesia remained inactive on the issue. Singapore (*Singapore's assistance to Indonesia*, case 5) failed to make amends funds and reassure Indonesia of its genuine solidarity when the pledged aid funds of US$ 10 billion remained largely undisbursed.

4.1.3. Solidarity costs, relational singaling, ingroup/outgroup behavior, myopic opportunism

Solidarity costs The term "solidarity costs" implies that there is no direct political or economic pay-off in return for a costly political or material contribution by one group member to the group as a whole or another group member, respectively.

ASEAN members generally were very reluctant – and often unwilling – to face high solidarity costs. Acceptance of economic and financial solidarity costs was considerably lower than in the diplomatic or political area.

The only really outstanding exception among the case studies is the case of *Myanmar* (case 4). Thus, ASEAN members (with the occasional exception of Thailand) were ready to face high diplomatic costs for the decision to admit Myanmar and subsequently fight for its international recognition and integration into intergovernmental processes such as the ASEAN-EU dialogue, ASEM and APEC. Some acceptance of solidarity costs – though to a lower degree and less stable – can be observed in the cases of *the South China Sea issue* (case 2) and, at least partly, *the haze* (case 2). Overall, ASEAN members are less likely to face political and economic solidarity costs in times of economic hardship or crisis.

Relational signaling As the case studies show, ASEAN has a mixed record of relational signaling. Whereas it was rather strong in the cases of *Aceh* (case 3) and *Myanmar*[529] (case 4), the cases of *the haze* (case 1) and the *South China Sea issue* (case 2) partly display a strong lack of mutually reassuring behavior. Thus, Singapore's media campaign against Indonesia in the case of *the haze* was an unusually aggressive behavior in terms of ASEAN relations. ASEAN members' complete failure to back the Philippines vis-à-vis China after the second Mischief Reef incident in 1998 came as a shock to the Philippines, since the country had to anticipate that it cannot really count on ASEAN's support against Chinese assertiveness, once it comes to the crunch. Minor armed clashes between ASEAN members in the Spratlys clearly eroded the notion of positive relational signaling in ASEAN. The cases of *East Timor* (case 3), *Singapore's assistance to Indonesia* (case 4), *Singapore's and Malaysia's position on AFTA/FTAs* (case 6), *ASEAN's solidarity with CLMV* (case 7) reveal that the ASEAN members' frequent rhetorical reference to the 'ASEAN way' suggests far more relational signaling than their behavior justifies. The cases of the *Anwar Ibrahim issue* (case 8) and *Indonesia's outbursts* (case 9) represent peaks

---

[529] As far as relational signaling is concerned in this case, the positive assessment applies only in a one-way direction, namely from ASEAN to Myanmar; in turn,Myanmar's behavior so far has given ASEAN no reason to expect much relational signaling or mutual reassurance in the future.

of negative, or absence of, relational signaling, as far as Malaysia, the Philippines and Indonesia (case 8) and Singapore and Indonesia (case 9) are concerned. The fact that these cases are seen as exceptional or remarkable in the eyes of observers, proves that they are not representative of ASEAN's general patterns of behavior. On the other hand, the fact that ASEAN relations occasionally could be derailed so easily shows that there is a high potential of covert distrust and animosity among major ASEAN members whose negative impact on ASEAN solidarity should not be underestimated.

Ingroup/ outgroup behavior   Generally, ASEAN displays a clear ingroup/outgroup distinction, a dividing line that is operative in terms of solidarity, too. Thus, ASEAN members have an ASEAN conscience that tells them to be solidary with fellow ASEAN members. The fact that ASEAN engaged collectively in solidarity projects such as developing a common code of conduct for the South China Sea, expressing support for Indonesia's position on Aceh, engaging in regional economic integration and backing the "frontline" state Myanmar against international isolation and sanctions shows that ASEAN members do share a concept of group solidarity that runs along the lines of ASEAN membership. Likewise, even though ASEAN members generally shrank back from costly aid projects, the fact that they launched (admittedly insufficient) initiatives and programs at all shows that they generally share the view that ASEAN solidarity should cover such aspects; they all seem to be essentially aware of the need for collective solidarity in a number of areas. Albeit, there is a strong implementation problem due to ASEAN nations' respective strong inward-looking focus on primary national interests, and ideas of ASEAN's purposes sometimes differ widely.

Group rituals/symbols   ASEAN members often refer to doing things the 'ASEAN way' or in the 'ASEAN spirit'. Their claimed mode of ASEAN-specific interaction functions as an important unifying symbol. The more ASEAN members' behavior openly discredits the 'ASEAN way', the more ASEAN runs the danger of losing its only unifying symbol.

As the case studies show, ASEAN members have in a number of ways violated the norms of the 'ASEAN way'. Especially since the economic crisis, ASEAN members' behavior shows that they have very often (too often) not been able to deal with increasing intra-ASEAN tensions in line with the ideals of the 'ASEAN spirit' and the 'ASEAN way'. What is worse, the 'ASEAN way' not only failed to guide ASEAN members with respect to proactive solidarity (i.e. getting ASEAN's act together in order to *actively implement* something together), but also failed to provide 'passive solidarity', i.e. the art of political acquiescence and refraining from comments on each other's affairs, a collective good ASEAN had previously prided itself in. Strong solidarity would have required ASEAN members to follow their unifying ideals of the 'ASEAN way' more closely.

Myopic opportunism/ opportunism   Myopic opportunism, i.e. *temporarily* neglecting group solidarity for the sake of realizing better individual alternatives, clearly was an issue in some of the case studies. In the case of the *South China Sea issue* (case 2), some opportunism was involved when the Philippines eagerly promoted the exclusion of the Paracel Islands from the ASEAN code of conduct (thereby acting against Vientam's interests) in 2000 and when Malaysia occupied and fortified reefs and shoals in the Spratlys in 1999. Further, there were several moments (especially in the time before the first Mischief Reef incident) when several ASEAN member states showed considerable reluctance to confront China, and this tendency culminated in 1998 when ASEAN members, for fear of risking to alienate the PRC, collectively failed to confront China over the second Mischief Reef incident. Thailand's and the Philippines' behavior in the case of *East Timor* (case 3) was partly a signal to the international community that they were reliable and democratic partners of the West in Southeast Asia.

If these examples were cases of *myopic* (short-term) opportunism, various ASEAN members also engaged in more permanent opportunism, i.e. they continuously neglected, circumvented and undermined ASEAN solidarity as a matter of principle. Thus, Malaysia largely sought to obstruct the process of finding a collective ASEAN response to the China threat in the *South China Sea* (case 2) and subverted ASEAN's solidarity by moving closer to China's position.

Likewise, Thailand's intervention in *East Timor* (case 3) was opportunistic in that the Thai government used the undefined status of the situation to set a precedent for its "flexible engagement" approach and to prove its reliability and democratic credentials to the international community, and in particular to its American friends.

Similarly, Malaysia undermined the AFTA project for the sake of protecting its national economy, and there have been no signs that this position is going to change in the future. With a view to Malaysia's readiness to permanently discredit AFTA, Malaysia's position may have to be classified not as opportunism rather than as new Malaysian obstructionism. Apparently, the Philippines and Indonesia took Malaysia's example as a pretext to seek exemptions from AFTA's liberalization scheme, too. So there seems to be even more ruinous opportunism at work in ASEAN (whether it turns out to be myopic or structural will depend on the policy preferences of these countries' governments).

4.2. ASEAN solidarity measured by ASEAN standards

Measured by their own standards (cp. fig. 1; assessment in section 4.1.1.), solidarity among ASEAN members was clearly deficient. Frequently, core members did not keep to the most basic norms of the organization and often acted beyond the limits of the 'ASEAN way'. Nevertheless, several case studies display that ASEAN members share a sense of what constitutes ASEAN solidarity, and that they are trying to live up to it, even though they are less ready to accept high solidarity costs these days. Accordingly, several case studies (*the haze*, case 2, *the South China Sea issue* , case 2, *East Timor/Aceh*, case3, *Myanmar*, case 4) revealed that countries acting in line with the norms are often in the majority, while a minority waters down or disturbs the overall impression of ASEAN solidarity. Thus, most of the members keep to the essentials of ASEAN solidarity most of the time, but increasingly not all ASEAN members keep to solidarity norms all of the time. Some ASEAN members, such as Malaysia and Myanmar, even display a tendency to permanently breach ASEAN solidarity for the sake of their own individual interests.

4.3. The state of ASEAN solidarity: the bird's eye view

4.3.1. Overall degree of ASEAN solidarity

As far as the case studies are concerned, ASEAN's solidarity was never consistently "high". The picture that emerges from the analysis rather suggests that overall solidarity among ASEAN members was frequently "deficient", i.e. weakly constituted. This means there was a sense of solidarity which, however, frequently failed to serve as the guideline for individual ASEAN members' behavior.

Thus, a ASEAN members frequently breached core norms of ASEAN and the 'ASEAN way', often shunned high diplomatic and economic solidarity costs, displayed a good deal of opportunistic behavior and – partly – sided with outsiders against the implicit interests of fellow ASEAN members. Nevertheless, wherever ASEAN was assessed as a group, the majority of ASEAN governments displayed at least a minimum of solidarity, whereas governments clearly breaching solidarity usually represented a minority (such as in cases 1, 2, 3, 4).

4.3.2. Relative stability of ASEAN solidarity

Overall, ASEAN members' solidarity appears to have followed changes in the region's political and economic environment. Whereas the economic crisis of 1998 and its aftermath had a diminishing impact on ASEAN solidarity,[530] there is some evidence that, prior to the Asian economic crisis, ASEAN's unity and solidarity even appreciated in the face of minor crises as long as the major economic and political parameters remained stable.[531]

Thus, before the crisis, ASEAN's solidarity record and prospects with regard to the South China Sea issue, economic integration (AFTA) and development aid to CLMV countries were better than after the crisis. As the analysis shows, ASEAN members' willingness to engage in crisis relief, economic and development aid dropped in times of general regional crisis and instability. During the crisis and in its aftermath, ASEAN members shunned high financial, economic – and frequently also diplomatic – solidarity costs and focused more on their short-term primary national (as opposed to longer-term regional) concerns. Thus, under the impact of major regional crises or disruption, ASEAN solidarity can be said to depreciate and become unstable.

However, this does not mean that solidarity is defunct. As defined in the outset of this analysis (cf. table 10), the criterion for complete solidarity failure is that a country's solidarity performance is clearly weaker than the external circumstances would suggest.[532] ASEAN solidarity, though effectively weakened and destabilized by the crisis, has not turned out to be defunct, although especially Malaysia under-performed in a number of cases. Myanmar's solidarity performance has also been exceptionally low.

Complete solidarity failure, such as Malaysia's behavior in the cases of the *South China Sea issue* (case 2) and *AFTA* (case 6), Thailand's defections from

---

[530] The cases of *the haze* (case 2) and of *Myanmar* (case 4) are exceptions to this tendency. In the former case, overall solidarity with Indonesia improved after 1998 as Singapore and the rest of ASEAN largely acquiesced on the haze issue. In the case of Myanmar, solidarity remained strong despite the economic crisis.

[531] A look at the case of the *South China Sea issue* (case 2) suggests that minor crises do not necessarily upset or impact negatively on ASEAN's solidarity, as long as the major political and economic parameters of the regional environment are friendly. Thus, in the years preceding the economic crisis, ASEAN suprised China with its vehement reaction to the first Mischief Reef incident and again adopted a unified stance when Vietnam called for ASEAN's assistance in an inicdent of Chinese explorative oil drilling in waters claimed by Vietnam. On the other hand, ASEAN's unity and solidarity in the South China Sea experienced a complete failure as the economic crisis stuck, and recovery has been slow ever since.

[532] I.e. deficient absolute solidarity in times of generally good external conditions has to be considered as unstable, whereas deficient absolute solidarity at times of general regional crisis can still be considered stable.

solidarity in the cases of *East Timor* (case 3) and *Myanmar* (case 4) have increased, but are not representative for overall ASEAN solidarity.

Overall, terms such as "fair weather solidarity" or "fair weather friends" do not apply to ASEAN. They are misleading and short-sighted because "fair weather" implies that ASEAN solidarity is based on superficial opportunism. However, ASEAN's history shows that not opportunism, but providing collective goods such as stability and security to Southeast Asia, are the main features of ASEAN cooperation.

4.3.3. Areas in which ASEAN solidarity is strongest/weakest

Seemingly, ASEAN solidarity has suffered in all areas since 1998. However, it also seems that it has suffered most with respect to economic integration (AFTA) and the readiness to provide financial and development aid to poorer members (CLMV) or members in concrete crisis (Indonesia). In the field of diplomatic and political solidarity, ASEAN's record is dissatisfactory, even though at first glance it seems to be slightly more stable (*the haze* after 1998, case 1; *South China Sea* after 1998, case 2; *Aceh*, case 3, Malaysia's and Singapore's support of Indonesia on *East Timor*, case 3; *Myanmar*, case 4). Nevertheless, there should be no illusions as to China's increasing influence, whose apparent divisive potential seems capable of diverting ASEAN solidarity even more in the future.

4.3.4. Implications for ASEAN members' appreciation of ASEAN's collective goods

With reference to the reasons for collective solidarity as described at the outset of this study (cf. fig. 2), it can be said that, as ASEAN solidarity is deficient and unstable, apparently ASEAN members' appreciation of, and trust in, the benefits they derive from ASEAN's collective goods is equally deficient and unstable.

The fact that, despite the heightened awareness of the strong interdependence in Southeast Asia, ASEAN solidarity has dropped (rather than increased) also suggests that ASEAN members perceive the grouping's utility to be insufficient for their respective national purposes.

As regional economic stability gained in importance after the beginning of the Asian economic crisis, ASEAN's diminished solidarity suggests that ASEAN members see ASEAN's relevance diminished in terms of providing economic stability and security. Thus, ASEAN partners will increasingly seek to establish links with external partners, such as the U.S., Japan, and China, a development that stands to diminish ASEAN solidarity even further.[533] Such a development would also reduce ASEAN's relevance in providing political unity, security and stability in the Southeast Asian region.

5. Conclusion

Evidence from the case studies suggests that overall ASEAN solidarity has to be classified as deficient and unstable (though not defunct!). Notably Malaysia and Myanmar displayed frequent strong deviances from solidarity.

This conclusion applies not only to ASEAN solidarity looked at in the light of the criteria of the bird's eye view perspective, but also if one applies exclusively ASEAN's own criteria for solidarity (cf. criteria in sections 2.1., 2.2. and their assessment in 4.1., 4.2.).

There is some evidence that ASEAN solidarity dropped considerably during the economic crisis and that – due to lasting symptoms of regional instability – recovery is slow in coming.

Further, with a view to ASEAN members' appreciation of ASEAN's collective goods (providing economic and political security and stability to Southeast Asia), weak solidarity among ASEAN members can only mean that they essentially doubt the Association's ability to provide these collective goods.

Trust in ASEAN's competence to provide economic stability and economic integration to Southeast Asia seems to be especially low. Thus, ASEAN solidarity can be expected to erode further as the region continues to face an economically critical condition and as significance of links with powerful economic and political partners outside of ASEAN (China, Japan, U.S.) increases.

---

[533] Both Singapore's – and increasingly also other ASEAN members' – efforts at forming bilateral FTAs with countries such as Japan and the U.S., and the ASEAN Plus Three initiative are indicative of this trend.

Chapter 5:

ASEAN –

POSITIONS VIS-A-VIS THIRD PARTIES

ASEAN – POSITIONS VIS-A-VIS THIRD PARTIES

1. Introduction

As the fourth reference point in the assessment of ASEAN's collective identity, this chapter addresses the question of ASEAN members' coherence or homogeneity in their dealings with, and attitudes towards, external third parties, i.e. non-ASEAN members. Considering that ASEAN provides no agreed mechanisms and principles for coordinating its respective member states' foreign policies and positions towards third parties, it is all the more interesting to see whether, and in how far, the five founding member states of ASEAN are distinguishable as a group adhering to certain implicit, shared views and attitudes vis-à-vis third parties or, alternatively, if commonalities and convergence of interests vis-à-vis external states are rather coincidential, arbitrary and transitory.

In this context, it seems particularly interesting to ask what positions the core ASEAN members (often referred to as ASEAN-5) have been taking vis-à-vis the large powers in the region, i.e. China, Japan and the U.S., whether they pursued similar approaches, and, if so, whether one can speak of coherent ASEAN positions and approaches vis-à-vis the major powers.

2. Procedure and evaluation

In a first step, each of the ASEAN-5 states is assessed individually with regard to its position on China, Japan and the U.S., respectively. This comparison will show in how far there are parallels in the ASEAN-5 states' policies and attitudes vis-à-vis these three powers. The second step refers to ASEAN's recent collective positions towards either of the three. The purpose of the latter is to see whether ASEAN's collective behavior vis-à-vis the three powers corresponds to the trends in the respective national trends. By juxtaposing both the respective national and the collective approaches, one can draw conclusions about the coherence and stability of current trends in ASEAN's collective behavior vis-à-vis external powers. A simple model may serve to illustrate the method of evaluation. If, for example, ASEAN's collective stance vis-à-vis a certain power displayed a clear long-term trend of high homogeneity while at the same time the individual national positions were highly heterogeneous, this would suggest a high degree of policy coherence and stability. Conversely, if all ASEAN-5 states pursued similar interests and policies vis-à-vis the three external powers, but failed to   adopt collective, coordinated ASEAN approaches, the degree of coherence could be said to be low, while the question of stability would not even arise. If the ASEAN-5 displayed a good deal of homogeneity in both their individual (bilateral) and collective (ASEAN) approaches, ASEAN would get good grades for coherence, but not necessarily for stability as well (as coherence might erode as and when interests and motivations begin to diverge).

3. The respective ASEAN-5 states vis-à-vis the three external powers

3. 1. The respective ASEAN-5 states vis-à-vis the U.S.

After a phase of reorientation in Southeast Asia following the end of the Cold War in the 1990s, the U.S. has come to play a more important role in the foreign and economic relations of all ASEAN-5 states (Indonesia, Malaysia, the Philippines, Singapore, and Thailand). At the turn of the millennium, following the events of the economic and financial crisis and the East Timor crisis, security and economic ties between the core ASEAN members and the U.S. have increased significantly. The Philippines and Singapore are increasingly relying on the American hegemon when it comes to economic and security questions. Since 1999, the Philippines has turned into one of the most fervent supporters of the U.S. in ASEAN. Thailand continues to be a safe Western ally. After several years of strong frictions, Indonesia is now cozying up to the American hegemon again, while Malaysia is increasingly giving up its belligerent posture vis-à-vis the United States and seeks to step up relations with the Bush administration.

Singapore   Singapore has left no doubts that the city state counts on support from the U.S. on various fronts. In the area of economic relations, it has vigorously pursued a bilateral free trade agreement as part of its efforts to promote a network of bilateral Asia Pacific free trade agreements.[534] With a view to China, Singapore has encouraged the U.S. to play a greater security role in the region. As Indonesia's economic instability and political uncertainties continue to worry Singapore, the city state has called on America to help stabilize the economic situation there. Overall, Singapore is "[t]he country with the most proactive policy of retaining a U.S. presence in ASEAN [...]."[535] By

---

[534] Cf. for example Dent (2001): 12.
[535] Ganesan (2000): 273.

playing the American card, Singapore encourages lasting U.S. commitment to the region.

> Singapore's Prime Minister Goh Chok Tong, in a June visit to Washington, made a plea for the U.S. to help find solutions to Indonesia's disarray, urged that it manage relations with China in ways that would ensure stability, and warned that if the U.S. did not give greater weight Southeast Asian concerns, it could find itself with diminishing influence in East Asia as a whole.[536]

In the face of regional instability since the economic crisis, Singapore has not only stepped up its relations with the American superpower in economic and diplomatic terms, but also in military terms. Thus, "[i]n January 1998, it announced that it would give American aircraft carriers and other warships access to its new Changi naval base [...]."[537] In 2000, the city state signed a bilateral Acquisition and Cross-Servicing Agreement intended to facilitate mutual logistical support, and for the first time joined Thailand and the U.S. in the "Cobra Gold" exercise.[538]

Despite charges of unilateralism and unsolidary behavior, predominantly by Malaysia and Indonesia, Singapore's leadership has not tired to point out that its pursuit of improved bilateral relations with the U.S. and other countries is always carried out with an eye to potential benefits to the ASEAN region. Indeed, in April 2002, *AFTA Watch* related that Trade and Industry Minister George Yeo announced that "Singapore plans to include Indonesia in a free trade pact it is negotiating with the United States. [... and that] [u]nder an eventual US-Singapore trade pact, Indonesian information technology (IT) products would enjoy simplified rules and duty-free access to the American market [...]."[539] Overall, it is clear that Singapore's foreign policy aims at tying ASEAN firmly into the U.S. project of Asia Pacific integration. At the same time, Singapore seeks to maintain good relations with both the U.S. and China.

The Philippines   The Philippines have come a long way since the time it kicked U.S. troops out of Subic Bay more than a decade ago. Since 1999,

---

[536] Breckon (2001a).

[537] Cheng (2001): 428.

[538] Huxley (2001): 206. Cp. also: Breckon (2001a).

[539] AFTA Online (2002): "Singapore backs economic integration: Trade pact with US to include economic integration".
An Agence France Press news report confirms Singapore's intentions to help integrate the Indonesian provinces of Bintan and Batam, an area that has drawn strong Singaporean investment in the past, into the envisioned Singapore-U.S. agreement.
(Agence France Press, 31 January 2002: Indonesia may ride on proposed US-Singapore free trade pact").

military and diplomatic ties have become significantly closer. This new-found favor for the American hegemon derives from mainly two factors: firstly, the Philippines feel more exposed to Chinese covetousness in the South China Sea than ever before. Past developments have shown that it cannot necessarily rely on its fellow ASEAN members' backing vis-à-vis China.[540] The U.S. is seen as the only guarantee against aggressive Chinese acts in the Spratlys. Labrador writes that the Philippines's position of weakness in dealing with China since the discovery of Chinese constructions on Mischief Reef in 1995 has

> led to a shift in Philippine perceptions of the U.S. military presence, setting the stage for the 1999 ratification of the U.S.-Philippines Visiting Forces Agreement and, for that matter, the return of Exercise Balikatan in 2000, an exercise conducted under the terms of the Mutual Defense Treaty.[541]

Secondly, the government relies on its ties with the U.S. to fight insurgencies by Muslim rebels in parts of the Philippines that have increasingly gotten out of control.[542] Sheldon Simon states: "The Philippines is particularly keen on obtaining U.S. arms and technical assistance to enhance its ability to suppress the Abu Sayyaf [...]."[543] Thus, it is not surprising that President Macapagal-Arroyo has consistently worked to boost U.S-Philippine relations:

> Well before her positive statements [in support of the U.S., M.H.] after Sept. 11, President Gloria Macapagal-Arroyo had pushed for closer relations with the United States, including security relations. In a major foreign policy speech July 12 she identified the military alliance with the U.S. as a "strategic asset for the Philippines" and said she would like to see a "blossoming" of the overall relationship [...].[544]

Lyall Breckon reports that the Philippine President, of all Southeast Asian leaders, was the one offering the "by far strongest backing" to the U.S. after the events of 11 September[545] and was duly "rewarded with a sizeable military and economic assistance package [of] [s]ome $100 million in military aid [...] immediately [... and] another $150 million under negotiation."[546] Clearly, to

---

[540] Cp. Labrador (2001): 228.

[541] Ibid.

[542] Against strong opposition at home, President Macapagal-Arroyo has pushed for, and received, U.S. backing and active military support in her countries' struggle against rebel groups.
(Cf. Tisdall (2002); Simon (2001).

[543] Simon (2001).

[544] Breckon (2001b).

[545] Ibid.

[546] Simon (2001).

achieve security and stability, the Philippines are increasingly depending on improved links with the U.S.

Thailand　　Thailand's economic and political ties with the U.S. underwent severe difficulties in the aftermath of the financial crisis. Among the contentious issues were differences over IMF policies, dissatisfactory U.S. economic aid to Thailand, U.S. rejection of an Asian Monetary Fund and American opposition to Thailand's candidate for the post of Director General of the WTO. When Prime Minister Thaksin took over power in Thailand in 2001, Thailand also moved perceptibly towards China, which may have worried the U.S. administration.

Nevertheless, the bilateral relationship has remained stable and has even experienced a boost since 2000. Thai politicians and elites have been eager to emphasize this circumstance.

As Kusuma Snitwongse points out, "[d]espite a growing relationship with China, Thailand has continued to maintain its alliance with the United States, symbolized by the holding of the annual 'Cobra Gold' joint military exercise [...]. Thai-U.S. relations remained strong."[547] Indeed, the "Cobra Gold" joint military exercise was upgraded in 2000 when "[f]or the first time it focused on peace-keeping and peace enforcement [...] and involved the participation of Singapore and observers from Australia, Indonesia, and the Philippines."[548] In the same year, the U.S. also backed Thailand's military in its border struggle with Myanmar and in the related war on drugs.[549] After September 11, although "Thailand's support was slower and more tentative" than that of the Philippines,[550] Thailand fully backed the U.S. war on terrorism agenda (and was duly praised for it by President Bush).

In economic terms, the bilateral relationship has been upgraded significantly in 2001 with the endorsement of the new Thai-U.S. Economic Cooperation Framework on 14 December 2001.[551] At the occasion of his visit to President Bush, Prime Minister Thaksin, pointing to the traditionally strong relations between the two countries, considered this framework to represent the basis for a strong "strategic partnership".[552]

---

[547] Kusuma (2001): 205, 206.
[548] "Thailand". In: Richard W. Baker, Christopher A. Mc Nally, Charles E. Morrison (eds.) (2001): 51.
[549] Cp. Montesano (2001): 179.
[550] Simon (2001).
[551] Cf. White House of the United States (2001): "U.S.-Thailand Joint Statement", 14 December.
[552] Thaksin (2001).

Thus, considering AFTA's collective weakness, Thailand, following Singapore's example, may be on the best way to concluding its own bilateral free trade agreement with the U.S.

Indonesia As Kivimäki shows, Indonesia's relations with the U.S. underwent a reversal after the Asian crisis, conditioned by the changes of the post-Cold War era in the 1990s. Thus, whereas during the era of bipolarity the U.S. had had a strong interest in injecting aid into the Indonesian economy so as to stabilize Suharto's regime and provide a suitable climate for cooperation, during the Asian crisis the U.S. made radical political and economic reform the precondition for a suitable climate of cooperation.[553] In short, Kivimäki (drawing on the title of an article by Bob Catley[554]) concludes that in its foreign policy stance vis-à-vis Indonesia, the U.S. turned from a "benign hegemon to an arrogant superpower".[555] Kivimäki also refers to his own interviews to show that many Indonesian elites rather overstated than underestimated the impact of U.S. policy decisions on Indonesia's economic condition.[556] Thus, Indonesia's governments since president Suharto have largely bowed to U.S. demands concerning economic and democratic reforms.

However, wide-spread perception of the U.S. patronizing Indonesia hurt nationalist sentiments and provoked strong resentment among political elites. Bilateral relations were strained after the U.S. took a firm stance during the East Timor crisis in 1999 and suspended bilateral military relations with Indonesia. In 2000, the relations deteriorated further when the suspension of military ties continued and the U.S. threatened to cut economic aid in the face of Wahid's indecisive movements on the East Timor question.

> Indonesian leaders were particularly angered by what they perceived as growing American interference in Indonesia's domestic affairs. In the aftermath of the Atambua incident, U.S. Secretary of Defense William Cohen warned Indonesia that international financial institutions could not continue their assistance unless the militia problem in East Timor was resolved. Such blunt warnings were seen as threats and provoked angry reactions in Jakarta. Toward the end of the year, it seemed that the United States had gradually replaced Australia as the main target of resentment and anger for Indonesia's political elites and society.[557]

---

[553] Kivimäki (2000): 527, 537, 545.
[554] Catley (1999).
[555] Kivimäki (2000): 545 f.
[556] Ibid.: 538 f.
[557] "Indonesia". In: Richard W. Baker, Christopher A. Mc Nally, Charles E. Morrison (eds.) (2001): p. 82.

Thus, president Wahid's term in office was marked by strong bilateral tensions with the U.S.

With the ebbing of the waves of the East Timor conflict, the situation has changed considerably since the end of 2000. Indonesia has seen the return of the IMF and Indonesia appears to be willing to swallow its prescriptions; military and economic relations with the U.S. have been rekindled, and the accession of Megawati Sukarnoputri to the presidency in 2001 has provided Indonesia with a head of government interested in being on good terms with the American hegemon.[558]

Nevertheless, Megawati is struggling with strong domestic opposition against her government's policy stance vis-à-vis the U.S. September 11 has only increased this trend. Her handling of the events of September 11 was symptomatic for Indonesia's ambiguous position: Whereas on the one hand she signaled full support and solidarity to the U.S., "pledged to strengthen cooperation in combating international terrorism"[559] and "denounced the attacks in the strongest possible terms" during a tour to Washington only one week after the attack, on the other hand "[b]ack home [...] she tempered her remarks by warning that the U.S. war on terrorism did not give one country the right to attack another."[560]

Criticism of Megawati's siding with the U.S. after 11 September came not only from the leadership of various Muslim organizations, but mainly from "secular nationalists" in her own political camp and from wide parts of the Indonesian armed forces (TNI) leadership.[561] Significantly, Indonesia's vice president Hamzah Haz undermined the credibility of Megawati's statements of support during her trip to Washington by announcing at home that he hoped "that the attacks would 'cleanse America of its sins'."[562] Similarly, the former Indonesian ambassador to the United States, Hasnin Habib, called on Megawati to stop Indonesia's bowing to superpower policies and demanded her to return to an independent and active foreign policy in line with the principles of the Bandung conference of 1955. The foreign policy committee of Indonesia's parliament adopted Hasnin Habib's position.[563]

Megawati is strongly interested in normalizing bilateral relations with the U.S. The Bush administration is therefore interested in stabilizing her political

---

Cp. also Liddle (2001): 219.
[558] Cf. Malley (2002): 131.
[559] Breckon (2001a).
[560] Ibid.
[561] Cf. Machetzki (2001): 587.
[562] Breckon (2001a).
[563] Cf. Machetzki (2001): 587.

position. As a sign of confidence, the U.S. has stepped up bilateral economic and military relations with Indonesia again in April 2002.[564]

Malaysia   Throughout most of the 1990s, Malaysia has become notorious for its critical view of U.S. attempts to expand its sphere of economic and political power in East Asia. Since the early 1990s, Mahathir promoted the idea of greater East Asian economic integration (including China) to counter the influence of the U.S.-dominated NAFTA bloc. By 1994, Malaysia had become openly critical of U.S. attempts to dominate the APEC agenda and turn the loose consultative forum into a free trade area. Within APEC, Malaysia and China became the two most vocal critics of the U.S., and Prime Minister Mahathir continued to promote his idea of an East Asian Economic Group in a modified version, as a separate caucus within APEC. In 1997/98, Mahathir sharply attacked the U.S.-centric global financial and economic structures and branded the U.S. preference for market liberalism and unregulated capital flows as ruinous to developing countries. He also strongly defied the role the IMF played in the crisis, calling for a separate Asian Monetary Fund. Tensions between Malaysia and the U.S. peaked in 1998, when Malaysia hosted the APEC summit during which Vice President Al Gore objected vocally to the imprisonment of former Deputy Prime Minister Anwar Ibrahim and openly sympathized with the Malaysian *reformasi* movement demanding more democratic structures. President Clinton had demonstratively chosen not to attend the APEC summit that year, thus documenting both the deep political gap between Malaysia and the U.S. and his low expectations concerning the outcomes of a summit hosted by one of its strongest critics. Through 2000, "Malaysia's foreign policy [...] continued to be shaped by championing the rights of the developing world against the perceived hegemonies of the West and globalization."[565]

Mahathir's strategy is to keep the U.S. at arm's length, as this both allows him to cater to domestic audiences and serves the purpose of remaining on good terms with various international partners, such as the member states of the Organizations of Islamic Countries (OIC) and, importantly, China. At the same time, despite bilateral tensions and occasional fierce rhetoric, Malaysia is well aware of the U.S. as both its most important economic partner and ultimate security shield to the region.

Thus, the U.S. continues to be the by far largest export market with the largest trade surplus for Malaysia. This means Malaysia has an interest in ensuring and expanding access to this market. Since Singapore has kicked off negotiations on

---

[564] Cf. Office of the United States Trade Representative, Washington, D.C. (September 2001): "U.S. Trade Representative Robert B. Zoellick Meets With Indonesian President Megawati To Discuss Strengthening U.S.-Indonesian Ties".

[565] Martinez (2001): 199.

a bilateral free trade agreement with the U.S. and has thus set an example for other ASEAN states such as Thailand and Indonesia, Malaysia has had an additional incentive to step up its bilateral relations with the U.S.

Table 28: Malaysia's trade balance with the U.S. from 1989 to February 2002, in millions of U.S. dollars

Year	Exports to U.S.	Imports from U.S.	Balance
2002 (January and February)	3,525.70	1,412.90	2,112.80
2001	22,336.40	9,380.20	12,956.20
2000	25,568.20	10,937.50	14,630.70
1999	21,424.30	9,060.00	12,364.30
1998	19,000.00	8,957.00	10,043.00
1997	18,026.70	10,780.00	7,246.70
1996	17,828.80	8,546.20	9,282.60
1995	17,454.70	8,816.10	8,638.60
1994	13,981.70	6,969.00	7,012.70
1993	10,563.00	6.064.40	4,498.60
1992	8,294.10	4,362.90	3,931.20
1991	6,101.50	3,899.90	2,201.60
1990	5,271.80	3,425.00	1,846.80
1989	4,744.10	2,870.40	1,873.70

Source: U.S. Census Bureau, 17 April 2002, http://www.census.gove/foreign-trade/balance/c5570.html [25/04/02].

Table 29: Malaysia's major export destinations (Feb. 2002), in millions of Ringgit Malaysia (RM)

Destination	Total value in February 2002	Total value in 2000
U.S.	4,782.50	67,672.30
Singapore	3,841.90	56,669.00
Japan	3,303.60	44,502.70
PR China	1,203.80	14,519.80
Netherlands	1,190.20	15,429.20
Hong Kong	1,135.60	15,298.60
Thailand	960.80	12,767.80
Rep. of Korea	893.80	11,157.30
Taiwan	831.90	12,117.10
UK	625.60	8,779.10

Source: MITI Malaysia, 15 April 2002, http://www.miti.gov.my/trdind/trade-t-2.htm [25/04/02].

Table 30: Malaysia's major imports, by origin (Feb. 2002), in millions of Ringgit Malaysia (RM)

Destination	Total value in February 2002	Total value in 2000
Japan	3,854.20	54,002.00
U.S.	3,493.30	44.840.90
Singapore	2,334.30	35,312.40
PR China	1,475.50	14,456.80
Taiwan	1,028.10	15,932.20
Rep. of Korea	989.10	11,239.20
Thailand	802.60	11,121.00
Philippines	752.00	6,989.30
Germany	732.60	10,423.70
Indonesia	615.00	8,517.20

Source: MITI Malaysia, 15 April 2002, http://www.miti.gov.my/trdind/trade-t5.htm [25/04/02].

Table 31: Malaysia's highest trade surpluses, by country (1999-2001), in millions of Ringgit Malaysia (RM)

Country	2001	2000	1999
U.S.	22,831.50	24,835.20	26,978.50
Singapore	21,355.60	23,878.50	18,267.10
Netherlands	12,963.50	13,419.10	14,424.60
Hong Kong	8,107.60	8,296.50	8,091.10
India	3.057.60	4,563.90	5,733.30
UAE	2,544.20	2,121.70	2,299.80
UK	1,907.40	5,485.50	6,434.80
Mexico	1,856.30	1,863.00	752.70
Australia	1,854.30	3,158.40	2,032.30
Thailand	1,646.80	1,498.10	1,104.30

Source: MITI Malaysia, 25 March 2002,
http://www.miti.gov.my/trdind/annu6.htm [25/0402].

Malaysia has also relied on the U.S. security umbrella in the region. According to the US State Department, "[d]espite sometimes strident rhetoric, the U.S. and Malaysia have a solid record of cooperation in many areas, including trade and investment, defense, counter-terrorism, and counter-narcotics."[566]

Following the Clinton administration's defeat, Prime Minister Mahathir has sought to strengthen Malaysia's ties with the U.S. and has solicited improved

---

[566] United States Department of Foreign Affairs (October 2000): "Background Notes: Malaysia".

relations with the Bush administration. The events of 11 September helped to reinforce this pursuit as the Bush administration discovered new commonalities with the Mahathir administration in its struggle against terrorism and was willing to push divisive questions of human rights and democratic values aside. Since then, bilateral relations have experienced a remarkable shift. At the margins of the APEC summit in 2001, Prime Minister Mahathir met privately with President Bush to condemn the terrorist attacks on the U.S. and discuss measures to fight terrorism. As Martinez relates, "[h]is meeting with Bush was a significant step in improving U.S.-Malaysia relations [...]. New American initiatives that prioritise national security over fundamental freedoms appeared to forge a common bond between the two nations."[567] Nevertheless, diplomatic sensitivities on both sides are still prominent. In February, Mahathir hoped to be able to meet Bush in Washington, but was denied the favor.[568] Instead, officials arranged a meeting on 14 May 2002. Whereas the White House acknowledged that "[a]s a modern, moderate, Muslim state, Malaysia plays an important role in the global war against terrorism and in regional security",[569] a former Malaysian diplomat indicated a turnaround in Malaysian-U.S. relations in a Malaysian newspaper article.

> Dr. Mahathir's official working visit to Washington next week marks a new milestone in bilateral relations, a clear shift in their priorities prompted by realpolitik. Dr Mahathir [...] wants to strengthen ties with Malaysia's largest trading partner.[570]

Overall, Malaysia economically and politically depends to a large degree on the U.S. But Mahathir's customary anti-hegemonial posture shows his ambiguous position vis-à-vis the U.S. and its Western allies. In the running-up to the Mahathir-Bush summit in May 2002, Karim Rasian showed that Malaysia's relations with the U.S. are both stable and limited at the same time:

> Mahathir remains an outspoken interlocutor for both developing nations and the Islamic world. His long-standing views on globalization and superpower hegemony, for example, will place him at odds with an

---

[567] Martinez (2002): 139.
The fact that Malaysia has taken a critical stance on the U.S. intervention in Afghanistan and was a signatory to the resolution of the Organization of Islamic Countries opposing any projection of U.S. military power to Islamic statesshould not mislead anyone into thinking Malaysia opposed Wahsington's agenda on terrorism. Mahathir has an image to lose as a critic of the West and a champion of Islamic and developing nations. His domestic power and international standing could erode if he chose to side too closely with the U.S. The Malaysian government's rhetoric and policies therefore differ in this respect.
[568] *Far Eastern Economic Review* (07 February 2002): "Bush-Mahathir Meet a No-Go".
[569] Press Secretary of the White House (16 April 2002): "Visit of the Prime Minister Mahathir of Malaysia".
[570] Abdullah (2002): "Reviving Malaysia-US ties".

increasingly unilateralist [U.S.] administration. After 20 years in office, Mahathir's views are unlikely to change overnight. [...]

Mahathir will want to strengthen Malaysia's ties with the largest trading partner, America. [...] Mahathir also recognizes that the U.S. is an important part of both Malaysian and Asean security and prosperity. Thus, bilateral relations are professional, cordial and – most importantly – unemotional [...]. Still, countries like Malaysia prefer a multipolar world and there are deep concerns about what is seen as U.S. adventurism and the negative impact of this on the burgeoning Asian superpower, China.[571]

Whereas the post-cold war environment has enabled Malaysia to assume a more independent foreign policy posture emphasizing the importance of exclusive forms of East Asian regionalism and a policy of opening up towards China, the Mahathir government basically remains a safe, if little enthusiastic patron of the U.S.

3.2. The respective ASEAN-5 states vis-à-vis Japan

Singapore   Singapore's official relations with Japan have never been better than they are at present, and yet, they couldn't be more twisted. On the one hand, the two countries are on the best political terms with each other and concluded the ground-breaking Japan-Singapore Economic Partnership Agreement in January 2002, which represents "the first regional trade agreement to be signed by Japan".[572] On the other hand, Singapore has assertively taken to pressuring an indecisive Japan to make more concrete economic liberalization commitments to ASEAN countries by using China as a lever to extol concessions from Japan. The latest coup in this regard was that Singapore engineered a common resolve by ASEAN leaders to agree, in principle, to China's proposal to form the ASEAN-China FTA. This decision, taken at the ASEAN Plus Three summit in November 2001, literally shocked and temporarily seemed to paralyze the Koizumi administration. Japan had been unprepared for this situation, as Prime Minister Koizumi's hurried tour of Southeast Asia in January 2001 proved. During this tour, Koizumi, whose objective it was to quickly counterbalance China's strategic advantage, signaled an overall shift of Japan's position vis-à-vis Southeast Asia, although he remained very unspecific about particular economic and free trade concessions to Southeast Asia. However, whereas at the November 2001 summit Japan had still rejected to talk about an ASEAN-

---

[571] Raslan (2002): "Mahathir Goes to Wahington".

[572] Statement by Prime Minister Junichiro Koizumi (13 January 2002).

Japan FTA at all, the prospect of an ASEAN-China FTA caused Japan to give in to Singapore's and other ASEAN members' demand to discuss an ASEAN-Japan FTA.[573]

Singapore's overall strategy in its conduct of relations with Japan is, in Prime Mister Goh's words, to "anchor Japan in Southeast Asia".[574] Singapore has realized that Japan's anchor in Southeast Asia will be all the deeper the less anxiety Southeast Asia displays about cooperating with China. This strategy of forging closer ties with Japan while assuming as much independence as possible serves three purposes. First, it keeps Japan committed to Southeast Asia; second, it keeps Southeast and East Asia firmly integrated in the Asia-Pacific context, as "Japan plays an important role in anchoring the US in East Asia"[575]; third, Southeast Asia's close ties to Japan and the West enable it to realize opportunities of cooperation with China more confidently and independently and deal with China from a position of relative strength.

Malaysia   Throughout the 1980s and 1990s, Japan was assigned the role of a potential leader of East Asia by Prime Minister Mahathir. As Milne and Mauzy have pointed out, "Mahathir came into office with a favorable disposition towards Japan [...]. He is much more pro-Japan than any other Southeast Asian leader."[576] Thus, Mahathir launched the "Look East" policy focused on Japan in the 1980s, reserved a special role for Japan as regional anchor in his concept of the East Asian Economic Caucus (EAEC) throughout the 1990s, supported and promoted Japan's idea of establishing an East Asian Monetary Fund and sustained the debate about monetary regionalism and the formation of a yen bloc in East Asia. Ironically, the ideas of Japan's self-styled friend and advocate, Mahathir, are not very popular in Japan itself these days, as Japan has never been really comfortable with Mahathir's ideas of an autonomous EAEC and abandoned the idea of an Asian Monetary Fund quickly after 1998. Indeed, whereas Japan is seeking to balance China's influence in East Asia by promoting Asia Pacific links, Mahathir appears to be holding on to his idea of Japan as a pan-East Asian player. Therefore, relations between Japan and Malaysia are warm and friendly at the surface, but seem to have actually cooled deep down. Thus, when Koizumi started his tour of Southeast Asia in January 2002, the two leaders could not conceal that their respective foreign policy prerogatives had little in common. As Lam Peng Er observed, at the bilateral summit in Kuala Lumpur on 10 January 2002,

---

[573] Cf. *Asia Times Online* (04 April 2002): "ASEAN eyes expanded FTA"; *Japan Times* (14 April 2002): "Japan Considering Creation of East Asia Free Trade Area Before 2010".

[574] Goh (2002): Speech, official dinner in honor of Prime Minister Koizumi, 13 January.

[575] Ibid.

[576] Mulne and Mauzy (1999): 123.

Malaysian Prime Minister Mahathir advocated an ASEAN Plus Three group [...] as a pan-Asian regional grouping Tokyo ought to support; Koizumi preferred an open and broader pan-Pacific community that encompasses Australia and New Zealand, while not excluding the U.S.[577]

Like most core ASEAN states, Malaysia is interested in better access to Japan's market and is therefore looking forward to the progress of talks on the proposed ASEAN-Japan trade agreement. Malaysia would also like to see more Japanese investments and ODA flowing to ASEAN. There is reason to speculate that Malaysia's decision to agree to negotiations about an ASEAN-China FTA was partly motivated by the desire to crack the Japanese market open and ensure Japan's financial and economic commitment to the region.

Thailand   Thailand relies heavily on Japanese FDI and ODA. In both sectors, Japan has been Thailand's largest source for decades. During the Asian crisis, Japan turned out to be Thailand's most reliable and generous partner, a circumstance that was highly appreciated in Bangkok.[578] Therefore, bilateral relations have been largely unproblematic. These structural dependencies cannot be expected to change in the foreseeable future. However, one important issue of contention between Thailand and Japan is the trade imbalance between the two economies, which has been in Japan's favor throughout the past decades (see table). Thailand therefore has a strong interest in reversing or at least neutralizing this trend. As the Thai Ambassador to Japan pointed out in this context in June 2001, Thailand is especially interested in increasing its share of agricultural exports to Japan and demands tariff reductions in this area.[579]

---

[577] Lam (2002).
[578] Cp. Kusuma (2001): 207.
[579] Cf. Sakthip Krairiksh (2001).

Table 32: Thailand's trade balance with Japan, 1975-2002 (in billions of yen)

Year	Imports from Japan	Exports to Japan	Balance (% of total trade)
2000	1,469	1, 142	-327 (12.52)
1999	1,285	1,008	-277 (12.08)
1998	1,222	1,068	-154 (6.72)
1997	1,764	1,157	-607 (20.78)
1995	1,850	950	-900 (32.14)
1990	1,315	599	-816 (42.63)
1985	488	246	-242 (32.97)
1980	435	257	-178 (25.72)
1975	284	215	-69 (13.82)

Source: Japan Statistical Yearbook 2002,
http://www.stat.go.jp/english/data/nenkan/zuhyou/b1201000.xls (Japan's exports 1975-2000),
http://www.stat.go.jp/english/data/nenkan/zuhyou/b1202000.xls (Japan's imports 1975-2000) [01/05/02].

Following Singapore's example, Thailand is now pursuing a bilateral free trade agreement with Japan. On 26 November 2001, Prime Ministers Thaksin and Koizumi signed an "Economic Partnership Framework" , which Thailand hopes will eventually evolve into a full-blown FTA. Whereas Japan in November still proved reluctant to advance FTA talks with Thailand, the Koizumi government made a turnaround on this issue. During a summit meeting on 15 April 2002, Koizumi, with a view to accelerating the Initiative for Japan-ASEAN Comprehensive Economic Partnership he had announced in January 2002, indicated his willingness "to launch a Working Group, which would use the Japan-Singapore Economic Partnership Agreement as a reference to review a partnership between Japan and Thailand."[580]

Politically, Japan has variously contributed to the stability of Thailand and its immediate Indochinese environment.[581]

The only issue that might harbor some potential for tensions between the two countries is Thailand's relations with China, which have been traditionally good and have improved rapidly in recent years. Prime Minister Thaksin has left no doubt that cooperation with China has a high priority for his government and is presently promoting what he termed a "strategic partnership" with China during

---

[580] Ministry of Foreign Affairs, Japan (15 April 2002): "Boao Forum for Asia, Summit Meeting between Prime Minister Junichiro Koizumi and Prime Minister Thaksin Shinawatra (Overview)".
[581] Cp. Kusuma (2001): 207.

a visit to Beijing in August 2001.[582] In the context of the Sino-Japanese rivalry, it is quite obvious that Thailand hopes the ASEAN-China FTA proposal will promote its own FTA negotiations with Japan.

Indonesia   Traditionally, relations between Indonesia and Japan have been smooth. Indonesia depends very much on Japanese FDI and bilateral trade with Japan. As Kong Yam Tam, considering the strategic options of ASEAN countries in forming FTAs with the U.S., Japan or greater China, noted in 1998, whereas the Philippines would stand to profit most if the U.S. was included in a regional FTA,

> Indonesia's gain in real GDP will be substantially improved whenever Japan is included as a member of the FTA. These are not peculiar phenomena, but are reflective of the heavy reliance of [...] Indonesia on the United States and Japan [...].[583]

Considering Japan's economic relevance to Indonesia, Indonesians have been wishing for Japan to forge closer ties with Southeast Asia. In terms of political stability in the region, Indonesia welcomes Japan's role as an ally of the U.S. The *Asia Pacific Security Outlook 1999* summarizes Indonesia's expectations:

> In general, Indonesians would like to see Japan play a leadership role in the region; the problem has been weak leadership in Japan. That much said, though, Indonesians clearly prefer that the Japanese role be limited to economics, as many are still reluctant to accept a Japanese military role. (However, support exists for Japanese participation in regional security.)[584]

Political relations between Japan and Indonesia have been good, even (or especially) during the East Timor crisis. An observer noted in 1999 that

> Tokyo has been characteristically quiet about the East Timor situation. [...] Although Japan has been criticized both at home and abroad for playing such a minor physical role in a problem in its figurative backyard, Tokyo's relatively passive stance likely will help smooth relations with the new government [of President Wahid, M.H.] in Jakarta.[585]

---

[582] Thayer (2001c).
[583] Tan (1998).
[584] "Indonesia". In: Baker, McNally and Morrison (eds) (1999): 83.
[585] Castellano (1999).

Through 2002, Japan continued to be Indonesia's largest bilateral ODA donor, creditor and investor.[586] Bilateral relations have been relatively smooth, both in economic and political terms. During the two bilateral summits on 28 September 2001 and 12 January 2002, Koizumi announced Japan's "Basic Aid policy for Economic Cooperation", which is to boost Japan's aid grants to Indonesia. Further, "regarding Indonesia's greatest concern, which is treatment of its debt from 2000, Prime Minister Koizumi asserted that it would be handled flexibly through debt rescheduling."[587]

However, Japan's recent pledges of support contrast with cuts in other areas. Thus, Indonesia and Japan may be poised for some contention if Japan implements its decision to substantially reduce its loans to Indonesia. And there is some doubt about Japan's commitment to its bilateral ODA schemes, too. As The Jakarta Post reported in January 2002,

> Mired in recession, Japan has considered reviewing its Official Development Assistance (ODA) policy toward Indonesia. Signs of this surfaced when Japan cut its pledge under the Consultative Group on Indonesia (CGI) to $720 million from $1.56 billion at the previous CGI meeting Japan along with the World Bank and the Asian Development Bank have been the biggest contributors under the CGI, which groups together Indonesia's sovereign creditors. Now, instead of spending more, Tokyo has shown signs of leaning toward receiving less from Indonesia under more generous debt restructuring terms.[588]

Although there can be no doubt that bilateral relations are basically stable, Indonesia might feel tempted to be more assertive and play the China card in the future in order to keep Japan truly committed to the cause of economic cooperation in the future. And indeed, in addition to the ASEAN leaders' adoption of the ASEAN-China FTA proposal, the continuing rapprochement between China and Indonesia came to a new high at the bilateral summit in March 2002, when the governments of the two countries edged visibly closer to each other.[589] An observer writing in The Straits Times suggested that the Sino-Indonesian rapprochement fitted into the present pattern of diplomatic realignments in China's favor among the states of Southeast Asia.

> The reciprocal visits of Chinese Premier Zhu Rongji to Indonesia last November and President Megawati to China last month signal their desire to put past bilateral troubles behind them. [...] China is eager to

---

[586] Cf. *The Jakarta Post* (03 April 2002b): "Mega forms team top boost economic ties with Japan",; *The Jakarta Post*, (03 April 2002b): " Japan to support RI at Paris Club".

[587] Japan, Ministry of Foreign Affairs, (2001a): "Japan-Indonesia Summit Meeting (Overview)".

[588] *The JakartaPost* (11 January 2002): "Japan to offer new aid for Indonesia".

[589] Breckon (2002).

expand its presence in the region as part of what it sees as its natural rivalry with Japan and the United States. Indonesia is eager to reduce its financial dependency on Japan and the US and develop foreign-policy alternatives to counterbalance the aggressive demands of Washington in the anti-terror struggle. [...] Japan was obviously shocked by China's proposed free trade area with Asean. It has always considered Southeast Asia its natural sphere of influence. But the region sees China in the ascendancy and Japan in [...] decline.[590]

Although I do not share Castle's view that there is a major realignment underway in Southeast Asia, I believe that Indonesia, as most other ASEAN states, might be more willing than in the past to tactically play the China card when dealing with the U.S. and Japan.[591] Generally, however, Indonesia is well-disposed towards Japan. President Megawati also welcomed Japanese Prime Minister Koizumi's initiative for wider Asia-Pacific economic integration including Australia and New Zealand.[592]

The Philippines The Philippines' relations with Japan are determined by three decisive parameters. First, the Philippines' fear of Chinese expansionism, especially with a view to the South China Sea; second, Japan's role as a balancer of China in East Asia and its close alliance with the Philippines' own major ally, the U.S.; third, FDI and economic aid flows from Japan to the Philippines and Southeast Asia. Due to Japan's stabilizing influence, bilateral relations have been smooth. Despite occasional political flare-ups about the still unresolved issue of Japan's conduct during WW II in the Philippines (the main issue being the question of the Filipino "comfort women"), relations have been stable. This was confirmed by the course of events in 2001 and 2002. Thus, in the immediate aftermath of the events of 11 September 2001, President Macapagal-Arroyo promoted a greater role for Japan in regional security and signaled her preference for a close Japanese-American alliance. During the bilateral summit on 14 September 2001, "President Arroyo stated that the presence of the United States was an important factor in the stability of the Asian and Pacific region and welcomed the strengthening of relations between Japan and the US in the area of security".[593] However, there has been some concern about substantial

---

[590] Castle (2002).

[591] The idea of Indonesia playing the China card is not too far-fetched. Kivimäki (2000: 546), for example, recommended Indonesia to play the pan-Asian card (focusing on cooperation with China and India) to regain some of its bargaining power vis-à-vis the U.S. (and hence the West): "By using the 'Asia card' in a sophisticated, unthreatening, but persistent way, Indonesia could win back some of its lost bargaining power." Indonesia might as well use improved bilateral ties with China in order to strengthen its position vis-à-vis Japan.

[592] Cf. *The Japan Times* (13 January 2002): "Koizumi's trade plan hailed by Megawati".

[593] Japan, Ministry of Foreign Affairs (2001b): "Japan-Philippines Summit Meeting (Outline)".

cuts of ODA to the Philippines as part of Japan's general ODA reduction policy. Thus, "[t]he Philippines appealed to Japan not to cut its ODA" when Koizumi toured Southeast Asia and met individually with the heads of government of the major ASEAN states in January 2002.[594] Further, the Philippines is still running a trade deficit with Japan and therefore supports ASEAN's pursuit of a free trade agreement with Japan.[595] The Philippines may already have discovered that Japan's rivalry with China gives it a lever to spur Japan's economic commitment to the Southeast Asian region. For example, at the occasion of a foreign policy briefing on 16 January 2002, Undersecretary of Foreign Affairs, Lauro Baja, hinted that, with a view to ASEAN states' cooperation with China and Japan in the ASEAN Plus Three process, "It is always better to have two important political and economic powers paying attention to us."[596] Overall, however, President Macapagal-Arroyo has left no doubt about the close bilateral relationship with Japan, which in May 2002 she considered to be "our closest neighbor outside of Asean",[597] as Japan remains "central to our future". In this context, the Philippine President noted that "as the Philippines' largest source of development assistance, Japan enabled the Philippines' rapid recovery during this past difficult year."[598] The Philippines are already profiting from the shock Japan received from ASEAN leaders' decision in late 2001 to negotiate a China-ASEAN FTA. Thus, Japan, in an effort to counterbalance China's growing influence, has offered to establish an economic partnership agreement (EPA) with the Philippines. During a visit by President Macapagal-Arroyo to Japan, both sides agreed to "create a working group to systematize the steps leading to an economic partnership agreement (EPA) between the two countries" similar to the one signed by Singapore and Japan earlier that year.[599]

3.3. The respective ASEAN-5 states vis-à-vis China

Singapore In 1990, Singapore resumed diplomatic relations with China. Unlike to other countries such as Indonesia, "the setting up of official ties with China was just a formality in view of the substantive economic and political

---

[594] Lam (2002).

[595] Cf. *Asia Times Online* (04 April 2002): "ASEAN eyes expanded FTA".

[596] Baja (2002): Statement at the Department of Foreign Affairs foreign policy briefing for the diplomatic corps, 16 January.

[597] Republic of the Philippines, Office of the Press Secretary (2000a): "GMA aims for more progressive, stable Asian environment in trip to Japan".

[598] Macapagal-Arroyo (2002): Speech at the 8th "The Future of Asia" conference, 21 May, Tokyo.

[599] Republic of the Philippines, Office of the Press Secretary (2002b): "Philippines, Japan to create working group to systematize economic agreement".

contacts in Sino-Singaporean relations that had built up over the years."[600] Starting out from this position, Singapore's relations with China continued to improve and expand throughout the 1990s.

Into the 2000s, Singapore's official position on China has been one of cautious optimism. The city state has largely played down its concerns about China's ascendancy as a political and economic power in the region and instead emphasized the positive political and economic implications of improved relations with China. This position resulted from the perception that China's influence in East Asia was there to stay and that therefore China needed to be dealt with in a forward-looking, non-confrontational and pragmatic way (a position shared largely by all ASEAN members).[601]

In economic terms, China's ascendancy presents a challenge to Singapore in at least two ways. On the one hand, China has emerged as a competitor to ASEAN countries in attracting inward foreign direct investments. On the other hand, Singapore is worrying about Singapore's and ASEAN's competitiveness in absorbing the increasing flow of outward FDI from China. While the former phenomenon (China's attraction of FDI) has become a commonplace when considering ASEAN-China relations, there has been little international awareness of the latter (ASEAN's need to position itself better to be able to attract outward Chinese FDI) so far.

Friedrich Wu and Yeo Han Sia argue that it must be Singapore's economic aim to "assimilate" China to the structures of the ASEAN Free Trade Area (AFTA) and the ASEAN Investment AREA (AIA) so as to significantly increase ASEAN's share in Chinese outward FDI which was at six percent in 1999.[602]

> Closer integration of ASEAN countries through the ASEAN Free Trade Agreement (AFTA) and ASEAN Investment AREA (AIA) would create a common marketplace that would ensure the region's attractiveness to foreign investors, including China. With the agreement between ASEAN and China on 6 November 2001 to begin negotiations on a[n] FTA in 2002, we will see the expansion of AFTA within the next ten years. The AFTA+1 [i.e. AFTA plus China, M.H.] arrangement is expected to yield considerable benefit for all member countries. [...] By assimilating China into AFTA and AIA, ASEAN will benefit from the expansion of two-way flow of goods, services, and investments. Capitalising on the stronger economic integration and geographical

---

[600] Lee Lai To (2001): 418.

[601] Cp. ibid.

[602] For this figure and Singapore's economic strategy concerning China, as outlined above, cf. Wu; Yeo (2001): "China's rising investment in Southeast Asia: How ASEAN and Singapore can benefit".

proximity would also make ASEAN a natural host for outward investments from China.[603]

In political terms, Singapore is seeking good relations with China while at the same time it sides very closely with the U.S. and Japan to balance China's growing political clout.

Malaysia   Since 1990, Prime Minister Mahathir has taken a benign foreign policy stance on China and has tried to boost bilateral relations in order to promote Malaysia's economic and political interests. This trend continued through 2002, despite Alan Boyd's erratic suggestion that Malaysia's arms-buildup was aimed at countering Chinese influence in the region.[604] Edging closer towards China and cooperating with the PRC has served Malaysia's purposes in various respects.

In the area of foreign policy, China's foreign policy paradigm of multipolarity and opposition to U.S. hegemony corresponded to Mahathir's post-Cold War interest in giving Malaysia a more independent foreign policy profile. In this context, the Mahathir government has seen China's emergence (which naturally also worried Malaysia as much as it worried most other ASEAN states) as a chance to promote greater East Asian integration as an alternative model to U.S. and Western economic and political domination of Asia.

Malaysia earned itself considerable credit with the Chinese government when it failed to condemn the Chinese government in the aftermath of the Tiananmen massacre. As early as 1991, Mahathir lobbied Deng Xiaoping during a state visit to support his idea of forming an East Asian Economic Caucus (EAEC). In 1993 and 1994, Malaysia and China emerged as the main critics of the U.S. trade liberalization agenda in APEC and objected to the Clinton administration

---

[603] Ibid.

[604] Malaysia's military build-up is aimed at reducing dangers emerging from the instability of its Southeast Asian neighbors rather than at deterring a potentially aggressive China. The rather unpredictable security situation in the Philippines and Indonesia represents a by far more immediate threat to Malaysia's security and domestic stability than the rather abstract and hypothetical China threat. Thus, the Philippines is struggling with terrorism in areas that border directly on Malaysia, and Malaysia is already struggling vehemently to curb and prevent illegal immigration from Indonesia. Before this background, Alan Boyd's assumption expressed in *Asia Times Online* that "he [Mahathir, M.H.]wants to send a message to China [...] that at least one ASEAN country is getting serious about defense, even if the rest of the region can't make up its collective mind" is far less credible than S. Jayasankaran's explanation in the *Far Eastern Economic Review* (which is based on intelligence from U.S. sources) that "the arms-buildup was aimed at more long-term threats, including piracy in the Malacca Strait and Muslim insurgencies in the southern Philippines and southern Thailand [...and that] the Malaysians were worried above all at the prospect of Indonesia's collapse [..., as] Malaysia shares a land border with Indonesia and has consistently had problems with Indonesian illegal immigrants." (Boyd 2002; Jayasankaran 2002).

taking over control and imposing its agenda on the APEC process. Overall, Liow assessed Malaysia's China policy in the following terms:

> The upturn in political cooperation between these two heretofore politically and ideologically antagonistic governments [those of Malaysia and China, M.H.] is a development that should be framed in the context of Mahathir's dominance over the Malaysian foreign policy process. Malaysia's political identification and cooperation with China have been a function of the prime minister's own political agenda, namely to construct a dynamic and independent Malaysian foreign policy. [...] For Mahathir, China would be a useful and important ally in his diplomatic confrontations with the West – in particular the U.S. [...][605]

Liow also shows that Malaysia has actively promoted genuine Chinese positions in ASEAN with regard to the Spratly islands question. Thus, at the 1999 ASEAN Ministerial Meeting, Malaysia took sides with China by insisting discussion of the South China Sea issue should not become internationalized at ARF level, but should be dealt with only bilaterally by the countries concerned. In this context, Malaysia also opposed the draft Code of Conduct presented by the Philippines and Vietnam and thereby alienated many fellow ASEAN members.[606]

Throughout the 1990s, bilateral contacts at the highest level have increased considerably, and China acknowledged the special status of its relations with Malaysia. Significantly, it was Malaysia who acted as coordinator for ASEAN-China relations when China first became a full ASEAN dialogue partner in 1996, and continued to act in this role in subsequent years until 1999. Bilateral relations peaked in 1999 when the two countries' governments announced "a twelve-point Sino-Malaysian Framework of Future Bilateral Cooperation" in June.[607] Later that year, both sides signed several cooperation and trade agreements, "signed a memorandum of understanding between Bank Negara Malaysia [National Bank of Malaysia, M.H.] and the People's Bank of China on setting up banks in each other's country"[608] and coordinated their views on regional affairs. Malaysia's long-term cooperation agreement with China represented one of the first two such agreements negotiated with ASEAN states.[609] Both parties made a point of demonstrating the harmonious nature of the two countries' bilateral relations. Whereas Mahathir defended the One China

---

[605] Liow (2000): 677-678.
[606] Cf. ibid.: 685-689.
[607] Thayer (1999a).
[608] Thayer (1999c).
[609] Thailand was the first ASEAN country to conclude a long-term cooperation agreement with the PRC (February 1999) and thus preceded Malaysia by some three months.

policy and vigorously justified China's decision to ban Falun Gong,[610] the Chinese leadership scratched Mahathir's back by giving him vocal support in pre-election times. Thus, when Mahathir visited Beijing in August 1999, "Premier Zhu Rongji honored his guest by referring to him as 'a good friend of China'".[611] In November the same year, Zhu visited Kuala Lumpur just "on the eve of Malaysia's tenth general elections", which caused the opposition leader to charge "Mahathir was 'playing the China card' in an effort to gain an electoral advantage."[612]

Through 2002, bilateral relations have remained cordial. Malaysia continued to promote its idea of an exclusively East Asian EAEC and thus remained a key partner in China's pursuit of forging closer relations with ASEAN in the context of ASEAN+1 and APT cooperation. Zhu Rongji's meeting with the king of Malaysia, Sultan Salahuddin Abdul Aziz Shah, in April 2001 symbolized the excellent state of the bilateral relationship.[613] Reportedly, at the Pacific Economic Basin Council meeting in May 2002, Mahathir noted that "Southeast Asian countries should not regard China as a 'black hole' sucking foreign investment from its neighbours [… and] that the world can't 'banish' China to some kind of economic limbo."[614] This remark is just another expression of Malaysia's long-standing integrative approach to the PRC.

Thailand Traditionally, Thailand's relationship with China is the least problematic one of all ASEAN-5 states. After Thailand had built a strategic political partnership with China throughout the 1980s, Thailand has also pursued the objective of establishing a strategic economic partnership with the PRC since the early 1990s.[615] Thus, Thailand has been edging closer toward China, both politically and economically for a considerable time now. Michael Vatikiotis reported in 1997 that

> "after Thai prime ministers get elected, China is almost always the first country outside Asean they visit. […] Since the end of the Cold War, Thailand has been moving closer to China, lured by the promise of its market and driven by large Thai-Chinese groups […]. "[616]

---

[610] Cf. Malaysian Prime Minister Mahathir (1999): "Reflections on my visit to China".
[611] Thayer (1999b).
[612] Thayer (1999c).
[613] Cf. People's Republic of China, Ministry of Foreign Affairs (2001): "Premier Zhu Rongji met with Malaysian Supreme Head of State", 26 April.
[614] *Far Eastern Economic Review* (16 May 2002): "China Briefing".
[615] Cp. Chulacheeb (1999).
[616] Vatikiotis (1997): 19.

In the same article, Vatikiotis also refers to a statement by Kusuma Snitwongse, a senior Thai think tank representative, in order to show Thailand's desire for close relations with China.

> In an expanded Asean, Thailand is hoping that closeness to China will enhance its role in the association, says Kusuma Snitwongse of the Institute of International and Strategic Studies at Bangkok's Chulalongkorn University. "Thailand wants a leading role in Asean, and Thailand can act as a bridge to China. The two are linked".[617]

Sukuma Snitwongse, in an article published in April 2001, gives an overview of the good progress Thailand has made in forging close ties with the PRC.[618] Thus, Thailand was the first ASEAN country to negotiate and sign a framework for long-term relations with China, the "Plan of Action for the 21st Century" on 05 February 1999.[619] The Chuan Leekpai administration was especially interested in winning China's support to curb drug trade from Myanmar. Both sides signed a "Memorandum of Understanding aimed at strengthening bilateral co-operation to fight the narcotics trade" on 09 October 2000.[620] However, despite generally friendly relations, the Chuan governement's insistence on its human rights stance in the Falun Gong question and its democratic posture accounted for bilateral frictions.

When prime minister Chuan Leekpai and his outspokenly democratic and Western-oriented foreign minister Surin Pitsuwan were voted out of office in landslide elections in 2001 and Thaksin Shinawatra acceded to power, Thailand's posture towards China changed recognizably. The Thaksin government has clearly focused on boosting economic relations and on balancing Thailand's trade deficit with China. It also had a strong interest in gaining China's support vis-à-vis Myanmar. Thayer reports that

> Bilateral trade between China and Thailand jumped from $4.3 billion in 1999 to $6.2 billion in 2000, making China Thailand's fourth largest trading partner. However, Thailand had a trade deficit of $533 million. Prime Minister Thaksin [in May 2000, M.H.] lobbied his guest [Chinese Premier Zhu Rongji, M.H.] for greater market access (for rice, rubber, shrimp, sugar, tapioca, and fruit), financial assistance, special quotas and tariff cuts, infrastructure investment, and assistance in stopping the illegal trafficking in [...] drugs [from the Golden Triangle, where China has considerable political influence, M.H.].[621]

---

[617] Ibid.: 20.
[618] Kusuma (2001).
[619] Thayer (1999a).
[620] Kusuma (2001): 204.
[621] Thayer (2001b).

In return for expected benefits, Thailand has put potentially divisive issues on the backburner. The most prominent example in this regard is that Thailand deferred to Chinese pressure and suppressed Falun Gong activities on Thai territory in early 2001.[622] Thayer describes the new Thai government's position vis-à-vis China in the following way:

> The Thaksin government came to power with a pro-business mandate. The Falun Gong episode served to confirm that his government would downgrade human rights and democracy issues in its foreign policy. Nowhere was this new emphasis more apparent than Thailand's relations with China. Shortly after taking office, Surakiat Sathirathai, the new foreign minister, declared that Thailand would conduct diplomacy the "Asian way" of face saving and non-confrontation. "China is the first country I plan to visit outside ASEAN," he said, "because I consider [it] will convey an important message that we greatly emphasize our ties with China."[623]

Since Thaksin's accession to power, Sino-Thai relations have been very harmonious due to Thailand's accommodating and deferential China policy. Thus, at a bilateral summit in August 2001, Thaksin called for "a strategic partnership not only politically but economically", whereas the Joint Communique of August 2001 denoted China's commitment to promote "large-scale bilateral cooperation projects and expand [...] bilateral trade and two-way investment". China also signaled its readiness to "facilitate the crackdown on drug-related crimes in the region".[624] Remarkably, Thailand has also turned out to be a very outspoken promoter of the envisioned ASEAN-China FTA. In this context, Thaksin has not only called for an early impelementation of the FTA in 2008 (instead of 2010, the official deadline agreed upon by leaders at the 2001 APT summit) during a meeting with ASEAN Secretary-General Rodolfo Severino in January 2001,[625] but also proposed to establish a separate Thailand-China FTA in case implementation of the ASEAN-China FTA should progress too slowly. In this context, Liu Jinsong, director of the political press section of the Chinese embassy in Thailand, reportedly related in May 2002 that "Beijing supported Thai Prime Minister Thaksin Shinawatra's initiative [of] setting up a Thailand-China bilateral FTA if the trade pact between mainland China and

---

[622] Cf. Thayer (2001a); Kusuma (2001): 205.

[623] Cf. Thayer (2001a).

[624] People's Republic of China and Kingdom of Thailand (2001): China-Thailand Joint Communiqué, Beijing, 29 August.

[625] *Chinadaily.com* (20 January 2001): "Thai PM proposes speedily open ASEAN-China free trade area".

Asean countries progressed to slowly."[626] Obviously, improving relations with China has become a beacon to Thailand's foreign policy over the last decades. The Thaksin government has clearly reduced the critical distance the predecessor government used to maintain vis-à-vis the PRC. Thus, with a view to China, Thailand is now continuing its previous course of massively cozying up to the influential East Asian neighbor.

Indonesia Since the resumption of diplomatic relations, China and Indonesia have made rapid progess in forging new bilateral ties, predominantly so in the aftermath of the economic crisis of 1997. As China has developed and articulated both a new economic and a strong political interest in forging closer ties with Indonesia, relations have improved considerably.

Politically, China's grand design of forging closer ties with ASEAN required boosting bilateral relations with Indonesia, ASEAN's by far most populous nation. Economically, Indonesia is also attractive to China both because of its potential to fuel China's growing need for energy resources (oil and gas) and because of its relative geographic proximity to the Chinese mainland.

Both the Wahid administration and the government of Megawati Sukarnoputri have realized China's eagerness to improve the bilateral relationship and have seen the benefits Indonesia might draw from closer relations with the giant neighbor. Thus, China appeared on President Wahid's political horizon as a potential partner and balancer of the West. When Wahid visited Beijing in October 1999, China and Indonesia concluded a

> long-term cooperation framework agreement along the lines of similar Chinese agreements with Malaysia and Thailand [...and] China offered a loan of U.S. $500 million to assist Indonesia in importing rice, agricultural equipment, and heavy machinery. Indonesia agreed to permit the Bank of China to resume operation in Jakarta . [...] Finally, in a speech delivered at Beijing University, President Wahid reiterated the call [...] for Asia – particularly China, India, Indonesia, Japan and Singapore – to strengthen their place in the world in order to avoid "the hegemony of one or two powers."[627]

As Smith shows, Wahid continued to consolidate Sino-Indonesian ties in 2000.

> In a more tangible sense, the biggest change [in post-Suharto Indonesia, M.H.] has been the improved relationship with the People's Republic of China (PRC). Gus Dur's first official visit (following a personal visit to Japan and the United States weeks earlier) was to China – a very

---

[626] Woranuj Maneerungse (2002): "China to protect its farm sector for now: Free trade except for agriculture, finance", *Bangkok* Post, 13 May.

[627] Thayer (1999c).

symbolic gesture of improving relations. In May 2000, Indonesia and China signed a Memorandum of Understanding to facilitate greater co-operation in politics, economics, tourism, and science on the fiftieth anniversary of diplomatic relations, although relations had been suspended between 1965 and 1990.[628]

Likewise, President Megawati Sukarnoputri has put great emphasis on intensifying relations with the PRC. Apart from heaps of symbolic shows of friendship and excellent relations on both sides, Megawati secured substantial deals and benefits during a visit to Beijing in March 2002. This visit marked a major landmark in the bilateral relations and signaled that the era of mutual suspicion and hostility is possibly finally over or has at least been put on the backburner. At the core of the five bilateral agreements signed during the visit was a major bilateral oil deal. Further, "[a]s many as 17 MOUs [Memorandums of Understandings, M.H.] were signed with a total value of US$ 1.14 billion on the business side alone, according to Megawati."[629] Significantly, China also granted $400 million in preferential loans to Indonesia. This contrasted very favorably with Japan's announcements in late 2001 and early 2002 to substantially reduce the extension of new loans to Indonesia. Further, China granted $6 million for technical and economic cooperation.[630] Another energy resources deal is already looming. Thus, Indonesia is competing with Australia and Qatar for a major long-term deal on the delivery of liquefied natural gas (LNG) to China and has good chances of securing the $10 billion project due to the newly intensified and very friendly relations with the PRC.[631] Thus, a CNN report quoted a Chinese Southeast Asia expert as commenting that "if they [Indonesia and China, M.H.] cooperate well, Indonesia may become a main supplier of oil to China in the future."[632] What is more, although clearly "[e]conomic and trade goals were at the top of the agenda, [...] she [Megawati, M.H.] was clearly seeking China's political support at a time when her government faced international criticism on issues ranging from antiterrorism to human rights."[633] China's continued wooing of Indonesia is already bearing

---

[628] Smith (2000): 513.

[629] Indonesian Weekly Netnews (2002): "President Megawati satisfied about results of her visit to China".

[630] For an overview of the outcomes and evaluations of the visit, cf.
Prabandari (2002): "Megawati, The dance and LNG"; BBC News (24 March 2002):"China pledges $400m to Indonesia"; Ruwitch (2002a): "Indonesia's Megawati arrives in China pushing trade"; Ruwitch (2002b): "Megawati seeks to strengthen ties with China"; Castle (2002): "Jakarta gains from rise of China, India";
Weaver (2002): "Loans a 'motivation' for Megawati in China".

[631] Cf. Prabandari (2002).

[632] Weaver (2002).

[633] Breckon (2002)

first fruits. If it continues, it may bring about a real change in the way the Indonesian elites perceive the Sino-Indonesian relationship. Thus, Hadi Soesastro, commenting on Megawati's ground-breaking visit to China in early 2002, demanded that the Indonesian govenrment engage more proactively with China:

> the [Sino-Indonesian, M.H.] relationship looks like a one-sided affair. This is also what a number of observers think about the agreed MOUs [Memorandums of Understanding, M.H.] which illustrate China's willingness to "give more than receive". This may show that we are not pro-active yet and therefore are placed on the receiving side only. China is real. Its development is awesome and at the same time scary. Because of that, China should be given serious attention. The Indonesian-China relationship is also a serious matter which cannot be treated ad hoc-style or in a perfunctory manner. Efforts have to be made[.] [W]ithout those, the relationship will remain empty.[634]

In summary, Indonesia has seen a strong policy turnaround regarding China within little more than a decade, and especially so since the end of the Suharto era. Recognition of China as a potential partner may very well result in closer political and economic cooperation in the future.

The Philippines The Philippines' relationship with China is the most problematic one of all ASEAN-5 countries. Territorial disputes in the South China Sea are still a very dominant issue that has caused the Philippines to side more closely with the United States. However, relations have improved due to China's strategy of accommodation and confidence-building vis-à-vis ASEAN. Despite sometimes intense diplomatic strive over incidences in the South China Sea, both sides managed to develop cooperative ties. Thus, in November 1999, President Estrada and Chinese Premier Zhu Rongji agreed in principle on the need for "a long-term framework document as a guideline for their [the Philippines' and China's, M.H.] bilateral relationship",[635] which was then signed during Estrada's visit to Beijing in May 2000.[636] The joint statement was part of a package of similar statements issued bilaterally by China and other ASEAN states. In late December 1999, both sides also agreed in principle to hold talks on a Code of Conduct for the Spratlys.[637]

Despite continuous bilateral rows and security problems with China, the Philippines has always kept to ASEAN's collective engagement approach vis-à-

---

[634] Soesastro (2002). Hadi Soesastro is Executive Director of the Centre for Strategic and International Studies (Indonesia).
[635] Thayer (1999c).
[636] For details of the joint statement, see Thayer (2000b).
[637] Thayer (1999c).

vis China. Very likely, the Philippines, aware of the lack of solidarity of other ASEAN members in the South China Sea question in the second half of the 1990s, had no other choice than either streamlining its China policy in accordance with the other ASEAN members or else risk being isolated politically.

After the removal of President Estrada from office, incoming president, Gloria Macapagal-Arroyo, has kept to the foreign policy course of the predecessor government and has continued working on a more relaxed bilateral relationship with China.

Economically, it is not clear what impact China will actually have on the Philippines. The Philippines' behavior vis-à-vis China is ambiguous. When President Macapagal-Arroyo was faced with the question whether or not to approve of China's ASEAN-China FTA proposals, she was rather hesitant to welcome the concept. Before the November 2001 summit, the Philippines' government diplomatically said it still had to study the benefits of the proposal to the Philippines. However, once the ASEAN leaders had taken the decision to enter into FTA negotiations with China, the Philippines claimed that it stood to profit greatly from economic cooperation and trade with China. Speaking at the annual "The Future of Asia" conference in Tokyo in May 2002, the Philippine President even envisioned an EU-style East Asian economic community:

> Philippine President Gloria Macapagal-Arroyo called for the creation of an East Asian economic bloc that would include both China and Southeast Asia. [...] Arroyo said China's economic growth will contribute to a complementary relationship in the manufacturing sector in Southeast Asia and become a "magnet" to attract industrial production and services on a long-term basis. She expressed strong expectations for a European Union-style economic community, integrating China and the Association of Southeast Asian Nations (ASEAN) [...].[638]

These remarks strongly resemble President Estrada's vision of an East Asian community, which he had promoted at the Manila APT summit in 1999, and echoed similar remarks by the long-standing former foreign minister, Domingo Siazon. On the whole, such remarks can be classified as empty rhetoric. Meanwhile, Arroyo's former doubts about the benefits and viability of an ASEAN-China FTA[639] has apparently given way to forward-looking optimism. In promoting closer China-ASEAN links, the president can now also rely on a study presented by her own government on the outcomes of the ASEAN-China FTA, which gives a positive outlook on China's economic impact on the region in the long term.

---

[638] *The Nihon Keizai Shimbun* (2002): "Arroyo Calls For Creation of E Asian Economic Bloc", 21 May.

[639] Cf. Breckon (2001c).

4. ASEAN's collective stance vis-à-vis the major powers

Following the analysis of individual ASEAN members' positions on the U.S., Japan and China, this section briefly looks at ASEAN's collective approaches to these major powers.

4.1. ASEAN vis-à-vis China

Within little more than a decade, ASEAN has passed significant stages in its approach to China. Back in 1990, the resumption of diplomatic relations between Indonesia and the PRC had been considered a major breakthrough for ASEAN on the account that it enabled ASEAN to collectively enter into dialogue with China at all. Today, the two sides are comfortably discussing East Asian and Sino-ASEAN economic integration between them. For pragmatic reasons, ASEAN countries, unlike the West, have preferred to engage China actively and constructively rather than emphasize the threat potential of their giant neighbor to the East. Beyond the mid-1990s, ASEAN actively contributed to breaking China's international isolation and promoted its integration into regional and global political and economic structures. Thus, ASEAN members lobbied for China's participation in APEC (to which it acceded in 1991). Subsequently,

> The relationship between ASEAN and the PRC entered a new phase when the former decided to establish a consultative relationship with the latter in 1993. Then, bilateral economic relations have improved over time, even though most ASEAN member states' economies and the PRC's economy are not considered highly complementary. Efforts to promote economic cooperation and boost trade and investment [...] officially began in 1995, when the first meeting of the Joint Committee on Economic and Trade Cooperation was held [...] in Jakarta. This Joint Committee serves as a forum for senior economic officials of ASEAN and the PRC to enhance mutual understanding and exchange ideas. In the meantime, economic interactions between ASEAN and the PRC took off, and the amount of bilateral trade began to increase."[640]

In March 1996, on Singapore's initiative, the first Asia-Europe Meeting (ASEM) saw China participating as part of a group of ten East Asian countries that now form ASEAN Plus Three (APT) group. In July that same year, China was accorded full ASEAN dialogue partner status at the 29th ASEAN Ministerial Meeting. As dialogue partner, China has participated in the annual ASEAN+1 (ASEAN and China) and ASEAN+10 (ASEAN and all dialogue

---

[640] Huang (2002): 1.

partners) Post-Ministerial Conferences (PMCs) as well as in ASEAN Regional Forum (ARF) meetings.[641]

Since 1997, Sino-ASEAN relations have undergone a major paradigm shift when ASEAN Plus Three (ASEAN and China, Japan, South Korea) held their first ever separate East Asian summit. Successive years have seen a surge of ASEAN's relations with China in the context of APT cooperation. In 1999, the APT joint statement was issued; in 2000, China proposed to forge an ASEAN-China FTA; since 2001, China has set up various currency exchange arrangements with Malaysia, Thailand and the Philipines as part of the APT currency exchange network. Sino-ASEAN relations experienced a new high in November 2001 when ASEAN leaders and the Chinese government agreed to start negotiations on the ASEAN-China FTA, which they said was to be concluded by 2010. Negotiations on the envisioned FTA began in 2002.

As China's economic potential looms, ASEAN members are continuing to expand bilateral dialogue and cooperation with the PRC, both collectively and individually. What is more, since the end of the Cold War, ASEAN's policy has been to catalyze dialogue between the major economic and political powers and China by means of promoting the PRC's participation in fora such as APEC, ASEM, ARF and ASEAN Plus Three.[642]

4.2. ASEAN vis-à-vis Japan

Japan is ASEAN's most important source of investments and ODA. Because of Japan's economic relevance to Southeast Asia and its role as a close ally of the U.S., ASEAN's collective political ties to Japan have been generally good. As a dialogue partner, Japan has contributed to various ASEAN projects and initiatives in the context of the ASEAN+1 (ASEAN and Japan) and ASEAN Plus Three process. ASEAN has been encouraging Japan to play a greater role in Southeast and East Asia, both in the economic and the political area. Economically, ASEAN hopes that Japan is able to restructure its own economy and open up its markets to Southeast Asia, especially in the agricultural sector.

Japan's economic stability and strength is seen as a guarantee for regional economic stability. In political terms, Western-leaning Japan is seen as a counterweight to emerging China. Lam Peng Er writes in this context that

> Southeast Asian states no longer have an allergic reaction to Tokyo' playing a larger political and security role in the region – insofar as it remains allied to the U.S. [...] In the next decade or two, the economic

---

[641] ASEAN Secretariat (undated d): "ASEAN-China Dialogue".
[642] Cp. also Webber (2001): 363, who states that "In the past, ASEAN itself has played a key role as a 'catalyser' of dialogue in the region, including the US [...]."

rise of China is unlikely to displace Japan in the region. [...] the Southeast Asian states would welcome Japan as a counterweight to China, especially when the latter is making rapid progress and emerging as a great power. [...] The best scenario for Southeast Asia is not "China rising, Japan declining." Ideally, it is "China rising, Japan recovering."[643]

Since 2001, ASEAN has made rapid progress collectively in forging even closer ties with Japan, apparently even closer than favored by Japan. By agreeing to establish a bilateral Sino-ASEAN FTA by 2010, ASEAN played the China card at the ASEAN Plus Three summit in November 2001 in order to make Japan more receptive to ASEAN's proposals for a bilateral ASEAN-Japan FTA. Since then, Japan has made a remarkable shift in its foreign economic policy towards ASEAN. The Koizumi administration is now willing to discuss upgrading the hitherto rather vague and insubstantial commitment to an Economic Partnership Agreement (EPA) with ASEAN to a full-fledged FTA. As the Chairman of the Japan External Trade Organization (JETRO) pointed out in a lecture at the Institute of International Economics in Washington in March 2002, there is a direct link between ASEAN's decision to establish the ASEAN-China FTA and Japan's turnaround:

As you know, on November 4, 2001, Chinese and ASEAN leaders agreed to start negotiating an FTA between them [...]. [...] [Nevertheless, M.H.] ASEAN might prefer Japan to China as an FTA partner because ASEAN products complement Japanese products, whereas they compete with Chinese products. However, [ASEAN countries may think that] Japan will not be able to conclude an FTA with ASEAN eventually because of its concern over ASEAN agricultural products [...]. Therefore, [they think] it is inevitable for ASEAN to sign an FTA with China [...]. But now, Japan has also started to study an FTA with ASEAN. Last September in Hanoi, METI Hiranuma agreed with his counterparts to start a joint governmental study on an Economic Partnership with Agreement between Japan and ASEAN. Of course, the EPA would include an FTA. Prime Minister Koizumi proposed his idea of a comprehensive economic partnership with ASEAN when he visited the ASEAN region and met with its leaders in January this year. His concept is to include not only trade and investment, but also science and technology, education, and tourism. [Therefore, for the next several years at least, Japan and China might be

---

[643] Lam (2002).

competing with each other trying to complete [the] EPA or FTA with ASEAN [...].[644]

The case of ASEAN's recent approach to Japan is a rare, but at the same time striking example of strategic foreign and economic policy coordination in ASEAN. Thus, ASEAN, as a collective, agreed to forge a China-ASEAN FTA while its objective, at least partially, was to play the China card so as to make Japan comply with all major ASEAN countries' requirement of improved access to the Japanese market. Thus, ASEAN-5 do not only display a high degree of interest convergence with respect to Japan, but have apparently also forged employed a strategic alliance in order to implement their objectives.

4.3. ASEAN vis-à-vis the United States

Throughout the 1990s, ASEAN members have increasingly developed common patterns of behavior vis-à-vis the U.S. which distinguished them as a group. First, there is ASEAN's position on China. Practically all members have adopted a constructive engagement policy and have objected to Western-style demonization and antagonisms concerning the PRC. ASEAN has also collectively resisted and defied U.S. and European pressure to suspend Myanmar's admission to the Association. Significantly, ASEAN members also displayed some coherence in dealing with the U.S. in 2001 and 2002, both in security and economic terms. Thus, ASEAN collectively condemned the terrorist attacks on the U.S.; when one of its members, Indonesia, was not forthcoming in fighting terrorist activities on its own territory, other ASEAN members, notably Singapore, but also Malaysia, exerted considerable pressure on the administration of Megawati, which was hesitant to take resolute action due to explosive domestic tensions. Another example is ASEAN-U.S. foreign economic relations. Thus, in addition to individual ASEAN members' pursuit of bilateral free trade agreements with the U.S., ASEAN has started collective talks on what U.S. trade representative and ASEAN economic ministers termed "an ambitious work programme designed to expand further the close trade and investment relationship between ASEAN and the United States" in early April 2002.[645] This new initiative could mark the beginning of negotiations on a U.S.-ASEAN FTA. Whereas at a meeting with ASEAN Economic Ministers on 04 April 2002, Zoellick "discussed an overall ASEAN-US free trade agreement",[646]

---

[644] Hatakeyama (2002).

[645] *Economic Intelligence Review* (April 2002):"America Leading The Way For ASEAN Free Trade".

[646] Bridges Weekly Trade News Digest (09 April 2002): "News from the Regions: ASEAN-US".

but dismissed the idea "as far too premature"[647], position papers circulated earlier by the semi-official U.S.-ASEAN Business Council and the American Chamber of Commerce in Singapore (AmCham) had called for a full-blown U.S.-ASEAN FTA modeled on the U.S.-Singapore FTA (USSFTA).[648] As long as all ASEAN-5 governments are continuing to edge closer towards the U.S. in the pursuit of improved market conditions and regional security, it is to be expected that they will increasingly seek to utilize the collective ASEAN channels to approach the U.S.

5. Conclusion

ASEAN-5 are currently displaying a high degree of motivational convergence with regard to the three major external powers, China, Japan and the U.S., both individually and collectively. Since the end of the Cold War, ASEAN-5 have not seen such a high degree of similar interests and motivations in dealing with the three powers. This convergence of interests has also had a clear impact on ASEAN's collective stance on these powers. Interestingly, all ASEAN-5 states are seeking to improve relations with both China, Japan and the U.S. at the same time, a motivational situation that is also reflected by ASEAN's collective approach to them.

With a view to the U.S., ASEAN's relations with the U.S. have never been severely at risk after the end of the Cold War. However, some ASEAN members had temporarily adopted very critical views of the U.S. in the 1990s, whereas others had edged even closer to the hegemon. Thus, the Philippines, Malaysia and Indonesia faced severe tensions with the U.S. over different issues at different stages. As for the Philippines, it was the aftermath of Subic Bay that continued to disturb the bilateral relationship; Malaysia's rejection of Western hegemonism had been a long-standing point of a certain bilateral hostility which had even intensified in the aftermath of the economic crisis; Indonesia's relations with the U.S. had been disturbed by America's insistence on economic reforms in (and perceived arrogance vis-à-vis) Indonesia in the aftermath of the crisis and America's position on East Timor. On the other hand, Singapore and Thailand had been rather accommodating to U.S. positions in the 1990s and into the new millennium. Individual ASEAN members' bilateral differences with America had also cooled down ASEAN's collective relations with the U.S. Between 1999 and 2002, economic and political factors calmed the waves of contention and, again at different stages, caused the governments of both the

---

[647] BBC News (05 April 2002): "US-Asian free trade zone no nearer".

[648] Cf. Kamarul (2002): "American Group proposes US-Asean free trade pact"; American Chamber of Commerce, Singapore (2002): "U.S.-Singapore Free Trade Agreement", 27 February.

Philippines, Malaysia and Indonesia to seek improved relations with the U.S., whereas Singapore edged even closer the Western *de facto* ally, both in economic and security terms. Since 1999, the Philippines has increasingly stepped up bilateral relations with the U.S. in order to gain American protection in the South China Sea and support in fighting the increasingly uncontrollable guerilla insurgencies in the provinces; Malaysia demonstratively made a point of seeking improved political and economic ties with the States in early 2002; Indonesia's relations with the U.S improved significantly with President Megawati Sukarnoputri seeking to boost bilateral economic and security ties. As bilateral economic and political ties with the U.S. improved, so did ASEAN's collective relations. Collectively, ASEAN condemned terrorism, sought closer security cooperation with the States and resumed negotiations with the Western partner on closer economic cooperation cooperation; there are already signs that the two sides might sooner or later start negotiating a bilateral U.S.-ASEAN FTA as part of the ongoing project of Asia-Pacific integration.

In the early 2000s, ASEAN also took the initiative to reinvigorate its traditionally good relations with recently relatively phlegmatic Japan. Throughout the 1990s, all ASEAN-5 states had been on good terms with Japan, and Japan emerged as the most proactive supporter of Southeast Asia during the economic crisis in 1997/8. Following Singapore's example, ASEAN has called for a Japan-ASEAN FTA. ASEAN's coordinated move in late 2001 to enter negotiations on a China-ASEAN FTA shocked Japan out of its complacency and reluctance to enter FTA negotiations with ASEAN. Apparently, ASEAN had intended this move to function as a wake-up call to Japan, and thus represents a remarkable act of foreign policy coordination.

With a view to China, both individual ASEAN countries and ASEAN as a whole has made rapid progress in forging bilateral relations. Whereas countries such as Thailand, Malaysia and Singapore have made headway in boosting their respective bilateral relations with the PRC, Indonesia only reluctantly joined ASEAN's mainstream engagement policy; the Philippines' relations with China continue to be hampered by the latter's aggressive forward orientation in the South China Sea question over most of the past decade. However, around the turn of the millennium, Indonesia has made quite considerably headway in its relations with China – which relies on friendly relations with Indonesia as part of its overall sunshine policy vis-à-vis ASEAN –, especially as the two countries may form a symbiotic relationship in the future, as China's market looms large as a likely destination for Indonesia's natural energy resources. The Philippines, in lack of an alternative, are also increasingly seeking to engage China by means of an economically and politically constructive relationship and this way arrive at more security and stability in the South China Sea. As all

ASEAN-5 states have moved closer towards China, both politically and economically, so has ASEAN as a collective. The rapid development of contacts and cooperation in the context of the ARF, ASEAN+1 (ASEAN and China) and ASEAN Plus Three (ASEAN plus China, Japan and Korea) is a clear sign of ASEAN's determination to collectively make a difference in regional and global affairs.

The larger picture that emerges is that, in the early years of the present decade, ASEAN members, both individually and collectively, are trying to improve their bilateral relations with all three powers at the same time. Apparently, they are hoping to profit economically and politically from being open to all sides. ASEAN countries stand to profit most from cooperation with each of the three powers if they are not being pushed to take sides for either of them. Thus, ASEAN-5 countries all have an interest in balancing and neutralizing the tensions and conflicts between the powers and will seek to reconcile them with each other as far as they are in a position to do so. On the other hand, there is some good reason to believe that the ASEAN countries, individually and collectively, will increasingly also seek to profit from all three power's interest in forging or maintaining stronger ties with Southeast Asian countries. There is some evidence that ASEAN has already started to discover ways of playing off China and Japan against each other.

To sum up, ASEAN as a group has shown that, as long as a majority of its members pursue complementary interests regarding third parties, it can develop remarkable synergies. ASEAN has also shown that it occasionally even serves as a body that socializes and partly also guides the foreign policy orientation of its members. Thus, in the case of ASEAN's constructive engagement policy vis-à-vis China, Indonesia was reluctant to embrace this stance at first, but then increasingly adopted a cooperative stance towards China. With regard to trade liberalization, the examples of Singapore's and Thailand's efforts to forge FTAs with the three powers, has apparently caused more reluctant ASEAN members, namely Malaysia, the Philippines and Indonesia, to follow suit. Thus, ASEAN apparently has a formative role in guiding its members' behavior and views of the world.

On the other hand, there is no guarantee of stability or sustainability in ASEAN's collective policies, as foreign policy making is not based on joint principles, but mostly *ad hoc*. At present, ASEAN members' interests vis-à-vis the three powers frequently converge, a development that makes ASEAN more decisive and able to act in concert. However, should the ASEAN members' respective motivations in dealing with the three powers change and develop into different directions, concerted approaches might give way to independent bilateral policies. In this sense, ASEAN offers no promise of steady and predictable foreign policy-making, as its members are guided more by national preferences and are not able to collectively build on the present coherence and continue from there to devise collective foreign policy coherence in the longer term.

Chapter 6:

ASEAN PLUS THREE:

WHAT THEY SAY, WHAT THEY MEAN, WHAT WE CAN EXPECT FROM THEM

ASEAN PLUS THREE: WHAT THEY SAY, WHAT THEY MEAN, WHAT WE CAN EXPECT FROM THEM

1. Introduction

This chapter sets out to throw some light on the ASEAN Plus Three (APT) process and its potential to catalyze East Asian economic and political integration. Ultimately, it asks if we can expect APT to emerge as the nucleus of an unfolding East Asian identity.

In a first step (entitled "What they say"), the analysis reconstructs the participating governments' represented official views on chances and limitations of the APT process. In a second step (entitled "What they mean"), the study will contrast the official views with an interpretation of APT participants' most likely actual motives and objectives to cooperate in the context of APT. In a third step, APT's main achievements and progress to date will be critically assessed. Against this backdrop, the fourth part seeks to come to conclusions about APT's performance with respect to the four indicators of identity as identified at the outset of this thesis (collective norms, pooling of sovereignty, solidarity and ingroup/ outgroup perceptions, including perceptions of third parties.

In conclusion, the study addresses the question of the relevance of ASEAN Plus Three as a political and economic entity in East Asia and what prospects and opportunities the APT process has in store for the evolution of East Asian regionalism.

2. What they say: Official objectives and agendas of the APT participants

This section attempts to give an overview of the various APT participants' objectives, agendas and positions concerning the APT process as represented and communicated to the international public by the respective governments and government-related elites.

It gives an outline of the views apparently shared communally by the major ASEAN member states (ASEAN-5) and proceeds by portraying each of the ASEAN-5 states in the light of their respective individual approaches to APT. Subsequently, it focuses on the "Plus Three" countries' represented views and positons on APT.

2.1. ASEAN members

Commonalities All ASEAN governments promote the view that ASEAN has a central role in providing a platform for integrated dialogue in East Asia across three dividing lines, namely the Southeast Asia - Northeast Asia divide, the tripartite intra-Northeast Asia divide (China - Japan - Korea), and finally the multiple divide between economic centers and peripheries across the region. The most important economic objectives promoted collectively by ASEAN members are to link up to economic centers and markets in Japan and China and to draw on Japanese funds for financial assistance and development aid. "Engaging" China, i.e. pacifying the dragon by enhancing political dialogue and economic cooperation, represents the main security objective.

Malaysia Since the early 1990s, Malaysia has been a fervent promoter of East Asian regionalism and the formation of an East Asian Economic Group or East Asian Economic Caucus (EAEG/ EAEC), and sees the EAEC embodied in the APT process that emerged in 1999.

The Mahathir government has always portrayed the EAEC as a forum with both an internal and an external dimension. Internally, the countries of the region were to be tied into a *Pax Aseana* and engage in enhanced dialogue and cooperation so as to respond to the demands of increasing interdependence. Externally, the group was supposed to develop a more unified stance on global political and economic issues. From the start, Mahathir opposed any Western influence in the EAEC. Thus, Australia and New Zealand had no place in his geographical and cultural notion of "East Asia", let alone the U.S. Likewise, the U.S. should have no role to play in the EAEC.[649]

In line with his traditional 'Look East' policy, Mahathir urged Japan to take on a leadership role in the regional forum. China was to be engaged in dialogue on regional cooperation rather than alienated and treated as a potential enemy.

When first introduced in 1991/92, Mahathir envisioned the EAEG/EAEC as an integrated economic bloc balancing Western predominance. This had drawn strong criticism from other ASEAN member such as Indonesia and Singapore. Subsequently, Malaysia had toned down its rhetoric. Between 1993 and 1996 Malaysia had promoted the EAEC as a loose consultative forum within APEC

---

[649] During an interview I did with Stephen Leong, senior adviser to the Malaysian government, in January 2001, Leong illustrated Malaysia's relations with the world using a model of concentric circles. It had Malaysia at the core, then, in expanding order from core to periphery, came the circle of bilateral relations, then ASEAN. The EAEC (together with the FPDA and the Indian Ocean Rim-Association For Regional Cooperation, IOR-ARC) was located on the third circle, whereas APEC (together with ARF, the Commonwealth and the Organisation of Islamic Conferences, OIC) was located on the fourth. The fifth level represented global multilateral institutions such as the WTO and the UN.

rather than an economic bloc, a free trade area or an economic community, respectively.[650] Malaysia's genuine (though usually not very specific) commitment to East Asian regionalism also informs its position on APT.

In the years following the Asian economic crisis of 1997, the government stepped up its rhetoric and called for "formalized" East Asian regionalism.[651] Since the APT process was put into place, Malaysia has been walking the rhetorical tightrope of seeking to balance its desire for a strong and more unified East Asia with its reluctance to build far-reaching regional regimes.

Thus, the Mahathir administration even kicked off public deliberation about the viability of East Asian monetary union and a common currency, promoted the idea of an Asian Monetary Fund (AMF) as a regional answer to the IMF's failed policies and also welcomed the APT currency swap arrangements. On the other hand, Malaysia invokes the so-called "Asian way" to evade regime-building and making uncomfortable commitments all too soon, for example in the area of regional trade liberalization. As Noordin Sopiee emphasized at "The Future of Asia" conference in 2001:

> [...] we must be determined and patient, non-Cartesian, with the stress not on producing paper but progress, not on building institutions but results, slowly evolving, slowly and quietly accomplishing, according to our "Asian way" (which so many say does not exist).[652]

With regard to China's proposal to establish an ASEAN-China Free Trade Area, Malaysia's government has been very reluctant to comment publicly. But as trade minister Rafidah Aziz indicated in March 2001, Malaysia's approach to economic integration within APT does not envision the formation of a free trade area:

> Rafidah stresses that Malaysia's concept of economic integration does not necessarily mean free trade areas (FTAs). Malaysia is not a proponent of FTAs. Instead, it favors a broader approach to economic integration which would generate a wider range of mutual support and benefits. "Trade liberalization does not mean happiness," she says emphatically. "Economic integration has been misinterpreted by some as a free frade area. I would like to dispel that, to deny that it means an FTA agreement."[653]

---

[650] Cp. Noordin Sopiee (1996). Noordin Sopiee's text represents merely a frame by putting lengthy Mahathir quotations in context. Noordin Sopiee is the head of ISIS and a close adviser to PM Mahathir.

[651] Cp. Leong (2000).

[652] Noordin Sopiee (2001).

[653] *Asia Times Online* (8 March 2001): "Momentum for East Asian economic community".

Seen in this light, it is not evident how APT should ever emerge as the "regional economic bloc rivaling the United States and the European Union" envisioned by Hew and Anthony[654]. Nevertheless, at the occasion of Japanese PM Koizumi's Southeast Asia tour in January 2002, PM Mahathir reaffirmed his vision of "ASEAN Plus Three as a necessary balance" to the EU and NAFTA.[655] The idea that ASEAN's APT initiative may be instrumental in bringing about a *Pax Aseana* for East Asia by catalyzing cooperation and reconciliation among the Northeast Asian countries, especially Japan and China, is central to the government's view. This view is also echoed by many think tank representatives in Malaysia.[656] Thus, Stephen Leong points out that

> [a]s co-operation between Germany and France has been a key factor in the EU's successful regional peace and prosperity, Sino-Japanese relations and Japanese-Korean co-operation through the EAEC can greatly contribute to common peace and prosperity in Asia. […] This is possible, for although China, Japan and Korea have problems getting along with each other, all three have the common denominator of having positive relations with ASEAN.[657]

Singapore   The government of Singapore clearly rejects the anti-American undertone of Malaysia's EAEC proposal and therefore is unhappy with the application of the term "EAEC" for the APT process. Indeed, Singapore's government has distanced itself repeatedly from Malaysia's EAEC concept.[658] For example, Singapore does not necessarily see APT as an East Asians-only club. Rather, the political establishment around Prime Minister Goh and Senior Minister Lee have emphasized the importance of transparency vis-à-vis the U.S. and establishing closer links between APT and Australia/New Zealand. Thus, SM Lee suggested to aim at "ASEAN Plus Three, Plus Two" cooperation, referring to the APT countries plus Australia and New Zealand. Rejecting the notion of an exclusive East Asian grouping, he said with a view to APEC that

---

Rafidah's rejection of regional free trade agreements agrees fully with PM Mahathir's view. In more diplomatic terms, he, for example, pointed out in November 2000 that "We think that there is a possibility of free trade and investment in that zone, but it's not going to happen any time soon" (quoted in Richardson 2000b).

[654] Hew and Anthony (2000). Hew and Anthony are two Malaysian think tank analysts from ISIS Malaysia.

[655] PM Mahathir, quoted in: "Japan, Malaysia seek common Asian voice", Yahoo News (10 January 2001): "Japan, Malaysia seek common Asian voice".

[656] Cf. Leong (2000): 80; cp. also: Hew and Anthony (2000).

[657] Leong (2000): 80.

[658] Cf. for example: Singapore, Ministry of Foreign Affairs (2000), 24 November.

It will be useful to have a sub-group within APEC of *East Asians and Australasians*, just like the sub-group on the Eastern side of the Pacific, of the United States, Canada and Mexico.[659] [Emphasis added, M.H.]

Singapore has also been promoting the formation of a free trade area between ASEAN and the Closer Economic Relations (CER) area of Australia and New Zealand, an idea that met with harsh opposition from Malaysia. The city state also insists that neither Australia nor Taiwan should be excluded *a priori* from the forum.[660]

Unlike the Malaysian government, which often portrays the U.S. in antagonistic terms, Senior Minister Lee emphasized the importance of the U.S. as an important partner in balancing China "if we are to have elbow room to ourselves".[661]

Prior to 2001, Singapore's position on APT was marked by cautious skepticism. In late 2000, Goh is quoted as saying that

I see no problem in ASEAN Plus Three evolving, if that's the desire of the leaders, into some kind of East Asia summit. But there are implications. I myself would not recommend a hasty evolution [...] [and concluded:] We need the United States to be in East Asia.[662]

Goh also warned that APT might eclipse ASEAN's relevance and recommended a very careful, gradual evolution towards an ASEAN-China Free Trade Area, as suggested by China.[663] Singapore portrayed the APT as the political consequence of increased political and economic interdependence within the region. However, Singapore depicted APT as a tool to *manage* and to adapt to external change rather than a vehicle to *induce* East Asian regionalism. In this respect, Singapore clearly differs from Malaysia.

Significantly, the government did not embrace the idea of the formation of an Asian Monetary Fund (AMF) as an alternative to the IMF.[664] As Shaun Narine relates, "Singapore Senior Minister Lee Kuan Yew has argued that any Asian fund would need the backing of the IMF simply because the IMF is able and willing to deliver the hard medicine to its "patients".[665]

---

[659] *The Straits Times* (21 November 2000): "SM Proposes APEC Sub-Grouping".

[660] Cf. Tay (2000): 234f., who very much promotes the Singaporean government's view of the new East Asian regionalism in his article.

[661] *The Straits Times* (21 November 2000): "SM Proposes APEC Sub-Grouping".

[662] Thayer (2000c).

[663] Cf. Richardson (2000b); Chua Lee Hong (2000).

[664] Cf. for example Deputy Prime Minister Lee's dismissive comments on the idea of an AMF, as portrayed in *The Straits Times* (08 March 2000).

[665] Narine (2001).

Government-related think tanks also cast doubt on the economic benefits of East Asian trade liberalization. Thus, Eric Teo from the Singapore Institute for International Studies (SIIS) notes:

> It is also unclear if ASEAN, Japan, China and South Korea all see an economic raison d'etre for an eventual 13-nation grouping in the future, even if it is based on open regionalism. [...] it may not be apparent for Japan or China [...] to see more rapid economic overtures to ASEAN, especially in the trade sector. ASEAN may also fear being "swamped" by Northeast Asian products and service providers should they liberalize their trade with the bigger economic powers.[666]

Teo suggests further that, from Singapore's view, essential challenges and obstacles to East Asian regionalism are to be found in

> the internal strains within ASEAN, the economic validity of such a future East Asian identity, some lingering uncertainties in the "triangular rapprochement" [...] in Northeast Asia, the "Taiwan political wild-card", American policy towards Asia [...] and the domestic debates on China's and Japan's roles in the region.[667]

In 2001, Singapore's government apparently displayed less reservations about the proposed ASEAN-China FTA. Returning from the ASEAN Plus Three summit in Brunei in November 2001, Prime Minister Goh strongly welcomed the APT leaders' decision to start negotiating an ASEAN-China Free Trade Area by 2002. "The more interlocked the economies of China and Asean are, the better it is for the long-term relationship between China and Asean." At the same time, he remained skeptical about the formation of an EAFTA, including Japan and Korea, diplomatically considering it as "something for the longer term".[668] Echoing Japanese PM Koizumi's views, PM Goh Chok Tong emphasized once more in January 2002 that he did not believe in the idea of molding East Asia into an economically integrated economic bloc.

> "What we fear most is that the world will be split into three economic blocs – FTAA, EU and East Asia – in the long term", Mr. Goh was quoted as saying. He said that to prevent this happening, both Singapore and Japan should establish FTAs with countries outside East Asia, to link the three blocs. Mr Goh said that Singapore was pursuing FTAs with the US and Australia and considering pacts with the EU and Mexico.[669]

---

[666] Teo (2001): 52.
[667] Ibid.
[668] *The Straits Times* (2001): "ASEAN, China plan FTA", 07 November, p. 1.
[669] Kwan (2002).

Further, Singapore's rhetorical support for the formation of the China-ASEAN FTA has been balanced by the government's frequent calls for closer economic integration in ASEAN so as to counter Chinese competition. Trade and Industry Minister George Yeo, for example, reportedly promoted this view once more during a visit to Indonesia in April 2002:

> [...] Yeo urged ASEAN members to move forward and forge an economic community loosely based on the European model. To compete against larger economies such as China, Singapore has no choice but to integrate its markets and make ASEAN "a common economic space for manufacturing and other sectors."[670]

The Philippines From early on, the Philippines has welcomed, and expressed its commitment to, an evolutionary development of an East Asian community. However, East Asian cooperation is explicitly not to alienate or frustrate the U.S.. In the area of regional security, the Philippines in November 1999 proposed to add a security dimension to APT by promoting an East Asia Security Forum designed to complement ARF efforts, particularly with a view to the South China Sea, but also the Taiwan strait and the Korean peninsula.[671] APT is clearly supposed to help "contain" (former President Ramos) and "tame" (Domingo Siazon) China's hegemonic ambitions. As Siazon (foreign minister under Ramos and Estrada, now ambassador under President Arroyo) pointed out,

> The continuing presence in East Asia of the United States as an Asia-Pacific power is [...] essential [...]. Recent moves by the United States to place more importance on its alliance with Japan are welcome. [...] Two decades of exceptional growth have made Beijing confident in projecting its influence abroad and in asserting its claims to China's "ancient territories" [...] Chinese adventurism would destabilize the whole region, but a cooperative China [...] would have enormous potential for good. [...] It is my hope that when the day of [Korean, M.H.] rapprochement dawns, an East Asian community would have grown sufficiently strong enough to tame any possible rivalry between Chinese, Japanese and Korean nationalism.[672]

Whereas the Philippine government hopes that APT cooperation may contribute to taking the sting out of Northeast Asian rivalries and pacify the region, it leaves no doubt that ultimately it relies on Japan and the West to balance China.

---

[670] Australian Associated Press (2002): "Singapore backs economic integration", 04 April.
[671] Cf. Rowena and Layador (2000): 441f.
[672] Siazon (2001).

As Fidel Ramos has pointed out, "[...] [N]o stable counterweight to China is possible without the American presence. Ultimately, it is the U.S.-Japan alliance that underpins Asia-Pacific security."[673] With regard to China, the Philippines hopes that APT dialogue will contribute to establishing a code of conduct for the South China Sea.

Like Singapore and Malaysia, the Philippines portrays East Asian regionalism as an unavoidable necessity, due to the strong interdependence among the countries of the region. The Philippines also portrays APT as a forum that in the longer term might – and should – develop into an East Asian community, i.e. a common market with a common currency in the longer term.[674] In November 1999, Foreign Minister Siazon told Reuter Television: "I see we will be having an ASEAN common market, then an East Asia free trade area, an East Asia common market and an East Asian currency."[675] Central Bank Governor Buenaventura in September 2000 even suggested to successively introduce an Asian Currency Unit on the way to a common currency, following the European Currency Unit (ECU)/Euro model for monetary union. He envisioned the eventual transfer of national monetary autonomy to an Asian Central Bank.[676] Similarly, Ambassador Siazon in June 2001 employed the model of the EU to describe his vision of East Asian regionalism, but indicated that East Asian integration would proceed along different lines.[677] Whereas governor Buenaventura envisioned a Regional Financing Agreement (RFA) "intended to complement existing international facilities by bridging the gap between short-term financial arrangements and medium-term schemes such as those of the IMF", Siazon frankly spoke of an Asian Monetary Fund (AMF).[678] Like his

---

[673] Special Representative of President Macapagal-Arroyo and former president of the Philippines, Fidel Ramos, pointed this out in a speech entitled "Security and Stability in the Asia-Pacific" at the World Economic Forum's Annual Meeting 2001, Davos, 29 January 2001. In this context, it is noteworthy that, subsequent to the events of 11 September, President Macapagal-Arroyo called for Japan to take a wider security role in East Asia., President Arroyo urged Japan, which she described as "our closest neighbor outside of Asean", to take a wider security role in East Asia. She said: "The Philippines supports wider collective responsibility in security for Japan in the region [...] This is one message I will bring to Japan [...]" (*Oman Daily Observer*, 13 September 2001: "Arroyo may urge Japan to take wider seurity role in Asia".)

[674] This view can be said to have prevailed in the Philippines since President Estrada's speech at the initial APT summit in Manila in 1999, in which he vaguely sketched a picture of economic and security cooperation as well as the evolution of an AMF, a common market and a single currency for East Asia (cf. Estrada 1999).

[675] Richardson (1999c). Richardson does not forget to express doubts about the credibility of such statements: "Mr. Siazon did not say when such developments would occur, but other analysts said it would take many years to bring down economic and political barriers in the region."

[676] Buenaventura (2000).

[677] Siazon (2001).

[678] Cf. ibid. (2001).

predecessor in office, Foreign Secretary Guignona promoted the view that "We hope the ASEAN+3 will eventually lead to wide-ranging areas of cooperation [...] in the economic, financial, socio-cultural and political-security fields."[679]

Thailand   Thailand portrays APT as one – but not the only one – necessary political answer to increased regional economic and political interdependence. Besides ASEAN, ARF and APEC, APT is seen as just another forum to deal with East Asian security and economic problems. Thus, like Singapore and the Philippines, Thailand thinks economic integration and trade liberalization should not stop at narrowly defined East Asian borders. Thailand's continued support for an AFTA-CER free trade area is a case in point. Indeed, the Thaksin government has already called for a wider "Asia Cooperation" including India and other South and West Asian countries.[680]

Nevertheless, Thailand appreciates APT's great potential to integrate Northeast Asia, particularly China, into a web of bilateral and plurilateral economic and political cooperation.

In contrast to its predecessor government, the government of Prime Minister Thaksin Shinawatra has demonstratively moved closer to China on a number of counts and sees APT as a welcome tool to boost relations with the large Eastern neighbor.[681] According to the Thai government, "China is the priority for Asean" with respect to forming free-trade areas.[682] The Thaksin government backed China's proposal of November 2000 to establish a China-ASEAN free trade area. In January 2002, Prime Minister Thaksin urged the early implementation of the proposed FTA.[683] With regard to China, joint development of the Mekong area and access to China's markets are on top of Thailand's agenda.

Thailand also hopes for financial and economic cooperation and free trade agreements with Japan. In this respect, Thailand encouraged Japan to engage in the discussion of an East Asian Free Trade Area.

Prior to the ascendancy of Thaksin Shinawatra as Prime Minister, the government of Chuan Leekpai supported the idea of an East Asian currency union. In July 2000, for example, Deputy Foreign Minister

---

[679] Cf. Department of Foreign Affairs, Philippines (2001).

[680] Surakiart (17 July 2001).

[681] Cp. for example Thayer (2001b); *Asia Times Online* (23 May 2001): "China, Thailand strengthen family bond".

[682] Boontipa Simaskul, Director-General of the Business Economics Department, quoted in: Woranuj Maneerungse (2001).

[683] *People's Daily* (2002): "Thai PM Proposes Speedily Open ASEAN-China Free Trade Area", 21 January. The report indicates the Thai News Agency (TNA), as its source of information.

Supachai Panitchpakdi [...] said he supports an initiative to establish an Asian common currency, similar to the launch of the euro. If Asia had its own common currency, it would be able to increase financial stability within the region and undercut the predominant role of the US dollar as a major medium of financial transactions.[684]

At the APT summit in November 2000, Supachai also promoted the idea of establishing an Asian Monetary Fund as a mid-to long-term objective.[685]

Whereas the Chuan Leekpai government was still focused on security issues as a field for APT cooperation,[686] the Thaksin government seems predominantly interested in the economic opportunities of the forum. Priority areas identified for cooperation with China are cooperation on agriculture, technology, HRD, investment and Mekong Basin development.[687] Due to its focus on economic issues, Thailand is unlikely to press China for political/ security dialogue.[688] Nevertheless, Thailand was pleased to see that, at the APT Foreign Ministers Meeting in 2001, China agreed to go beyond mere economic and cultural cooperation within APT and expand the dialogue to the political area as well.[689]

Indonesia   The Indonesian government has made only a few and very general references to APT. As president, Wahid promoted sometimes obscure ideas of Asian regionalism which apparently no-one in Indonesia nor anywhere else in the region was ready to share.[690] His Foreign Minister, Alwi Shihab, largely declined to deliberate publicly about APT. To the author's knowledge, the

---

[684] Naranart Phunangkanok; Thanong Khantong (2000).

[685] Cf. Yonan and Areddy (2000): "Leaders of ASEAN Plus Three Endorse Currency Swap Plan".

[686] Cf. Surin (2000b).

[687] Kingdom of Thailand, Ministry of Foreign Affairs (2001): "Main Points of Proposals and Suggestions Raised by the Prime Minister of Thailand", informal paper on Thailand's agenda for the 7th ASEAN summit in November 2001.

[688] Since its accession to power, the Thaksin government has steered a remarkably accommodating course vis-à-vis China. For the sake of maintaining good relations and extracting economic concessions for Thailand, Thailand's deferrence to China's interests even went so far as to deny refuge to Falun Gong activists and suppress Falun Gong activities on Thai territory. (cp. Thayer 2001a).

[689] An interview I conducted with officials at the Department of ASEAN Affairs at the Ministry of Foreign Affairs in November 2001, confirmed this view.

[690] Cp. Smith (2000): 512. Cp. also Wahid's (in)famous speech delivered in the larger context of the ASEAN summit in November, in which he – in an apparent rage of irrationality – had severely offended and threatened Singapore, promoted racist pro-Malay and anti-Chinese views and suggested to form a separate so-called West Pacific Forum, which he envisioned to include countries such asPapua New Guinea, East Timor, Australia, Zealand and possibly the Philippines, which he generously invited to join. (Lengthy extracts form the speech appeared under the headline "Why Gus Dur is not happy with Singapore", *Straits Times*, 27 November 2000).

administration of Megawati Sukarnoputri has not yet offered any elaborate views on APT.

Generally, a look at speeches by Indonesian government representatives (at ASEAN level and elsewhere) shows that regional fora such as APEC and ARF are regularly referred to, whereas APT is hardly ever mentioned.

Nevertheless, government-affiliated think tanks and elites (Ali Alatas, Hadi Soesastro and Jusuf Wanandi) have a quite positive view of the APT process.[691] They seem to agree that Indonesia has to be essentially interested in the formation and evolution of the APT.

Thus, they expect APT to develop into an institutional frame to manage inevitable economic and political interdependence among East Asian countries. Although APT is seen as an important tool to achieve both sustainable peace and prosperity, it is to focus mainly on issues such as economic, financial and development cooperation. According to Alatas, APT even should form an East Asian Free Trade Area and establish an Asian Monetary Fund.

East Asian regionalism is to be open and non-exclusive. Thus, in the medium to longer term, Australia and New Zealand, but also Taiwan should be allowed to join. The importance of the U.S. and APEC are frequently emphasized. APT is to complement rather than eclipse APEC relations.

For the time being, in the political area APT is expected to enhance trust and create an atmosphere of cooperative benevolence. Economic cooperation is to present the basis for enhanced security. Further, in the short to medium term APT should concentrate exclusively on economic and financial, not on security and potentially divisive political issues.

With a view to regional peace and stability, reconciliation among Northeast Asian countries, especially Japan and China, is seen as a major goal for APT. In this context, China is portrayed as an emerging regional great power that needs to be contained through positive engagement and balanced integration.

2.2. The 'Plus Three' countries

South Korea   Korea's government welcomes APT as the basis for an increasingly institutionalized regional body for economic, political and security cooperation.[692] To Korea, intra-APT dialogue on security is of high importance, especially with regard to the Korean peninsula. Rhetorically, the government envisions the forum as developing into a more comprehensive community of

---

[691] Alatas (2001); Soesastro (2000); Wanandi (2000); cf. Wanandi's comments at an ASEAN think tank roundtable entitled "'We Must stick Together' - ASEAN's top minds consider how to keep the organization relevant", *Asiaweek*, 26 (2000), 34, 1 September.

[692] Cf. for example Korea.net (2000): "Reference Materials for the ASEAN Plus 3 Summit and State Visits to Singapore".

values and institutions.[693] Korea has also shown great interest in a Japan-Korea FTA, which is frequently portrayed as a first step towards a Northeast Asian FTA with China, which, in turn, could be the foundation of an East Asian FTA including Southeast Asia[694] (and potentially also New Zealand).[695] In the official discourse, East Asian community-building is to be open and transparent to outsiders, especially the U.S.. Japan's and Korea's membership is portrayed as a guarantee for a U.S.-centric world view.[696] Consequently, the objectives of contributing to open regionalism in APEC and cooperating for a new WTO trade liberalization round feature very high on Korea's APT agenda.

On the other hand, Korea is not content with the structure of international financial institutions such as the IMF and the World Bank. Therefore, APT is portrayed as a chance to improve the existing international financial architecture and thus help prevent financial crises by means of coordinating East Asian countries' interests and represent them more cohesively in the international arena. Korea is not promoting the establishment of an Asian Monetary Fund, but has urged reform of the IMF and the World Bank and demanded more participation rights for East Asian countries on the grounds that "emerging countries have been often overlooked."[697] East Asian regional cooperation is only seen as one of many playing fields. A high official of the Ministry of Foreign Affairs and Trade pointed out that

> Korea, which learned from its foreign exchange crisis in 1997 about the serious consequences that can result from globalization and the lack of a sound financial regulatory system, strongly desires reform of the international financial system. Accordingly, Korea actively participates in G-20 meetings and has presented various initiatives to promote regional cooperation in APEC and ASEAN+3, [in] the belief that regional initiatives should be pursued in parallel with global efforts. [...]
> Korea believes that the formula for determining a country's voting rights in the IMF should be adjusted to reflect the growing significanc of

---

[693] Cp. Mitton (1999).

[694] In a keynote speech at the APT summit in November 2001, President Kim Dae-jung proposed "creating an East Asia Free Trade Area to insitutionalize cooperation among the East Asian countries" (arrival statement by President Kim Dae-jung on returning to Korea from the APT summit in Brunei, Korea.net, 06 November 2001).

[695] Cp. Won (2001): 92, 94.

[696] Mitton (1999).

[697] Thus the South Korean Minister of Finance and Economy, Jin Nyum (2000). This view is also expressed by Kong; Wang (eds.) (2000) in their "Introduction". They claim that, in Korea's view, "the IMF needs to be more democratic, transparent, and accountable. Emerging market member countries and their citizens need greater voice in the formulation of IMF policies [...]"(p. 15).

newly emerging countries [...]. [...]cooperation among Asian countries can help prevent a recurrence of financial crises.[698]

Further, the annual separate Northeast Asian summits (breakfast meetings) that have been established within the APT process are portrayed as an important means of establishing trust between the leaders of Korea, Japan and China through informal dialogue and initially focusing exclusively on economic issues. The Korean government describes the ultimate purpose of APT as managing interdependence among the countries of the region and providing peace and stability in the region.

Japan   Japan's public statements on APT are surprisingly neutral in tone. Government speeches and statements focus predominantly on short- to mid-term technical and material aspects of cooperation rather than on a longer-term vision for APT. Japan likes to emphasize its readiness to provide development aid and assistance to Southeast Asia. The fields of cooperation idenitified in the 1999 Joint Statement on East Asia Cooperation represent Japan's guideline to which it keeps without swerving into enthusiastic visions for the future.

Japan is focused on supporting ASEAN's various cooperation schemes and in cooperating in the areas of transnational problems such as piracy, drug-trafficking and HIV as well as IT and HRD, such as Mekong River Basin development, the Initiative for ASEAN Integration (IAI), etc. In this context, Japan likes to emphasize its role as a benefactor of ASEAN countries. Talk of establishing an AMF has disappeared from the official rhetoric.

As FM Makiko Tanaka pointed out in 2001, APT countries needed to engage in finding common ground, but cooperation among participants should be developed gradually. Japan wishes the process to be "'open' in the sense that it should be transparent to non-member countries and coherent and complementary to the global system."[699] Beyond economic issues, APT is expected to engage in political and security dialogue among the Northeast Asian countries. Despite Japan's necessarily prominent role in implementing the currency swap arrangements, neither monetary nor economic integration (such as an EAFTA) played a role in public Japanese statements on APT.

While Japan has failed to develop clear ideas for the future development of APT, there can be no doubt about the importance it attributes to strengthening its ties with ASEAN, partly for economic reasons and partly to balance China's growing influence in Southeast Asia. Significantly, Japan is signaling that it is seeking cooperation with APT countries, but by all means wants to prevent APT from integrating into an economic bloc. Prime Minister Koizumi, on a tour of

---

[698] Cho (2001).

[699] Tanaka (2001): "Statement by Her Excellency Makiko Tanaka, Minister for Foreign Affairs of Japan on the occasion of the ASEAN +3 Meeting", 24 July.

Southeast Asia in January 2002 pointed out APT merely represents a starting point for a wider "East Asian community" including Australia and New Zealand:

> Japan, China, Korea, Australia, New Zealand and the 10 Asean countries should evolve into a new East Asian 'community' of nations that 'acts together and advances together', suggested Japanese Prime Minister Junichiro Koizumi yesterday. [...] In time, the grouping could co-opt other important partners such as India, he added. But he warned that success would not come overnight, adding that the first of many steps would be to start discussions within the 'Asean + 3' framework.[700]

Apparently, Japan is working against an exclusively East Asian forum as envisioned by Malaysia and China.[701]

China   Since the formal inception of the APT process in 1999, China has pursued a policy of building a strong bilateral China-ASEAN axis within the forum. At the APT summit in November 2000, Prime Minister Zhu also expressed China's interest in forging a bilateral China-ASEAN free trade area.[702] Since then, China has vigorously pursued FTA talks with ASEAN.

The Chinese government supports cooperation in the areas laid down in the APT agenda of 1999. Prime Minister Zhu pointed out in November 2000 that

> [...] the Ten Plus Three mechanism may serve as the main channel for regional cooperation, through which to gradually establish a framework for regional financial, trade and investment cooperation, and furthermore to realize still greater regional economic integration in a step by step manner.[703]

With a view to improving Northeast Asian relations in the context of APT, China has also agreed to hold annual trilateral summit meetings with Japan and Korea to discuss cooperation among the three.

In the area of security, China has signaled its readiness at the bilateral and plurilateral level to make concessions which previously had been unthinkable. Thus, apart from promising various bilateral initiatives in economic and

---

[700] Low (2002).

[701] Japan is ever more frequently applying the term "East Asian community" in a not strictly East Asian context. For example, in advance of Koizumi's trip to Australia, Japanese officials, according to an Australian Associated Press news report, related that "Japan is set to propose a major expansion of economic relations with Australia as part of a broader effort to create an East Asian economic community" (Australian Associated Press, 03 April 2002: "Japan to push Howard on trade").

[702] Zhu Rongji's statements as quoted in Thayer (2000c).

[703] Ibid.

financial cooperation, Prime Minister Zhu Rongji in November 2001 reiterated his government's willingness to accede to the ASEAN Treaty of Amity and Cooperation and the Southeast Asian Nuclear Weapon Free Zone treaty (SEANWFZ). What is more, Zhu also affirmed that the PRC was "willing to complete consultations with ASEAN on the norm[s] of behavior [i.e. the previously strongly contentious issue of a Sino-ASEAN Code of Conduct, M.H.] in the South China Sea region as quickly as possible."[704]

With a view to APT cooperation, Zhu pointed out in November 2001 that "the three [Northeast Asian] countries can bring into play their respective advantages while giving support to ASEAN's integration process" and signaled China's readiness to discuss political and security issues in the context of the forum, starting out with non-traditional security issues and transnational crime initially and gradually proceeding to more sensitive issues:

> [...] efforts should be made to gradually carry out dialogue and cooperation in the political and security fields. [...] Our dialogue and cooperation in the political and security fields could begin by focusing on these areas first, with their contents gradually enriched as [we] go on.[705]

Clearly, China's moves with regard to ASEAN and APT show that the PRC is presently anxious to please ASEAN leaders and eager to enhance trust and confidence-building with the states of Southeast Asia.

3. What they mean: A sober assessment of APT participants' motivation to cooperate

This section asks for the actual motives and objectives guiding the various countries in the APT process.

3.1. ASEAN

ASEAN has been left weakened by increasing division among ASEAN members and failing to actually deepen ASEAN economic and political integration in the aftermath of the economic crisis of 1997. Thus, ASEAN has been under strong internal and external pressure to prove its relevance as a regional actor. Against this backdrop, the APT initiative provides a welcome opportunity for ASEAN to brush up its international reputation, as initial

---

[704] Zhu Rongji (2001b).
[705] Zhu Rongji (2001a).

success and shows of goodwill in the APT context are much easier to achieve than substantial progress in the many – and hitherto rather disappointing – projects of ASEAN integration.

In more positive terms, the APT process clearly represents a chance for ASEAN countries to confront the trend of increasing bilateralization and diversification of its members' relations with the two poles of East Asia – China and Japan – and thus coordinate and represent Southeast Asian interests vis-à-vis these two poles more effectively.[706]

Political considerations

In the area of non-traditional security issues, Southeast Asian governments can expect APT to contribute to regional stability by institutionalizing both multilateral and bilateral dialogue and cooperation on development assistance, regional economic stability and transnational issues (e.g. maritime piracy and cross-border drug trafficking). Southeast Asia also stands to benefit from dialogue at APT level, as it might contribute to more relaxed relations between the governments of Northeast Asia and help them overcome deep-rooted cultural, historical and political barriers. APT also follows ASEAN's constructive integration approach towards China,[707] since it is focused on engendering regional stability and security by engaging China in a web of mutually beneficial and inconspicuous relations with its Southeast Asian and Northeast Asian neighbors. In this context, Prime Minister Goh Chok Tong of Singapore indicated that the ASEAN-China FTA proposal, apart from economic considerations, also had a strong political aspect to it:

> Both sides [ASEAN and China, M.H.] also recognize the long-term geopolitical benefits of locking fiendly relations between China and

---

[706] Indeed, there seems to be a clear trend towards increasing bilateralization of ASEAN members' relations with China and Japan. Singapore has been exposed to criticism from other ASEAN members for its decision to pursue a bilateral free trade agreement with Japan. Malaysia, since the early 1990s, has sought to improve relations with China, occasionally even at a cost to ASEAN's cohesiveness (for instance with regard to the South China Sea issue). Likewise, the Thaksin government in Thailand has displayed a tendency to accommodate China's political agenda (such as making concessions in the area of human rights by suppressing Falung Gong activities in Thailand) for the sake of improved bilateral economic ties and Chinese support in resolving contentious transnational issues with Myanmar. Further, the Mekong Basin states such as ASEAN newcomers Myanmar and Laos are increasingly exposed to China's growing economic and political influence.

[707] ASEAN has previously been instrumental in facilitating China's participation and cooperation in APEC, ASEM, the ARF, ASEAN Plus One meetings, and now APT.

Asean [...] The more interlocked the economies of China and Asean are, the better it is for the long-term relationship [...].708

ASEAN can also expect APT to reverberate positively on the the ASEAN Plus One dialogues (where ASEAN meets separately with China, Japan and South Korea), as both China and Japan are interested in enhancing their respective bilateral cooperation profiles with ASEAN.

ASEAN member states' preference for informal relations and the absence of a collective APT agenda suggests that ASEAN will not seek to formalize or institutionalize the APT process further. Rather than intending APT to evolve into a full-blown organization with clear objectives, ASEAN will be comfortable with APT evolving as a cluster of regional synergies and various forms of cooperation around which ideally an ever-tighter web of informal diplomatic contacts and exchange can be nurtured and cemented.

Economic considerations

Considering the difficulties ASEAN members are facing in meeting their own trade liberalization schedules within AFTA, it is hard to imagine that ASEAN could manage to collectively conclude any significant free trade agreements with China and/ or Japan in the foreseeable future (even though China and ASEAN, at the APT summit in November 2001, announced just that, namely to look into establishing an ASEAN-China Free Trade Area within ten years' time). Indeed, as Lim Say Boon observes, talk about the ASEAN-China FTA may even distract ASEAN from its own integration project:

> [...] at a time when Asean is in urgent need of economic reform, the [China-ASEAN FTA] plan could end up a distraction from the more urgent task at hand – to speed up the removal of residual trade and considerable investment restrictions within Asean itself.709

According to Lim, the economic rationale of the proposed China-ASEAN FTA to many ASEAN economies is not evident:

> [...] given the fierce competitiveness of the China juggernaut, there must be serious concerns that such an arrangement may result in serious dislocation of Asean industries. [...] serious damage to significant industries seems almost inevitable [...]. Indeed, the gradual implementation of the Asean-China free trade area – proposed over 10 years – may do Asean more harm than good.710

---

708 Goh Chok Tong, as quoted in *The Straits Times* (07 November 2001): "Asean, China Plan FTA".
709 Lim Say Boon (2001).
710 Cf. Ibid.

Interestingly, a number of ASEAN countries do not want the ASEAN-China FTA at all. The dividing line between proponents and reluctant followers of the envisioned FTA seems to be similar to the one concerning the question of intra-ASEAN trade liberalization in AFTA. As Breckon notes,

> It is not clear [...] that the ASEAN countries will actually gain from an FTA with China. China's labor costs are lower than those in almost all the Southeast Asian economies, and it will probably be reluctant to export capital that it needs at home to create jobs for its own expanding workforce. Prior to the November [APT] summit, Malaysia, Indonesia, and Vietnam all expressed reservations about an FTA with China, fearing that Chinese products would swamp their own industries. Philippine President Gloria Macapagal-Arroyo noted that the ASEAN-China FTA idea would have to be studied carefully. Singapore was the most aggressive in pushing for agreement and was supported by Thailand.[711]

The picture seems familiar from ASEAN integration efforts: whereas Malaysia is at the core of those seeking to apply the brakes, Thailand and Singapore are making an effort to accelerate the FTA process.[712] Interestingly enough, Malaysia's legendary enthusiasm for East Asian integration cooled considerably at the concrete prospect of closer economic integration with China.

The fact that ASEAN leaders (most of them only very reluctantly) nevertheless endorsed the idea of the proposed ASEAN-China FTA at the 2001 APT summit indicates that in many ways the rhetorical endorsement of the proposal is much more a public relations initiative than an economic policy. Thus, ASEAN can demonstrate that it is still a relevant political actor in the region. Politically, continued discussion of the ASEAN-China FTA project may be intended to play off China against Japan in order to get the reluctant partner to engage in free trade talks with ASEAN countries, either bilaterally or collectively. Thus, from ASEAN's perspective, taking into account Japan's outright denial to discuss the issue of free trade agreements with ASEAN at the APT summit in 2001, Japan may have been the main addressee of the China-ASEAN FTA initiative. Japan's position reveals that presently there is no scope for the idea of a more comprehensive and integrated East Asian Free Trade Area. As the next section shows, Japan is interested in integrating APT into Asia-Pacific structures including the U.S. Not surprisingly, initial high-flying visions of an integrated East Asian economic community or a common currency for East Asia (as

---

[711] Breckon (2001c).

[712] Interestingly, Malaysia's reluctance contrasts with its otherwise enthusiastic promotion of East Asian regionalism and its notorious political strive for the formation of an East Asian Economic Grouping or Caucus (EAEG/ EAEC). It indicates that Malaysia's hesitant position on the envisisoned ASEAN-China FTA is based exclusively on economic considerations.

promoted by President Estrada at the APT summit in 1999 in Manila) have lost currency in ASEAN.[713]

Development assistance

ASEAN may also benefit from APT in the area of Japanese financial development assistance. By agreeing to contribute the lion's share to ASEAN initiatives aimed at reducing the economic gap between old and new ASEAN members (such as the Initiative for ASEAN Integration, IAI), Japan is fast becoming ASEAN's sole paymaster.[714] In so far, APT represents a welcome additional political framework to support the flow of Japanese development aid to ASEAN.[715] China's financial development assistance, which can be measured in millions rather than billions of U.S. dollars, has been symbolical rather than substantial.

3.2. Japan

Looking at Japan's interest and potential role in the APT process, the most important question to consider is in how far APT advances, i.e. provides additional value to, Japan's relations with Southeast and Northeast Asian countries. Essentially, this means asking in which respect APT contributes to Japan's political/security and economic interests in the region.

Political considerations

With a view to the political benefits of APT to Japan, one can establish the following motives:

---

[713] Cp. for example Webber (2001): 341.
As a collection of studies carried out by scholars from APT countries shows, there is absolutely no case for a common currency or deeper monetary integration in East Asia (cf. Khairul Bashar and W. Möllers, eds. 2000). Thus, visionary enthusiasm about the opportunities of regional economic integration has to be seen in the light of political signaling rather than economic reasoning.

[714] ASEAN countries themselves are both unable and unwilling to contribute substantial financial support to the IAI. Even Singapore, the initiator of the IAI and richest nation in the ASEAN club, has limited its contributions to providing and maintaining training facilities for scholars and government servants from the so-called CLMV countries (Cambodia, Laos, Myanmar, Vietnam). Singapore has made it clear that it is not willing to engage in any kind of financial assistance. Similarly, Thailand and Malaysia are focusing exclusively on providing education and training facilities.

[715] Practically, the existence of the APT has only a marginal impact on Japan's assistance to ASEAN, since ASEAN and Japan are maintaining close ties in the context of the ASEAN Plus One process.
(In the ASEAN Plus One process ASEAN meets separately with China, Japan and South Korea.)

First, APT provides a novelty in that it has established separate summit meetings of the leaders of Northeast Asia, i.e. China, Japan and South Korea. It is unlikely that these three countries would have been established regular annual summit meetings without the existence of APT. Although the summits (so far held in the manner of informal meetings among the Northeast Asian leaders) have been rather unfocused so far, this direct link between Northeast Asian leaders may eventually evolve as a valuable diplomatic instrument for defusing tensions and improve mutual understanding. Thus, Japan has promoted the idea of institutionalizing the Northeast Asian summit:

> Japan appears especially anxious to strengthen ties with its two [North] East Asian neighbours – as reflected by the fact that Tokyo is the reported initiator of the idea of a new three-way forum, as well as by Japanese Prime Minister Junichiro Koizumi's recent official visits to Beijing and Seoul.[716]

This indicates that the Japanese government has serious hopes for the platform to evolve as a useful tool for stabilizing East Asian relations.

Second, Japan needs to participate proactively in the APT process if it wants to play a political role commensurate with its present status as the dominant economic power in Southeast Asia. ASEAN members expect Japan to support the APT process, both with a view to integrating China into global and regional structures and taking over a role as sponsor of regional initiatives of financial cooperation (such as the swap arrangements) and development assistance (such as Japan's contributions to the IAI). Japan must be interested in meeting ASEAN countries' expectations, as it needs to improve relations with, and secure access to, Southeast Asia so as to provide a sound political environment for expanding Japanese business operations and production networks in the region.

The third benefit of the APT to Japan is the chance to contribute substantially to the stability of East Asian, and particularly the Southeast Asian, economies. Thus, Japan has sought to improve the financial stability of Southeast Asian countries after the crisis of 1997. Its proposal to establish an Asian Monetary Fund (AMF) and, after that project had been abandoned, the implementation of the so-called Miyazawa Plan, represented the world-wide most substantial initiatives to back (South)East Asian currencies.[717]

---

[716] *The Business Times* (05 November 2001): "New Trilateral forum among East Asian nations in the works".

[717] While Japan had indicated its readiness to grant US$ 100 billion to an AMF, the Obuchi government earmarked US$ 30 billion as stand-by credits for Malaysia, Indonesia, the Philippines, Thailand and Korea under the Miyazawa initiative. Remarkably, the Miyazawa Plan was accompanied by a public relations offensive against the policies and operative principles of the IMF. In the course of this campaign, the Japanese government even

It is widely recognized that the financial crisis and Japan's reaction to it (especially the AMF proposal and the Miyazawa initiative) have catalyzed the formation of the APT process. Japan's genuine concern for financial stability in Southeast Asia and Korea has not subsided. Indeed, Japan contributed much to the forum's prestige when it helped draw up the Chiang Mai initiative and subsequently concluded bilateral currency swap agreements with a number of East Asian countries.

Economic considerations

Apparently, Japan does not envision APT as becoming the seedbed for an East Asian free trade area or economic bloc. The Koizumi government's reluctance to discuss multilateral free trade agreements at the 2001 APT summit in Brunei clearly confirmed this position. The Koizumi government is not interested in discussing the issue of an ASEAN-Japan FTA or even an EAFTA with its APT partners. Instead, it prefers selective bilateral approaches to trade liberalization (such as the FTA negotiations with Singapore). On the whole, it appears that in the economic area, Japan's main interest is to ensure the economic security of Southeast Asia as a base for Japanese production and business networks, not regional bloc-building in East Asia.

Limits to Japan's engagement in East Asia

As has been frequently noticed, the strong cultural and political differences between Northeast Asian countries, as well as Japan's political and economic ties to the U.S., will preclude Japan from adopting a more distinctive East Asian perspective in the foreseeable future.

Although there is a recognizable trend toward greater economic and political awareness of East Asia among Japanese elites, this trend does not appear to greatly affect Japan's political identity and foreign policy orientation. Whereas observers of Japan generally acknowledge increased activism in the East Asian region, they also agree that there are no signs that Japan is presently undergoing a major paradigm shift towards identifying itself as a predominantly East Asian country. Japan's greater regional engagement is seen as a complement, rather than an alternative, to Japan's traditionally pro-Western orientation.

As Maswood states,

> [...] even as Japan interacts more extensively with East Asian countries, Japanese foreign policy objectives are not served by policies that instigate institutionalized regionalism [since] [t]his may jeopardize

---

promoted the establishment of an Asian Monetary Fund (AMF) whose eligibility criteria were to be defined by East Asian governments and modeled on the particular needs of East Asian economies. At last, however, Japan distanced itself from the AMF idea so as not to drive a wedge between itself and the U.S.

Japan's relations with with the United States and it is unlikely that Japan will abandon its western orientation for regionalism. Japanese interests are not to initiate policies that culminate in a tightly organised regional structure or an economic bloc. Instead, Japan can be expected to pursue a form of regionalism that dampens regional identity and is consistent with the current directions of US-Japan relations. [...]

The option of an Asian identity is not as far fetched as it sounds. The regional countries, particularly China, are becoming increasingly important for Japan.

[...] Japan will have to devise a formula for reconciling its trans-Pacific interests with the issue of regional identity.[718]

While Blechinger concedes that Japan's stronger economic focus on East Asia has significantly raised awareness of, and an interest in, the region among Japanese business and political elites, she nevertheless concludes that Japan's main foreign policy focus cannot be expected to change essentially in the foreseeable future:

[...] given the fact that the Japanese economy strongly relies on exports and that Japan has important interests in Asia and the United States, it may be argued that mainstream opinion in the Japanese domestic discourse supports an Asia Pacific, rather than an exclusively Asian, identity for Japan. Considering the current state of regional integration and security cooperation in Asia, no dramatic changes in Japanese foreign policy are to be expected in the near future.[719]

Although Blechinger and Leggewie admit that "After the crisis, the compromise between Japan's foreign policy and economic elites rather shifted toward an outspoken commitment to the Asian region" and although they expect that "the process of political and economic cooperation and integration in Asia will continue and will become of more central importance for Japanese foreign

---

[718] Maswood (2001a): 7, 13, 15.

[719] Blechinger (2001): 88f.

Whereas Blechinger (2001) and Blechinger; Leggewie (2000) assert that Japan's identity will be determined mainly by the Japan-U.S. axis, Blechinger (2000: 81) surprisingly also argues that East Asian regionalism, represented by ASEAN Plus Three, may eventually "contribute to the formation of a regional identity and thus invigorate East Asian regionalism"). This apparent contradiction can easily be resolved if one implies that Blechinger's concept of identity is a concentric model with a core identity in the center that allows for various other layers of identity. Thus, the core of Japanese identity would be located at the national level, whereas the second concentric circle of identity would imply Japan's identity as an industrialized, pro-Western country, and Japan's evolving East Asian identity may be a new, third layer of identity located furthest from Japan's core identity.

policy than before", they at the same time predict that Japan "will fulfill this role not as a rival, but as a partner to the US [...]."[720]

Evidence of Japan's strategic opposition to China in APT

Japan's tactical behavior in APT suggests that its strategic opposition to China will prevent APT from developing into a more closely-knit and integrated grouping or community and that there is no common East Asian identity in the making that deserves the name. Rather, one of the main reasons for Japan's participation in APT is to balance the influence of China in Southeast Asia. Thus, Prime Minister Koizumi reacted to the announcement by the heads of government of ASEAN countries and China to attempt to launch a common ASEAN-China FTA within ten years' time by launching a promotional tour to Southeast Asia during which he advocated a model of regional integration focused on the Asia Pacific region rather than East Asia. In line with this approach, Japan is presently turning away from, and de-emphasizes, any "Asia First" approaches. As Robyn Lim points out,

> Still, Japan is stuck with the consequences of its misguided regional policies, promoted by "Asia First" proponents [...]. The Asean+3 to which Japan belongs in fact is a reincarnation of the old East Asia Economic Caucus. Because the EAEC excluded the U.S., it was bound to be dominated by China. That's why Koizumi is seeking to dilute Asean+3, presumably in order to consign it to well-deserved oblivion. He has proposed an East Asian community that would include Australia and New Zealand as core members. And in his keynote address in Singapore, he proposed that such a community should not be exclusive, but should enjoy close partnership with the U.S.[721]

While few observers would probably agree with Lim's view that Japan is trying to water down APT, many agree that Japan is actually trying to balance China's growing influence in East Asia by opening up the forum as much as possible, rather than advancing the cause of exclusive regional integration.[722]

In April 2002, the Koizumi administration launched what it called the "ASEAN plus five" initiative. At the first glance, this proposal appears to aim at establishing an East Asian Free Trade Area when what it is really aiming at is an Asia-Pacific trade area. The envisioned free trade zone, which is to be launched before 2010, is to include the APT members plus – significantly – also Taiwan. "In the future, the area could be extended to Australia and New

---

[720] Blechinger; Leggewie (2000): 320.

[721] Robyn Lim (2002).

[722] Cf., for example, Kajita (2002).

Zealand, as well as the United States [...], officials said.[723] Japan's "ASEAN plus five" move is clearly designed to check China's advances in the area of pursuing a separate FTA with ASEAN and give the APT project an irreversible Asia-Pacific orientation. Whereas Koizumi's first reaction to China's advance immediately after the November 2001 APT summit had been to establish closer ties with ASEAN, the Japanese government has now changed course, without, however, yielding its original objective, namely to check China. As the *Japan Times* comments in a lengthy article on Japan's "ASEAN five" initiative,

> Japan recently [i.e. in January and February 2002, M.H.], pitted itself against China in seeking a free-trade agreement with ASEAN, but the officials said they now regard that as a step toward the ultimate goal of an East Asia market, with an undercurrent of competition for leadership with China. [...] Japan hopes to take the initiative with ASEAN and South Korea, adding to the one with Singapore, as their economic systems are somewhat closer to Japan's than they are to China's, they [the Japanese officials, M.H] said. [...] Separately from the East Asia study group, Japanese and ASEAN officials are studying ways to conclude an FTA and will submit a report to their leaders in November. Japan and South Korea agreed on a similar study last month[724]

Since the 2001 APT summit, FTAs with ASEAN and South Korea. Japan's objectives within APT remain the same, but the strategy has changed. Whereas Japan prior to the summit rejected the idea of free-trade arrangements, it is now seeking to establish ties with South Korea and ASEAN by means of free-trade arrangements in order to counter the PRC's influence and integrate them more closely with a greater Asia Pacific area.

Conclusion: Overall assessment of Japan's role as an East Asian player within APT

The APT harbors interesting opportunities for Japan to enhance its political and security relations with its Northeast Asian neighbors and help stabilize the economic environment in the Southeast Asian region. Japan will therefore continue to support mechanisms of regional monetary stability and promote cooperation with its APT partners at various levels. As Lam Peng Er put it, Japan will continue to "rely on the ODA carrot as a key instrument of its foreign policy".[725] Its APT commitments can be expected to be strongest in the area of

---

[723] *Japan Times* (2002): "Japan Considering Creation of East Asia Free-Trade Area Before 2010", 14 April.
[724] Ibid.
[725] Lam (2001): 129.

economic cooperation and financial and development assistance to Southeast Asia.[726]

However, whereas Japan is willing to spend liberally on regional monetary and economic stability and ODA projects, its engagement in the region is guided by its political ties with the U.S.. Observers of Japan's foreign policy vis-à-vis East Asia basically agree that, although Japan has become more proactive, and is willing to assume a more independent posture in its foreign policy approach towards East Asia, it essentially avoids acting independently of American interests and concerns in the region. Therefore, regardless of whether Japan's foreign policy is seen as rather *reactive* or *proactive* as regards East Asia,[727] Japan stands for strong financial and political support for non-exclusive East Asian regionalism, and will strongly oppose and discourage any kind of exclusive pan-Asian regionalism. In this sense, Japanese leadership within the APT would preclude the formation of a "core" (as opposed to a complimentary or "peripheral") East Asian identity.

3.3. China

Political considerations

To the People's Republic, the APT process represents a potentially effective way to pursue several objectives at once.

First, there is China's post-Cold War policy of striving for what is frequently referred to as a "multipolar" world order, a term denoting China's opposition to perceived U.S. hegemony.[728] As Wang Hongying shows, China's decision making elites regard limited multilateralism as an effective tool to promote multipolarity and to reassure Southeast Asian countries of its reliability as a responsible, cooperative international player:

> [The] Chinese attitude toward multilateralism is quite instrumental, as indicated by the official discourse. [...] Chinese IR scholars and policy makers are sraightforward with the practical reasons for their limited endorsement of multilateralism. Their reasoning includes the use of multilateral arrangements to counter-balance US-led military alliances and to undermine American dominance in the region, and to appease

---

[726] Although Japan has reduced its overall ODA world-wide, it has allocated a greater proportion of its total ODA funds to ASEAN countries; in the context of the APT process, Japan has indicated that Southeast Asia can even expect an increase in Japanese ODA.

[727] Cp. the individual contributions in Maswood (2000b), and discussion of the same, in Maswood (2001a).

[728] Cp. Wang Hongying (2000): pp. 74, 78.

Southeast Asian nations and to ameliorate their perception of China as a threat.[729]

If multilateralism in general is seen as an effective means to further the PRC's interests, it is evident that China must be especially interested in playing a role in APT, where strategic opponents such as the U.S. have no place and where shows of political goodwill and support to ASEAN are likely to yield high diplomatic returns. Unlike APEC, APT represents an exclusively East Asian forum. Unlike APEC, the APT has no fixed objectives, agendas, obligations, regimes or implementation schedules and is process-oriented rather than outcome-oriented. In the APT forum, China does not find itself under pressure to perform; indeed, the PRC, unlike Japan, is not expected to actually *do* anything but show political goodwill and make token contributions. This is an ideal ground for China to raise its profile and image in Southeast Asia, as APT imposes little economic and political costs, while at the same time it presents an opportunity to both promote "multipolarity" and disperse Southeast Asian fears of the "China threat".

Second, from a Chinese perspective, the Northeast Asian summit within the APT represents a convenient platform for informal exchange with the leaders of Japan and Korea on current political, economic and security issues. Yet, despite the indubitable advantages of such a dialogue platform, it cannot be ruled out that the main motive for Chinese participation in the process is to make a symbolic show of political goodwill intended to keep ASEAN countries happy and polish up China's political image internationally.

Economic considerations

China's economic initiatives under the APT umbrella serve both political and economic objectives.

At the APT summit in Manila in 1999, Prime Minister Zhu Rongji proposed the idea of launching an ASEAN-China FTA. A joint ASEAN-China study reported favorably on the potential economic benefits such an FTA could be expected to yield to both ASEAN countries and China, whereupon the heads of government of the ASEAN nations and the PRC jointly endorsed the idea at the APT summit in Brunei in November 2001.[730]

To kick-start the ASEAN-China FTA, China unilaterally offered to open its market to all ASEAN countries for an initial period of five years, during which no reciprocal market liberalization is expected from ASEAN countries. Thus, China reaffirmed its interest in forming an ASEAN-China FTA.

Economically, the proposed FTA would make sense for China, since it would reinforce China's competitiveness vis-à-vis the Southeast Asian economies.

---

[729] Ibid.: 80.
[730] Cf. ASEAN-China Experts Group on Economic Cooperation (2001).

Favorable economic conditions, such as low labor and production costs, strong inflow of FDI and increasingly advanced means of industrial production, would boost additional Chinese exports to – and thus create a trade surplus with – the developing countries of Southeast Asia (who, as Kong Yam Tan puts it, "are increasingly being squeezed in the middle of the industrial ladder [, i.e.] [t]hey do not yet have the skill and technological base to compete with the NIEs [while] [o]n the other hand, the other cheap labour countries like China [...] are rapidly catching up").[731] Numerous Southeast Asian companies could be expected to relocate their production sites to China (thus diverting investments, employment opportunities and vocational training facilities from their home countries).[732]

To kick-start the ASEAN-China FTA, China unilaterally offered to open its market to all ASEAN countries for an initial period of five years, during which no reciprocal market liberalization is expected from ASEAN countries. Thus, China reaffirmed its interest in forming an ASEAN-China FTA. The extension of reduced tariffs would come at a relatively low cost to China, as the initial benefits granted to ASEAN economies largely just precipitate China's WTO liberalization commitments by a few years. As a commentary in *The Straits Times* points out,

> To expedite the [China-ASEAN FTA] process, China made a unilateral concession by offering to open its market to the Asean countries five years before these economies were ready to reciprocate. The cost of this concession is minimal because China, after its entry to the World Trade Organization (WTO), will have to open its markets for commodities and services before 2005-06 anyway.[733]

Thus, China's initiative, as a by-product of its WTO accession rather than a genuine APT commitment, is less substantial than it appears at first and constitutes a mere token commitment to East Asian reigonalism.

Politically, even if the ASEAN-China FTA was never actually implemented, China would nevertheless benefit from the proposal,[734] as the initiative boosted

---

[731] Tan (2000): 244.

[732] Conversely, only Singapore, as a financial and trade center in Southeast Asia, could expect to attract, and profit from, substantial investments by Chinese companies.

[733] Ching Cheong (2001).

[734] While a number of Southeast Asian leaders did not receive the initiative with great enthusiasm, they nevertheless endorsed it at the APT summit in 2001. This suggests that they either really intend to implement the proposal (despite the expected detrimental impact on their respective national economies) and form an FTA or, more likely, they formally consented to the proposal, never actually expecting the ASEAN-China FTA to materialize. This would not be unusual for ASEAN, as characteristically, ASEAN is notorious for its decision-making style according to the "AFTA motto" ("Agree First, Talk After"), a term coined by observers of the ASEAN Free Trade Area process).

China's international reputation as a promoter of East Asian regionalism in times of economic slowdown and saved the otherwise unspectacular 2001 APT summit from exposing the lack of other significant initiatives or achievements.

To sum up: If the ASEAN-China FTA, against all odds, actually turned out to be viable concept, China would stand to win in several respects: it would earn itself a reputation as a reliable international player, prove its leaderhship qualities in East Asia and carry an invaluable strategic victory in its struggle for the "multipolarization" of global economic and security structures, i.e. secure a greater role for China in the international arena.

Especially at times of economic slowdown and recession in Southeast Asia, China's offer to grant temporary unreciprocal market access to Southeast Asia must be tempting for Southeast Asian governments, since, for a limited period of three to four years, they could expect some additional revenue from investments by Chinese companies and an increase of exports to China. This could help China to develop a positive profile in the conduct of regional affairs.

Since it is very unlikely that an East Asian Free Trade Area (EAFTA) may evolve over time, China's FTA proposal to ASEAN also carries a competitive note with regard to Japan: whereas China has taken the intitiative, Japan remains passive on plurilateral free trade talks in East Asia.

3.4. South Korea

Political considerations

Korea's call for greater East Asian regionalism and cooperation is credible, considering that the government envisions regionalism as being complementary to, rather than opposing, the existing global architecture and pursues a Japan-Korea axis within the forum. On the one hand, Korea's call to widen the scope for East Asian emerging economies in reforming the global financial architecture and assume a greater role in institutions such as the IMF and the World Bank (rather than promoting an Asian Monetary Fund) may be heard much more clearly in Washington and the capitals of Europe if expressed collectively by APT countries. On the other hand, Korea, like Japan and the ASEAN states, does not wish East Asia to turn into an economic or political bloc. In this regard, the typical Korean view seems to be that

> [...] a one-sided regionalist approach will be detrimental to multilateralism, as this will imply another large-scale regional bloc next to the EU [...] and NAFTA [...]. A further fragmentation of [the] world economy will not do any good to the outward-oriented East Asian

economies. Therefore, the East Asian countries are rather encouraged to adopt a balanced approach between regionalism and multilateralism.[735]

The ROK, which has already drawn closer to China's political orbit due to the immense pull of the PRC's economic dynamic,[736] will increasingly have to walk the tightrope of having to accommodate both the U.S. and China (the former being its largest trade partner and most important security shield, the latter its most dynamic economic partner).[737] As Snyder reports, Korea is presently adapting to the necessities of its changed economic environment. Thus, on the one hand, Korean analysts are calling for a foreign policy aimed at reconciling the U.S. and the PRC, and on the other emphasize the need to de-link economic and security policies so as to make South Korea more independent economically in its dealings with China. Snyder therefore concludes that, "given the intermittently confrontational track of the U.S.-PRC relationship, the issue of how to deal with China is gradually becoming a likely source of future differences in the U.S.-ROK relationship." However, he also points out that "[d]espite China's growing trade with China, Seoul knows that the foundation for a prosperous trade relationship with China is its security relationship with the United States and under current circumstances will choose [this] relationship when pressed to do so."[738] South Korea's slackening, but nevertheless still dominant inclination towards (and reliance on) the United States will keep the ROK from pursuing strategies of exclusive political or economic integration in East or Northeast Asia, as such a move would have not only economic but also major political implications, especially if we accept that, as Frank-Jürgen Richter (Asia Director of the World Economic Forum) puts it, "a China-Korea-Japan FTA would have significant geopolitical impact [... and] would diminish American influence in this economically powerful region."[739] However, Korea will seek to expand bilateral and plurilateral cooperation with China in the context of APT wherever it is economically convenient and politically viable.

With a view to the security situation on the Korean peninsula, South Korea must have a strong interest in improving Northeast Asian dialogue at all levels so as to promote stability there. In this respect, Korea certainly appreciates the chances provided by both the Northeast Asian summit and programs of economic cooperation within APT.

---

[735] Park (2001): 146.

[736] Snyder (2001a) points out that the PRC surpassed Japan as South Korea's second largest trade partner after the U.S. and that South Korean imports from and exports to China continue to grow "dramatically". Further, China has surpassed the U.S. as a destination for Korean investments. He also describes the positive political impact of China's grown economic power on Sino-Korean bilateral relations.

[737] Cp. ibid.

[738] Ibid.

[739] Richter (2002).

Economic considerations

Apart from all rhetoric of aiming to form an East Asian Free Trade Area (EAFTA) with China, Japan and Southeast Asia, Korea is actually only marginally interested in establishing an EAFTA including China and ASEAN; its *real* interests have surprisingly little to do with East Asian regionalism.

First, the pursuit of a Korea-Japan FTA has been a chief South Korean objective for several years, and the ROK has conducted serious bilateral talks with Japan on the issue since 1998. The Korea-Japan FTA is expected to "reduce the existing trade imbalance" with Japan, increase Japanese investments in Korea and "gain greater access to Japan's technological infrastructure."[740] Second, Korea's other main and long-standing interest is to gain access to the NAFTA markets by establishing an FTA with the U.S. Third, Korea sees no viable alternative to these two FTAs; the envisioned East Asian FTA is seen as a long-term vision rather than a practicable enterprise. Thus, a discussion paper published by the Korea Institute of International Economic Policy (KIEP) in September 2001 points out that both China and the ASEAN FTA presently lack the potential for substantial additional trade liberalization and unreservedly dismisses the notion that an EAFTA could materialize in the short to medium term out of hand. The study conludes that

> [...] the U.S. and japan are considered to be the most feasible and desirable FTA partners for Korea. Recently, there have been prevailing talks on a 'Korea-China FTA' or an 'ASEAN+3 FTA' in order to create a regional trading arrangement in East Asia. However, this may not be feasible in the short run for two main reasons. The first problem is China's capacity. [... After substantial tariff cuts in the course of its WTO accession,] China may find it hard to make an additional tariff cut to zero in order to form an FTA with Japan and Korea. Moreover, since China maintains relatively higher actual tariff rates for Korea and Japan than for other countries, a complete elimination of tariffs for China to form a 'Korea-Japan-China FTA does not seem feasible in the short run. The second problem is the compatibility of the said 'ASEAN+3 FTA with the WTO. [As] [t]he FTA among ASEAN countries, namely AFTA is [merely] a preferential trading arrangement among developing countries [and as such incompatible with the] GATT Article XXIV [...], AFTA should first be transformed into an FTA under the terms and conditions of GATT Article XXIV covering "substantially all the trade," which requires significant time and commitments. [741]

---

[740] Rhee (2000): 73.
On the expected political and economic benefits of a Japan-Korea FTA both for Korea and Japan, see Fukagawa (2000).
[741] Sohn and Yoon (2001), Executive Summary; cf. also pp. 38f.

South Korea is now focused on forging bilateral FTAs with Japan and the U.S. In this context, APT regionalism can only represent a complement to its overall Asia Pacific orientation (with focus on the U.S.). A point in case for Korea's non-exclusive Asia Pacific orientation are its other pursuits of FTAs with countries such as Chile and New Zealand (both of which are APEC countries). Significantly, although the Korean government employs friendly official rhetoric supportive of the idea of a Northeast Asian free trade area and has entered serious negotiations about a bilateral Japan-Korea FTA, there have been no serious bilateral talks about a Korea-China free trade agreement yet, nor has a bilateral study group been established yet. Observers who believe that there is a chance for an APT free trade area to be established, have to rely on coffee cup reading rather than on facts. Thus, Snyder observes that

> Sino-Korean trade promotion activities and information sharing/coordination continued to expand, including consultations among Chinese and Korean financial securities regulators and financial supervisory commission

and speculates that

> [i]n addition, the decision to launch three-way coordination meetings among Japanese, Chinese, and Korean economic ministers [...] is the first practical step toward pursuing a China-Japan-Korea free trade zone.[742]

Observers within and outsides of Korea are confident that, telling by the current dynamic of the economic relations, Korea and China or all three Northeast Asian countries together do have the potential to eventually form a mutually beneficial FTA.[743] But in the end, it takes more than mere potential, namely political trust, reliability and mature relations, to establish successful economic integration.

Prospects for Korea's behavior in APT

Summing up, Korea is experiencing a major shift of its economic environment with China emerging as an ever-more important economic partner. However, Korea's ultimate political reliance on the U.S. and the American role as largest trade partner ensure Korea's continued general Asia Pacific orientation. Nevertheless, the changed economic conditions after the crisis and the economic ascendancy of China are likely to create the need for a more independent

---

[742] Snyder (2001a).
[743] Cp. Richter (2002), who argues that a Northeast Asian FTA as a "win-win" proposition; cp. further: Sohn and Yoon (2001): 26f.; Snyder (2001b).

Korean foreign and economic policy. Korea can therefore be expected to capitalize on the increased opportunities of *ad hoc* dialogue, political and economic cooperation and coordination and maybe even on or the other occasional single-issue coalition. The forum may also be conducive to security talks concerning the Korean peninsula and improve the climate for the envisioned Japan-korea FTA. However, the time is not yet ripe for advanced economic and political integration. Talk of an East Asian Free Trade Area remains elusive for the foreseeable future.

4. Achievements and limitations of the APT project to date

From the time of the first group summit of ASEAN member states plus China, Japan and South Korea in 1997, the APT process developed a remarkable intitial dynamic. In 1998, the summit was followed up by the "Joint Statement on East Asia Cooperation" of 1999, the first document ever issued in the context of East Asian cooperation. Subsequently, summits and foreign and finance ministers' meetings were institutionalized on a regular basis.[744] These developments were followed up by the Chiang Mai initiative, the decision to implement currency swap arrangements and a catalog of various other forms of plurilateral and bilateral contacts and cooperation. However, there is reason to believe that APT is already running out of steam due to an apparent lack of common resolve and direction.

4.1. The Chiang Mai Initiative

In May 2000, APT Finance Ministers surprised the global public when they launched an initiative to form a network of regional bilateral currency swap and repurchase arrangements designed to shield regional currencies from strong and unexpected depreciation. The so-called Chiang Mai initiative distinguished APT from other regional and transregional cooperative arrangements (particularly APEC and ASEM) in so far as it was the only forum that seemed not only to address the issue of financial stability and crisis prevention but whose member countries were apparently also ready to assign (and risk the loss of) a considerable portion of their own foreign reserves to this end.

Indeed, at a first glance the figures are impressive and made some observers, such as Heribert Dieter, wax almost lyrical about the opportunities of an APT

---

[744] Cf. Hund and Okfen (2001).

liquidity fund.[745] For example, Dieter showed that if East Asian countries really were to put their heart into the swap initiative and attributed ten to fifteen or twenty percent of their joint foreign reserves to a liquidity fund, this would suffice to effectively fend off any liquidity crises:

> In March 2000, the central banks of the Asean countries, together with China, Japan and South Korea, collectively had foreign reserves of well over $800 billion. [...] By comparison, the entire Eurozone currently has reserves of about $340 billion. Even if only 10%-20% of East Asia's reserves were available for the regional fund, participating economies could easily overcome any liquidity crisis without help from Washington.[746]

However, very soon it became clear that APT members did not really think in those dimensions. Instead of the 80 to 160 billion dollars Dieter thinks an effective mechanism would require, APT members are intending to commit only a fraction of this amount to the scheme. By April 2002,

> Japan ha[d] [...] "signed bilateral swap deals with China (for $3 billion), South Korea ($2Billion), Thailand ($3 billion), the Philippines ($3 billion) and Malaysia ($1 billion), while China and Thailand also ha[d] a $2 billion swap agreement.[747]

In December 2001, China had assigned US$2 billion to a bilateral swap with Thailand.[748] The PRC is also in the process of negotiating a similar agreement with the Philippines.[749]
South Korea is currently disucssing swaps with China, Malaysia, the Philippines and Thailand.[750] Thus, the APT swaps scheme accounted for an overall US$ 16 billion in April 2002, which leaves prospects for the overall scheme at an estimated $26 billion to $30 billion once the presently envisioned swaps are implemented.
Japan's commitments under the swap agreements so far are bound to be largely ineffective, since disbursement of the lion's share is tied to IMF eligibility criteria. Rather than devising a more flexible and regionally adapted alternative to the IMF (an "Asian" fund), Japan tied the new swap arrangement to an

---

[745] Cf. Dieter (2000a); Dieter (2000b).
[746] Dieter (2000a). Dieter (2000b) has slightly different figures that, however, point into the same direction.
[747] *Business World Online*, (04 April 2002):"Southeast Asian integration lacks key factor: unity".
[748] *People's Daily* (07 December 2001): "China, Thailand Sign Currency Swap Agreement".
[749] AFTA Online (17 April 2002).
[750] *Business World Online* (04 April 2002): "Southeast Asian integration lacks key factor: unity".

institution which, in the eyes of many Asians, had become a symbol of inflexibility and failed regulatory policies during the Asian financial crisis. Japan's money therefore would only add to the bulk of IMF funds available *after* a crisis has struck, instead of supplying money early and effectively *before* a crisis can unfold. For example, although Japan has earmarked US$2 billion as an emergency fund to back the Korean won[751], Dieter points out that "[w]ithout IMF consent, South Korea [...] would be able to draw just $200 million, a sum hardly sufficient to fight a liquidity crisis."[752] Considering the lack of progress, Dieter, who had initially been so enthusiastic about – and willing to believe in – the opportunities of an AMF-type liquidity fund and who had praised Japan's leadership qualities, had come to see the swap arrangements as a "toothless tiger" by mid-2001.[753]

Other observers similarly believe that the scheme is a symbol for good neighborly relations rather than an effective tool. Thus, the *Financial Times* commented on the Japan-China swap deal that

> [t]he swap facility is considered to be largely symbolic [...], since Japan and China hold the largest levels of foreign reserves [...]. In addition, China's capital account is not convertible, meaning that the yuan is not vulnerable to speculative currency attacks.[754]

At large, the whole net of actual and intended swaps has meanwhile come to be seen mostly as political symbolism. As one out of a great number of similar media reports related in April 2002,

> [...] analysts say [...] the currency safety net is little more than a symbolic gesture with little practical use [Although] [m]ore deals are on the way [...,] the agreements mean little in practice. Now that most regional countries have floating currencies, a repeat of the 1997 economic meltdown is seen as unlikely. And the amounts of money involved remain largely ineffectual. [...] The main significance of the swap web, analysts say, is that some of its proponents see it as a precursor to an Asian Monetary Fund [...] Few, however, see much hope for an AMF any time soon.[755]

Summing up, the promise of the Chiang Mai initiative has not been realized so far. Progress is still possible, if not necessarily likely. As there are no signs that East Asian countries might allocate substantial portions of their foreign

---

[751] Cf. figures given by Rowley (2001).

[752] Dieter (2001).

[753] Ibid.

[754] Sevastopulo (2002).

[755] *Business World Online* (04 April 2002). Martinez (2002: 140) shares the view that the swap arrangements are of little practical, but rather symbolic value.

currency reserves to the swap arrangements and that Japan will switch the points for a fine-tuned East Asian liquidity fund as a real alternative to the IMF, the swap deals cannot be expected to significantly enhance economic stability or economic relations in East Asia.[756]

4.2. Financial monitoring and early warning systems

Effective crisis prevention through regional currency swaps would require both financial and economic monitoring in the region. However, the Chiang Mai initiative has so far failed to act upon APT members' common resolve to establish financial and economic surveillance and an early crisis warning mechanism. Admittedly, the APT Finance Ministers' Meeting in May 2001, "recognizing the importance of enhanced monitoring of the economic situation in our region in implementing the BSA [Bilateral Currency Swap Arrangements, M.H.] [...] agreed to establish a study group" on the issue,[757] but it is highly doubtful that participating governments will be ready to release relevant sensitive economic data in the end. The low profile of the ASEAN Surveillance Process (ASP) – ASEAN's attempt at installing economic monitoring among Southeast Asian nations – provides reason to be pessimistic about any effective monitoring at APT level.

4.3. The proposed ASEAN-China Free Trade Area

In November 2000, Chinese Prime Minister Zhu Rongji proposed the establishment of an ASEAN-China Free Trade Area, whereupon a joint study group was established that came up with a favorable report presented prior to the ASEAN/ APT summit in November 2001, at which occasion the respective heads of government endorsed the plan. The decision to establish an ASEAN-China FTA by 2011 emerged by general consensus rather than by formal agreement. The heads of state also declined to make specific provisions, or set a schedule for, further steps toward the implementation of the envisioned FTA.

Despite the favorable study group report, there is little evidence that ASEAN economies stand to benefit economically from the envisioned FTA. Indeed, ASEAN members such as Malaysia, Indonesia and Vietnam, but also the Philippines, have been openly skeptical. The pattern that emerges is that both Singapore and Thailand, who have already concluded or are pursuing bilateral

---

[756] Cp. Dieter; Higgott (2001). Dieter and Higgott are rather skeptical concerning the opportunities for an East Asian liquidity fund (p. 49f.).
[757] ASEAN + 3 Finance Ministers: Joint Ministerial Statement, 9 May 2001, Honolulu (USA), http://www.aseansec.org/economic /jms_as+3fmm.htm [07/06/01].

FTAs with several partners world-wide, such as the U.S., Japan, Australia, New Zealand and other economies in Latin America, are adopting a free-trade stance vis-à-vis China because it corresponds to their general preference for trade liberalization,[758] whereas other ASEAN partners are reluctant because they fear economic disadvantages from an ASEAN-China FTA. This pattern clearly indicates that regionalism is not the driving force behind the FTA pursuits. Rather, ASEAN member states are pursuing their own national preferences, regardless of who they are dealing with. Singapore and Thailand have adopted a free-trade stance vis-à-vis the whole world (including China), and negotiations about the envisioned ASEAN-China FTA has already spurred Japan's commitment to Southeast Asia in the areas of financial assistance, economic cooperation and recently even free trade talks. Similarly, Malaysia, despite its decade-long promotion of East Asian regionalism, seems to fear actual progress towards East Asian regional (economic) integration, thus following the essentially anti-integrationalist stance it already adopted in the context of ASEAN integration.[759]

4.4. State of the discussion about the East Asia Free Trade Area (EAFTA)

Until very recently, the idea of establishing an EAFTA was merely a visionary fancy with little impact on APT relations. However, China's proposal to establish an FTA with ASEAN has provoked a strong reaction from Japan, which is fearing to lose influence in the region. The latest Japanese proposal to establish an "ASEAN plus five" free-trade area by 2010 (see section 3.2.) has brought new life into the debate about the EAFTA. However, Japan has unmistakably pointed out that an EAFTA can only be the first step on the way toward a wider Asia-Pacific free-trade area (including Taiwan, the U.S., Australia and New Zealand). Japan and China are thus pitched against each other as strategic opponents within APT. Thus, it is becoming increasingly clear

---

[758] With a view to Singapore's economic security approach, Dent remarks that "Singapore [...] not only practices free trade but ardently promotes it within every audience of its economic diplomacy." (Dent 2001: 11.)

[759] As a matter of fact, Malaysia's promotion of East Asian regionalism increasingly appears to be a means of deflecting integration elsewhere rather than promoting it. Just at the time when APEC started discussing Asia-Pacific integration and trade liberalization in the early 1990s, Malaysia began playing the (anti-Western) East Asian card. When ASEAN intended to finalize AFTA at the end of the 1990s, Malaysia discredited the scheme by failing to meet its agreed-upon commitments to reduce tariff rates for sensitive goods, while Prime Minister Mahathir's government emphasized wider East Asian integration. When China eventually proposed closer economic integration, Malaysia was not prepared to follow, but could not really oppose the idea, either, since this would have damaged its credibility.

that APT, in its present shape, does not have the potential to evolve as an economic bloc or community that stands by itself.

4.5. Development cooperation

Development cooperation is one of APT's most promising and least controversial projects. Especially Japan has promised all sorts of ODA, allocating funds and expertise to major ASEAN initiatives such as Mekong development, the Initiative for ASEAN Integration (IAI) and ASEAN initiatives designed to provide infrastructure and education to the newcomer ASEAN countries. Despite overall cuts in its world-wide ODA, Tokyo seems willing to sustain and even upgrade its financial engagement in Southeast Asia, and clearly is the only significant provider of ODA to the region within APT. China's financial assistance to ASEAN has been largely symbolic, but the PRC supports training facilities and technical assistance to various infrastructure projects, mainly in the Mekong area.

Besides support for some new ASEAN projects, APT has dusted off the "usual suspects" of cooperation initiatives, such as the Kunming Rail project (a veteran in political shows of goodwill), whose objective it is to implement a direct rail link between Singapore and China.

4.6. Institutionalization

To date, the APT process has developed only very few institutions, although the process itself can be said to be firmly established through regular summit and ministerial meetings. As mentioned, APT dialogue has also brought about annual meetings among Northeast Asian heads of government. In November 2001, Kim Dae-jung, Junichiro Koizumi and Zhu Rongji further agreed to hold regular trilateral economic ministers' meetings, which are to be attended by finance and trade ministers.[760] Collectively, the heads of governments gathered at the 2001 APT summit in Brunei resolved to establish an APT Secretariat, but it is to be expected that further institutionalization will at best be very slow in coming, as APT participants emphasize the principle of informality and voluntary cooperation.

---

[760] *Korea Now* (19 November 2001): "ASEAN+3 Working with the Neighbors: Korea, China, Japan agree to hold regular economic ministers' meetings".

5. East Asian Identity in the Making?

In the light of the previous analysis, this section examines whether APT represents a likely basis for the emergence of a specifically East Asian or APT identity. In order to do so, it assesses three indicators, namely collective norms, APT participants' readiness to "pool" sovereignty (i.e. transfer sovereignty from the national to the regional level) and, finally, whether APT participants share a clear ingroup/ outgroup distinction.

5.1. Collective norms

Collective norms, defined as the code of justified expectations about appropriate behavior within a given group, represent the backbone of any collective identity. If there was to be a specific East Asian or APT identity, it would therefore have to be based on a set of specifically East Asian or APT norms marking the governments of the participating countries as a distinct group.

In reality, APT participants collectively subscribe to only a few and very general norms (though this already represents some progress, considering the various and sometimes long-standing political, historical and cultural antagonisms in the region). Thus, participating governments expect from each other to show political goodwill and readiness to engage in bilateral and multilateral dialogue and cooperation related to economic, financial and political stability and other non-traditional security issues, both with a view to regional and global concerns. Further, Northeast Asian countries are expected by ASEAN countries to engage in trilateral dialogue among themselves so as to provide more political stability to East Asia as a whole; the Northeast Asian partners of ASEAN understand – and have largely accepted – that they are expected to play this role if they do not want to risk disappointing their Southeast Asian neighbors. The APT process also relies on participating governments' readiness to settle contentious issues exclusively by peaceful means. Non-compliance with this norm would naturally erode the non-compliant government's credibility and destabilize the APT process as such; notably China would presently be unwilling to pay such a price, as it has been seeking to improve relations and build trust and confidence with its Southeast Asian neighbors. With a view to procedural norms, the principles of informality and voluntariness represent paramount procedural principles of APT.

Interestingly, an implicit prerequisite for China's participation in the APT, and thus a *sine qua non* for the APT process, is APT participants' acceptance of the "one-China" principle. Failure to support the PRC's line in this question would seriously erode the foundations of the APT process.

The norms shared collectively by APT governments are very general and rudimentary. However, as long as all participants, for whatever reasons, have a genuine interest in keeping the process going, these norms will have to be respected by all. Adherence to these norms could, in turn, develop into a stable framework for dynamic socialization processes and political stability in the region. So far, however, given the heterogeneous composition of the forum, APT's collective purposes and norms appear to be too thin as to form the basis for a particular East Asian identity (a core identity) that might assume prevalence over APT participants' various other identities in the long run.

5.2. Is there a basis for APT solidarity?

It would be a mistake to assume that APT can be expected to develop into a grouping whose members are linked by a firm bond of solidarity.[761] The general rivalry between Japan and China alone precludes APT from developing into an all-East Asian solidary group as they will compete with each other for influence and position themselves strategically in the forum. However, the strategic opposition between these two East Asian giants may paradoxically cause them to make long-term political "investments" in the region (i.e. assign political and economic resources to APT countries without expecting direct material returns), as they are seeking to find more acceptance as responsible and cooperative partners and increase their influence in Southeast Asia. As a result, Japan and China will be mimicking solidarity with Southeast Asia. If the external conditions of APT cooperation remain stable, there is a slight chance that sustained mimicry may eventually even bring about a soialization process converting mimicry into more authentic forms of solidarity.

5.3. Pooling of sovereignty

Pooling of sovereignty within the APT context is extremel unlikely. As ASEAN countries have so far been very reluctant to transfer sovereignty from the national to the regional level and thus left initiatives such as the ASEAN Free Trade Area (AFTA), the ASEAN Investment Area (AIA) and the ASEAN Surveillance Mechanism (ASP) largely ineffective, they can hardly be expected to devise East Asian regional regimes and mechanisms requiring them to cede national sovereignty to a supranational level. Japan has made it clear that it has no interest in institutionalized economic integration in East Asia. It is also

---

[761] Solidarity is defined here as the degree of member states' readiness to accommodate collective interests or another member state's needs, especially if this implies yielding vested national interests.

unlikely that China might cede some of its national powers and prerogatives to regional institutions or endorse regional regimes that require strict compliance. Rather, the insistence of all APT participants on informality indicates that there is not going to be any kind of transfer of national sovereignty from the national to the regional level in the foreseeable future.

5.4. Ingroup/ outgroup distinction

Any collective identity will be the stronger the more members share commonalities distinguishing them as a separate group. As Weller points out, the significance of a collective identity depends on the degree to which such commonalities establish a clear line between *ingroup* and *outgroup*.[762]

The distinction between ingroup and outgroup is not very pronounced in APT. Rather than a manifestation of an East Asian identity, APT represents an attempt by a number of increasingly interdependent states to discuss issues of regional stability and engage in confidence building, mutual reassurance and in exploring common ground for cooperation. However, APT states have not significantly closed ranks or undergone any other remarkable foreign policy swings indicating a growing sense of East Asian unity.

Whereas many observers identified the Asian side at the first Asia-Europe Meeting (ASEM) in 1996 as a manifestation of the EAEC and, as such, as a precursor of an increasingly integrated and proactive East Asian bloc, there is no sign so far that East Asia may evolve as a third unified bloc in an increasingly tripolar world order. Japan will continue to consider itself an essentially Western country. Close ties with the U.S. will remain its prime foreign policy orientation. Similarly, South Korea cannot be expected to leave the safe haven of its pro-Western foreign policy orientation for the rough seas of uncertain Northeast Asian relations. On the other hand, China's pursuit of global multipolarity will continue to pit the PRC against what it perceives as American hegemony in the region.

Observers of East Asia generally agree that rivalry between Japan and China precludes or strongly limits greater APT coherence.[763] As Webber puts it,

> APT is likely to be plagued by a similar constellation of 'duelling' would-be hegemons that has weakened APEC. [...] ASEAN is unlikely to be able to serve as a powerful motor of East Asian integration where

---

[762] Weller (1999): 254.

[763] Cf. for example Tay (2001b): 212. Tay holds that the two major dividing lines going through APT are, first, the differences between pro-Western countries and China regarding the role of the U.S. and, second, the Sino-Japanese rivalry (pp. 211f.).

Japan and China do not judge closer cooperation in any case to be in their own respective interests.[764]

ASEAN countries can be expected to hide their concerns about China's growing influence behind a policy of constructive engagement and general openness towards the unpredictable Eastern neighbor, as they have done since the early 1990s. Nevertheless, they will not become genuine friends of China and will seek to balance improving relations with China by ensuring their individual ties with the West, i.e. the U.S. (and in extension Japan), remain intact and shield them from perceived dangers from the East. Ultimately, most APT nations' wide-spread perception of the U.S. as an insurance of last resort against China leaves a wide gap permanently dividing the membership of APT. As Cheng has pointed out,

> Japan and South Korea will obviously be very concerned with the Bush Administration's position on the "ASEAN plus 3" process; and they would not like to see the process weaken the American presence in Asia, as well as their relations with the United States. At the same time, even the most enthusiastic proponents of East Asian regionalism in ASEAN, namely, Singapore and Malaysia, have been trying to tone down its significance. [...] Singapore has been working hard to facilitate the maintenance of the U.S. military presence in the region, and it started negotiations on a U.S.-Singapore Free Trade Agreement in December 2000. Similarly, Prime Minister Mahathir, while endorsing the idea of closer co-operation between ASEAN and the three Northeast Asian states, has also indicated that "it is not going to happen any time soon", and that such an arrangement should not put developing countries at risk.[765]

In this context, it has to be noted that, as relations with China improved, some Southeast Asian countries, such as Thailand, the Philippines, and Singapore have deliberately balanced this development by stepping up bilateral political, military and economic ties with the U.S. in recent years.[766] Therefore, rather than East Asian integration or even bloc-building, the real purpose of APT cooperation is to bridge the gap between China and the rest of APT for the sake of regional security.

---

[764] Webber (2001): 363.

[765] Cheng (2001): 433.

[766] For Thailand's recent relations with the U.S., Japan and China, see Kusuma (2001): 204ff. For the Philippines' security agenda vis-à-vis the U.S., cp. "The Philippines", in Richard W. Baker; Christopher A. McNally; Charles Morrison (2001): p. 52.

As Weller has pointed out, one decisive factor for the political relevance[767] of a given collective identity is the absence of alternative identities. As alternative identities blur the distinction between ingroup and outgroup, the political relevance of a given collective identity is strong when the individual identity subjects do not adhere to possibly conflicting alternative identities and weak when the opposite is the case.

This implies that even if there actually was a processes of collective identity formation in the making within APT or East Asia, such a particular identity would be outweighed by the APT participants' older and stronger identities for a long time to come. At present, however, there is no reason to speculate about the potential impact an evolving East Asian identity may have on the political behavior of East Asian countries, as no such identity formation process is currently underway.

6. Conclusion: What we can expect from them

A look at the political discourse among APT states shows that the majority of participants prefer East Asian cooperation with a pro-Western Asia-Pacific orientation rather than exclusive forms of East Asian regionalism. Only Malaysia and China seem to prefer the latter.

Judging from Japan's and China's behavior vis-à-vis ASEAN, it seems that, within APT, Japan and China represent strategic opponents competing for influence in Southeast Asia, rather than engaging in East Asian community-building. Whereas China has aggressively pursued a strong China-ASEAN axis within APT by promoting an ASEAN-China FTA, Japan is seeking to balance China's efforts by stepping up its political and economic cooperative profile in the region.

With a look at the achievements of the forum in the area of building regional cooperative regimes, it seems that after a good start with promising initiatives such as the Chiang Mai initiative to establish regional currency swap arrangements or economic surveillance mechanisms, progress has been very slow.

With regard to economic integration, the proposed ASEAN-China FTA is far from certain, the concept represents a dividing line going through APT rather than a first step toward East Asian integration. The decision by ASEAN and PRC leaders at the 2001 APT summit to establish the ASEAN-China FTA has triggered fierce competition between Japan and China for influence in East Asia. Nevertheless, although APT has not shifted the points for closer

---

[767] Political relevance denotes that a collective identity determines the political behavior of the identity subjects. The German term applied by Weller (1999) is "handlungsbestimmend".

integration of APT as a separate entity, the distinct dynamic of the APT process has already begun to change the political and economic landscape in East Asia. Thus, Japan has apparently been forced to give up its reluctance to discuss trade liberalization with Southeast Asian APT members and is now struggling to integrate the forum into Asia-Pacific structures so as to preclude Chinese domination. This means that APT might already be on the way toward closer integration, albeit not in terms of an economic bloc in its own right, but as a building bloc for an Asia-Pacific trade area (possibly similar to the APEC FTA previously envisioned by the U.S.). If an East Asian FTA should actually emerge due to Japan's "ASEAN plus five" initiative, it will very likely be a transitory state towards an Asia-Pacific FTA. As regards the ASEAN-China FTA, it is not at all certain if it is going to become an effective concept due to strong reservations by central ASEAN members such as Malaysia, the Philippines and Indonesia.

With a view to Southeast Asia's place within APT, ASEAN members find themselves in a position of increased strength both vis-à-vis Japan and China, as they seem to profit politically and economically from the rivalry between the Northeast Asian giants, which requires them to accommodate their Southeast Asian neighbors.

As regards the promotion of regionalism, within the structures of APT there is wide scope for various forms of regional cooperation, ranging from development assistance and economic cooperation to dealing with transnational and security problems. Northeast Asian relations may improve through enhanced trilateral dialogue among China, Japan and Korea within the APT process. Overall, APT is much more an exercise in overcoming mutual distrust, promoting dialogue and stabilizing political relations in East Asia than about exclusive forms of political or economic integration.

Chapter 7:

CONCLUSION

CONCLUSION

1. Summary

This study addressed the question of the substance and quality of collective identity between ASEAN governments after more than three decades of ASEAN cooperation and assessed the intergovernmental ASEAN Plus Three process with a view to its prospects of developing a specific, politically relevant collective East Asian identity. Collective identity between states was defined as a clearly perceptible (i.e. observable) distinction between ingroup and outgroup. Its respective strength and political relvance depend on both the clarity and prominence of the the ingroup/ outgroup distinction on the one hand and its formative impact on the perceptions and behavior of its respective identity subjects (i.e. degree to which the individual group members' perceptions are also formed by alternative, "interfering" identities). The four indicators of collective identity between states underlying the approach chosen in this study were collective norms, readiness of members to pool sovereignty, solidarity and positions vis-à-vis outsiders (i.e. non-members).

In the case of ASEAN, four separate studies on each of these four indicators depicted the collective identity of ASEAN after more than three decades of cooperation. In the case of APT, a single study on the expectations and motives of the various member states' governments and a reflection on its chances and limitations resulted in an assessment of the prospects of formation of a politically relevant East Asian identity.

The analysis of the ASEAN members' discourse on ASEAN norms showed that the traditional ASEAN norms of the "ASEAN way" remain largely in place, even though in the course of the norms debate that ensued in the aftermath of the Asian economic crisis of 1997 there have been differences among ASEAN members about the appropriate interpretation of some norms or the relative weight of particular norms in situations where they conflicted with others. Crucially, the ASEAN norms debate was carried out on the basis of the traditional ASEAN norms, and even the most ardent promoters of a more flexible handling of the "ASEAN way" did not doubt its general validity.

The study on pooling of sovereignty in ASEAN showed that all of ASEAN's mechanisms of closer regional cooperation and integration, including the ASEAN Free Trade Area (AFTA), stop short of transferring national sovereignty and authority to central collective institutions. Many ASEAN members are still afraid of making commitments they cannot withdraw at any time without risking to be reprimanded by, or face sanctions of, supranational

ASEAN authorities and institutions. The still paramount insistence on absolute national sovereignty runs counter to, and marks the limits of, ASEAN's various ambitious objectives of regional integration as outlined in the ASEAN Vision 2020 of 1997 and the Hanoi Plan of Action of 1998. Thus, AFTA's regulatory mechanism for the Common Effective Preferential Trade scheme (CEPT) was softened rather than tightened in 2001, practically allowing ASEAN members to interminably defer liberalization commitments. The ASEAN Surveillance Process (ASP) remains largely ineffective as ASEAN members, for fear they could be forced to submit sensitive national data, insist on voluntary submission of data. Torn between the need for coherence and effectiveness on the one hand and most member states' distrust to any kind of centralization on the other, attempts at institutionalized crisis management and conflict resolution, such as the establishment of the deliberately still-born ASEAN Troika and the High Council (envisioned since more than two decades but never actually implemented), remain indecisive at best. The Initiative for ASEAN Integration (IAI) remains a half-hearted approach to support the poorest ASEAN countries, as the old ASEAN countries shun high cost commitments and rules-based aid mechanisms.

The study on ASEAN solidarity focused on eight case studies, each of which examined situations of contention and conflict between two or more ASEAN states and evaluated the behavior of the parties involved. The case studies focused on the question whether the observed behavior was both in line with ASEAN-specific norms, i.e. corresponded to the socially codified behavior any ASEAN member can typically expect from every other ASEAN member and also agreed with more general standards of solidarity as represented by the five situations of solidarity (as introduced in the text). Overall, the solidarity study suggests that there is a certain base-line solidarity among ASEAN members which derives from a sense of belonging to the same grouping. However, whereas the case studies provide some evidence of relatively stable solidarity prior to the crisis (an assertion that is only partly substantiated by the analysis), solidarity in post-crisis ASEAN can be said to be relatively unstable and deficient, as serious norm breaches occcurred frequently and ASEAN members' general readiness to accept high economic or political solidarity costs was rather limited. There were also occasional crude cases of unsolidary behavior and opportunism affecting the foundations of the relations between member states, eroding the basis of trust and reliability. The fact that two ASEAN members, Malaysia and Vietnam, even disregarded the central ASEAN norm of resolving disputes by peaceful means and engaged in military incidents over territorial claims in the South Chna Sea shows that ASEAN members are sometimes still grappling with the very basics of peaceful coexistence.

ASEAN members' motivations and foreign policy interests vis-à-vis the regional great powers, i.e. the U.S., China and Japan, displayed many similarities at the beginning of the 21st century. Their frequently complementary respective foreign policy interests and agendas also encouraged more cohesive collective approaches to these three powers. Thus, after a period of frequently strained bilateral ties and discord between ASEAN members such as Indonesia, the Philippines and Malaysia and the U.S. in the 1990s, these states have recently sought to mend relations with the hegemon. ASEAN is presently pursuing improved trade relations with the U.S. and trying to engage the U.S. in FTA talks. With a view to China, ASEAN members have consistently pursued a distinctive policy of cautious, but constructive engagement and more predictable (friendly) relations with the East Asian neighbor, both at the bilateral and collective level. This attitude continues through 2002 and has even intensified at the collective level, with the establishment of the ASEAN Plus Three process and the official collective resolve of the ASEAN heads of government to follow China's initiative and engage in negotiations on an ASEAN-China FTA. As regards Japan, ASEAN members have expressed their interest in forming a free trade agreement with Japan and have – not at last through engaging in the APT process and stepping up ASEAN-China relations and promoting the ASEAN-China FTA – built up considerable collective pressure on Japan to show more economic commitment to the region and consider ASEAN-Japan FTA negotiations. Thus, as long as ASEAN members have shared interests and motives in dealing with external powers, ASEAN can serve as an effective consultative forum in the area of concerted approaches to foreign and foreign economic policy making. However, in the absence of more comprehensive collective policy approaches, such coherence can be expected to become unsustainable as and when national perceptions of third parties begin to diverge again.

Prospects for the formation of a specific East Asian identity through ASEAN Plus Three cooperation are rather limited. APT partners are too diverse and guided by different strategic interests as that they could form a politically relevant East Asian economic or political bloc in the foreseeable future. As two oppositional regional poles with rivaling strategic interests in Southeast Asia, Japan and China will seek to maximize their influence in APT and thus woo ASEAN as best they can. Paradoxically, the strategic rivalry between Japan and China can be expected to enhance APT cooperation as such and thus make the forum sustainable. However, the two poles' pull in opposite directions will not allow for closer pan-East Asian integration. The concrete findings of the analysis of APT were that most APT states advocate East Asian regionalism with a view to tieing East Asia into (U.S.-oriented) Asia-Pacific structures, whereas China is promoting more exclusive forms of pan-East Asian regionalism, but actually is primarily concentrating on establishing a strong China-ASEAN axis. Within ASEAN, Malaysia appears to be promoting more exclusive forms of pan-East Asian bloc-building (and considers APT to represent its original EAEC concept), but its motives in doing so remain rather hazy, as it seems essentially opposed to actual projects of closer East Asian integration. Japan is seeking to balance China's efforts and step up its political and economic profile in the region. A look at the achievements of APT so far suggests that there is wide scope for additional regional cooperation, ranging from development assistance and economic cooperation to dealing with transnational problems. However, progress in the area of the APT currency swap arrangements and mechanisms of economic and financial surveillance have been rather modest and ineffective to date. Considering that APT partners are still struggling with such basic tasks as promoting mutual trust and confidence-building, APT provides a large playing field to engage in various multilateral and bilateral cooperation exercises (though not integration). In this context, Northeast Asian relations may also improve through enhanced trilateral dialogue between China, Japan and Korea. With a view to economic integration, the proposed ASEAN-China FTA has triggered fierce competition between Japan and China and thus further divided the APT membership. Moreover, it is not at all certain whether the ASEAN-China FTA plan is going to work out in the end, not at last because of strong reluctance on the side of Malaysia, Indonesia and the Philippines. Nevertheless, regardless of APT's internal divisions and uncertainties, its dynamic has already started to change the political and economic landscape of East Asia. Thus, ASEAN has been able to enhance its leverage vis-à-vis Japan and China, profiting from their strategic opposition. Japan's reluctance to discuss trade liberalization with ASEAN members is already crumbling, as it is struggling to anchor the larger part of the APT membership more firmly in Asia-Pacific structures so as to preclude Chinese domination. Should Japan's "ASEAN plus five" model emerge as the basis of an East Asian FTA, it will represent a first step towards an Asia-Pacific FTA rather than an autonomous East Asian bloc. With a view to the five indicators of identity underlying this study, APT thus does not look set to develop a great potential in the areas of specific collective East Asian norms, institutionlization and pooling of sovereignty, genuine solidarity, and coherence vis-à-vis external parties.

2. Discussion

Relations between ASEAN states are firmly rooted in a set of collective norms that have helped sustain the ASEAN process for more than three decades. However, since the economic crisis of 1997, ASEAN has found it difficult to adapt traditional norms, which protect absolute national sovereignty, reject centralization and interference in each others' internal affairs and enforce decision making on the basis of the smallest common denominator, to

ASEAN's new challenges and objectives of closer and more systematic political and economic cooperation and integration. Thus, in the post-crisis period, ASEAN norms seemed to obstruct rather than promote the implementation of the new ASEAN agenda (as outlined in the ASEAN Vision 2020 and the Hanoi Plan of Action).

If unresolved, this norms deadlock will, as in the past, prevent ASEAN from pooling sovereignty and thus from turning into a more vertically integrated community. However, inflexible and antiquated as the ASEAN norms may seem, they represent the basis and vantage point of all ASEAN cooperation and remain accepted by all ASEAN members, even those demanding their adaptation to contemporary needs of deepening regional integration.

In the post-crisis period, differences between reform-oriented and more conservative ASEAN members about the interpretation of ASEAN norms and the future course of ASEAN integration have frequently caused intra-ASEAN tensions and were left largely unresolved. As a result, ASEAN appeared to be lacking cohesion and a common sense of direction. ASEAN members' frustration with this situation, enhanced by bleak economic prospects, appears to be mirrored by frequently deficient and unstable solidarity between ASEAN members in the aftermath of 1997. Certainly, solidarity among ASEAN members was lowest between 1998 and 2000. Since then, the situation seems to have relaxed.

The collective and respective individual postures and motivations of the ASEAN-5 states in dealing with the great powers in the region, i.e. the U.S., Japan and China, suggest a basic consensus about ASEAN's general disposition with regard to all three. Thus, as the region's main trading partner and security shield, the U.S. was seen as the main anchor for regional stability throughout the 1990s and beyond. However, this general disposition was frequently overshadowed as various core ASEAN member states' (such as the Philippines, Malaysia and Indonesia) bilateral relations with the increasingly less benign hegemon underwent serious strains and tensions at different times and for different reasons in the 1990s. Currently, bilateral strains between various ASEAN members and the U.S. appear to be on the mend, and ASEAN members have started bilaterally and collectively to pursue the conclusion of free trade agreements with the Bush government.

With a view to Northeast Asia, ASEAN members have always looked to Japan for economic and development assistance. During the economic crisis, Japan was the only ASEAN partner that came forth with substantial commitments to stabilize Southeast Asian economies. Since the crisis, ASEAN members, bilaterally and collectively, have increasingly called for Japanese economic assistance and access to the Japanese market. Most recently, ASEAN appears to have successfully instrumentalized the ASEAN Plus Three process to extol pledges of greater commitments to Southeast Asia from Japan. As regards

China, ASEAN members, both bilaterally and collectively, have engaged in cautious, but clearly constructive and optimistic engagement with China from the early 1990s on. In the course of this policy, bilateral and collective contacts with the respectfully accommodated East Asian neighbor have steadily intensified, most recently culminating in the ASEAN Plus Three process and ASEAN's collective determination to conduct serious negotiations on a China-ASEAN FTA. In the early 2000's, ASEAN members' positions vis-à-vis formative third parties appear to have converged recognizably, a development that is mirrored by the smoothing U.S.-Southeast Asian relations, the establishment of the ASEAN Plus Three process and subsequent dynamization of the ASEAN Plus One processes with the Northeast Asian dialogue partners of ASEAN.

In conclusion, ASEAN cooperation is based on collective norms, which have been internalized by at least the core ASEAN members and serve as the anchor point in the political debate about the future of the association. However, these norms are in need of revision, which has caused frictions between reform-oriented and more traditionalist member states. Unless the norms are revised, pooling of sovereignty cannot effectively be implemented in ASEAN. All major ASEAN initiatives for regional integration lack effectiveness because of many ASEAN member states' unwillingness to transfer national sovereignty and authority to regional institutions and mechanisms. Thus, ASEAN's very identity stands in the way not of widening ASEAN cooperation, but of effective deepening and regional integration. Erosion of ASEAN solidarity in the aftermath of 1997 suggests that more than three decades of socialization in ASEAN were not enough to establish genuinely stable relations between ASEAN members. Especially in times of trying crises ASEAN member states seem prone to neglect solidarity. However, while ASEAN cooperation provides important advantages to its member states on the one hand and on the other makes few direct demands on its members – and as each member can basically withdraw from its commitments (though not the normative code of ASEAN) – at any time, there is no actual risk of eventual deterioration or even dissolution of the association as such. Therefore, ASEAN can be expected to weather trying periods at very low input level, while ASEAN members will turn away from actual problems and seek to locate other, more promising areas of mutually beneficial (and non-binding) cooperation instead. ASEAN's focus on getting its act together in the area of its collective external relations appears to be a case in point: while internal integration is stuck due to strong intra-ASEAN differences, ASEAN, in lack of a grand design or strategy, has found a new tactical purpose in optimizing its external relations through more coordinated approaches to China, Japan and the U.S. Thus, ASEAN's loose structures of regional cooperation require it to frequently shed its skin and redefine its policies. This low-input and flexible-purpose network has good chances of sustaining a certain base-line of regional stability, but rather as a neighborhood watch group than an economically and politically integrated community of states. Likewise, ASEAN members' identification with the association can be considered strong enough to stick to the process as such and (though sometimes possibly only in lack of alternatives) find some comfort in its sustained existence. However, ASEAN members are not ready to cede national prerogatives to the collective. Therefore, ASEAN's collective identity can be likened to a thinly constituted, elastic and wide-meshed, but essentially firm net. Its chances of eventually evolving as a more thickly and tightly constituted collective identity appear to be rather limited.

In the case of ASEAN Plus Three, the findings of this study do not suggest that there is a specific East Asian identity in the making. Rather than generating identity, the forum is governed by strong polarization between Japan and China, whose respective main purpose in cooperating within APT is to compete for strategic and tactical influence in Southeast Asia. Within APT, Japan and China are mainly focused on accommodating ASEAN's need for functional and economic cooperation with Japan and China and political stability in the East Asian region. In the same vein, the fact that China, Japan and Korea have started to engage in separate intra-Northeast Asian dialogue may be seen as largely a gesture of goodwill on the side of Japan and China who both seek to develop a profile as responsible and reliable partners of ASEAN. Thus, basically all APT initiatives, from the Chiang Mai initiative to the various forms of development cooperation, are designed to solve Southeast Asian problems and have little direct impact on Japan and China. Nor does APT dialogue stand to essentially alter relations between the two Northeast Asian rivals.

Far from representing a process expressive of, or generating, East Asian identity, APT is a forum that, paradoxically, thrives on the deep divisions going through its membership. Thus, China and Japan participate because they cannot and do not want to leave the stage to the strategic opponent. On the other side, ASEAN is currently profiting from this rivalry in that it has found a lever to stir both sides' commitment to Southeast Asia by playing off the two sides against each other. Thus, the emergence of the APT process has been paralleled by increased activity in the area of the separate ASEAN Plus One talks with the respective Northeast Asian dialogue partners. The most striking example in this context is ASEAN's decision to agree to bilaterally negotiate an ASEAN-China FTA, which caused Koizumi to launch a diplomatic counter-offensive in a tour of Southeast Asia, during which he signaled Japan's readiness to drop its opposition to discussing bilateral trade liberalization with ASEAN. Against this general backdrop, there is little room for the evolution of specific collective East Asian norms, solidarity, shared positions vis-à-vis relevant third parties (especially the U.S.) or even progressive pan-East Asian regional integration.

Considering all these circumstances, any postulation of an unfolding and increasingly relevant East Asian identity would be clearly misguided.

Appendix:

BIBLIOGRAPHIC
REFERENCES

REFERENCES

ASEAN Documents:

- Agreement on the Common Effective Preferential Tariff Scheme for the ASEAN Free Trade Area, Singapore, 28 January 1992, at http://www.aseansec.org/economic/afta/afta_ag2.htm [13/12/00].

- Agreement on the Common Economic Effective Preferential Tariff Scheme for the ASEAN Free Trade Area, Singapore, 28 January 1992, http://www.aseansec.org/economic/afta_ag2.htm [13/12/00].

- Framework Agreement on Enhancing Economic Cooperation, Singapore, 28 January 1992, http://www.aseansec.org/economic/afta/afta_sg1.htm [13/12/00].

- Framework Agreement on the ASEAN Investment Area, Manila, 07 October 1998, http://www.aseansec.org/economic/fwagr_aia.htm [13/12/00].

- Declaration of ASEAN Concord, Denpasar (Bali), 24 February 1976.

- Treaty of Amity and Cooperation in Southeast Asia, Denpasar (Bali), 24 February 1976.

- Protocol Amending the Treaty of Amity and Cooperation in Southeast Asia, Manila, 15 December 1987.

- ASEAN Declaration (Bangkok Declaration), Bangkok, 08 August 1967, http://www.aseansec.org/history/leaders67.htm [03/03/00].

- ASEAN Plan of Action for Energy Cooperation 1999-2004, 1 July 1999, http://www.nepo.go.th/inter/ASEAN-PlanOf%20Action.html [11/05/01].

- ASEAN Regional Haze Action Plan (1997), December, http://www.aseansec.org/function/pa_haze.htm [02/07/01].

- ASEAN Vision 2020, ASEAN Summit, Kuala Lumpur, 15 December 1997, http://www.aseansec.org/summit/vision97.htm [03/03/00].

- ASEAN Regional Haze Action Plan, December 1997, http://www.aseansec.org/function/pa_haze.htm [02/07/01].

- Framework Agreement on the ASEAN Investment Area, Makati (Philippines), 07 October 1998, http://www.aseansec.org/economic/fwagr_aia.htm [13/12/00].

- Hanoi Plan of Action, Hanoi, 1998, http://www.aseansec.org/summit/6th/prg_hpoa.htm [29/02/00].

- Joint Ministerial Statement, Fifth ASEAN Finance Ministers Meeting, Kuala Lumpur, 7-8 April 2001, http://www.aseansec.or.id/economic/jps_5afmm.htm [02/05/01].

- Joint Press Statement, 14th AFTA Council Meeting, Chiang Mai, 4 October 2000.

- Protocol on Dispute Settlement Mechanism, Manila, 20th November 1996, http://www.aseansec.org/economic/dsm.htm [13/12/00].

- Protocol Regarding the Implementation of the CEPT Scheme Temporary Exclusion List, 4th Informal ASEAN Summit, Singapore, 23 November 2000, http://www.aseansec.org/summit/infs4_tel.htm.

- Protocol Regarding the Implementation of the CEPT Scheme Temporary Exclusion List", Fourth ASEAN Informal Summit, Singapore, 23 November 2000, http://www.aseansec.org/summit/infs4_tel.htm [27/11/00].

- Terms of Understanding on the Establishment of the ASEAN Surveillance Process, Washington, D.C., 4 October 1998, http://www.aseansec.org/economic/term_fin.htm [26/02/01].

- Treaty of Amity and Cooperation in Southeast Asia, Indonesia, 24 February 1976, http://www.aseansec.org/summit/amity/76.htm [03/03/00].

ASEAN Plus Three Documents:

- Joint Statement on East Asia Cooperation, Manila, 28 November 1999, http://www.aseansec.org/summit/inf3rd/js_eac.htm [21/02/00].

- Joint Ministerial Statement of the ASEAN+3 Finance Ministers Meeting, Honlulu, 09 May 2001, http://www.aseansec.org/economic/jms_as+3fmm.htm [07/06/01]

- Press statement by the Chairman of the 7th ASEAN Summit and the 5th ASEAN+3 Summit, Bandar Seri Begawan, 05 November 2001 (manuscript received in print at the occasion of a visit at the Ministry of Foreign Affairs in Bangkok in December 2001).

- Press statement by the Chairman of the 7th ASEAN Summit and the three ASEAN+1 Summits, Bandar Seri Begawan, 06 November 2001 (manuscript received in print at the occasion of a visit at the Ministry of Foreign Affairs in Bangkok in December 2001).

General References:

- Abdullah, Ahmad (2002): "Reviving Malaysia-US ties", *Business Times*, Singapore, http://www.emedia.com.my/Current_News/BT/Wednesday/Sport/200205 08025750 [13/05/02].

- Acharya, Amitav (1997): "Ideas, Identity, and institution-building: from the 'ASEAN way' to the 'Asia-Pacific way'?, *The Pacific Review*, 10, 3, pp. 319-346.

—— (1999): "Realism, Institutionalism and the Asian Economic Crisis", *Contemporary Southeast Asia*, 21, 1, pp. 1-29.

- Aditjondro, George J. (2000): "Suharto's Fires", *Inside Indonesia*, Jan-Mar 2000, http://www.insideindonesia.org/edit65/aditijondro.htm [02/07/01].

- AFTA Council (2000): Joint Press Statement, 14th AFTA Council Meeting, Chiang Mai, 4 October, http://www.aseansec.org/economic/aem/31/eco_ac14.htm [24/11/00].

- AFTA Online: (23 February 2001): "Malaysia blocks Australia and New Zealand", http;//www.aftaonline.com/cvrstryfeb23.html [11/05/01].

—— (2002): "Singapore backs economic integration: Trade pact with US to include economic integration", AFTA Watch, http://www.aftaonline.com/aftawatch.html [04/04/02].

—— (17 April 2002): "Economic Developments – Currency swap talks with South Korea and China", country report on the Philippines, http://www.aftaonline.com/country reports.html [17/04/02].

- Agence France Press (21 February 2001): "Malaysia issues warning on economic links", www.singapore-window.org/sw01/010220af.htm [04/05/01].

—— (16 November 2001): "Thailand vetoes ASEAN support for Myanmar over ILO sanctions", http://www.freespeech.org/bai/news/newsint/nov00int161100.html [08/05/01].

—— (31 January 2002): "Indonesia may ride on proposed US-Singapore free trade pact", http://www.google.de/search?q=cache:eqIvUH3S3NoC:asia.news.yahoo. com/020131/afp/020131044522indonesia.html+indonesia+singapore+us+ fta&hl=de [04/07/02].

- Aggestam, Lisbeth (1999): *Role Conceptions and the Politics of Identity in Foreign Policy*, ARENA Working Paper no. 99/8, http://www.arena.uio.no/publications/wp99_8.htm [05/06/01].

- Alatas, Ali (1998): "We Have Solidarity", interview with Ali Alatas, *Asiaweek.com,* 25 December, http://www.cnn.com/ASIANOW/asiaweek/98/1225/nat4.html [26/06/2000].

—— (1999a): Statement at the Ceremony of Cambodia's admission to ASEAN, Hanoi, 30 April, http://www.asean.or.id/news/accam_in.htm [10/07/00].

—— (1999b): Opening Statement, 32nd AMM, Singapore, 23 July, http://wwwaseansecorg/amm/amm32osi.htm [19/06/00].

—— (2001): "'ASEAN Plus Three' Equals Prosperity and Peace", Trends in Southeast Asia series, no. 2., Singapore: Institute of Southeast Asian Studies, January, paper delivered at the Regional Outlook Forum organized by ISEAS, Singapore, 5 January, http://www.iseas.edu.sg/trends221.pdf [19/10/01].

- American Chamber of Commerce, Singapore (2002): "U.S.-Singapore Free Trade Agreement", 27 February, http://www.amcham.org.sg/Home/position.htm [28/05/02].

- *Antara* (1 October 1999): "Malaysia wants ASEAN to handle East Timor peace-keeping job", http://www.indonesia-ottawa.org/news/Timtim/ET-N.antara_100199.htm [07/03/01].

- Anuraj Manibhandu: "China, Japan plan to fund Asean initiatives", *Bangkok Post*, 26 November 2000, http://www.bangkokpost.com/261100/261100_News12.html [27/11/00].

- Anwar, Dewi Fortuna (2000): "National versus Regional Resilience? An Indonesian Perspective". In: *Southeast Asian Perspectives on Security*, ed. Derek da Cunha, Singapore: Institute of Southeast Asian Studies, pp. 81-97.

- ASEAN Calendar 2001 and ASEAN Calendar 2002, as provided by the ASEAN Secretariat, http://www.aseansec.org/general /calendar/jan02.htm , http://www.aseansec.org/general /calendar/feb02.htm, http://www.aseansec.org/general /calendar/mar02.htm, http://www.aseansec.org/general /calendar/apr02.htm, http://www.aseansec.org/general /calendar/may02.htm, http://www.aseansec.org/general /calendar/jun02.htm, http://www.aseansec.org/general /calendar/jul02.htm, http://www.aseansec.org/general /calendar/agus02.htm, http://www.aseansec.org/general /calendar/sept02.htm,

http://www.aseansec.org/general /calendar/oct02.htm,
http://www.aseansec.org/general /calendar/nov02.htm,
http://www.aseansec.org/general /calendar/dec02.htm,
http://www.aseansec.org/general /calendar/jan01.htm,
http://www.aseansec.org/general /calendar/feb01.htm,
http://www.aseansec.org/general /calendar/mar01.htm,
http://www.aseansec.org/general /calendar/apr01.htm,
http://www.aseansec.org/general /calendar/may01.htm,
http://www.aseansec.org/general /calendar/jun01.htm,
http://www.aseansec.org/general /calendar/jul01.htm,
http://www.aseansec.org/general /calendar/agus01.htm,
http://www.aseansec.org/general /calendar/sept01.htm,
http://www.aseansec.org/general /calendar/oct01.htm,
http://www.aseansec.org/general /calendar/nov01.htm,
http://www.aseansec.org/general /calendar/dec01.htm.

- ASEAN Economic Ministers (2001): Joint Press Conference of the 7th AEM Retreat Statement", 3 May.

- ASEAN Eminent Persons Group (2000): *Report on Vision 2020: The People's ASEAN*, 4th Informal ASEAN Summit, 24 November, http://www.aseansec.org/summit/infs4_epg.htm [13/12/00].

- ASEAN Finance Ministers (1998): "Terms of Understanding on the Establishment of the ASEAN Surveillance Process, Washington, D.C., 4 October, http://www.aseansec.org/economic/term_fin.htm [26/02/01].

—— (2001): Joint Ministerial Statement, Fifth ASEAN Finance Ministers Meeting, Kuala Lumpur, 7-8 April, http://www.aseansec.or.id/economic/jps_5afmm.htm

- ASEAN Foreign Ministers (2000): Joint Communique, 33rd AMM, Bangkok, 25 July, http://www.aseansec.org/politics/pramm33.htm [09/02/01].

- ASEAN Heads of Government (2000): Press Statement by the Chairman, 4th ASEAN Informal Summit, Singapore, 25 November.

- ASEAN Ministerial Meeting on Haze, 3rd (1998): Joint Press Statement, 4 April.

- ASEAN Secretariat (1995): *AFTA Reader*, vol.2, Jakarta.

—— (2000): "ASEAN Free Trade Area", Jakarta, information received via email from Nora'in Asli, an ASEAN Secretariat official, on 12/02/01.

—— (undated a): "ASEAN Investment Area: An Update" http://www.aseansec.org/general/publication/aia_upd.htm [26/02/01].

—— (undated b): "The ASEAN Secretariat: Basic Mandate, Functions and Composition", http://www.aseansec.org/politics/asec_rlst.htm [07/03/01].

—— (undated c): "The ASEAN Troika", http://www.aseansec.org/amm/as_troika.htm [13/12/00].

—— (undated d): "ASEAN-China Dialogue", Jakarta, http://www.aseansec.org/view.asp?file=/dialog/mchi.htm [23/05/02]

—— (undated e): "ASEAN Investment Area: An Update", http://www.aseansec.org/general/publication/aia_upd.htm [26/02/01].

—— (undated f): "The ASEAN Secretariat: Basic Mandate, Functions and Composition", http://www.aseansec.org/print.asp?file=politics/asec_rlst.htm [04/07/02].

—— (undated g): "The ASEAN Troika", http://www.aseansec.org/amm/as_troika.htm [13/12/00].

- ASEAN+3 Finance Ministers (2001): "Joint Ministerial Statement", 9 May, Honolulu (USA), http://www.aseansec.org/economic /jms_as+3fmm.htm [07/06/01].

- ASEAN+3 Heads of Government: Joint Statement on East Asia Cooperation, Manila, 28 November 1999, http://www.aseansec.org/summit/inf3rd/js_eac.htm [21/02/00].

- ASEAN-China Experts Group on Economic Cooperation (2001): "Forging Closer ASEAN-China Economic Relations in the Twenty-First Century", report submitted October, http://www.aseansec.org/newdata/asean_chi.pdf [18/03/02].

- *Asia Pacific Management News* (29 October 1997): "Stir over Singaporean and Malaysian aid to Indonesia", http://www.ampforum.com/news/apmn102.htm [22/05/01].

- *Asia Times Online* (8 March 2001): "Momentum for East Asian economic community", http://www.atimes.com/se-asia/CC08Ae01.html [05/02/02].

—— (23 May 2001): "China, Thailand strengthen 'family' bond", http://www.atimes.com/se-asia/CE23Ae03.html [26/05/01].

—— (04 April 2002): "ASEAN eyes expanded FTA", http://www.atimes.com/se-asia/DD04Ae01.html [29/04/02].

- *Asiaweek* (1 September 2000): "'We Must stick Together' - ASEAN's top minds consider how to keep the organization relevant", 26, 34, http://www.asiaweek.com/asiaweek/magazine/2000/0901/asean.roundtable.html [18/04/02].

- Associated Press (16 March 2000): "China, Asean agree on Spratlys code", http://www.inquirer.net/issues/mar2000/mar16/news/news_5.html [10/07/00].

- Australian Associated Press (03 April 2002): "Japan to push Howard on trade", http://news.ninemsn.com.au/Business/story_28803.asp [18/04/02].

—— (04 April 2002): "Singapore backs economic integration", http://www.aftaonline.com/aftawatch.html [04/04/02].

- Austria, Myrna S.; John Lawrence V. Avila (2001): *Looking Beyond AFTA: Prospects and Challenges for Inter-Regional Trade*, Philippine Institute for Development Studies (PIDS) Discussion Paper Series, no. 2001-10, April, http://dirp4.pids.gov.ph/ris/pdf/pidsdps0110.PDF [29/08/01].

- Badawi, Abdullah (1998a): Opening Statement, 31st AMM, Manila, 24 July, http://202.186.32.3/KLN/statemen.nsf/d9696fa2492631ddc82565a9001ea b29/538f824c45090f81c825664c00143a26?OpenDocument [15/06/00].

—— (1998b): "'Stick To Tradition' – A top diplomat gives his views", *Asiaweek.com*, 25 December, http://www.cnn.com/ASIANOW/asiaweek/98/1225/nat2.html [26/06/2000].

- Baja, Lauro L. Jr. (2002): Statement at the Department of Foreign Affairs foreign policy briefing for the diplomatic corps, 16 January, http://www.dfa.gov.ph/archive/speech/usec/fpbriefing.htm [06/05/02].

- Baker, Richard W.; Christopher A McNally; Charles E. Morrison (eds.) (1999): *Asia Pacific Security Outlook 1999*, Tokyo, New York: Japan Center for International Exchange (JCIE).

—— (2001): *Asia Pacific Security Outlook 2001*, Tokyo, New York: Japan Center for International Exchange (JCIE).

- *Bangkok Post* (26 November 2000): "China, Japan plan to fund Asean initiatives", http://www.bangkokpost.com/261100/261100_News12.html [27/11/00].

—— (5 May 2001): "Asean must move towards integration", http://www.bangkokpost.net/050501/050501_News23.html [08/05/01].

—— (13 May 2002): "China to protect ist farm sector for now", http://www.google.com/search?q=cache:irJm2e-q0q8C:www.bangkokpost.net/Business/13May2002_biz43.html+thaksin+china&hl=de [15/05/02].

- Bayuni, Endi M. (2000): "Singapore investors wait for more signals from Indonesian Government", *Jakarta Post*, 7 March, http://indonesia-ottawa.org/economy/OPINION/singaporeinvestment.html [22/05/01].

388

- BBC News (30 April 2001): "Thai-Burmese tensions at ASEAN meet", http://news.bbc.co.uk/hi/english/world/asia-pacific/newsid_1304000/1304414.stm [08/0501].

—— (3 May 2001): "Burmese talks feared stalled", http://news.bbc.co.uk/hi/english/world/asia-pacific/newsid_1310000/1310628.stm [08/05/01].

—— (24 March 2002): "China pledges $400m to Indonesia", http://www.news.bbc.co.uk/hi/english/world/asia-pacific/newsid_1891000/1891007.stm [17/05/02].

—— (05 April 2002): "US-Asian free trade zone no nearer", http://news.bbc.co.uk/hi/english/business/newsid_1912000/1912961.stm [28/05/02].

- Berg, Wolfgang (1999): "Kollektive Identität. Zugänge und erste Überlegungen". In: *Kulturunterschiede. Interdisziplinäre Konzepte zu kollektiven Identitäten und Mentalitäten*, ed. Heinz Hahn, Frankfurt: IKO - Verlag für Interkulturelle Kommunikation, pp. 217-238.

- Berthier, Serge (1999): "The only way for ASEAN", interview with Rodolfo Severino, ASEAN Secretariat homepage, http://www.asean.or.id/secgen/aseanway.htm [20/08/00].

- Bessho, Koro (1999): *Identities and Security in East Asia*, New York: Oxford University Press [Institute for International and Strategic Studies, Adelphi Paper 325].

- Bilson Kurus (1993): "Understanding ASEAN: Benefits and Raison d'Etre", *Asian Survey*, 33 (1993), 8, pp. 819-831.

- BizAsiaNews (16 May 2000): "Non-tariff Barriers rising in Asean Free Trade Area", http://www.bizasia.com/gen/articles/stand_art.htm?ac=FC9R7-7 [16/05/01].

- Blechinger, Verena (2000): "Flirting with Regionalism: Japan's Foreign Policy Elites and the East Asian Economic Caucus". In: *Facing Asia: Japan's Role in the Political and Economic Dynamism of Regional Cooperation,* ed. V. Blechinger and J. Leggewie, Munich: Iudicum, pp. 57-86.

——; Jochen Leggewie (2000): "Action and Direction, direct and Indirect Leadership: Re-evaluating Japan's Role in Asian Regional Cooperation". In: *Facing Asia: Japan's Role in the Political and Economic Dynamism of Regional Cooperation,* ed. V. Blechinger and J. Leggewie, Munich: Iudicum, pp. 297-324.

—— (2001): "Between Bilateralism and Regionalism: Business and the State in Japan's Relations with Asia". In: *Interdependence in the Asia Pacific*, ed. Bert Edström, Stockholm: The Swedish Institute of International Affairs, 2001 [Conference Papers 28], pp. 71-90.

- Boekle, Henning; Volker Rittberger; Wolfgang Wagner (1999): *Normen und Außenpolitik: Konstruktivistische Außenpolitiktheorie*, Univ. of Tübingen [Working Paper Series on International Politics and Peace Research, no. 34].

- Boyd, Alan (2002): "ASEAN's military buildup threatens détente with China", *Asia Times Online*, 8 May, http://www.atimes.com/se-asia/DE08Ae03.html [08/05/02]

- Brandmaier, Frank (2000): "Myanmar: stumbling block in EU, ASEAN talks", *Dawn*, 13 December, http://www.dawn.com/2000/12/13/int14.htm [08/05/01].

- Brandon, John J. (1999): "Lifting Southeast Asia's haze", *Christian Science Monitor online*, 19 September, http://www.csmonitor.com/durable/1999/09/p11s1.htm [02/07/01].

- Breckon, Lyall (2001a): "U.S. – ASEAN Relations: Wanted: More Attention from the United States", *Comparative Connections*, 3, 2, http://www.csis.org/pacfor/cc/0102Qus_asean.html [03/04/02].

—— (2001b): "Solid in Supoprt for U.S. ... So Far", *Comparative Connections*, 3, 3, http://www.csis.org/pacfor/cc/0103Qus_asean.html [03/04/02].

—— (2001c): "China-Southeast Asia Relations - Gains for Beijing in an Otherwise Gloomy Quarter", *Comparative Connections*, 3, 4, http://www.csis.org/pacfor/cc/0104Qchina_asean.html [23/01/02].

—— (2002): "China-ASEAN Relations: Courtship and Competition", *Comparative Connections*, 4, 1, http://www.csis.org/pacfor/cc/0201Qchina_asean.html [08/05/02].

- *Bridges-Weekly Trade News* Digest (09 April 2002): "News from the Regions: ASEAN-US", vol.6, no.13, http://www.ictsd.org/weekly/02-04-09/story3.htm [28/05/02].

- Buenaventura, Rafael B. (2000): "Some Thoughts on the Prospect for Asian Economic Cooperation", speech at the "First International Conference on Asian Political Parties", Manila, 19 September, http://www.bsp.gov.ph/archive/Speeches_2000/SomeThoughts.htm [18/04/02].

- *Business Recorder* (6 October 2000): "Southeast Asia struggles to defuse trade dispute", http://www.brecorder.com/story/S00DD/SDJ06/SDJ06170.htm [15/05/01].

- Busse, Nikolas (1999): "Constructivism and Southeast Asian Security", *The Pacific Review*, 12, 1, pp. 39-60.

―― (2000): *Die Entstehung von kollektiven Identitäten: Das Beispiel der ASEAN*, Baden-Baden: Nomos.

- Buszinsky, Leszek (1998): "Thailand and Myanmar: the perils of 'constructive engagement'", *The Pacific Review*, 11, 2, pp. 290-305.

- Camroux, David (2001): "Die ASEAN vor dem Ende"[The near end of ASEAN], *Le Monde Diplomatique*, German version, 16 February, http://monde-diplomatique.de/mtpl/2001/02/16/a0030.stext?Name=askHDg22b&idx=0 [25 April 2001].

- Castellano, Marc (1999): "Japan cheers new Indonesian leadership", *JEI Report* [Japan Economic Instititute], no. 41, 29 October, http://www.jei.org/Archive/JEIR99/9941w4.html [03/05/02].

- Castle, James (2002): "Jakarta gains from rise of China, India", *The Straits Times*, Singapore, 12 April, http://www.google.com/search?q=cache:vRNc-RHc4dEC:straitstimes.asia.1.com.sg/analysis/story/0,1870,113639,00.html [03/05/02].

- Catley, Bob (1999): "Hegemonic America: The Arrogance of Power", *Contemporary Southeast Asia*, 21, 2, pp. 157-175.

- Chairman of the 4th ASEAN Summit: "The Way Forward: Initiative For ASEAN Integration", Press Statement, 4th ASEAN Informal Summit, Singapore, 25 November 2000, http://www.asean.or.id/summit/infs4_cps.htm [02/05/01].

- Chairman of the 7th ASEAN Summit and the 5th ASEAN+3 Summit: Press statement, Bandar Seri Begawan, 05 November 2001 (obtained in print at the occasion of a visit at the Ministry of Foreign Affairs in Bangkok in December 2001).

- Chanda, Nayan (1994): "Divide and Rule: Beijing Scores points on South China Sea", *FEER*, 11 August, p. 18.

――; R. Tiglao; J. McBeth (1995): "Territorial Imperative", *FEER*, 158 (1995), 8, 23 February, pp. 14-16.

- Chandrasekaran, Rajiv (2002): "Indonesia and U.S. wind up talks on resuming military relations", *International Herald Tribune*, 26 April, http://www.iht.com/articles/55888.htm [02/05/02].

- Chang Li Lin; Ramkishen S. Rajan (1999a): "Regional Responses to the Southeast Asian Financial Crisis: A Case of Self-Help or No Help?", Singapore: Institute of Policy Studies, 1 June, http://www.swissasiafoundation.org/publicat/pb_47rr.pdf [20/03/2000] [also published in *Australian Journal of International Affairs*, 53 (1999), 3, pp. 261-282].

——; Ramkishen S. Rajan (1999b): *Regional Responses to the Southeast Asian Economic Crisis: A Case of Self-Help or No-Help?*, Singapore: Institute of Policy Studies (IPS) Working Paper no. 8, June, http://www.ips.org.sg/pub/wp8.pdf [20/11/00].

——; Ramkishen S. Rajan (2000): *Regional Versus Multilateral Solutions to Transboundary Environmental Problems: Insights from the Southeast Asian Haze*, Centre for International Economic Studies Discussion Paper No.41, Adelaide: University of Adelaide, October 2000, http://pandora.nla.gov.au/parchive/2001/S2001-Mar-8/www.adelaide.edu.au/CIES/0041.pdf [02/07/01].

- Cheng, Joseph Y.S. (2001): "Sino-ASEAN relations in the Early Twenty-first Century", *Contemporary Southeast Asia*, 23, 3, pp. 420-451.

- Cheng, Michael et al. (1998): "Foreign Policy: Loans to Indonesia (1998)", Socratic Circle, Singapore, http://www.socraticcircle.org.sg/resources/papers/loans.html [22/05/01].

- *Chinadaily.com* (20 January 2001): "Thai PM proposes speedily open ASEAN-China free trade area", http://www.chinadaily.net/news/2002-01-20/52891.html [16/05/02].

- Ching, Cheong (2001): "China gains big in FTA deal with ASEAN", *The Straits Times*, Singapore, 30 November, p. 27.

- Cho, Whan-Bok (2001): "Globalization and Outlook for Korea's Economic Diplomacy", *Korea Focus*, 9, 2, http://www.kofo.or.kr/KoreaFocus/content.asp?no=363&title=VOL0902%20%20%20&category=ess [21/04/02].

- Chua, Lee Hong (2000): "'Two big ideas' to boost East Asia", *Straits Times*, Singapore, 27 November, http://straitstimes.asia1.com.sg/primenews/story/0,1870,5860,00.html [27/11/00]

- Chuan, Leekpai (1998): Opening Address, 6th ASEAN Summit, Hanoi, 15 December 1998.

—— (2000): Opening Address, AMM, Bangkok, 24 July, http://www.aseansec.org/amm/amm33wel.htm [24/07/00].

- Chulacheeb, Chinwanno (1999): "Thailand-China Economic Relations: From Strategic Partnership to Economic Partnership", International University of Japan (IUJ) Research Institute Working Paper, Asia Pacific Series, no. 6, May, http://www.iuj.ac.jp/research/wpap006.cfm [15/05/02].

- Clad, James (2000): "Fin de Siecle, Fin de l'ASEAN?", *PacNet*, 9, 3 March, http://www.nyu.edu/globalbeat/asia/Pacnet030300.html [19/06/01];

- Cohen, Margot; Murray Hiebert (1997): "Where There's Smoke …", *Far Eastern Economic Review*, 2 October, p. 28-29.

—— (2001): "Reality Bites: Asean says its more developed members must help the others. A low-cost basic approach is best", *FEER*, 16 August, http://www.feer.com/2001/0108_16/p028region.html [04/09/01].

- Corben, Ron (1999): "Thailand-East Timor", correspondent report, *Voice of America*, 19 October, http://www.fas.org/man/dod-101/ops/war/1999/10/991019-timor2.htm [11/06/01].

- Cossa, Ralph A. (1998): "Mischief Reef: A Double Betrayal", *PacNet* no. 49, 22 December 1998, http://www.nyu.edu/globalbeat/asia/Cossa122298.html [31/05/01].

- Cotton, James (1999): "The 'haze' over Southeast Asia: Challenging the ASEAN Mode of Regional Engagement", *Pacific Affairs*, 72 (1999), 3, pp. 331-352.

- Country Watch (undated): "Minister: Indonesia, Singapore agree to settle differences quietly", report based on news dispatches by the *Jakarta Post*, http://www.countrywatch.com@school/as_wire.asp?vCountry=154&UID=690894 [19/03/02].

- Crispin, Shawn W. (2000): "Ties that Bind", *FEER*, 10 August, http://www.feer.com/_0008_10/p22region.html [24/04/01].

——; Bertil Lintner (2001): "Something for Nothing - Talks between Burma's junta and Aung San Suu Kyi are faltering as Japan leads Asia in breaking with a Western-led ban on bilateral aid", *Far Eastern Economic Review*, 10 May, http://www.feer.com/_0105_10/p028region.html [08/05/01].

- Darmp, Sukontasap (1997): "ASEAN's Problem of Common Interest", *The Nation*, 6 June, http://www.sintercom.org/sef97/myanmar_news.html [14/05/01].

- Dent, Christopher M. (2001): "Singapore's Foreign Economic Policy: The pursuit of Economic Security", *Contemporary Southeast Asia*, 23, 1, pp. 1-23.

- Dieter, Heribert (2000a): "Asia's Monetary Regionalism", The 5th Column, *Far Eastern Economic Review*, 06 July, http://www.feer.com/2000/0007_06/p30.html [06/09/01].

—— (2000b): "Ostasien nach der Krise: Interne Reformen, neue Finanzarchitektur und monetärer Regionalismus", *Aus Politik und Zeitgeschichte*, no. 37/38, pp. 21-28.

—— (2001): "East Asia's Puzzling Regionalism", The 5th Column, *Far Eastern Economic* Review, 12 July, p. 29. (http://www.feer.com/_0107_12/p029fcol.html [05/07/01].

——; Richard Higgott (2001): "Ostasiens Weg in eine Währungsunion", *Internationale Politik* [International Politics], 56, 4, pp. 45-50.

- Dolven, Ben (1999): "Friend or Foe? Singapore tries to figure out Indonesia's new leaders", *FEER*, 25 March, http://www.feer.com/9903_25/p22foreign.html [24/04/01] or http://www.moe.edu.sg/neu/online/pub-content-feer.html [16/05/01].

——; John McBeth (1998): "Ties fray as S'pore cools towards Indonesia", *FEER*, 9 July, in: Singapore Window, http://www.singapore-window.org/80709fe.htm [05/02/01].

- Dosch, Jörn (1996): "Die ASEAN – Kooperations- und Integrationsleistungen, Perspektiven". In: Kooperation, Regionalismus und Integration im asiatisch-pazifischen Raum, ed. Guido Eilenberger, Manfred Mols, Jürgen Rüland, Hamburg: Institut für Asienkunde, 1996, pp.103-120.

—— (1997): *Die ASEAN: Bilanz eines Erfolges, Akteure, Interessenlagen, Kooperationsbeziehungen*, Hamburg: Abera [also: PhD thesis, University of Mainz, 1996].

——; Manfred Mols (1998): "Thirty Years of ASEAN: achievements and challenges", *The Pacific Review*, 11, 2, pp. 167-182.

- Dupont, Alan (2000): "ASEAN's Response to the East Timor Crisis", *Australian Journal of International Affairs*, 54, 2, pp. 163-170.

- *Economic Intelligence Review* (April 2002): "America Leading The Way For ASEAN Free Trade", as re-released by AsianInt.com, http://www.aisaint.com/top/TOP983.asp [28/05/02].

- EEPSEA/ WWF (1999): "The Indonesian Fires and Haze of 1997: The Economic Toll", Research Report, Singapore: ISEAS, August, http://www.eepsea.org/publications/research1/ACF62.html [02/07/01].

- Estrada, Joseph E. (1999): Welcome Remarks at the Summit Opening Ceremonies, 3rd ASEAN Informal Summit, Manila, 28 November, http://www.aseansec.org/summit/inf3rd/prg_wel.htm [10/07/00].

- Fabiola Desy Unijadijaja; Tiarma Siboro (2002): "Distrust hurts Indonesia-Singapore relations, says analyst", *Jakarta Post*, 23 February, http://www.thejakartapost.com/yesterdaydetail.asp?fileid=20020223.B10 [25/02/02].

- *Far Eastern Economic Review* (24 December 1998): "'Tis the Season", p. 18.

—— (07 February, 2002): "Bush-Mahathir Meet a No-Go", *FEER* Intelligence , http://lamankm2.tripod.com/cgi-bin/forum.cgi?print=6690 [25/04/02] (originally: http://www.feer.com/articles/2002/0202_07/p008intell.html [08/02/02].

—— (16 May 2002): "China Briefing", section entitled Southeast Asia, http://www.feer.com/articles/2002/0205_16/p022china.html [13/05/02].

- Finnemore, Martha; Kathryn Sikkink (1998): "International Norm Dynamics and Political Change", *International Organization*, 52, 4, pp. 887-917.

- Fukagawa, Yukiko (2000): "Japan-Korea FTA as a New Initiative in East Asia: Beyond Bitterness", Tokyo, May, Global Communication Platform (GLOCOM) homepage, http://www.glocom.org/opinions/essays/200005_fukagawa_jp_kr_fta/index.html [16/01/02].

- Funston, John (1999): "Challenges Facing ASEAN in a More Complex Age", *Contemporary Southeast Asia*, 21, 2, pp. 205-219.

- Gan, Ivan (1999): "Smoke gets in Asean's eyes", *Asia Times Online*, 14 August, http://www.atimes.com/se-asia/AH14Ae01.html [02/07/01].

- Ganesan, N. (2000): "ASEAN's relations with Major External Powers", *Contemporary Southeast Asia*, 22, 2, pp. 258-278.

- Goh, Chok Tong (1998): Opening Statement, 6th ASEAN Summit, Hanoi, 16 December, www.aseansec.org/summit/6th/prg_opsn.htm [13/06/00].

—— (1999a): "ASEAN – Meeting the Challenges Ahead", Keynote Address, 32nd AMM, Singapore, 23 July, http://www.gov.sg/mfa/amm/speeches/1999072300.html [15/06/00]. [GohAMM99]

—— (1999b): "Finally Being His Own Man", Interview with Goh Chok Tong, *Asiaweek.com*, 25 November, http://www.cnn.com/ASIANOW/asiaweek/interview/goh.chok.tong/index.html [21/06/00].

—— (1999c): Transcript of remarks by the Prime Minister of Singapore to the media after the 3rd ASEAN Informal Summit, Manila, 28 November, http://app.internet.gov.sg/scripts/mfa/pr/read_content.asp?View,379, [sic!] [15/06/00].

—— (2002), speech at the official dinner in honor of Prime Minister Koizumi, Singapore, 13 January, http://www.gov.sg/singov/announce/130102pm2.htm [30/04/02].

- Guerin, William A. (2000): "Singapore vs. Indonesian relationship – Is racism the problem?", *Business Indonesia Suratkabar.com*, 12 November, http://www.suratkabar.com/arsip/bill/1112.shtml [02/05/01].

- Guyot, James F. (1997): "Burma in 1996: One Economy, Two Politics", *Asian Survey*, 37, 2, pp. 188-193.

—— (1998): "Burma in 1997: From empire to ASEAN", *Asian Survey*, 38, 2, pp. 191-196.

- Haacke, J. (1999): "The concept of flexible engagement and the practice of enhanced interaction: intramural challenges to the 'ASEAN way'", *The Pacific Review*, 12, 4, 581-611.

- Habibie, B.J. (1998): Opening Statement, 6th ASEAN Summit, Hanoi, 15 December, http://www.aseansec.org/summit/6th/prg_opid.htm [13/06/00].

- Hatakeyama, Noboru (2002): "Japan's New Regional Trade Policy – Which country comes after Singapore?", Second annual Whitman International Lecture, Institute of International Economics, Washington, D.C., 13 March, http://www.iie.com/papers/hatakeyama0302.htm [27/05/02].

- Hechter, Michael (1987): *Principles of Group Solidarity*, Chapter II: "The Problem", Berkeley: Univ. of California Press.

- Henderson, Jeannie (1999): *Reassessing ASEAN*, London: Oxford Univ. Press [Institute for International and Strategic Studies, Adelphi Paper 328].

- Hernandez, Carolina G. (1996): "The Philipines in 1995: Growth Amid Challenges", *Asian Survey*, 36, 2, pp. 142-151.

- Hew, Denis; Mely C. Anthony (2000): "ASEAN and ASEAN+3 in Postcrisis Asia", *NIRA Review*, 7, 4, pp. 21-26, http://www.nira.go.jp/publ/review/2000autumn/hewanthony.pdf [05/02/02].

- Hiebert, Murray /John McBeth (1997): "Trial By Fire: Smog crisis tests Asean's vaunted cooperation", *Far Eastern Economic Review*, 16 October, p. 16.

- Hu, Wixing; Gerald Chan; Daojian Zha (2000): *China's International Relations in the 21st Century: Dynamics of Paradigm* Shift, New York: University Press of America.

- Huang, Kwei-Bo (2002): "The China-ASEAN Free Trade Area: Background, Framework and Political Implications", Taipei: Taiwan Research Institute, Division of Strategic and International Studies [Peace Forum, Essays], http://www.dsis.org.tw/peaceforum/papers/2002-02/APE0202001e.pdf [10/05/02].

- Hund, Markus; Nuria Okfen (2001): "Vom East Asian Economic Caucus (EAEC) zu ASEAN Plus Three" [From EAEC to APT]. In: *Multilateralismus in Ostasien-Pazifik: Probleme und Herausforderungen im neuen Jahrhundert*, ed. Hanns W. Maull and Dirk Nabers, Hamburg: Institut für Asienkunde [Institute of Asian Affairs], pp. 68-86.

- Huxley, Tim (2001): "Singapore in 2000: Continuing Stability and Renewed Prosperity amid Regional Disarray", *Asian Survey*, 41, 1, pp. 201-207.

- Inbaraj, Sonny (1997): "The media's repsonsibility for East Timor", *The Nation* (Bangkok), 30 March, http://202.44.251.4/nationnews/1997/199703/19970330/3571.html [07/03/01].

—— (2000): "Asean's commitment to East Timor faces tough test", *Asia Times Online*, 1 February, http://www.atimes.com/se-asia/BB01Ae01.html [11/06/01].

- Indonesian Weekly Netnews (2002): "President Megawati satisfied about results of her visit to China", http://www.google.com/search?q=cache:Qg72bBy_e9wC:httpd.chello.nl/~p. groenewegen/new_page_3.htm [17/05/02].

- Irawan Abidin (2000): "The Stakes Between Singapore and Indonesia", Homepage of the Embassy of the Republic of Indonesia in Ottawa (Canada), 05 December, http://www.indonesia-ottawa.org/Perspective/December/120500_JP_01.htm [16/05/01].

- James, Colin (2000): "Tariff Terminator - A free-trade agreement between Singapore and new Zealand aims at shaking up Asean", *FEER*, 17 August, http://www.feer.com/_0008_17/p26region.html [21/12/00].

- Japan, Ministry of Foreign Affairs (2001a): "Japan-Indonesia Summit Meeting (Overview)", 28 September, http://www.mofa.go.jp/region/asia-paci/indonesia/pv0109/overview.html [03/05/02].

—— (2001b): "Japan-Philippines Summit Meeting (Outline)", 14 September, http://www.mofa.go.jp/region/asia-paci/philippine/pv0109/summit.html [06/05/02].

—— (2002): "Boao Forum for Asia, Summit Meeting between Prime Minister Junichiro Koizumi and Prime Minister Thaksin Shinawatra (Overview)", 15 April, http://www.mofa.go.jp/region/asia-paci/china/boao0204/thailand.html [01/05/02].

- Japan, Japanese Embassies homepage: "Japan's Role in [the] Asian Financial Crisis", a list with major contributors' pledges to the various by early 1998, http://www.embjapan.org/JCONASIA.html [27/08/01].

- Jayakumar, S. (1997): Opening Statement, 30th AMM, Kuala Lumpur, July, http://app.internet.gov.sg/scripts/mfa/pr/read_content.asp?View,95, [sic!].

—— (1998): "Stick to Basics", Opening Statement, 31st AMM, Manila, 24 July, http://app.internet.gov.sg/scripts/mfa/pr/read_content.aspView,99, [sic!].

—— (1999a): "Redefining ASEAN", Speech at the ceremony of Cambodia's admission to ASEAN, Hanoi, 30 April, http://www.asean.or.id/news/accam_sg.htm [10/07/00].

—— (1999b): Remarks on return from the AMM Foreign Ministers' Retreat, Singapore, 23 July, http://www.gov.sg/mfa/amm/speeches/1999072302.html [15/06/00].

—— (2000): Opening Statement, 33rd AMM, Bangkok, 24 July, http://www.aseansec.org/amm/amm33osg.htm [24/07/00].

- Jayasankaran, S. (2002): "Malaysia: Call for Arms", *Far Eastern Economic Review*, 16 May, http://www.feer.com/articles/2002/0205_16/p020region.html [09/05/02].

- Jepperson, Ronald L.; Peter J. Katzenstein; Alexander Wendt (1996): "Norms, Identity, and Culture in National Security". In: *The Culture of National Security: Norms and Identity in World Politics*, ed. Peter J. Katzenstein, New York: Columbia Univ. Press, pp. 32-75.

- Jin, Nyum, Minister of Finance and Economy, Republic of Korea (2000): "Keynote Speech". In: *Reforming the International Financial Architecture: Emerging Market Perspectives*, ed. Il Sa Kong and Yunjong Wang, Seoul: Korea Institute for International Economic Policy (KIEP).

- Job, Brian L. (1999): "ASEAN Stalled: Dilemmas and Tensions Over conflicting Norms", paper prepared for delivery at the 1999 Annual Meeting of the American Political Science Association, Atanta, Sept. 2-5, 1999, http://pro.harvard.edu/ abstracts/016/016001JobBrian00.html [01/08/00].

- Johnson, Douglas (1997): "Drawn into the Fray: Indonesia's Natuna Islands Meet China's Long Gaze South", *Asian Affairs*, 24, 3, pp. 153-161.

- Joyner, Christopher C. (1999): "The Spratly Islands Dispute in the South China Sea: Problems, Policies, and Prospects for Diplomatic Accommodation", in: Ranjeet K. Singh (ed): *Investigating Confidence-Building Measures in the Asia-Pacific Region*, Washington: Stimson Center, May [Report No. 28], pp. 53-108, http://www.stimson.org/pubs/cbm/cbmgen/cbmapspratly.pdf [25/05/01].

- Kajita, Takehiko (2002): "Japan's new ASEAN policy comes as China rises", *The Japan Times Online*, 15 January, http://www.japantimes.com/cgi-bin/getarticle.pl5?nb20020115a3.htm [11/04/02].

- Kamarul, Yunus (2002): "American Group proposes US-Asean free trade pact", *Business Times*, Singapore, 18 March, http://www.myglobal.gov.my/DocPublic/Trade/US-Asean18.doc [28/05/02].

- Kamlin, Muhamad (1991): *The Meaning of Integration in the ASEAN Region*, Faculty of Arts and Social Sciences, University of Brunei Darussalam, Working Paper no. 8, 1991.

- Kavi,Chongkittavorn (2000a): "East Timor is Asean's new catalyst", *The Nation*, 21 February, http://202.44.251.4/nationnews/2000/200002/20000221/4214.html [07/03/01].

—— (2000b): "Working together to try to bring Burma in from the cold", *International Herald Tribune*, 1 August, p. 6.

- Khairul Bashar and Wolfgang Möllers (eds). (2000): *A Common Currency For East Asia: Dream or Reality?*, Kuala Lumpur: Asian Institute for Development Communication and Konrad Adenauer Foundation.

- Khin Nyunt (1999): "We Restored Order", Interview with Khin Nyunt, *Asiaweek.com*, vol.25, n.50, 17 December, http://www.cnn.com/ASIANOW/asiaweek/interview/khin.nyunt/index.html, continued on http://www.cnn.com/ASIANOW/asiaweek/interview/khin.nyunt/khinnyunt2.html [21/06/2000].

- Khoo, How San (2000): "ASEAN as a Neighborhood Watch Group", *Contemporary Southeast Asia*, 22, 2, pp. 279-301.

- Kim, Dae-jung (2001): Arrival statement by the President upon returning to Korea from the APT summit in Brunei, Korea.net, 06 November, http://www.korea.net/kwnews/pub_focus/print.asp?cate=01&serial_no=1975 [11/04/02].

- Kingdom of Thailand, Ministry of Foreign Affairs (1998): "Thailand's Non-Paper on Flexible Engagement", http://thaiembdc.org/pr/pr743.htm [27/06/00].

—— (2001): "Main Points of Proposals and Suggestions Raised by the Prime Minister of Thailand", informal paper on Thailand's agenda for the 7th ASEAN summit in November, received on 12 November 2001 during a visit at the MFA.

- Kivimäki, Timo (2000): "U.S.-Indonesian Relations During the Economic Crisis: Where has Indonesia's Bargaining Power Gone?", *Contemporary Southeast Asia*, 22, 3, pp. 527-569.

- Koizumi, Junichiro (2002): Statement by the Japanese Prime Minister, 13 January, http://www.kantei.go.jp/foreign/koizumispeech/2002/01/13singapore_e.html [30/04/02].

- Kong, Il Sa; Yunjong Wang (eds.) (2000): *Reforming the International Financial Architecture: Emerging Market Perspectives*, Seoul: Korea Institute for International Economic Policy (KIEP), p. 20 [Conference proceedings 00-04, seminar held 9-11 September].

- Konrad Adenauer Stiftung (Konrad Adenauer Foundation) (1999): "No Alternative to Regionalism", interview with Rodolfo Severino, August, www.kas.de/publikationen/multimedial/aktuell/severino_komplett.html [10/07/00].

- *Korea Now* (19 November 2001): "ASEAN+3 Working with the Neighbors: Korea, China, Japan agree to hold regular economic ministers' meetings", http://kn.koreaherald.co.kr/SITE/data/html_dir/2001/11/19/200111190008.asp [11/04/02].

- Korea.net (2000): "Reference Materials for the ASEAN Plus 3 Summit and State Visits to Singapore and Indonesia", Policy Updates, November, http://www.korea.net/2k/focuson/pub_focus/content.asp?cate=03&serial_no=151 [19/10/01].

- Kraft, Herman (2000): "ASEAN and Intra-ASEAN Relations: Weathering the Storm?", *The Pacific Review*, 13, 3, pp. 453-472.

- Kreuzer, Peter (1999): "Der Konflikt um das Südchinesische Meer", *Die Friedens-Warte*, 74 (1999), 4, pp. 491-509.

- Kusuma, Snitwongse (2001): "Thai Foreign Policy in the Global Age: Principle or Profit?", *Contemporary Southeast Asia*, 23, 2, pp. 189-212.

- Kwan, Weng Kin (2002): "PM Goh, Koizumi call for Japan-Asean pact", *The Straits Times*, Singapore, 10 January.

- Labrador, Mel C. (1996): "The Philipines in 1995: Growth Amid Challenges", *Asian Survey*, 36, 2, pp. 142-152.

—— (2001): "The Philippines in 2000: In Search of a Silver Lining...", *Asian Survey*, 41, 1, pp. 221-229.

- Lam, Peng Er (2001): "Japan's diplomatic initiatives in Southeast Asia". In: *Japan and East Asian Regionalism*, ed. S. Javed Maswood, London/New York: Routledge, pp. 118-131.

—— (2002): "Japan-Southeast Asia Relations: Trading Places?: The Leading Goose & Ascending Dragon", *Comparative Connections*, 4, 1, http://www.csis.org/pacfor/cc/0201Qoa.html [16/04/02].

- Langhammer, Rolf J. (2001a): "European Enlargement: Lessons for ASEAN". In: *ASEAN Enlargement: Impacts and Implications*, ed. Mya Than; Carolyn L. Gates, Singapore: Institute of Southeast Asian Studies, pp. 102-127.

—— (2001b): "Is ASEAN Still Relevant? Some Thoughts from a European Perspective". In: *ASEAN Beyond the Regional Crisis: Challenges and Initiatives*, ed. Mya Than, Singapore: Institute of Southeast Asian Studies, 2001, pp.283-288.

- Lau, Leslie (2001): "Thai Premier pledges to forge closer ties with KL", *The Straits Times*, Singapore, 25 April, http://straitstimes.asia1.com.sg/0,1870,39346,00.html? [25/04/01].

- Lee ,Valerie (1999): "Southeast Asian deal on Spratlys scuppered", *Reuters*, 20 July 1999, http://www.malaysia.net/lists/sangkancil/1999-07/msg00827.html [03/05/01].

- Lee, Lai To (1999a): *China and the South China Sea Dialogues*, Westport (Connecticut) and London: Praeger, 1999.

—— (1999b): "Singapore in 1998: The Most Serious Challenge Since Independence", *Asian Survey*, 39, 1, pp. 72-79.

—— (2001): "The Lion and the Dragon: a view on Singapore-China relations", *Journal of Contemporary China*, 10, 28, pp. 415-425.

- Lee, Hsien Loong (2000): "ASEAN Post-Crisis: Rebuilding Confidence and Prosperity", Speech by the Deputy Prime Minister of Singapore, Bangkok, 30 November, http://www.gov.sg/sgip/Announce/bangkok.htm [12/01/00].

- Leifer, Michael (1999): "The South China Sea Stalemate", paper delivered at the Workshop on the Conflict in the South China Sea, Oslo, 24-26 April 1999, http://www.sum.uio.no/southchinasea/Publications/pdf-format/leifer.pdf [31/05/01].

- Leong, Stephen (2000): "The East Asian Economic Caucus (EAEC): 'Formalized' Regionalism Being Denied", in: *National Perspectives on the New Regionalism in the South*, ed. Björn Hettne et al., London: Macmillan, pp. 57-107.

- Lepsius, M. Rainer (1999): "Bildet sich eine kulturelle Identität in der Europäischen Union?". In: *Identität und Interesse: Der Diskurs der Identitätsforschung*, ed. Walter Reese-Schäfer, Opladen: Leske und Budrich, pp. 91-99.

- Liddle, R. William (2001): "Indonesia in 2000: A Shaky Start for Democracy", *Asian Survey*, 41, 1, pp. 208-220.

- Lim, Kit Siang (1996): Statement by the Parliamentary Opposition Leader in Malaysia, 3 November, http://www.malaysia.net/dap/sg133.htm.

- Lim, Robyn (2002): "Japan Re-Engages Southeast Asia", *Far Eastern Economic Review*, 24 January, http://www.feer.com/articles/2002/0201_24/p026fcol.html [17/01/02].

- Lim, Say Boon (2001): "Asean-China FTA a distraction?", article appeared parallelly in *The Straits Times* (Singapore), 3 December, and *The Korea Herald*, 4 December, http://www.koreaherald.co.kr/SITE/data/html_dir/2001/12/04//200112040018.asp [23/01/02].

- Liow, Joseph Chin Yong (2000): "Malaysia-China Relations in the 1990s: The Maturing of a Partnership", *Asian Survey*, 40, 4, pp. 672-691.

- Low, Ignatius (2002): "Wanted: An E. Asian community", *The Straits Times*, Singapore, 15 January.

- Macapagal-Arroyo, Gloria (2002): Speech at the 8th "The Future of Asia" conference, Tokyo, 21 May, http://www.news.ops.gov.ph/japan_conference.htm [22/05/02].

- Machetzki, Rüdiger (2001): "Der 11. September 2001: Auswirkungen in Indonesien" [The impact of September 11 on Indonesia], *Südostasien aktuell*, 20, 6, pp. 586-588.

- Mahathir, Mohamad (1998): Opening Statement, 6th ASEAN Summit, Hanoi, 15 December, http://www.aseansec.org/summit/6th/prg_opmy.htm [13/06/00].

- Mahathir, Mohamad (1999): "Reflections on my visit to China", Dr. Mahathir's World Analysis column, *Manichi Shimbun*, 6 September, www.manichi.co.jp/english/mahathir/08.html [13/05/02].

- Malaysia Directory (25 November 2000): "No Myanmar, no meeting, ASEAN tells EU", http://ww8.malaysiadirectory.com/news/10/112505.html [08/05/01].

- Malaysia, Ministry of Industry and Trade (MITI) (2001): "Developments in the implementation of the CEPT Scheme for ASEAN Free Trade Area", updated 01 Feb 2001, www.miti.gov.my/trade/mtmain.htm [12/03/01].

- Mallet, Victor (1999): *The Trouble With Tigers: The Rise and Fall of South-East Asia*, London: Harper Collins.

- Malley, Michael S. (2002): "Indonesia in 2001: Restoring Stability in Jakarta", *Asian Survey*, 42, 1, pp. 124-132.

- Marshall, Andrew (2002): "Southeast Asian integration lacks key factor: unity", Reuters, 03 April, http://asia.news.yahoo.com/020403/reuters/nbkk298227.html [04/04/02].

- Martinez, Patricia (2001): "Malaysia in 2000: A Year of Conflict", *Asian Survey*, 41, 1, pp. 189-200.

——, Patricia (2002): "Malaysia in 2001: An Interlude of Consolidation", *Asian Survey*, 42, 1, pp.133-140.

- Maswood, S. Javed (2001a): " Japanese foreign policy and regionalism", in: *Japan and East Asian Regionalism*, ed. S. Javed Maswood, London: Routledge.

—— (2001b): *Japan and East Asian Regionalism*, London/ New York.

- McBeth, John (1996): "Burma Road", *FEER*, 12 December, p. 18.

—— (2000): "Wahid and Sukarno's Gold", *FEER*, 14 December, http://www.google.de/search?q=cache:Lrt5rexbPoUC:www.feer.com/articles/2000/0012_14/p034region.html [21/03/02].

——; Trish Saywell (2001): "Gas Gateway", *FEER*, 22 February, http://www.feer.com/_0102_22/p054money.html [16/05/01].

- McDevitt, Michael (1999): "China and the South China Sea: A Conference Summary Report", *PacNet* no. 15, 16 April, http://www.nyu.edu/globalbeat/asia/Mcdevitt041999.html [25/05/01].

- Mehta, Harish (2001a): "ASEAN urged to close gap between old and new members", *Business Times*, Singapore, 04 May 2001, http://business-times.asia.com.sg/news/story/0,2276,6556,00.html [09/05/01].

—— (2001b): "FTAs ensure others, Asean stay engaged", *Business Times*, Singapore, 9 May, http://business-times.asia1.com.sg/news/story/0,2276,7020,00.html [09/05/01].

- Menon, Jayant (2000): "The Evolving ASEAN Free Trade Area: Widening and Deepening'", *Asian Development Review*, 18, 1, pp. 49-72.

- Mitton, Roger (1999): "Interview: Hong Soon-young", interview with the Foreign Minister of Korea, *Asiaweek.com*, 17 December, 25, 50, http://www.asiaweek..com/asiaweek/interview/hong.soon.young/index.html [18/04/02].

- Mohan, Srilal (1999): "Singapore-Indonesia ties sink to chilly depths", *Asia Times Online*, 05 March, http://www.atimes.com/se-asia/AC05Ae01.html [02/05/01].

- Mohd. Haflah Piei (2000): "The ASEAN Experience in Economic Integration (1967-1999)". In: *A Common Currency for East Asia: Dream Or Reality?*, ed. Khairul Bashar and Wolfgang Möllers, Kuala Lumpur: Asian Insitute for Development Communication, 2000, pp. 1-28.

- Montesano, Michael J. (2001): "Thailand in 2000: Shifting Politics, Dragging Economy, Troubled Border", *Asian Survey*, 41, 1, 171-180.

- Mulne, R.S. and Diane K. Mauzy (1999): *Malaysian Politics under Mahathir*, London: Routledge.

- Murphy, Dan (2001): "Southeast Asian nations dance to different tunes", *Christian Science Monitor* Electronic Edition, http://www.csmonitor.com/durable/2000/11/24/text/p9s1.html [27/11/00].

- Mya Than and George Abonyi (2001): "The Greater Mekong Subregion: Cooperation in Infrastructure and Finance". In: *ASEAN Enlargement: Impacts and Implications*, ed. Mya Than and Carolyn L. Gates, Singapore: Institute of Southeast Asian Studies, pp. 128-163.

- Naranart Phunangkanok; Thanong Khantong (2000): "ASEAN+3 in regional cooperation talks", news dispatch, 29 July, http://www.members.tripod.com/thanong/07292000.htm [04/09/01].

- Narine, Shaun (2001): "ASEAN and the Idea of an 'Asian Monetary Fund': Institutional Uncertainty in the Asia-Pacific". In: *Non-Traditional Security Issues in Southeast Asia*, ed. Andrew T. H. Tan and J. D. Kenneth Boutin, Singapore: Institute for Defense and Strategic Studies (IDSS), pp. 227-256.

- Nathan, Dominic (1997): "Diary of Disaster: People kept in the haze for too long", *The Straits Times Interactive* Haze News, Singapore, 12 October, http://www.bssc.edu.au/learning_areas/xchange/1997/issues/singapore/diary.htm [02/07/01].

- Nguyen Dy Nien (2000): Statement at the Opening Ceremony, 33rd AMM, Bangkok, 24 July, http://www.aseansec.org/amm/amm33ovn.htm [24/07/00].

- Nguyen Manh Cam (1999a): Statement at the Ceremony of Cambodia's admission to ASEAN, Hanoi, 30 April, http://www.asean.or.id/news/accam_vi.htm [10/07/00].

—— (1999b): Speech, 32nd AMM, Singapore, 23 July, www.aseansec.org/amm/amm32osv.htm [19/06/00].

- Nischalke, Tobias Ingo (2000): "Insights from ASEAN's Foreign Policy Co-Operation: The 'ASEAN Way', a Real Spirit or a Phantom?", *Contemporary Southeast Asia*, 22, 1, pp. 89-112.

- Noordin, Sopiee (1996): *EAEC: Fact and Fiction*, Kuala Lumpur: Institute of Strategic and International Studies (ISIS) Malaysia.

- Noordin, Sopiee (2001): "Ten Commandments For East Asian Regional Cooperation", speech at the conference "The Future of Asia", organized by *Nikkei Shimbun*, 8 June, http://www.nni.nikkei.co.jp/FR/NIKKEI/inasia/future/2001speech_sopiee.html [18/04/02].

- *Oil&Gas Journal* (4 October 1999): "Singapore Power secures Indonesia gas supply", 97, 40, p. 38.

- *Oil&Gas Journal Online* (15 January 2001): "Singapore, Indonesia signal improved ties at gas delivery ceremony", http://www. .... [16/05/01].

- *Oman Daily Observer* (13 September 2001): "Arroyo may urge Japan to take wider seurity role in Asia", http://www.middleeastwire.com/world/stories/20010913_3_meno.shtml [12/10/01].

- Park, Sung-Hoon (2001): "Regionalism and Economic Integration in East Asia: Current Status and Future Policy Options", in: *Asia-Europe on the Eve of the 21st Century*, ed. Chirathivat, Suthiphand, Singapore: Institute of Southeast Asian Studies (ISEAS), pp. 133-146.

- Pathan, Don (1997): "PM Steers Clear of VN-China drilling dispute", *The Nation*, 31 March, http://202.44.251.4/nationnews/1997/199703/19970331/3608.html [07/03/01].

- *People's* Daily (21 January 2002): "Thai PM Proposes Speedily Open ASEAN-China Free Trade Area", http://english.peopledaily.com.cn/200201/21/eng20020121_89049.shtml [23/01/02].

- *People's Daily* (07 December 2001): "China, Thailand Sign Currency Swap Agreement", http://english.peopledaily.com.cn/200112/06/eng20011206_86099.shtml [05/04/02].

- People's Republic of China, Ministry of Foreign Affairs (2001): "Premier Zhu Rongji met with Malaysian Supreme Head of State", 26 April, http://www.fmprc.gov.cn/eng/10016.html [15/05/02].

- People's Republic of China; Kingdom of Thailand (2001): "The China-Thailand Joint Communiqué", Beijing, 29 August, http://www.chinaembassy-india.org/eng/17357.html [15/05/02].

- Phan Van Khai (1998): Keynote Address, 6th ASEAN Summit, Hannoi, 15 December, http://www.aseansec.org/summit/6th/prg_keyn.htm [13/06/00].

- *Philippine Daily Inquirer* (01 October 1999): "Lame Excuse", http://www.iidnet.org/apcet/news-pdieditorial.htm [07/03/01].

- Prabandari, Purwani D. (2002): "Megawati, The dance and LNG", *Tempo* [Indonesia], no. 30, 02-08 April, http://www.google.com/search?q=cache:7rT0amoSs84C:www.tempointer active.com/majalah/eng/eco-5.html [17/05/02].

- Radio Singapore International (13 February 2001): "Economic implications of the Indonesia-Singapore gas deal", transcript of an interview with Dr. Mike Nahan, Executive Director of the Institute of Public Affairs in Melbourne, http://rsi.com.sg/en/programmes/newsline/2001/02/13_01.htm [02/05/01].

- Ramcharan, Robin (2000): "ASEAN and Non-Interference: A Principle Maintained", *Contemporary Southeast Asia*, 22, 1, pp. 61-88.

- Rajan, Ramkishen (1999): *Financial and Macroeconomic Cooperation in ASEAN: Issues and Policy Initiatives*, Centre for International Economic Studies (CIES) Working Paper No. 99/29, Adelaide: University of Adelaide, December.

- Ramos, Fidel (2000): "The World to Come: ASEAN's Political and Economic Prospects in the New Century", Address at the Economic Strategy Institute's Global Forum 2000, Washington, D.C., 17 May, http://www.asean.or.id/secgen/articles/sp_fvr2.htm [10/07/00].

—— (2001): "Security and Stability in the Asia-Pacific" at the World Economic Forum's Annual Meeting, Davos, 29 January, http://www.dfa.gov.ph/archive/speech/fvr/fvr_dinner.htm [06/03/02].

- Raslan, Karim 2002: "Mahathir Goes to Wahington", *Far Eastern Economic Review*, 09 May, http://www.feer.com/articles/2002/0205_09/p023fcol.html [02/05/02].

- Republic of the Philippines, Department of Foreign Affairs (2001): "VP and DFA Sec. Guingona's replies to questions submitted by the Manila Bulletin for the DFA Day Special Supplement", http://www.dfa.gov.ph/archive/anniv103/man_bul.htm [18/04/02].

——, Office of the Press Secretary (2002a): "GMA aims for more progressive, stable Asian environment in trip to Japan", http://www.news.ops.gov.ph/today/.htm [20/05/02].

——, Office of the Press Secretary (2002b), "Philippines, Japan to create working group to systematize economic agreement", http://www.ops.gov.ph/japanvisit2002/news3.htm [22/05/02].

- Reuters (22 November 1999): "ASEAN defends hands-off policy on Aceh", http://www.mastiffassociation.org/nes/pacrim/ra21b.htm [11/06/01].

—— (2001a): "Malaysia", Reuters country profiles, http://www.alertnet.org/thefacts/countryprofiles/303296?version=1 [25/04/02].

—— (22 July 2001): "ASEAN finalises integration plan but stuck on Spratlys", http://sg.news.yahoo.com/010722/3/19jxc.html [24/07/01].

—— (23 July 2001): "Australia takes bilateral tack on Asian free trade", http://www.google.com/search?q=cache:eo8BGGapeFM:sg.news.yahoo.com/010723/3/19lpa.html+Singapore+FTA+ASEAN&hl=de [29/08/01].

- Reyes, Alejandro (2000a): "Who's Afraid of a Little Candor? - ASEAN Day For: The Secretary-General's Report", *Asiaweek.com*, July 28, http://www.asiaweek.com/asiaweek/intelligence/2000/07/28/.

—— (2000b): "Tariff Troubles - Exemption Rules are undermining AFTA", *Asiaweek*, 1 September, http:/www.asiaweek.com/asiaweek/magazine/2000/0901/asean.tariff.html [08/03/01]

—— (2000c): "Keeping Up With the Singaporeans - Rather than attack the Lion City, neighbors should learn from it", *Asiaweek*, 8 December, http://www.asiaweek.com/asiaweek/magazine/2000/1208/viewpoint.html [08/03/01].

- Rhee, Chong-Yun (2000): "Northeast Asian Economic Cooperation and Korea-Japan Free Trade Area", *Korea Focus*, 8, 4, pp. 62-74.

- Richardson, Michael (1998): "A Nervous ASEAN Will Approach China Over Expansion in Spratlys", *International Herald Tribune*, 14 December, http://www.iht.com/IHT/MR/98/mr121498.html [14/05/01].

—— (1999a): "On Eve of Annual Talks, ASEAN Members Are Split Over Spratlys Dispute", *International Herald Tribune*, 23 July, http://www.iht.com/IHT/MR/99/mr072399a.html [27/06/00].)

—— (1999b): "East Timor Leaders Oppose a Malaysian-Led Force", *International Herald Tribune*, 3 November, http://www.etan.org/et99c/november/01-6/3eleadrs.htm [11/06/01].

—— (1999c): "Wary of Rivals, East Asia Weighs Closer Integration: Security and Free Trade Pacts under discussion", *International Herald Tribune*, 26 November, http://web.nps.navy.mil/~relooney/3040_1122.htm [21/04/02].

—— (2000a): "Investment in Southeast Asia Plunges", *International Herald Tribune*, 27 July, http://62.172.206.162/IHT/MR/00/mr072700a.html [alternatively, http://www.iht.com/IHT/TODAY/THU/FIN/crisis.2.html [27/07/00].

—— (2000b): "Asian Leaders Cautious on Forging New Regional Partnerships", *International Herald Tribune*, 27 November, http:/www.Iht.com/articles/2561.htm [27/11/00].

—— (2001): "Gas Sparks Southeast Asian Ties", *International Herald Tribune*, 16 January, http://www.iht.com/articles/7643.html.

- Richter, Frank-Jürgen (2002): "Prospects for an Asian Nafta", The 5th Column, *Far Eastern Economic Review*, 18 April 2002, http://www.feer.com/articles/2002/0204_18/p027fcol.html [11/04/02].

- Rowena, Maria A.; Luz G. Layador (2000): "The Emerging ASEAN Plus Three Process: Another Building Block for Community Building in the Asia Pacific?", *The Indonesian Quarterly*, 28, 4, pp. 434-443.

- Rowley, Anthony (2001): "Asean+3 group boosts currency defences", *The Business, Times* Singapore, 11 May, http://business-times.asia1.com.sg/news/story/0,2276,7402,00.html? [11/05/01].

- Rüland, Jürgen (1995a): "Die Gemeischaft Südostasiatischer Staaten (ASEAN): Vom Antikommunismus zum regionalen Ordnungsfaktor", *Aus Politik und Zeitgeschichte*, B13-14, pp. 3-12.

—— (1995b): "Der Stellenwert der Asean für die Außen-, Sicherheits- und Wirtschaftspolitik der Mitglieds- und Beobachterstaaten", *KAS-AI*

(*Konrad Adenauer Stiftung –Auslands Informnationen*), 9/1995, pp. 49-65.

—— (2000a): "ASEAN and the Asian crisis: theoretical implications and practical consequences for Southeast Asian regionalism", *The Pacific Review*, 13, 3, pp. 421-451.

—— (2000b): "Allianz der Einzelgänger: Die ASEAN-Staaten zwischen Freihandel und Protektionismus " [Alliance of Loners: ASEAN Nations between free trade and protectionism], *Freitag*, 49, 01 December.

- Ruwitch, John (2002a): "Indonesia's Megawati arrives in China pushing trade", Reuters, 24 March, http://www.google.com/search?q=cache:BnXv1^t4XdzAC:biz.yahoo.com/rf/020324/pek75625_1.html [17/05/02].

- Ruwitch, John (2002b): "Megawati seeks to strengthen ties with China", AFP/Reuters, 25 March, http://www.google.com/search?q=cache:cAfnGaMWtZQC:asia.news.yahoo.com/020325/reuters/asia-96782.html [17/05/02].

- Sakthip Krairiksh (2001): "Economic Relations between Thailand and Japan", speech at Keio University, Fujisawa Campus, 14 June, http://www.thaiembassy.or.jp/test2/embassy/greeting/otherspeech/doc/speech%20at%20Keio2.htm [02/05/02].

- Salil, Tripathi (2000): "Seeds of the next crisis - In letting AFTA stall, ASEAN shows it has learned nothing", *Asiaweek*, 18 August, http://www.asiaweek.com/asiaweek/magazine/2000/0818/viewpoint.html [08/03/01].

- Saywell, Trish (2001): "Even the Best Are Helpless", *FEER*, 09 August, http://www.feer.com/2001/0108_09/p012region.html [02/08/01].

- Schmitt-Egner, Peter (1999): "Regionale Identität, Transnationaler Regionalismus und Europäische Kompetenz. Theoretische, methodische und normative Überlegungen zum Verhältnis von Regionaler und Europäischer Identität." 129-158.

- Schofield, Clive (2000): "A Code of thConduct for the South China Sea?", *Jane's Intelligence Review*, 27 October, http://www.janes.com/security/regional_security/news/jir/jir001027_1_n.shtml [08/05/01].

- Seri Syed Hamid Albar (1999a): Speech at the Ceremony of Cambodia's admission to ASEAN, Hanoi, 30 April, http://www.asean.or.id/news/accam_ml.htm [10/07/00].

—— (1999b): Opening Statement, 32nd AMM, Singapore, 23 July.

—— (2000): Opening Statement, 33rd AMM, Bangkok, 24 July, http://www.aseansec.org/amm/amm33omy.htm [24/07/00].

- Sevastopulo, Demetri (2002): "Japan and China sign currency swap deal", *Financial Times* (*FT.com*), 28 March, http://news.ft.com/ft/gx.cgi/ftc?pagename=View&c=Article&cid=FT3SQ VF6CZC&live=true&tagid=FTDZ14FSNUC [28/03/02].

- Severino, Rodolfo (1998a): Remarks, 8th Southeast Asia Forum, Kuala Lumpur, 15 March, http://www.asean.or.id/secgen/visi2020.htm [10/07/00].

—— (1998b): "Weathering the Storm: ASEAN's Response to Crisis", *FEER* Conference on "Weathering the Storm: Hongkong and the Asian Financial Crisis", Honkong, 11 June, http://www.asean.or.id/secgen/sg_feer.htm [10/07/00].

—— (approx. 1999): "The Only Way For ASEAN", interview by Serge Berthier, http://www.asean.or.id/secgen/aseanway.htm [10/07/2000].

—— (1999a): "No Alternative to Regionalism", interview with Rodolfo Severino, Secretary-General of ASEAN, August, Konrad Adenauer Foundation Speeches and Interviews [Reden und Gespräche] Series, http://www.kas.de/publikationen/multimedial/aktuell/severino_komplett.h tml [10/07/00].

—— (1999b): "Regionalism: The Stakes for Southeast Asia", Address, Institute of Defense Studies, Singapore, 24 May, http://12.4.115.99/ASEAN2/ASEANOverview/Severino_Speeches_Regi onalism.htm [10/07/2000].

—— (1999c): "Thinking ASEAN", interview with Rodolfo Severino, *Philippine Graphic Magazine*, 29 November, http://www.aseansec.org/secgen/articles/sg_gqa.htm [10/07/2000].

—— (1999d): "The ASEAN Way in Manila", *Far Eastern Economic Review*, 23 December, http://www.aseansec.org/secgen/articles/sg_feer.htm [10/07/2000].

—— (2000): "Sovereignty, Intervention and the ASEAN Way", Address, ASEAN Scholar's Roundtable, Singapore, 3 July, http://www.asean.or.id/secgen/sg_siaw.htm [10/07/2000].

- Shihab, Alwi (2000a): "The Indonesian Foreign Policy Outlook", Keynote Address, Conference in Observance of the National Press Day, Jakarta, 17 February, http://www.dfa-deplu.go.id/policy/statements/menlu/speeches/natpress-17feb00.htm [02/08/00].

—— (2000b): Briefing by the Foreign Minister to Foreign Ambassadors in Jakarta on Aceh, Maluku and Irian Jaya, Jakarta, 7 July, http://www.deplu.go.id/new/persalwishihab-12july00.htm [02/08/2000].

—— (2000c): Opening Statement, 33rd AMM, Bangkok, 24 July, http://www.aseansec.org/amm/amm33oid.htm [24/07/00].

- Siazon, Domingo (1999a), "ASEAN in the Next Millennium", Opening Statement, 32nd AMM, Singapore, 23 July, http://www.dfa.gov.ph/oth/aseanmm.html [16/06/00].

—— (1999b): "We Have to Change", interview with Domingo Siazon, *Asiaweek.com*, 10 December, http://www.cnn.com/ASIANOW/asiaweek/interview/domingo.siazon/index.html, continued on http://www.cnn.com/ASIANOW/asiaweek/interview/domingo.siazon/siazon2.html [21/06/00].

—— (2000a): Transcript of an interview with Domingo Siazon, ChannelNewsAsia.com, 3 February, http://www.channelnewsasia.com/analysis_prog/incon/incon_dsiazon.htm [10/07/00].

—— (2000b): "Building a Community of Peace", Opening Statement, 33rd AMM, Bangkok, 24 July, http://www.mfa.go.th/amm33/speech/philip.htm [27/07/00].

—— (2001): "East Asia Needs Innovative Diplomacy", speech at the conference "The Future of Asia", Tokyo, 7 June, http://www.nni.nikkei.co.jp/FR/NIKKEI/inasia/future/2001speech_siazon.html [20/04/02].

- Siboro, Tiarma; Fabiola Desy Unijadijaja (2002): "Distrust hurts Indonesia-Singapore bilateral relations, *The Jakarta Post*, 23 February, http://www.thejakartapost.com/yesterdaydetail.asp?fileid=20020223.B10 [25/02/02].

- Siegwart Lindenberg (1998): "Solidarity: Its Microfoundations and Macrodependence. A Framing Approach". In: *The Problem of Solidarity: Theories and Models*, ed. Patrick Doreian and Thomas Fararo, Amsterdam: Gordon and Breach, 1998, pp. 61-112.

- Siemers, Günter (2001): "Myanmar vor einer Aussöhnung?", *Südostasien aktuell*, 20, 2, pp. 171-180.

- Sim, Susan (1998): "Visit off to good start for ties", *Straits Times*, Singapore, 6 August, http://www.huaren.org/focus/id/080698-05.html [26/05/01].

- Simon, Sheldon (1998): "The Economic Crisis and ASEAN Political and Security Concerns", Memorandum for the President, paper prepared for The Aspen Strategy Conference on Political and Security Implications of the East Asian Crisis, Aspen, Colorado, August 13-15, http://csf.colorado.edu/isa/isn/23-3/simon.html [16/05/01].

—— (2001): "U.S.-Southeast Asia Relations: Mixed Reactions in Southeast Asia to the U.S. War on Terrorism", *Comparative Connections*, 3, 4, http://www.csis.org/pacfor/cc/0104Qus_asean.html [03/04/02].

- Singapore News (2001): "Bilateral FTAs spark freer trade in the region", Week 3-9 March, http://www.google.com/search?q=cache:xTdpJNBLgv4:www.gov.sg/sgnews/bites3mar.html+singapore+FTA+malaysia&hl=de [03/09/01].

- Singapore Window (28 November 2000): "Singapore's trade initiatives undermine ASEAN economic policy", http://www.singapore-window.org/sw00/001128st.htm [10/04/01].

- Singapore, Ministry of Foreign Affairs (2000): "Transcript of remarks to the media by PM Goh on the discussion of the ASEAN+3 Summit", 24 November, http://app.internet.gov.sg/scripts/mfa/pr/read/_script.asp?View,674, [04/12/00].

- Singh, Daljit (2000): "Southeast Asia in 1999: A False Dawn?". In: *Southeast Asian Affairs 2000*, ed. Daljit Singh, Singapore: Institute of Southeast Asian Studies, pp. 3-24.

——; Tin Maung Maung Than (eds.) (1999): *Regional Outlook Southeast Asia 1999-2000*, Singapore: Institute of Southeast Asian Studies (ISEAS).

- Sisavath, Keobounphanh (1998): Opening Statement, 6th ASEAN Summit, Hanoi 15 December, http://www.aseansec.org/summit/6th/prg_opla.htm [13/06/00].

- Smith, Anthony L. (1999): "Indonesia's Role in ASEAN: The End of Leadership?", *Contemporary Southeast Asia*, 21, 2, pp. 238-260.

—— (2000): "Indonesia's Foreign Policy Under Abdurrahman Wahid: Radical or Status Quo State?", *Contemporary Southeast Asia*, 22, 3, pp. 498-526.

- Snyder, Scott (2001a): "China-Korea Relations: Keeping the Eye on the (WTO) Prize While Containing Consular Crises", *Comparative Connections*, 3, 4, http://www.csis.org/pacfor/cc/0104Qchina_skorea.html [12/04/02].

—— (2001b): "China-Korean Relations: Economic Interest Uber Alles: Hitting the Jackpot through Sino-Korean Partnership", *Comparative Connections*, 3, 2, http://www.csis.org/pacfor/cc/0102Qchina_skorea.html [12/04/02].

- Soesastro, Hadi (2000): "Indonesia, ASEAN and East Asia", *The Jakarta Post*, 30 November, http://www.indonesia-ottawa.org/Perspective/November/November_30_JP.htm [19/10/01].

—— (2002): Indonesia-China Relations – But Where is the Beef?", *Kompas* [Indonesia], 01 April, http://www.kompas.com/kompas-cetak/0204/01/ENGLISH/indo.htm [17/05/02].

- Sohn, Chan-Hyun; Jinna Yoon (2001): *Korea's FTA (Free Trade Agreement) Policy: Current Status and Future Prospects*, Seoul: Korean Institute for International Economic Policy, Discussion Paper 01-01, September, http://www.kiep.go.kr/Project/publish.nsf/ewebview11/0B7AFA727EDA7AEE49256AE900261B32/$file/dp01-01.PDF [16/01/02].

- Somsavat Lengsavad (1999): Opening Statement, 32nd AMM, Singapore, 23 July, http://www.aseansec.org/amm/amm32osl.htm [19/06/00].

—— (2000): Opening Statement, 33rd AMM, Bangkok, 24 July, http://www.aseansec.org/amm/amm33ol.htm [29/09/00].

- Stahl, Bernhard (2001): "Die Gemeinschaft Südostasiatischer Staaten (ASEAN)". In: *Multilateralismus in Ostasien: Probleme und Herausforderungen im neuen Jahrhundert*, ed. Hanns W. Maull and Dirk Nabers, Hamburg: Institut für Asienkunde [Institute of Asian Affairs], pp. 23-67.

- Storey, Ian James (1999): "Creeping Assertiveness: China, the Philippines and the South China Sea Dispute", *Contemporary Southeast Asia*, 21, 1, pp.95-118.

—— (2000): "Indonesia's China Sea Policy in the New Order and Beyond: Problems and Prospects", *Contemporary Southeast Asia*, 22, 1, pp. 145-174.

- Stratfor (2000): "Singapore's trade initiatives undermine ASEAN economic policy", Stratfor Analysis, 28 November, Singapore Window, http://www.singapore-window.org/sw00/001128st.htm [10/04/01].

- Stubbs, Richard (2000): "Signing on to liberalization: AFTA and the politics of regional economic cooperation", *The Pacific Review*, 13, 2, pp. 297-318.

- Suchitra, Punyaratabandhu (1998): "Thailand in 1997: Financial Crisis and Consitutional Reform", *Asian Survey*, 38, 2, pp. 161-167.

- Suh, Sangwon (1999): "Unease Over East Timor: Indonesia's neighbors question their roles", *Asiaweek*, 25, 41, 15 October, http://www.asiaweek.com/asiaweek/magazine/99/1015/easttimor.html [11/06/01].

- Sukhumbhand, Paribatra (1998): "Engaging Myanmar in ASEAN", address by the Deputy Minister of Foreign Affairs at the Conference 'Engaging Myanmar in East Asia', Manila, 29 November, http://www.thaiembdc.org/pressctr/statemnt/others/dfm_1198.htm [08/05/01].

- Surakiart Sathirathai (2001): "Towards an Asia Cooperation Dialogue", keynote address of Thailand's Minister of Foreign Affairs, Insitute of Defence and Strategic Studies, Singapore, 17 July, http://www.thaiembdc.org/pressctr/statemnt/others/fmacd071701.html [15/10/01].

- Surin, Pitsuwan (1998a): "Currency Turmoil in Asia: The Strategic Impact", Remarks at the 12th Asia Pacific Roundtable, Kuala Lumpur, 1 June, http://www.mfa.go.th/Policy/fm01.htm [31/05/00].

—— (1998b): "Thailand's Foreign Policy During the Economic and Social Crisis", Keynote address at the Seminar in Commemoration of the 49th Anniversary of the Faculty of Political Science, Thammasat University, 12 June, http://www.mfa.go.th/Policy/fm02.htm [13/06/00].

—— (1998c): Press Briefing on Flexible Engagement, Manila, 24 July, http://thaiembdc.org/pr/pr705.htm [27/06/00].

—— (2000a): "Heeding ASEAN's Legacy", *Far Eastern Economic Review*, 17 February, http://www.aseansec.org/secgen/articles/sp_hal.htm [10/07/00].

—— (2000b): "Setting ASEAN's Future Agenda", *The Bangkok Post*, 16 July, http://www.bangkokpost.net/160700/160700_Perspective07.html [19/07/00]. [SurBP2000]

—— (2000c): Opening Statement, 33rd AMM, Bangkok, 24 July, http://www.aseansec.org/amm/amm33oth.htm [24/07/00].

- Suthiphand, Chirathivat *et al.* (1999): "ASEAN Prospects for Regional integration and the Implications for the ASEAN Legislative and Institutional Framework", *ASEAN Economic Bulletin*, 16, 1, pp. 28-50.

- Syed Seri Hamid Albar (1999): Opening Statement, 32nd AMM, Singapore, 23 July, http://202.186.32.3/KLN/statemen.nsf/d9696fa2492631ddc82565a9001ea b29/6358fba0c085e5b6c82567b70011682d?OpenDocument [15/06/00].

- Tan, Kong Yam (1998): "Regional Trading Arrangements in the Asia-Pacific Region: Strategic Options for a Weakened ASEAN, research paper, National University of Singapore, http://216.239.35.100/search?q=cache:I8Ra0hO1e-UC:www.brandeis.edu/global/research/tan.htm [29/04/02].

—— (2000): "Regional Trading Arrangements in the Asia Pacific Region:Strategic Options for a Weakened ASEAN". In: *Regional Cooperation & Asian Recovery*, ed. Peter Petri, Singapore: Institute of Southeast Asian Studies, pp. 224-248.

- Tanaka, Makiko (2001): Statement by Her Excellency Makiko Tanaka, Minister for Foreign Affairs of Japan on the occasion of the ASEAN +3 Meeting, 24 July, http://www.mofa.go.jp/region/asia-paci/asean/conference/asean3/state0107.html [18/04/02].

- Tasker, Rodney (1995): "A Line in the Sand", *FEER*, 6 April, pp. 14f.

- Tay, Simon S.C. (1997):"The haze and Asean cooperation", *The Straits Times*, Singapore, 1 October, http://www.moe.edu.sg/neu/online/pub-content-hazeasean2.html [02/07/01].

—— (1998): "What Should Be Done About the Haze?", *Indonesian Quarterly* 26, 2, pp. 99-117.

—— (2000a): "Security Cooperation and Crisis Management in the ASEAN Regional Forum: Realists in Normative Enterprises", paper presented at the USIP-IDSS Conference on The US and Southeast Asia: Towards a Common Agenda for Preserving Peace, Singapore, 1-2 April 2000, http://www.siiaonline.org/pdf/security%20Cooperation%20and%20Crisis%Management.pdf [23/01/01].

—— (2000b): "ASEAN and East Asia: A New Regionalism?". In: *A New ASEAN In A New Millennium*, ed. Simon S.C. Tay, Jesus Estanislao, Hadi Soesastro, Jakarta: Centre for Strategic and International Studies, pp. 228-239

——; Estanislao, P. Jesus; Hadi Soesastro (eds.) (2000): *A New ASEAN In A New Millennium*, Jakarta: Centre for Strategic and International Studies.

—— (2001): "The Relevance of ASEAN: Crisis and Change". In: *Reinventing ASEAN*, ed. S.S.C. Tay; J. P. Estanislao; Hadi Soesastro, Singapore: Institute of Souheast Asian Studies, 2001.

—— (2001b): "ASEAN and East Asia: A New Regionalism?". In: *Reinventing ASEAN*, ed. S. S. C. Tay; J. P. Estanislao; Hadi Soesastro, Singapore: Institute of Southeast Asian Studies, 2001, pp. 206-225.

——; J. P. Estanislao; Hadi Soesastro (eds.) (2001): *Reinventing ASEAN*, Singapore: Institute of Souheast Asian Studies [2nd, updated and revised edition of *A New ASEAN In A New Millennium*, Jakarta: Centre for Strategic and International Studies, 2000].

- Teo, Eric (2001): "The Emerging East Asian Regionalism", *Internationale Politik und Gesellschaft* [International Politics and Society], 1/2001, pp. 49-53.

- Thaksin, Shinawatra (2001): "Building a U.S.-Thai Strategic Partnership for the 21st Century", keynote address at a dinner organized by the U.S.-ASEAN Business Council and the Asia Society, Washington, D.C., 14 December, http://www.us-asean.org/Thailand/thaksinvisit01/speech.htm [05/04/02].

- Than Shwe (1998): Statement, 6th ASEAN Summit, Hanoi, 15 December, http://www.aseansec.org/summit/6th/prg_opmm.htm [13/06/00].

- Thayer, Carlyle A. (1999a): "China-ASEAN Relations: Some Progress, along with Disagreements and Disarray", *Comparative Connections*, 1, 2, http://www.csis.org/pacfor/cc/992Qchina_asean.html [08/05/02].

—— (1999b): "Beijing Plans for a Long-Term Partnership and Benefits from Anti-Western Sentiment", *Comparative Connections*, 1, 3, http://www.csis.org/pacfor/cc993Qchina_asean.html [08/05/02].

—— (1999c): "China Consolidates Long-Term Regional Relations", *ComparativeConnections*, 1, 4, http://www.csis.org/pacfor/cc/994Qchina_asean.html [08/05/02].

—— (2000a): "Tensions Promote Discussions on a Code of Conduct", *Comparative Connections*, 2, 1, http://www.csis.org/pacfor/cc/001Qchina_asean.html [10/07/00].

—— (2000b): "China Consolidates its Long-Term Bilateral Relations with China", *Comparative Connections*, 2, 2, http://www.csis.org/pacfor/cc/002Qchina_asean.html [08/05/02].

—— (2000c): "ASEAN Plus Three: An Evolving East Asian Community?", *Comparative Connections*, 2, 4, http://www.csis.org/pacfor/cc/004Qchina_asean.html [15/04/02].

—— (2001a): "China - ASEAN Relations: Regional Rivalries and Bilateral Irritants", *Comparative Connections*, 3, 1, http://www.csis.org/pacfor/cc/0101Qchina_asean.html [18/04/02].

—— (2001b): "China-ASEAN Relations: Making the Rounds", *Comparative Connections*, 3, 2, http://www.csis.org/pacfor/cc/0102Qchina_asean.html [08/10/01].

—— (2001c): "Developing Multilateral Cooperation", *Comparative Connections*, 4, 3, http://www.csis.org/pacfor/cc/0103Qchina_asean.html [01/05/02].

- *The Business Times*, Singapore (3 May 2001): "Singapore won't be 'back door to Afta'", http://business-times.asia1.com.sg/news/story/0,2276, 6365-988919940,00.html [09/05/01].

—— Singapore (05 November 2001): "New Trilateral forum among East Asian nations in the works", p. 2.

- *The Jakarta Post* (15 January 2001): "Indonesia and Singapore leaders launch joint energy project", http://www.indonesia-ottawa.org/economy/Economicissues/leaderenergyproject.html [22/05/01].

—— (11 January 2002): "Japan to offer new aid for Indonesia", obtained through Corfina News Clips, http://www.corfina.com/financial_news/january_02/jan_11_02.htm [03/05/02].

—— (03 April 2002a): "Japan to support RI at Paris Club", obtained through Corfina News Clips, http://www.corfina.com/financial_news/april_02/april_03:02.htm [03/05/02].

—— (03 April 2002b): "Mega forms team top boost economic ties with Japan", obtained through Corfina News Clips, http://www.corfina.com/financial_news/april_02/april_03:02.htm [03/05/02].

- *The Japan Times* (13 January 2002): "Koizumi's trade plan hailed by Megawati", http://www.japantimes.co.jp/cgi-bin/getarticle.pl5?nn20020113a2.htm [03/05/02].

—— (14 April 2002): "Japan Considering Creation of East Asia Free Trade Area Before 2010", http://www.taiwansecurity.org/News/2002/JT-041402.htm [18/04/02].

- *The Nation*, Bangkok (09 May 2000): "Asean 'not ready' to deal with Burma", http://202.44.251.4/nationnews/2000/200009/20000905/12999.html [07/03/01].

—— (24 July 2000): "Regional Perspective: Asean must confront new-old member split", http://nationmultimedia.com/Monday/ed2.html [24/07/00].

- *The Nihon Keizai Shimbun* (21 May 2002): "Arroyo Calls For Creation of E Asian Economic Bloc", http://www.nikkei.co.jp/FR/NIKKEI/inasia/future/2002news2.html [21/05/02].

- *The Star*, Malaysia (2001): "Smugglers still playing the risk game", Friday, 09 March.

- *The Straits Times*, Singapore (20 October 1999): "Lee Kuan Yew on East Timor: 'Look the other way'", Singapore Window, http://www.singapore-window.org/sw99/91020st.htm [10/05/01].

—— (8 March 2000): "Asian monetary fund not practical - BG Lee says that although the IMF is not perfect, it is better to improve on it, rather than to set up an alternative", http://straitstimes.asia1.com.sg/money/sinb13_0308.html [13/03/00].

—— (04 May 2000): "No Myanmar, no EU-ASEAN talks", http://straitstimes.asia1.com.sg/asia/sea14_0504.html [04/05/00]

—— (19 July 2000): "Thailand to push for 'troika' plan to act in crises", ,http://straitstimes.asia1.com.sg/asia/sea4_0719.html.

—— (26 July 2000): "Asean creates new rapid response team", http://straitstimes.asia1.com.sg/primenews/pri3_0726.html. [27/07/00].

—— (26 July 2000): "ASEAN expresses support for Indonesian unity", 25 July 2000. Cp. "Asean backs Indonesia against provinces", http://straitstimes.asia1.com.sg/asia/sea8_0726.html [26/07/00].

—— (26 July 2000): "New Asean members want development", http://straitstimes.asia1.com.sg/asia/sea/10_0726.html [26/07/00].

—— (21 November 2000): "SM Proposes APEC Sub-Grouping", http://www.abaconline.org/news/SMAPEC.htm [18/04/02].

—— (27 November 2000): "Why Gus Dur is not happy with Singapore", http://straitstimes.asia1.com.sg/asia/story/0,1870,6192,00.html [27/11/00].

—— (24 January 2001): "Extracts from Prime Minister Goh Chok Tong's interview with *The Straits Times*, as published on 24 Jan 2001", http://www.gov.sg/sgip/intervws/0101-04.htm [09/05/01].

—— (07 April 2001): "Ministers close to haze pact".

—— (09 May 2001): "Group to discuss rights in Myanmar and layoffs", http://straitstimes.asia1.com.sg/asia/story/0,1870,42413,00.html? [09/05/01].

—— (09 May 2001): "S'pore and Phnom Penh to boost ties", http://straitstimes.aisa1.com.sg/primenews/story/0,1870,42402,00.html? [09/05/01].

—— (17 May 2001): "ASEAN ministers meet to fight haze", http://www.haze-online.or.id/News&Events/straitstimes_01may17.htm [02/07/01].

—— (21 July 2001): "Manila urged to follow S'pore on FTA", http://www.google.com/search?q=cache:QSXLhtqH7k:straitstimes.asia.com.sg/asia/story/0,1870,58572-995752740,00.html+Singapore+FTA+ASEAN&hl=de [29/08/01].

—— (7 November 2001): "ASEAN, China plan FTA", p. 1.

- *The Sun on Sunday*, Malaysia (14 January 2001): "Rice glut may swamp farmers", p. 15.

- *The Times of India* (15 February 2001): "Singapore, Indonesia expand agriculture cooperation", http://www.timesofindia.com/150201/15aspc6.htm [16/05/01].

—— (10 March 2000): "Malaysia against Aceh independence", http://www.timesofindia.com/100300/10worl6.htm [11/06/01].

- Thomas, Gary (1999): "Aceh/ASEAN", correspondent report, *Voice of America*, 22 November, http://www.fas.org/man/dod-101/ops/war/1999/11/991122-aceh1.htm [11/06/01].

- Tisdall, Simon (2002): "U.S. aims its sights on Philippines", *Guardian Unlimited*, 24 January, http://www.guardian.co.uk/elsewhere/journalist/story/0,7792,638602,00.html [04/04/02].

- U Win Aung (1999): Statement, 32nd AMM, Singapore, 23 July, http://www.aseansec.org/amm/amm33omya.htm [29/09/00].

—— (2000): Opening Statement, 33rd AMM, Bangkok, 24 July, http://www.aseansec.org/amm/amm32osu.htm [19/06/00].

- Uday, Khandeparkar (1997): "Singapore, Philippines defend ASEAN expansion", Reuters, http://www.sintercom.org/sef97/myanmar_news.html [14/05/01].

- Ufen, Andreas (2000): "Verhaltenskodex für Spratly-Inseln wahrscheinlich", *Südostasien aktuell*, 19, 5, p. 369.

- Umbach, Frank (2000): "ASEAN and Major Powers: Japan and China - A Changing Balance of Power?". In: *International Relations in the Asia-Pacific: New Patterns of Power, Interest, and Cooperation*, ed. J. Dosch and M. Mols, New York and Münster: St. Martin's Press and LIT Verlag, 2000, pp. 171-214.

- UNEP (2001): "Haze Negotiations Begin Today", ROAP/01/02, News Release, 19 March, Eco-list environmental journalists homepage, http://lists.isb.sdnpk.org/pipermail/eco-list/2001-March/001107.html.

- Unger, Leonard (1986): "The International Role of the Association of Southeast Asian Nations". In: Alan K. Henderson: *Negotiating World Order: The Artisanship and Architecture of Global Diplomacy*, Wilmington (Delaware), pp. 149-163.

- United States, Department of Foreign Affairs (2000): "Background Notes: Malaysia", October, http://www.state.gov/www/background_notes/malaysia_0010_bgn.html [25/05/02].

——, Office of the Trade Representative (2001): "U.S. Trade Representative Robert B. Zoellick Meets With Indonesian President Megawati To Discuss Strengthening U.S.-Indonesian Ties", press release 01-72, Washington, D.C., September. http://www.ustr.gov/releases/2001/09/01-72.htm [02/05/02].

——, White House (2001): "U.S.-Thailand Joint Statement", press release, Office of the Press Secretary, 14 December, http://www.whitehouse.gov/news/releases/2001/12/20011214-7.html [05/04/02].

——, White House (2002): "Visit of the Prime Minister Mahathir of Malaysia", statement by the Press Secretary of the White House, 16 April, http://www.whitehouse.gov/news/releases/2002/04/20020416-10.html [25/04/02].

- Valencia, Mark J. (2001): "Blue-Water Brawls: The latest on disputes in the South China Sea", security report, Taiwan government homepage, http://publish.gio.gov.tw/FCR/current/r0105p40.html [26/05/01].

—— ; Jenny Miller Garmendia (2000): "Old disputes heighten chance for war in South China Sea", *Honolulu Advertiser*, 23 April, http://www.honoluluadvertiser.com/2000/Apr/23/opinion5.html [03/05/01].

- Van Dyke, Jon M. / Mark J. Valencia (2000): "How valid are the South China Sea claims under the Law of the Sea convention?". In: *Southeast Asian Affairs 2000*, ed. Daljit Singh, Singapore: Institute of Southeast Asian Studies, 2000, pp. 47-63.

- Vatikiotis, Michael (1996): "Seeds of Division", *FEER*, 17 October, pp. 16-17.

—— ; Murray Hiebert (1997): "Drawn to the Fray", *FEER*, 3 April.

—— (1997): "Tributary Trade: Thailand's Chavalit seals a trade-off with China", *Far Eastern Economic Review*, 17 April, pp. 19-20.

—— ; Rodney Tasker (1995): "Hang On Tight", *FEER*, 28 December 1995/ 4 January 1996 (double editon), pp. 16-17.

- Wanandi, Jusuf (1999): "ASEAN's Challenges for Its Future", *Pacnet Newsletter* no.3, 22 January, http://www.csis.org/pacfor/pac0399.html [01/08/00].

—— (2000): "East Asian Institution-Building", paper delivered at the 2000 annual meeting of the Trilateral Commission, Tokyo, http://www.trilateral.org/annmtgs/trialog/trlgtxts/t54/wan.htm [20/09/01].

- Wang, Hongying (2000): "Multilateralism in Chinese Foreign Policy: The Limits of Socialization?". In: *China's International Relations in the 21st Century: Dynamics of Paradigm Shifts*, ed. Wixing Hu, Gerald Chan, Daojian Zha, Lanham/ New York/ Oxford, University Press of America, pp. 71-91.

- Weaver, Lisa Rose (2002): "Loans a 'motivation' for Megawati in China", CNN.com, 26 March, http://asia.cnn.com/2002/WORLD/asiapcf/east/03/25/china.indon/?related [17/05/02].

- Webber, Douglas (2001): "Two funerals and a wedding? The ups and downs of regionalism in East Asia and Asia-Pacific after the Asian crisis", *The Pacific Review*, 14, 3, pp. 339-372.

- Weller, Christoph (1999): "Kollektive Identitäten in der internationalen Politik. Anmerkungen zur Konzeptualisierung eines modischen Begriffs". In: *Identität und Interesse. Der Diskurs der Identitätsforschung*, ed. Walter Reese-Schäfer, Opladen: Leske und Budrich, pp. 249-277.

—— (2000): "Kollektive Identitäten in der Menschenrechtspolitik: Zur Analyse der Entstehung einer asiatischen Identität", paper delivered to a workshop entitled 'Die Menschenrechtspolitiken Japans, Indonesiens und der Philippinen: Spiegel asiatischer Identität?' ['The Human Rights Politics of Japan, Indonesia and the Philippines: Reflecting an Asian Identity?'], Institute of Asian Affairs, Hamburg, 29 June, http://www.human-rights-politics-and-east-asia.de/Aktivitaten/weller/hauptteil_weller.html [03/06/02].

- Wendt, Alexander (1994): "Collective Identity Formation and the International State", *American Political Science Review*, 88, 2, pp. 384-396.

—— (1999): *Social Theory of International Politics*, Cambridge and New York: Cambridge University Press [Cambridge Studies in International Relations, no. 67].

- Wesley, Michael (1999): "The Asian Crisis and the Adequacy of Regional Institutions", *Contemporary Southeast Asia*, 21, 1, pp. 54-73.

- West, Andrew (2000): "Singapore should not be condemned by its neighbors, rather its economic practices should be copied by them", *Capitalism Magazine*, 7 December, http://www.capitalismmagazine.com/2000/december/west_asean.htm [07/03/01].

- Wheatley, Alan (2001): "Onus on ASEAN to perk up on trade, investment", Pacific Basin Economic Council (PBEC) homepage, 30 April, http://www.pbec.org/clips/2001/010430lees.htm [29/08/01].

- Whiting, Allen S. (1997): "ASEAN Eyes China: The Security Dimension", *Asian Survey*, 37, 4, pp. 299-322.

- Wichmann, Peter (1996): *Die Politischen Perspektiven der ASEAN: Subregionale Integration oder Supraregionale Kooperation?*, Hamburg: Institut für Asienkunde [Mitteilungen des Instituts für Asienkunde no. 262].

- Won, Yong-Kul (2001): "East Asia Economic Integration: A Korean Perspective", *The Journal of East Asian Affairs* [Korea], 15, 1, pp. 71-96, here: pp. 92, 94.

- Woranuj, Maneerungse Saritdet Marukatat (2001): "China priority for free-trade", *Bangkok Post*, 20 June, http://www.google.de/search?q=cache:4R32HoHUK2kC:www.capitalrice .com/news.asp%3FPage%3Drice%26News_ID%3D27+%22China+priori ty+for+free-trade%22+bangkok+post&hl=de [16/04/02].

—— (2002): "China to protect its farm sector for now: Free trade except for agriculture, finance", *Bangkok Post*, 13 May, http://www.google.com/search?q=cache:irJm2e-q0q8C:www.bangkokpost.net/Business/13May2002_biz43.html [15/05/02].

- Wu, Friedrich; Yeo Han Sia (2001): "China's rising investment in Southeast Asia: How ASEAN and Singapore can benefit", feature article, Ministry of Trade and Investment, Economics Division, Singapore, http://www.mti.gov.sg/public/PDF/CMT/NWS_2001Annual_China.pdf [09/05/02].

- Yahoo Financial News—Asian Markets (2000): 'Political troubles threaten to overshadow economic agenda at summit',19 November, http://www.asia.biz.yahoo.com/news/asian_markests/political_troubles_threaten_to_overshadow_economic_agenda_at_summit.html [23/11/00].

- Yahoo News (10 January 2001): "Japan, Malaysia seek common Asian voice", http://www.google.de/search?q=cache:adrG1_xE1GsC:sg.news.yahoo.com/020110/1/2a4hn.html [06/03/02].

- Yeo, Han Sia (2001): "China's rising investment in Southeast Asia: How ASEAN and Singapore can benefit", feature article, Ministry of Trade and Investment, Economics Division, Singapore, http://www.mti.gov.sg/public/PDF/CMT/NWS_2001Annual_China.pdf [09/05/02].

- Yonan, Alan Jr./ James T. Areddy (2000): "Leaders of ASEAN Plus Three Endorse Currency Swap Plan", Dow Jones Newswires, 25 November, http://asia.biz.yahoo.com/news/asian_markets/dowjones/article.html?s=asiafinance/news/001125/asian_markets/dowjones/Leaders_Of_Asean_Plus_Three_Endorse_Currency_Swap_Plan.html [27/11/00].

- Yuwadee, Tunyasiri (2001): "Chavalit may visit Burma ahead of PM - to lay groundwork for patching up ties", *The Bangkok Post*, 26 May, http://www.bangkokpost.com/today/260501_News02.html [26/05/01].

- Zhu, Rongji (2001a): "Strengthening East Asian Cooperation and Promoting Common Development", address at the 5th APT summit, Bandar Seri Begawan, 5 November, http://www.chinaembassy-indonesia.or.id/eng/20836.html [06/04/02].

—— (2001b): "Jointly Creating a New Situation in China-ASEAN Cooperation", transcript of an address by the Chinese Prime Minister to ASEAN leaders at the bilateral ASEAN Plus One summit on 6 November, http://www.china.org.cn/baodao/english/newsandreport/2001dec/23-1.htm [05/04/02].

www.ingramcontent.com/pod-product-compliance
Lightning Source LLC
LaVergne TN
LVHW062301060326
832902LV00013B/1994